Mathematically speaking, if you want to become a millionaire by the age of 40 and you start working at the age of 20, you will need to save $136.98 per day (7 days per week).

I'm writing this book to teach you how to become a millionaire but I'll let you do your own math.

1. What do you want your net worth to be?

   _____

2. How many days are you willing to invest in becoming a multi-millionaire?

   _____

3. How much money do you plan on saving every day?

   _____

4. What problems do you plan on solving (services or products) in exchange for the millions that you plan on earning?

   _____

5. How much profit do you plan on earning per service or product that you offer?

   _____

6. How many products or services do you need to sell to your ideal and likely buyers in order to achieve your financial goals?

   _____

7. What will you do with your time once you've achieved the financial goals you have?

   _____

8. How many hours per week are you willing to work in exchange for the money that you wish to earn?

   _____

A MILLIONAIRE'$ GUIDE

HOW TO
BECOME
= SUSTAINABLY =
RICH

A Step-By-Step Guide to Building a Successful, Money-Generating, and Time-Freedom Creating Business

It's not about where you came from or what kind of car you are driving today. It's about where you are going. I started my entrepreneurial journey inside a 1989 Ford Escort

"Don't read this book unless you are passionate about becoming rich while simultaneously creating both time and financial freedom. I'll teach you the systems but you must supply the B.O.O.M.! (the BIG, OVERWHELMING OPTIMISTIC, MOMENTUM)."

~ **Clay Clark**

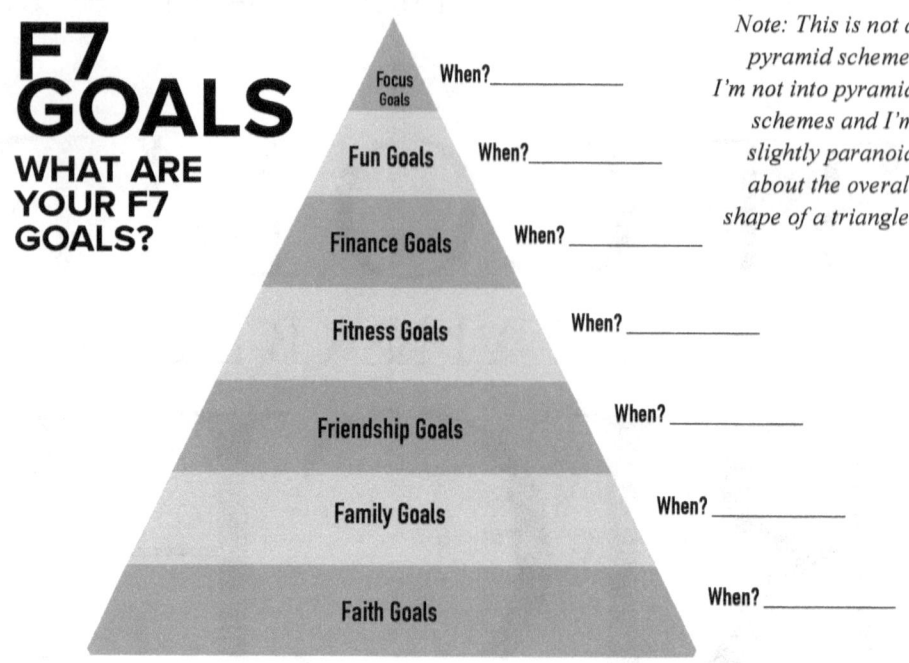

How to Become Sustainably Rich: A Millionaire's Step-by-Step Guide to Building a Successful, Time Freedom-Creating Business

ISBN: 979-8-9864278-2-9

Clayton Menendez Publishing
Published by Thrive Publishing
3920 West 91st Street South
Tulsa, OK 74132

By default, 96% of businesses fail.
INC. MAGAZINE
https://www.inc.com/bill-carmody/why-96-of-businesses-fail-within-10-years.html

STOP THROWING GUTTER BALLS!

① ESTABLISH REVENUE GOALS

What are your yearly gross revenue goals?

_____

What are your total weekly gross revenue goals?

_____

② DETERMINE THE BREAK-EVEN NUMBERS

Number of customers/sales to break even?

_____

③ DEFINE WORK WEEK: NUMBER OF HOURS

How many hours are you willing to work?

_____

What are your boundaries?

_____

⑥ CREATE 3-LEGGED MARKETING STOOL

Leg 1 _____

Leg 2 _____

Leg 3 _____

⑤ IMPROVE BRANDING

On a scale of 1-10, with 10 being the highest, how highly would you rate your website, print pieces, and social media?

_____

④ DEFINE YOUR UNIQUE VALUE PROPOSITION:

Who are your top 3 competitors?

_____

Have you mystery shopped your competitors?

_____

⑦ CREATE A SALES CONVERSION SYSTEM

Sales scripts? _____

Recorded calls? _____

One sheets? _____

Pre-Written emails?_____

Lead trackers?_____

⑧ DETERMINE SUSTAINABLE CUSTOMER ACQUISITION COSTS

What does it cost to obtain each customer?

_____

Do you have a tracking sheet? _____

Weekly advertising spend? _____

⑨ CREATE REPEATABLE SYSTEMS, PROCESSES, AND FILE ORGANIZATION

What daily, core, repeatable, actionable processes are not documented into script or checklist form?_____

What processes and systems are not repeatable?

_____

Do you have checklists for all positions?

⑫ CREATE HUMAN RESOURCES AND RECRUITMENT SYSTEMS

• Who are your A players? _____
• Who are your B players? _____
• Who are your C players? _____
• When is your weekly staff meeting? _____
• When is your weekly group interview? _____

⑪ CREATE A SUSTAINABLE AND REPETITIVE WEEKLY SCHEDULE

When is your w weekly group interview?_____

When is your daily group huddle?_____

⑩ CREATE MANAGEMENT EXECUTION SYSTEMS

What people on your team will not do their jobs?

_____

Do you have merit-based pay installed? _____

⑬ CREATE YOUR ACCOUNTING AND AUTOMATE THE EARNING OF MILLIONS

Are you using Clay Clark's Ultimate tracking sheet?_____

⑭ DETERMINE THE POINT OF ACHIEVING FINANCIAL SUCCESS?

F7 GOALS

1-Faith _____

2-Family _____

3-Friendship _____

4-Fitness _____

5-Finances _____

6-Fun _____

7-Focus _____

THE EMOTIONAL
TRADE-OFFS OF A SUCCESSFUL PERSON

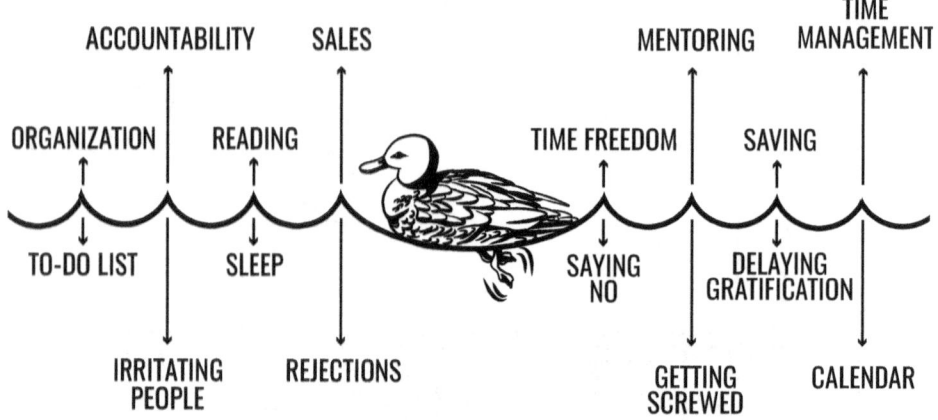

ACCOUNTABILITY SALES MENTORING TIME MANAGEMENT

ORGANIZATION READING TIME FREEDOM SAVING

TO-DO LIST SLEEP SAYING NO DELAYING GRATIFICATION

IRRITATING PEOPLE REJECTIONS GETTING SCREWED CALENDAR

"Diligence is the difference maker."

- Proverbs 10:4

$ HOW TO GET CASH FOR YOUR BUSINESS FAST $

1. **Kabbage**

2. **Oklahoma Capital Bank / Regent Bank**

3. **Equity Line**

4. **Walt Disney / Sam Walton Method** (Ask people you know)

5. **Lori Montag (Zany Bands) Method** (Sell your house and put it toward your business)

6. **Nuclear Winter Method** (Fire everyone you do not need)

7. **Clay Clark Method** (Turn your air conditioning and other non-vitals off [cable, dinners out, etc.] to be able to put that money toward the business

Dedication

"Brevity is the soul of wit."

- William Shakespeare

I dedicate this book to you and my dad. I dedicate this book to you because unless you are a sick, twisted freak, you are reading this book because you are passionate about success.

My dad delivered pizzas, worked odd jobs, and moved away from our family for a short period of time to Minnesota to help take care of our family when he couldn't find a decent paying job that matched the skills sets he paid to learn while graduating from a four-year college. Dad, my goal with this book is to mentor millions of people just like you about what they need to do to provide for their families in a way that produces financial and time freedom abundantly. I love you. Thank you for delivering those pizzas. I don't understand why God allowed you to lose the ability to use your hands, to take care of yourself, to chew food or to breathe on your own, but I'll interrogate Him when I get there.

To all of the people who made fun of my father for delivering those pizzas and who made fun of me for stuttering severely as a kid, I hope this book inspires and helps you, too.

In fact, over the years I have helped apartment owners, air conditioning installers, bakeries, basketball coaching programs, gun dealers, photographers, commercial real estate & residential real estate agents, insurance agents, home remodelers, event planners, financial planners, precious metals dealers, automotive sales, and more.

YEARLY GROWTH

$191,017.96
3 EMPLOYEES
2019

$646,514.25
238.5%
7 EMPLOYEES
2020

$1,075,799.44
66.4%
15 EMPLOYEES
2021

$1,900,767.09
76.7%
18 EMPLOYEES
2022

BACK TO BASICS
BUILDERS

Joe Burbey
Owner / Founder
www.HomeRemodelingMilwaukee.com

Eric Trump, Kash Patel, General Flynn, Aaron Antis, and Clay Clark Take a Team America Photo at General Flynn & Clay Clark's Reawaken America Tour (2022).

Author Note

YOU CAN EITHER LEARN FROM MENTORS OR MISTAKES

If you do not choose to implement the systems found within this book, you have the option of spending 20 years learning these SUCCESS SYSTEMS through the pain of trial and error with a side of bankruptcy and soul-crushing financial woes. You could exhaustively read and apply the actionable items found within the informative pages of the Harvard Business Review, as I did. You could invest thousands of hours of time reading the autobiographies of the world's most successful people, as I have done. You could go back to school and earn your master's degree while being taught by professors who are too scared of the world of business to actually leave the campus to attempt to apply what they are teaching. You could even invest years and countless hours attempting to contact the world's most successful people to convince them to become your business mentor, as I did. You could drag yourself and your family to expensive mindset-changing and upsell focused seminars, as I did. My friend, you could even sprint naked through the minefield of business as a highly motivated idiot just as I once did while trying to convince my wife that I was learning through trial and error.

The choice is yours – learn from me or learn from your mistakes. Now, who's with me?

Sincerely,

Clay Clark
Founder of DJConnection.com, EpicPhotos.com,
EITRLounge.com, MakeYourLifeEpic.com, the
Thrivetime Show Podcast,
the Thrive15.com Online Business School,
the Reawaken America Tour, etc.

"The time will never be perfect for you to start achieving massive success. You must act now because you will be dead soon."

-Clay Clark

THOMAS EDISON DEVELOPED 10,000 FAILED EXPERIMENTS BEFORE
DEVELOPING THE FIRST PRACTICAL MODERN LIGHT BULB.

"TEMPORARY FAILURES ARE A PREREQUISITE TO SUCCESS."
-NAPOLEON HILL

Contents

I STARTED BUILDING WEALTH AT THE
AGE OF 16. WHEN WILL YOU START?

PHASE 2

PHASE 3

CHAPTER 20: HOW TO CONVERT 282

CHAPTER 21: THE 7 NINJA MOVES 288

CHAPTER 22: A NOTE FROM JERRY VASS 296

CHAPTER 23: SCALING PRODUCTION. 298

CHAPTER 24: STAYING ORGANIZED 306

CHAPTER 25: ACCOUNTABILITY 318

CHAPTER 26: SETTING PRICES 330

BECOME AN AUTOMATIC MILLIONAIRE

Automate your savings and you will win: If you decide to invest $200 per week every two weeks for the next thirty five years you are on the planet and you earned an annual return of just 10% you find yourself as the proud owner of an account worth $1,678,293.78

Your business is just a vehicle to get you to your goals. The vehicle exists to serve you.

Your business is just a vehicle you build to get your where you want to go. You absolutely must know your F7 goals or you will never magically drift to success. What are your goals for your faith, your family, your friendships, your fitness, your finances, fun, and focus?

Clay Clark
(Founder of Thrive15.com, former U.S. SBA Entrepreneur of the Year, host of the Thrive Time Show and America's #1 Business Coach)

Chapter 1

Do You Need a Business Coach?

"Unless you have a psycological disorder you should be building a business to create both time and financial freedom for both you and your family and that's what I do well. In fact, while I'm writing this page of content for you I am generating approximately $1,000 per hour from my various business ventures in the Hair, Real Estate, Buying and Selling Gold, Dog Training, Consulting, Automotive Repair, and Vehicle Repair and other various industries."

- Clay Clark
(Founder of several multi-million-dollar businesses.)

"ALL THE SMILES IN THE WORLD AREN'T GOING
TO HELP YOU IF YOUR PRODUCT OR SERVICE IS
NOT WHAT THE CUSTOMER WANTS."
-THE SERVICE PROFIT CHAIN

YOUR PRODUCTS AND SERVICES CAN'T SUCK.

What Are You Actually Going to Learn?

In this powerful book, I, the founder of Thrive15.com, former U.S. Small Business Administration Entrepreneur of the Year, and a man who has successfully coached clients in practically every industry imaginable (Bakers, Cosmetic Surgeons, Consultants, Dentists, Gym Owners, Lawyers, Online Retailers, Personal Trainers, Real Estate Professionals, Retailers, Neurologists, Speakers, etc.) will show you how to overcome the obstacles, limiting beliefs, and system failures that nearly every business owner encounters along the way. In this book, you'll learn how to:

 Build a duplicable and scalable business model capable of working without you.

 Systematically enhance each aspect of your business to greatly reduce costs and to dramatically increase profits.

 Build systems that are scalable and sellable (meaning that somebody else would actually want to buy your business someday).

 Discover your company's hidden opportunities and lowest hanging fruit for quick growth.

 Enhance both the cash flow and workflow of your business.

 Receive bonus – and unsolicited – parenting tips from a man raising five kids and 38 chickens while he participates in the ownership, equity, and system enhancement of nine different businesses.

Are You Going to Use a GPS or Spend Your Time Chronically Lost?

I've written this book with the stated goal of "providing people with the world's most POWERFUL AND EFFICIENT BUSINESS BOOK EVER" (while at the same time, demonstrating my extreme humbleness). This book provides you with a step-by-step guide that you can refer to time and time again and that will serve as your virtual business GPS and navigation system. Back in the day before global positioning systems had become available on every smartphone and before I had enough disposable cash to fill up the gas tank whenever I want, I used to get so lost that I would occasionally run into Yoda and every other wise hermit seeking to escape the world by moving to the outskirts of humanity. But when GPS became readily available, I now had a choice. Was I going to allow billion-dollar, precise and proven satellite technology to guide me to my desired destinations, or was I going to be a jackass? I chose to be a jackass for six more months, then I started using a GPS after my sanity was called into question. You have that same choice today. Will you follow a proven system or be a jackass?

Clay Clark is the founder of Thrive15.com and a former U.S. Small Business Administration Entrepreneur of the Year. He has been the speaker of choice for many of America's largest companies including Hewlett Packard, O'Reilly Auto Parts, Valspar Paint, Maytag University, Oxi Fresh, and many others. Clay and his businesses have been featured in Forbes, Entrepreneur, Fast Company, Bloomberg and countless other media outlets. Clay, his wife, five kids, 38 chickens, four goats, and his seven turkeys all live in Tulsa, Oklahoma.

IF YOU DON'T GET UP EARLY YOUR SUCCESS WON'T
BE REALIZED UNTIL LATE IN LIFE.

U.S. Small Business Administration

SBA
Your Small Business Resource

Oklahoma District Office
301 NW 6ᵗʰ Street, Suite 116 Oklahoma City, OK 73102   405/609-8000 (fax) 405/609-8990

February 21, 2007

Mr. Clayton Thomas Clark
DJ Connection Tulsa, Inc.
8900 South Lynn Lane Road
Broken Arrow, Oklahoma 74102

Dear Mr. Clark:

Congratulations! You have been selected as the **2007 Oklahoma SBA Young Entrepreneur of the Year.** On behalf of the U.S. Small Business Administration (SBA), I wish to express our appreciation for your support of small business and for your contributions to the economy of this State.

In recognition of your achievement, **an awards luncheon will be held Tuesday, May 22, 2007** at Rose State College in Midwest City, Okla. The luncheon is sponsored by the Oklahoma Small Business Development Center. Two complimentary luncheon tickets have been reserved for you and one guest.

Arrangements for the luncheon are still being finalized. You will be notified of the details as soon as they become available. You are encouraged to bring family, friends, and business associates. Upon presentation of your award, you will have the opportunity to make acceptance comments.

Also, for our awards brochure, please email an electronic photo of yourself to darla.booker@sba.gov by Friday, March 16.

Again, congratulations on your outstanding accomplishment.

Sincerely,

Dorothy (Dottie) A. Overal
Oklahoma District Director

Clay Clark interviews NBA great David Robinson about David's path to achieving business success after he concluded his Hall of Fame NBA career.

Results from Implementers and Doers (Just Like You)

"Our experience working with Clay Clark and his team has been nothing short of amazing. When our team first met Clay, I expressed that if we were able to move the needle and get results, we would be working together for a very long time. Clay and his team listened to our problems and custom built a program specifically for us. So far this season, we have experienced a 42% increase in corporate sponsorship sales, a 10% increase in season ticket sales, and over a 103% increase in group tickets sales! We have also had a 21% increase in people actually attending the games thus resulting in a 27% increase in concession and novelty sales. Our program focused on search engine optimization, an increased social media presence, targeted online ads, digital retargeting ads, and the implementation of the Dream 100 system. Beyond that, Clay's team redesigned our website making it more visually appealing and user friendly for our online visitors by creating a dynamic visual experience. Our slogan for Tulsa Oilers hockey is 'Feel The Boom'; thanks Clay for giving us that BOOM!"

Taylor Hall
Tulsa Oilers | General Manager | www.tulsaoilers.com
Proud ECHL affiliate of the National Hockey League's Winnipeg Jets

• •

"It was one of the best presentations I've ever seen. I've seen Jack Canfield and I've seen Tony Robbins, and I can tell you that Clay made a far greater impact on me than any of those other speakers, as great as they are and as great as they were at that time."

Lance Dawson
Mortgage Broker
www.mortgagearchitects.ca

"Vision without execution is hallucination."
- *Thomas Edison*
(American inventor and businessman. He developed many devices that greatly influenced life around the world, including the phonograph, the motion picture camera, and the long-lasting, practical electric light bulb.)

"To achieve success you must implement proven systems and processes that will produce consistently profitable and often times boring results. If excitement is what you seek try skydiving and pay for it using profits from your boring and profitable business."

- Clay Clark

"You certainly were the on-site leader that we needed for this calling campaign. By watching you work with these students and seeing the result, I became reassured that hiring you to do exactly what you did was the right thing to do. Your team brought in over $120K in gifts and pledges, which may be an all-time ORU phonathon record! But I'll have more for you later. I smile to think how funny you were and what a GREAT job you did for us. Again, thanks for everything....and don't drink too much Red Bull!"

Jesse D. Pisors, B.A. (1996) M.A. (2005)
Director of Alumni & Ministerial Relations and Annual Fund
Oral Roberts University

• •

"I had the pleasure of working with Mr. Clark in 2010 when I managed over 2.2 million square feet of downtown office and retail space. I can recommend him highly and without reservation. I had hired Mr. Clark to rebrand the portfolio and reach out to prospective tenants. Throughout the course of the campaign, Mr. Clark was a consummate professional. He conducted market research, built a website, and coordinated obtaining pictures, print materials, and gaining media attention within what I would deem record time. Within the first week of Mr. Clark going public with the campaign, he generated hundreds of prospective tenants. Mr. Clark's positive attitude is contagious. He is a hard worker, and he is genuinely a great guy to work with. I hope that in the near future I will have the opportunity to work with Mr. Clark again."

David Atkinson
One Place, LLC | 120 W. 3rd Street | Tulsa, OK 74103

• •

"In terms of our website, we weren't even on Google and now we are the top in Google search results. Already 70 kids signed up for camp. Could have 80-90 before it's over. The site really gives us a big time look. I'm happy with it."

Don Calvert
Founder of Score Basketball | ScoreBBall.com

"I own Facchianos Bridal and Formal attire and have had to pay thousands of dollars in the past to have websites built that were subpar and not what I needed for my business, until Clay taught me how to do it myself. Now my company website comes up on the search engines in the first three searches. It has changed my business overnight on how many times our phone rings. It can change the life of your business to be in control of your website."

Jennifer Thompson
Owner/Bridal Stylist | Facchianos Bridal and Formal Attire

• •

"The attendees all left with pages and pages of takeaways. They really enjoyed the energy, and the SPECIFIC ACTION POINTS you gave everybody. You and our Accounting Presenter got top marks. You really made this year's training EPIC."

Anitra Nichols
Maytag University | 100 S. Anaheim Blvd. Suite #250 | Anaheim, CA 92805

• •

"We've gone into overdrive to get Brenda trained. We've had a record month!! We've collected $60,000. We have quite a bit pending insurance as well. Can't wait to finish all the numbers!! That's awesome! Thank you, Clay, for all that you do! We had over 30 leads in March alone!"

Jennifer Cushman
Office Manager | Face & Body Cosmetic Surgery and Medical Spa | www.FaceandBody.net

• •

"You single-handedly saved this event (Tulsa Sports Charity Fundraisers for Hall of Fame Basketball Coach Eddie Sutton).... He also asked if they could do an 'Eddie's Worst Scowl' contest with the TV stations, and I thought he would love that... I think they are now drinking from your Kool Aid!!!"

Stephen E. Sutton
Vice President of Spirit Bank | Public Sector / Financial Associations Portfolio Manager

"We were able to move to the top of Google searches in the competitive mortgage Internet search category, we got featured on the news twice and we closed nearly 35% more loans within the first six months. The contact management system, search engine strategy, and PR system you set up are producing results. Our only issue now is scaling. Let's talk."

Adnan Sheikh
Founder | President | ZFG Mortgage | www.ZFGMortgage.com

• •

"So far we've generated $63,600 of additional annual gross revenue as a result of the ACCESS plan you helped us create. We are closing in on $10K in monthly revenue. I just signed up an additional ACCESS client and it's the 2nd one that I've landed in the last 30 days from LinkedIn. And the only thing I'm doing on LinkedIn is the Myth versus Law and the Legal Mumbo Jumbo. I'm not doing any other activity. So that appears to really be working in that medium. So I'm making $850 a month off of my free LinkedIn subscription. So I'm kind of excited. So I just wanted to let you know that some of what we are doing is working."

Scott Reib
Attorney at Law | ReibLaw.com

"Being top in Google has impacted our business tremendously. Knowing that we're top in Google makes it so much easier for our clients to search and if they use certain keywords that pertain to our business, we're the first ones that come up on that page. We get a lot of phone call and website traffic. I would suggest every one takes this program seriously."

- MYRON KIRKPATRICK
(Founder of White Glove Auto - WhiteGloveAutoTulsa.com)

"Hi Clay. You have no idea how you blessed me with our conversation and the book recommendations. When I was in Tulsa, the Brazilian government made a sudden change in the regulations for the housing market that drove a lot of people out of business.

"We pretty much had to reinvent our business to survive. February through June were not fun... However, God blessed us and we were able to survive and prosper. We have now about 20 employees working on three different construction sites. The principles in the books you recommended and the ones I 'caught' during our conversation have helped me a lot!

"I often tell my wife: 'If Clay Clark can run five businesses, then why can't I run a business and a ministry?' You have been an inspiration! Thanks my friend!"

Rubens Cunha
Brazilian Missionary

• •

"Clay Clark has been instrumental throughout in providing me with business guidance at the right times! He has moved both of my companies to the top of Google searches and helped me to be featured in countless media outlets and publications. I have a big vision in what God has called me to do and sometimes as an entrepreneur you can dream so big that you can lose focus. With three successful companies, I knew that it was time for growth and sustainability so that we could reach the people that we needed to reach. I truly believe that God brings certain people into your life at certain times and I thank God for bringing Clay at a time of need. Clay has been instrumental in combining his business savvy with my big vision. The bottom line is that I am in business to help people...but I am also in business to make money, and that is what Clay has helped me do! If you are considering bringing Clay on for anything business related, it will be the best investment you ever make."

Jonathan Conneely
"Coach JC" | Founder / President, JJC Enterprises

"Wow. Wow. Wow. Thank you for your input and for working so hard for me behind the scenes while we were back and forth for this (for the TV show, "The Voice"). I'm humbled and overwhelmed with gratitude. So glad to know you and your sweet family. Thanks for believing in me!"

Amanda Preslar
Founder of PreslarMusic.com

• •

"Clay, I just want you to know that this last year has been unbelievable. I've gone from poverty thinking to just a small measure of wealth thinking and, as the book said, the universe has discovered me!!! I've never felt so free! I truly have become what T. Harv Eker calls, 'a money magnet'! And it's only the beginning. We have seven revenue streams now and each of them are growing and contributing daily. Thank you Clay Clark! My life is expanding and you have been a major influence on me! Have a great day, my friend!"

Clay Staires
Professional Speaker/Trainer and Growth Expert
The Leadership Initiative | www.claystaires.com

• •

"Thank you so much for all your hard work and success on this campaign. We have raised over $100,000 for the WPS (matched)! Thank you!"

Yvette Webb
Development Event Coordinator | Oral Roberts University

• •

"Clay is a force to be reckoned with. He is a contagious, mind-expanding, 'get off your blessed assurance' motivating business coach that is positively changing my world and soon to be the whole world. I doubled my business every year I worked with Clay Clark, and I went from less than 10 clients to over 100 clients as a direct result of the systems and processes Clay Clark taught me. We grew from $10,000 per month to over $100,000 per month of revenue as a direct result of working with Clay. He actually taught my first consultant everything he knows."

Tim Redmond, CEO
Redmond Growth Initiatives | www.RedmondGrowth.com

"Best emcee and entertainer we have ever used. From the time the first guest walked into the room until the last guest left, you electrified the room with your energy! Thank you for taking our event to the NEXT LEVEL (as you like to say)!"

Angie W.
Event Planning Team | 11th Annual Zenith Awards | Apartment Association

. . . .

"Thanks for all your help last year; we've done a lot of work, reading and investing and the results are truly amazing. Our best staff ever, continuous increases, and overall happiness like never before (and yes more profitable than we've been in years, and while in a down economy)! I feel like we now have entirely new understanding on the importance of culture in the workplace. Do you have any more books you could recommend?! Thanks again Clay!"

Dave Bauer
www.mymaytagstore.com

. . . .

"I have come to realize that foundational sales principles work, regardless of what you're selling. I work at a coffee shop and my boss told me 'Hey, we really need to sell more coffee beans.' So I started employing the creative use of imagery, humor, phrasing and tried and true sales methods taught to me by Clay Clark and the book he recommended I read, Soft Selling in a Hard World. I made posters describing the different coffees with funny pop culture references along with legitimate consumer reviews of each coffee. I also began using 'the 90-second close.' Our store shot up to the spot of #1 in whole bean sales out of 613 stores in our entire region. Not only that, but we are averaging 5 pounds sold out of every 100 customers that come into the store, whereas the average store in the US sees 1 to 1.5 pounds sold per every 100 customers that come in. These numbers don't lie and they just point to the fact that a proper training in sales by someone who knows what they are doing and who has a track record to prove it can make you succeed in sales in whatever business realm you find yourself in, even the coffee shop business."

Scott T.
Store Manager & Barista | Starbucks Coffee

"I'm getting lots of referral traffic from Facebook and social media. My website and biz cards look awesome. The $50 referral program is working great and I have my templates for responding to emails and my sales pitch down pat."

Dominick Cooper
Founder of Launch Academy | http://launchacademytulsa.com/

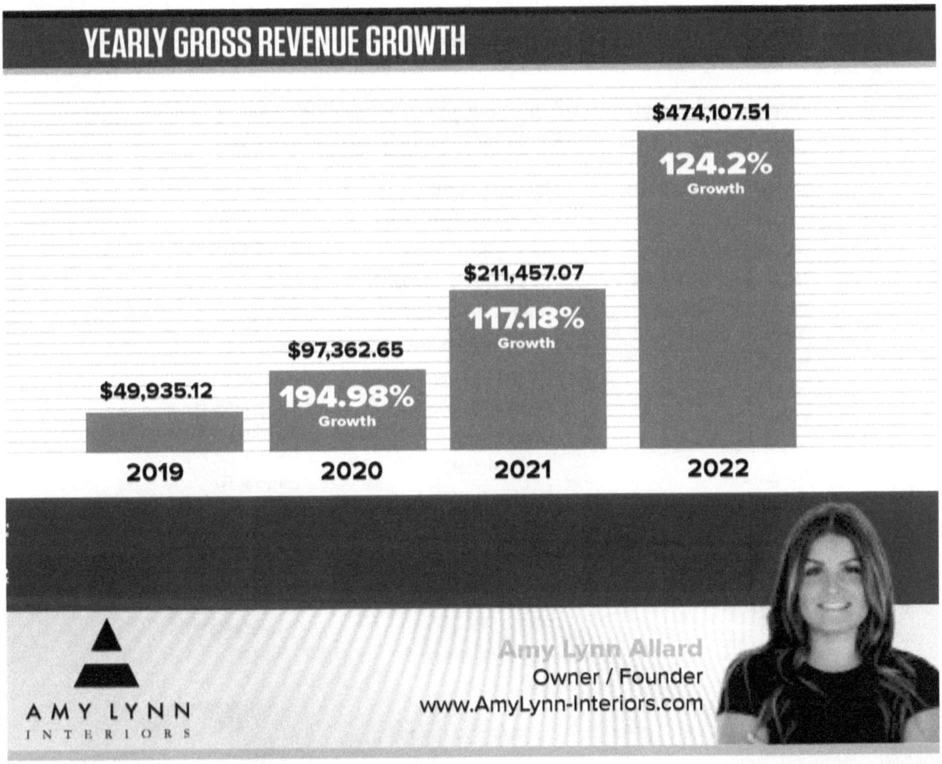

YEARLY GROSS REVENUE GROWTH

$474,107.51

124.2%
Growth

$211,457.07

117.18%
Growth

$97,362.65

194.98%
Growth

$49,935.12

| 2019 | 2020 | 2021 | 2022 |

AMY LYNN
INTERIORS

Amy Lynn Allard
Owner / Founder
www.AmyLynn-Interiors.com

"The missing ingredient for nearly all of the 1,000-plus clients I have worked with directly to improve their businesses is pigheaded discipline and determination. We all get good ideas at seminars and from books, radio talk shows and business-building gurus. The problem is that most companies do not know how to identify and adapt the best ideas to their businesses. Implementation, not ideas, is the key to real success."

CHET HOLMES
Former business partner of billionaire Charlie Munger and the best-selling author of The Ultimate Sales Machine

* *

"You won't reap a harvest if you don't sew the seeds."

Clay Clark

If you take off for your birthday, your spouse's birthday, your anniversary, the days before and after each national holiday, two weeks for vacation, and when you don't feel good while starting or growing a business (before you make your millions), you will be poor.

Circle the days you took off this past year from sowing seeds, and determine how realistic it is for you to plan on reaping a harvest this year.

The day before New Year's Eve.

New Year's Eve.

New Year's Day.

The day after New Year's Day.

The day before Martin Luther King, Jr. Day

Martin Luther King, Jr. Day

The day after Martin Luther King, Jr. Day

The day before President's Day

President's Day

The day after President's Day

The Thursday before Good Friday

Good Friday

The Saturday before Easter

Easter

The day after Easter

The day before Memorial Day

Memorial Day

The day after Memorial Day

The day before Independence Day

Independence Day

The day after Independence Day

The day before Labor Day

Labor Day

The day after Labor Day

The day before Columbus Day

Columbus Day

The day after Columbus Day

The day before Veterans' Day

Veterans' Day

The day after Veterans' Day

The Monday of the week of Thanksgiving

The Tuesday of the week of Thanksgiving

The Wednesday of the week of Thanksgiving

Thanksgiving

Black Friday

The day before Christmas Eve (Known as Festivus for all of your Seinfeld fans)

Christmas Eve

Christmas Day

The day after Christmas

7 days that you don't feel like coming in because you feel sick

104 weekend days off

"You can't get much done in life if you only work on the days when you feel good."

JERRY WEST
Hall of Fame basketball player and legendary NBA executive

"Lazy hands make for poverty, but diligent hands bring wealth."

PROVERBS 10:4

"Rise and Grind."

CLAY CLARK

Some authors don't need a "Hype Man." But until he's famous, Clay does.

FOREWORD BY BEST-SELLING AUTHOR, CLIFTON TAULBERT

As I listened to my introduction by former United States Supreme Court Judge Sandra Day O'Connor, I was literally pinching myself. No one knew better than I that I could have failed. Instead, I had become a businessman and an author; thus my reason for being in the nation's capital. I was standing in the James Madison Room in the Library of Congress where after my introduction, I would give a lecture on my recently released book, Eight Habits of the Heart. It all seemed surreal.

I had grown up in the Mississippi Delta during the era of legal segregation when fieldwork was the industry of choice offered me. Somehow I had managed to THRIVE when merely surviving would have been just as acceptable. Early on in my young life I had gravitated toward an entrepreneurial way of thinking—a way of thinking that quite frankly took me out of the norm of many of my peers and placed me on a path to success. I graduated from high school as first in my class when many of my peers were simply dropping out—oftentimes due to the circumstances beyond their control. My thinking dictated my actions.

After a successful stint in the United States Air Force—the 89th Presidential Wing - that same way of thinking followed me to Oklahoma. It led to my early involvement with a small Oklahoma oil field company where one of the partners invented the Stairmaster Exercise System and many years later, it led me to be an investor in one of Oklahoma's more successful de novo banks. Clay Clark understands this way of thinking and feels compelled to share its value with others.

Clay Clark's passionate book is about what is possible for our lives. Clay is a man I have known since he was a very young boy. I watched him grow up and quite frankly over the last decade or so, achieve beyond my wildest thoughts. Looking back at my own life and the obvious limitations I faced, I should have known that if you plan, focus, and head in the right direction, you will get to your destination. I watched Clay do this, as did all of Tulsa and now beyond. I remember when not even thirty years of age, just a young guy with a growing DJ business, he threw his hat in the Tulsa mayoral race. Had this been Glen Allan, Mississippi, my hometown of less than five hundred people—and many not voting, I could have understood this. We never had a mayor, and with his gift of conversation, he probably could have been elected in my Delta hometown. But this was Tulsa, Oklahoma, where former mayors had cut their teeth in the oil industry and held family names that were well known. That little fact didn't seem to bother Clay. He passed out his red, white and blue "stuff" with a flashing smile. He was in the race. It was then that I realized that he was in control of his destiny and was driven by his own internal dreams for himself. I never forgot his courage to do so. In this book, he reminds us all of the "courage" we have and in so doing, he takes away every excuse not to act courageously on our own behalf...to THRIVE, if you will.

This book is Clay's conversation—the written word of his life and his beliefs. While reading the manuscript, I could see and hear him talking aloud and flashing that smile—that I am sure he'll one day find a way to market. He doesn't believe in the underutilization of his talents and gifts—a flashing smile notwithstanding. He has been recognized nationally by the White House as Oklahoma's Small Business Entrepreneur of the Year and he still hasn't reached that seasoned age of forty. He has learned to leverage his business acumen and finds himself in multiple successful business partnerships. So I was not surprised at all when he set out to launch THRIVE UNIVERSITY—the place to get what you need to know to get you where you want to go. Those are his words. This book, though, extends his winning talks beyond sold-out conferences to thousands more nationwide and around the world. Through his THRIVE UNIVERSITY, he will open up passageways for others to live beyond the "just surviving" mentality. He celebrates success wherever it is found. He understands the hard work and dedication required. He really does admire Napoleon Hill and fills his life with his actionable quotes. They are all through this book. As I look at Clay's success and his larger than life vision for his future, he is well on his way to emulating the man he so admires and quite frankly, placing himself in a similar position of being admired and quoted as his life and businesses continue to THRIVE.

Oftentimes, people offering advice simply trust that the message is understood and then move on; not Clay Clark. He is committed to being in your face for your success. Not afraid of repetitive conversation and in-your-face humor, he is committed to each reader getting the message and more importantly, implementing the actions steps set forth in this book and those voiced at THRIVE15.com. To embrace and implement the action steps in this book or from THRIVE15.com is the much-needed precursor to implementing the action steps around your "big idea." This man gets emotional over your business success—maximizing your talents and potential. He remembers his dorm-room start and fully celebrates yours. Quoting Clay, "My friend, as you can tell by now, running a successful business is about so much more than just having a 'big idea.' Your 'big idea' is important, but the overwhelming majority of what will make your business succeed or fail has little to do with the 'big idea' itself and everything to do with the execution of the 'big idea.'" Clay leaves us no doubt that action on our part matters. His life as well as his insightful consulting encounters are a clear window through which we can look and see what is possible in many of our lives if one is willing to put in the time and effort necessary to turn ideas into reality. Clay clearly points out that our "want to" becomes the driver of our actions or lack of actions.

Yes, I could have failed had I not embraced the notion that execution of a plan mattered. Clay is right. His life challenges us to not settle, but to THRIVE. In so doing, we place ourselves in a position to light the darkness for others. It is in our reach to others that we truly maximize our existence on this planet. If I were still home in the Delta doing the same thing, I doubt seriously if I would be able to light the pathway for myself or others. Today I am lighting the darkness as a businessman and writer, telling others what is possible for their lives. Clay's passionate plea for others to move beyond merely surviving comes from an honest place of caring. Why fail when you can THRIVE? Thank you, Clay, for not being afraid to step out beyond the ordinary and for inviting us along on your remarkable journey.

Clifton L. Taulbert

President of The Building Community Institute | Bestselling author of Once Upon A Time...
When We Were Colored (which was later turned into a major motion picture of the same name) |
Pulitzer-Nominated Author

"EVERYTHING ELSE BECOMES UNNECESSARY IN A
BUSINESS IF NOBODY SELLS ANYTHING."
- CLAY CLARK

Clifton Taulbert (Best-selling author, award-winning entrepreneur and man who was once not allowed to walk in through the front door or banks as a results of legal segregation who went on to open up his own bank)

"Books are like eggs. Sometimes you have to crack them open to get anything out."

- Clifton Taulbert

(He is best known for his books Once Upon a Time When We Were Colored and Eight Habits of the Heart: Embracing the Values that Build Strong Communities. Taulbert offers courses in Character Education and Building Strong School Communities through Knowledge Delivery Systems, an online resource for educators. A former Oklahoma Banker, Taulbert is president and founder of The Freemount Corporation, a consulting company focused on human capital development and organizational effectiveness. Since the founding of the company, his philosophy has been embraced by such companies as Lockheed Martin, Bank of America, Baxter Healthcare, Pacific Coast Gas, the U.S. Department of Defense, the U.S. Department of Justice, the Federal Bureau of Investigation and K-12 and post-secondary academic leadership around the world-from China to the Mississippi Delta.)

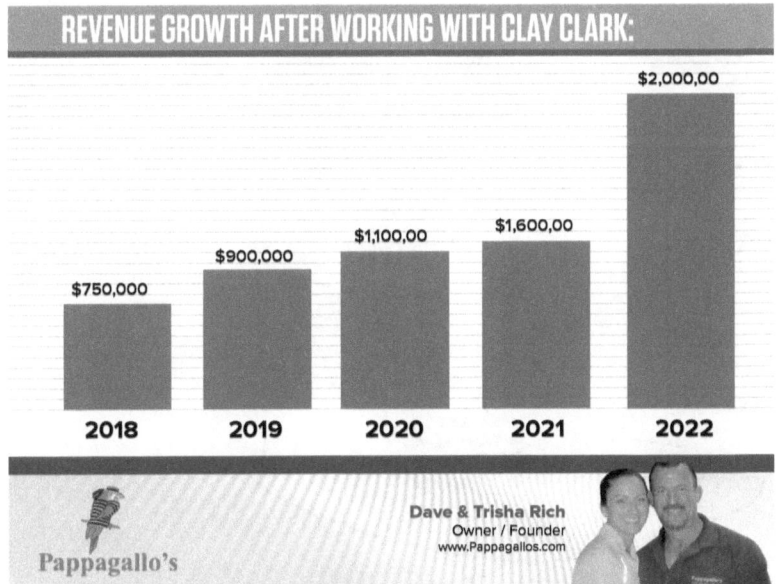

REVENUE GROWTH AFTER WORKING WITH CLAY CLARK:

2018	2019	2020	2021	2022
$750,000	$900,000	$1,100,00	$1,600,00	$2,000,00

Pappagallo's

Dave & Trisha Rich
Owner / Founder
www.Pappagallos.com

"Success is a choice you must make every single day. What time are you willing to wake up every day in order to find the time to work your business?." - *Clay Clark* (Founder of Thrive15.com)

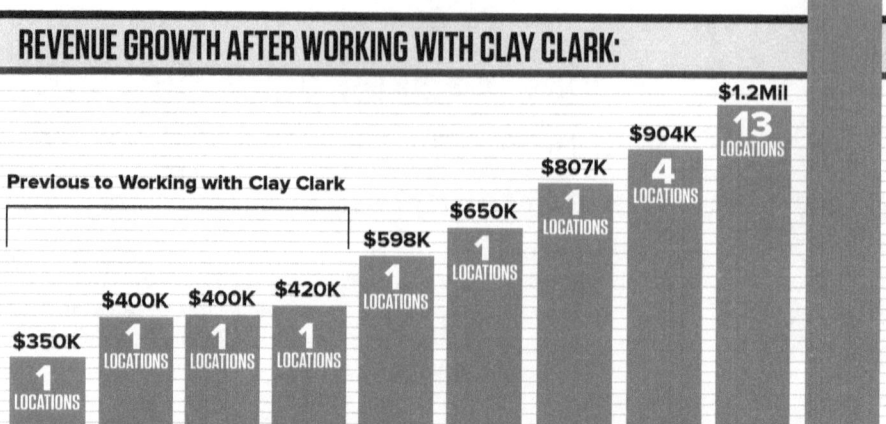

REVENUE GROWTH AFTER WORKING WITH CLAY CLARK:

Previous to Working with Clay Clark

2013	2014	2015	2016	2017	2018	2019	2020	2021	2022
$350K 1 LOCATIONS	$400K 1 LOCATIONS	$400K 1 LOCATIONS	$420K 1 LOCATIONS	$598K 1 LOCATIONS	$650K 1 LOCATIONS	$807K 1 LOCATIONS	$904K 4 LOCATIONS	$1.2Mil 13 LOCATIONS	

TIP TOP K9

Rachel & Ryan Wimpey
Owner / Founder
www.TipTopK9.com

PLAN FOR THE WORST AND
HOPE FOR THE BEST.

"CONTROL YOUR OWN DESTINY OR
SOMEONE ELSE WILL."
- JACK WELCH

Chapter 2

Introduction

Today I'm known as the founder of the Thrivetime Show Podcast, the founder of the ReAwaken America Tour, the former U.S. Small Business Administration's Entrepreneur of the Year, a writer for Entrepreneur.com, and a guy who's had his businesses featured in Fast Company, Forbes, and Bloomberg. However, I am actually a man-bear-pig who grew up in and out of poverty and who had to take both Algebra and his ACT three times just to get into college. My friend, if I can do this, you can too and I'm excited to show you how.

Definition Magician:
Poverty – "pov-er-ty" – The state of being extremely poor

The word "poverty" means different things to different people. Having traveled around the world, I have unfortunately met people who don't have access to clean drinking water and who live outside in the elements permanently. However growing up, my family was what I would call "American poor."

We were not homeless, but only because of the generosity of countless family and friends who wanted to help my mom and dad because they were good people and of high integrity. As a kid, I remember numerous times when our bills were paid by somebody else and our clothes were provided by somebody else, but we were never homeless. I remember when my father, then in his late 30s, chose to deliver pizzas to provide for our family rather than go on government

> "You must walk to the beat of a different drummer. The same beat that the wealthy hear. If the beat sounds normal, evacuate the dance floor immediately! The goal is to not be normal, because as my radio listeners know, normal is broke."

-Dave Ramsey
(Bestselling author, national radio talk show host, and financial expert)

assistance. I remember the kids taunting me on the school bus about this and I remember feeling helpless. I remember making up stories and outright lies about what my dad did for a living so that I could defend him in some way. I remember repeatedly thinking to myself, "Someday you morons are going to be poor too and when you are, I will be glad."

Fast-forward to my middle school and high school years. My family moved from Oklahoma to Minnesota so my mom could go to work for her sister We still never had money in the budget for the things I wanted, so I started selling gum and candy out of my locker in middle school. Our principal (I believe his name was Mr. Johnson) eventually banned the use of gum at school and thus I quickly learned about the Law of Supply and Demand. Because it was essentially illegal to have gum and candy, everyone now wanted it and I was the "go-to guy." I made thousands of dollars selling gum and candy and I eventually moved up into the t-shirt game. Our local high school only sold lame, soulless, and politically correct t-shirts that were approved by our athletic department, so I started producing shirts that really captured the soul of the student body. I produced classy shirts that taunted our opponents and that the kids wanted to buy. In order to produce the shirts that the students wanted for which I had already taken orders, I had to learn all about Photoshop, kinds of t-shirts, heat presses, inventory management, order forms, and cash management.

"You can't connect the dots looking forward. You can only connect them looking backward. So you have to trust that the dots will somehow connect in your future. You have to trust in something — your gut, destiny, life, karma, whatever."

-*Steve Jobs*
(Co-founder of Apple, the founder of NeXT and the former CEO of Pixar)

Fast-forward again to 1999, I was a non-Christian believer (at the time). Yet I still decided to attend a private Christian college called Oral Roberts University because it was as far away from my parents as I could get. My best friend and I agreed to be roommates and because the school was based in the town in which I was born. Oral Roberts University is known for being the college that

Homer Simpson's neighbor, Ned Flanders, graduated from, the college that Kathie Lee Gifford (of Regis and Kathie Lee and the Today Show) attended, and that the Grammy Award winning recording artist Ryan Tedder (frontman for OneRepublic and songwriter for Adele, Beyoncé, U2, and countless others) graduated from. The school was named for its charismatic and Pentecostal televangelist founder, Oral Roberts. During my time at ORU, I discovered that approximately 80% of your college courses have no practical application to your life after college and that attempting to pay your own way through college is very tough.

> "Start where you are, with what you have. Make something of it and never be satisfied."
>
>  *-George Washington Carver*
> (The famous inventor who was born into slavery and who went on to invent countless uses for peanuts and sweet potatoes, which helped empower millions of poor families who then grew these crops as both their own source of food and income)

In order to pay my way through college, I started a company called www.DJConnection.com. I grew the business to the point that we were actually providing entertainment for thousands of events per year (as many as 80 events on many weekends) before I decided to sell the company. I started out my DJ business by carrying around a backpack full of flyers. I would shove these flyers promoting my next dance party underneath the doors of each and every college student three times before each event. I held these events at the local Marriott Hotel located at the corner of 71st and Lewis in Tulsa, which was basically walking distance for most of the student body.

I did not have a business license to promote these events. I did not have the proper insurance in place to house over 500 people in one place at one time. I did not own any of my own DJ equipment (I didn't even know how to properly operate the DJ equipment). But I had nothing to lose, so I produced incredible events that people loved to attend.

> "Learn from people who know the way and aggressively implement proven systems and processes until you achieve your goals. Don't make excuses. Show up everyday and diligently put in the work."
> - *Clay Clark*

Since selling www.DJConnection.com, I've gone on to start many successful ventures (www.EITRLounge.com, www.EpicPhotosTulsa.com, and www.MakeYourLifeEpic.com, just to name a few) and to coach thousands of business owners through the process of developing the duplicable and scalable best-practice business systems they need to have in place to grow. I've spent the majority of my working hours in conference rooms, workshops, and on the stage at public speaking events. However, when my son was born blind and since my dad lost the ability to use his arms, his legs, to feed himself, and even the ability to breathe on his own, it has become increasingly clear to me that my time on this planet is limited and I must teach these provable systems to people like you, faster.

PBS, CNNMoney, and countless news outlets have published articles showing that half of U.S. adults no longer believe in the American dream.[1] This is why I feel like I have a lot of work to do.

My friend, this can be your year and your time to thrive. However, YOU must commit to learning the proven systems, processes, controls, and strategies that you need to know to turn your big visions into reality, otherwise your big ideas will never become your reality. Once you learn these systems, you will find yourself enjoying more time freedom owning a company that is both fun to own and operate.

> "Hope when that moment comes, you'll say...I did it all. I did it all. I owned every second that this world could give. I saw so many places, the things that I did. With every broken bone, I swear I lived."
>
> -*Ryan Tedder*
> ("I Lived" by OneRepublic)

"Desire is the key to motivation, but it's the determination and commitment to unrelenting pursuit of your goal - a commitment to excellence - that will enable you to attain the success you seek."

-Mario Andretti
(Retired Italian American world champion racing driver, one of the most successful Americans in the history of the sport. He is one of only two drivers to win races in Formula One, IndyCar, World Sportscar Championship and NASCAR - the other being Dan Gurney).

Conflicting emotions often get in the way of implementing the motions you need to take. Sign the commitment letter below[2] and you'll begin to notice your life changing for the better.

I _____ *(first and last name)* commit to dedicating myself to investing the time needed to learn and implement these proven business systems and strategies into my own life and business.

Signature: _____

Date: _____

For accountability, take a picture of this signed page and email it to us at info@ThriveTimeShow.com.

**Quick disclaimer:
For your overall benefit, I have filled this book with 100% true examples and case studies taken from my work with real clients, real families, and real people like you. However, to protect the privacy and confidentiality of Thrivers all around the world, I have changed a few of the variables (names, genders, industries, and locations). Nevertheless, these are still 100% fact-based stories.

A Quick Summary of this Book

This book has been written to help you achieve massive, quick, and sustainable growth. However, if you really do desire to greatly enhance your life, your business, and your amount of financial and time freedom, you must give me permission to help by taking the actions prescribed in this book.

Phase 1 – Decrease Your Business' Reliance Upon You

In order to build these world-class and duplicable systems, we are going to need to reduce your business' reliance upon you. The first portion of the book will show you how. We will provide you with the practical tools, downloadables and templates that you need along the way, however you must commit to taking the action needed to turn your dreams into reality.

Phase 2 – Unlock Your Company's Fast and Sustainable Growth Potential by Listening to Your Customers

During this portion of the book, we will show you how you can clearly identify the low-hanging fruit and the sustainable growth potential that is currently hidden within your own business, simply by listening to your current customers.

Phase 3 – Take the Limiters Off of Your Growth

Here we will teach you how to quickly identify and eliminate actual barriers, limiting beliefs, and systems that are causing your business to become stuck or to grow at a very slow annual growth rate. During this portion of the book, we will deep-dive into the very practical areas of HR, leadership, sales, marketing, Internet optimization, and much, much more.

Phase 4 – Optimize Your Personal Happiness and Personal Life Satisfaction

During this phase of the book, I will teach you how to optimize your quality of life in such a way that you are eager to start each day because you know it will be a day filled with meaning and purpose. Unfortunately, I have had the opportunity meet with thousands of clients all over the world who have copious amounts of money but very little time freedom and satisfaction with their overall quality of life. This doesn't have to be your reality.

"Before I knew how to build business systems that were not dependent upon on me. I used to pride myself on working at each and every trade show that our team went to. My wallet was happy, but my wife was not. Now, I know that you can truly have both time and financial freedom. You can build a business model that is capable of working without you."

- Clay Clark
(3-Time Algebra-taker and the former U.S. SBA Entrepreneur of the Year)

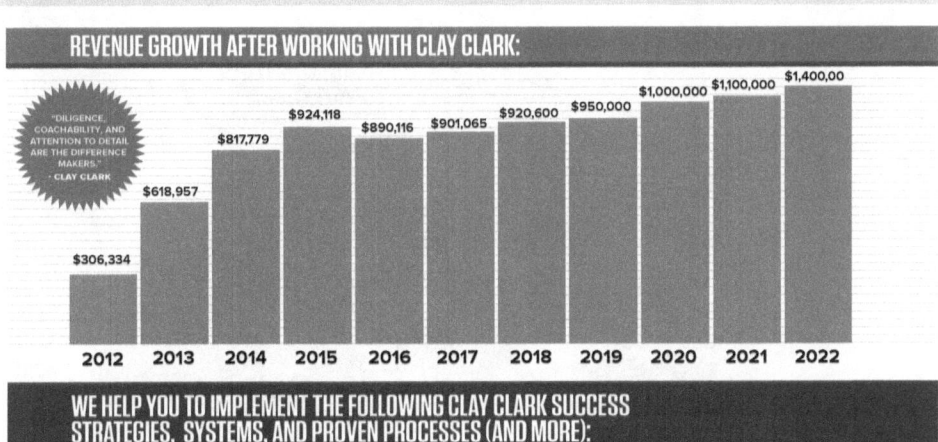

REVENUE GROWTH AFTER WORKING WITH CLAY CLARK:

"DILIGENCE, COACHABILITY, AND ATTENTION TO DETAIL ARE THE DIFFERENCE MAKERS." - CLAY CLARK

2012	2013	2014	2015	2016	2017	2018	2019	2020	2021	2022
$306,334	$618,957	$817,779	$924,118	$890,116	$901,065	$920,600	$950,000	$1,000,000	$1,100,000	$1,400,00

WE HELP YOU TO IMPLEMENT THE FOLLOWING CLAY CLARK SUCCESS STRATEGIES, SYSTEMS, AND PROVEN PROCESSES (AND MORE):

AMERICAN DOCUMENT SHREDDING

Kelly Herneisen
Owner / Founder
www.weshredonsite.com

IMPLEMENTING PROVEN SYSTEMS = SUCCESS

16,000% Growth

David & Stacy Whited
Owners / Founders
www.FlyoverConservatives.com

FLYOVER

"WE'VE EXPERIENCED A 16,000% INCOME/GROWTH."
DAVID & STACY WHITED

"TIME IS THE SCARCEST RESOURCE OF THE MANAGER;
IF IT IS NOT MANAGED, NOTHING ELSE CAN BE MANAGED."
- PETER F. DRUCKER

"TIME IS YOUR MOST PRECIOUS ASSET."

Phase 1

$1,509,027.64

$335,756.14

$70,432

2019   2020   2021

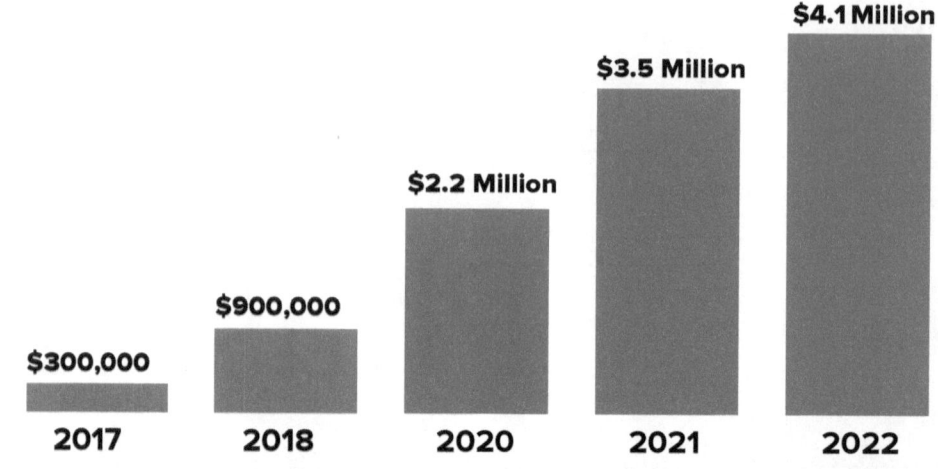

"BE LIKE A POSTAGE STAMP.
STICK TO IT UNTIL YOU GET THERE."
—HARVEY MACKAY

Chapter 3

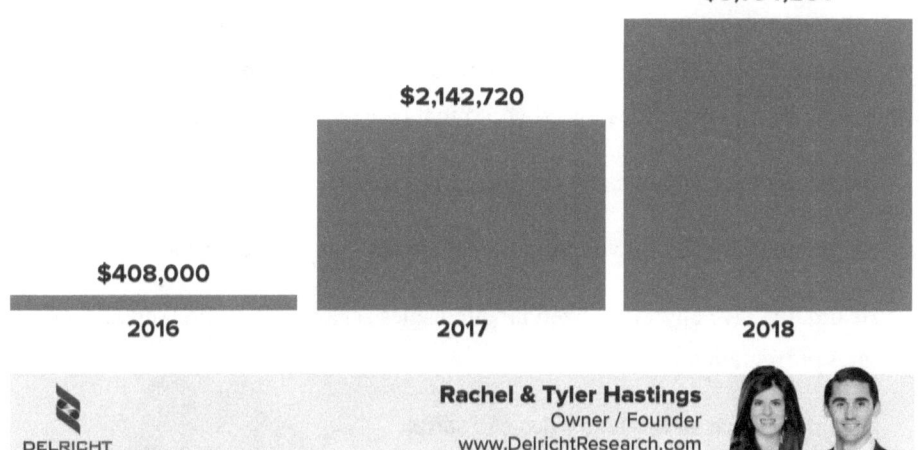

$3,784,260

$2,142,720

$408,000

2016   2017   2018

Rachel & Tyler Hastings
Owner / Founder
www.DelrichtResearch.com

DELRICHT

Decreasing Your Business' Reliance Upon You

Years ago I was working with a business owner based in Texas who had absolutely worked himself into exhaustion. He ran a soccer coaching facility and was approaching 60 years of age. During college, he had been a standout and full-scholarship player, and business just seemed to follow him wherever he went following his Division 1 career. However, as his business grew, his physical body began to deteriorate from years of hard use and natural aging. This coach who was once able to demonstrate every drill first-hand was now forced to hire younger coaches to teach the kids the moves, drills, and systems that he had spent a lifetime creating. Furthermore, for the first time in his life, he was now facing major competition from another coaching facility in town.

His banker referred him to me and soon thereafter, we sat down to conduct our standard 29-Point

"No one lives long enough to learn everything they need to learn starting from scratch. To be successful, we absolutely, positively have to find people who have already paid the price to learn the things that we need to learn to achieve our goals."

-Brian Tracy
(Bestselling author and world-renowned speaker)

Business Self-Evaluation (which you can access for free by visiting www.Thrive15. com/TreasureTrove). His overall score of 58% indicated that he had many problems (which we call "opportunities for growth") that he needed to address including:

1. He did not have any turnkey marketing systems.

2. He did not have any proven turnkey advertisements he used throughout the year.

3. He did not have any formalized inbound sales scripts, pre-written emails, or sales presentation processes.

4. He did not have an inbound sales call script.

5. He did not have an outbound sales call script.

6. He did not have a formalized up-selling / cross-selling sales presentation script.

7. He did not have a systematic customer "wow experience" baked into his workflow. He did not have a documented workflow at all.

8. He did not have a way to scalably deliver his coaching services without physically being the coach.

9. He did not have any understanding of his break-even point, his goal achievement point, when his taxes were due, and how much money he was making or losing each week.

10. He had no concept of his overall profitability per customer.

11. He did not have a cause-based marketing or public relations campaign in place.

12. He did not have any file organization or existing nomenclature rules in place.

13. He did not have talent recruitment and scripted job posting, inquiring, responding, or interviewing processes in place.

14. He did not have an ongoing training program in place for his staff.

15. He was not being intentional about developing banking relationships or friendships with those who have the ability to invest in businesses.

16. He was not doing anything intentionally to become a leader that his employees would follow.

17. He did not have a management, follow-up, or delegation system in place.

18. He did not have a system in place to motivate himself and keep himself engaged and excited about the vision of his company.

19. He did not have a time management system in place to block out distractions and to create time to focus on the important aspects of his business.

20. His overall growth was stagnant.

21. He was spending everything he made and was actually behind in many of his financial responsibilities.

22. He did have a proof of concept and he knew from first-hand experience that people were willing to pay for professional soccer coaching services. Especially, if a parent believed that their kid had the potential to play soccer at the Division 1 NCAA college level on a full-scholarship basis.

23. He did not have any documented processes in place indicating how the company would eventually scale (expand rapidly) to different markets in the event that their marketing efforts were successful and their trainings were shown to be effective.

24. He did not have financial peace, and in fact, was actually quite stressed out financially most of the time.

25. He did not have any formalized goals for his life in the areas of Faith, Family, Finances, Fitness, and Friendships.

26. He did not have any formalized or accurate checklists in place and thus, all questions from employees and customers were consistently being directed toward him.

27. He did have effective communication skills, yet he was terrible at communicating with his loyal, ongoing customers in an effective manner (via text message, email, social media, and mass voicemail).

28. He had very little documentation for anything including his passwords, processes, the service experience delivery, the bathroom cleaning checklists, and the actual coaching process itself.

> "Resources are what he uses to do it, processes are how he does it, and priorities are why he does it."

> -*Clayton M. Christensen*
> (Professor at Harvard Business College)

29. He did not have customer relationship management software in place, despite having worked with over 10,000 paying customers throughout his 30-year career.

30. To make long story short, this incredible man was a loyal father, a committed husband, and an outstanding coach, but he was way down the road toward something I call the "Proven Path to Small Business Death" which includes:

   a. Running out of health.
   b. Running out of money.
   c. Running out of time.

> "Most entrepreneurs are merely technicians with an entrepreneurial seizure. Most entrepreneurs fail because you are working IN your business rather than ON your business."

> -*Michael Gerber*
> (Bestselling author of the E-Myth book series)

However, I am proud to say that nearly four years after our first meeting, this is no longer the case. This client has made SIGNIFICANT improvement in 25 of the 29 areas of weakness we originally discovered in his 29-Point Business Evaluation and he is finally financially free. Recently he unfortunately had to have another surgery, but when he did, he had a team of employees and a staff prepared, trained, and ready to fill in for their mentor and leader.

My friend, have you ever taken a timeout from the busyness of your day to ask yourself why it seems as though a few people have a natural ability to move from one successful venture to another with little or no drama, while most business owners seem to never be able to figure out the magic formula? Why do some college basketball coaches seem to win everywhere they go, while others just can't seem to ever win? Over the years, I've had the opportunity to become friends with the legendary Hall of Fame Division 1 college basketball coach, Eddie Sutton, who was able to take four schools to the NCAA Tournament and to take both Arkansas and Oklahoma State to the Final Four. During his career, he was one of only eight college basketball coaches to have ever won over 800 games. That was because he knew HOW TO WIN. Athletic directors knew that no matter where Eddie Sutton coached, he was going to win because he knew the methodology, the resources, the systems, the processes, and the priorities needed to win.

My friend, you must become like one of these legendary coaches. YOU MUST LEARN THAT THE PARALLELS AND COMMON DENOMINATORS FOUND IN RUNNING MOST BUSINESSES FAR OUTWEIGH THE DIFFERENCES OF EACH BUSINESS TYPE AND INDUSTRY. The great entrepreneurs have learned this and their wallets are much bigger as a result. For example, one of my clients now owns a sushi bar, a neurological center, a testosterone clinic, a cosmetic surgery business, and a liquor store. What do all these businesses have in common? They all allow him to exchange goods and services for the monetary compensation we all seek.

For your benefit, I need for you to take the following pledge:

I, _____, believe that although my business does have unique variables and specialized aspects, I know that the similarities of successful businesses greatly outweigh their differences. I realize that saying, "Yes, but my type of business is very different" is not helpful and is a limiting belief.

Signed: _____ Date: _____

Refusing to implement the proven systems that we will teach you during this book would be a lot like a super small Division 1 athletic director telling Coach Eddie Sutton during the peak of his career that he couldn't possibly help his team or his program to win more games because he had only coached at Creighton, Arkansas, Kentucky, and Oklahoma State. My friend, if this is the mindset you have, you need to go out and get one of those police-grade tasers and unleash it on your own inner thigh while in the middle of a church service. Doing that would be dumb and everybody would see how dumb you are, just like it's dumb and everybody can see how dumb you are when you are working 80 hours per week because you believe that you are only one on the planet capable of doing what you do.

> "If you are willing to do only what's easy, life will be hard. But if you're willing to do what's hard, life will be easy."
> -*T. Harv Eker*
> (Bestselling author of Secrets of the Millionaire Mind)

Unless you are a professional athlete who is playing at the all-star level or unless you are the Artist Known as Prince (whom we just lost recently), you can teach people to do your job. It's hard to teach people to dress up like a purple figure skater and then create iconic and legendary music for decades in a row, but it's not hard to teach people to do your job.

What if You Were Abducted by Aliens for 30 Days?

I realize that asking you "what would happen to your business if you were abducted by aliens" may cause you to wonder what is wrong with me and if I have a firm grasp on reality. However, just for a second, let's suppose that you were abducted by aliens for 30 days who were focused on picking your brain, trying to figure out what the mullet is all about, why the heck Americans use a representative delegate system for determining the presidency of the United States, and why we are willing to exchange goods and services in exchange for a paper (fiat) currency.

Definition Magician:
Fiat – "fee-aht" – A paper currency made legal tender by a fiat of the government, but not based on or convertible into precious metal based coin.

My friend, throughout the years I have asked thousands and thousands of people this question and I almost always hear the same, terrible answer. Most business owners would be totally out of business if they were unable to work for 30 days. Think about all of the energy, time, and effort you have invested in your business and your entire business would be totally gone if you were abducted by aliens for 30 days. Time and time again, I meet with business owners who have built owner-based business systems that only work if the owner invests long hours. These business owners explain to me that they have no time freedom, no financial freedom, and they definitely do not have an exit strategy for the business.

However, most of these same business owners tell me that the reason they even decided to start a business was so that they could achieve both financial and time freedom. At the end of the day, if the success of a business is judged based upon whether it has achieved its purpose to create the time and financial freedom that the owner desired, then that business would actually need to be considered a failure.

Now, if we were playing third grade soccer, I'm sure a socialist referee would give us a 2nd place trophy and some ice cream to keep us from considering the profundity

> "Most people are sitting on their own diamond mines. The surest ways to lose your diamond mine are to get bored, become overambitious, or start thinking that the grass is greener on the other side. Find your core focus, stick to it, and devote your time and resources to excelling at it."
>
>  *-Gino Wickman*
> (The bestselling author of the book Traction: Get a Grip on Your Business)

that your business is currently failing you. But this isn't third grade soccer – this is your livelihood. Time to face reality.

Take the test. How long would your business last if you were abducted by aliens for 30 days? www.ThriveTimeShow.com/TreasureTrove

Don't Feel Bad, but Don't Get Stuck

As a dude who started his first business out of his college dorm room and who has personally launched over a dozen successful ventures during my lifetime, I will say that every business has to start with a highly-motivated individual who is willing to scratch and claw his or her way into profitability. However, once you begin to figure out what works, you must have the knowledge, discipline, and focus needed to document your workflow, your operational systems, and your turnkey marketing moves that have been proven to work time and time again. If you don't do this, you will become trapped inside of your own success.

Remember my fabulous friend, you are trying to build a duplicable business vehicle that is capable of growing and producing revenue for you without you personally doing all of the work. Building a business vehicle that is dependent upon you is much like renting a super expensive luxury car to take your kids to Disney World, and then arriving at the park only to discover that you don't have enough money left in your

"The difference between great people and everyone else is that great people create their lives actively, while everyone else is created by their lives, passively waiting to see where life takes them next. The difference between the two is living fully and just existing."

-Michael Gerber
(Bestselling author of the E-Myth book series)

account after renting the Lamborghini (which your wife advised you not to rent in the first place) to afford admission into the park. In an attempt to save face, you may tell your kids, "Hey kids, it's no big deal. Let's just go to Taco Bell and you can have anything you want to eat and we'll eat it while driving fast in this Lamborghini." Big letdown.

> "Drifting, without aim or purpose, is the first cause of failure."
> **-Napoleon Hill**
> **(Bestselling author of** *Think and Grow Rich* **and** *Outwitting the Devil*)

My friend, not only is this example insane, it's also just as crazy to build a business that is totally reliant upon you. Your business exists to allow you to achieve your faith, family, financial, fitness, and friendship goals, and that is it. Be careful here, because if you are not very intentional YOU WILL BECOME SO BUSY WORKING IN THE BUSINESS THAT YOU WON'T BE ABLE TO FIND ANY TIME TO WORK ON THE BUSINESS.

Build Your Business with the End in Mind

I GUARANTEE THAT YOU WILL ACHIEVE SUCCESS IF YOU FOLLOW THE PRACTICAL STEPS OUTLINED IN THIS BOOK, however you must have your vision for your life fully cemented into your mind at all times as you are building your business. My friend, I love my life because I know what I want and I know what I'm about all day, everyday. I know what I call my "F7 Goals."

You must intentionally know and take the time to clearly write down your F7 Goals because you will certainly never "drift" toward the achievement of them. For me personally, I know my goals for my Faith, Family, Finances, Friendships, Fun, and Fitness. I'm a dad with five kids, chickens, goats, turkeys, trees, land, and I prefer spending time alone with my family, reading the Bible, engaging only in mutually beneficial friendships, watching podcasts, watching all documentaries, and chasing

YOU ARE HERE X — — — — → WHERE DO YOU WANT TO GO?

"An organization's capabilities reside in two places. The first is in its processes—the methods by which people have learned to transform inputs of labor, energy, materials, information, cash, and technology into outputs of higher value. The second is in the organization's values, which are the criteria that managers and employees in the organization use when making prioritization decisions."

-Clayton Christensen
(Harvard Business Professor)

my wife around whenever possible (that's how you create five kids, you see). My friend, if you are going to go through the HELL of starting a business, you must make sure that you build a thriving business model that is not dependent upon you for the delivery of every aspect of the business' value to customers. So I'm going to challenge you here for a moment. Take the assessment. What are your F7 Goals?

As your business begins to grow, you will be forced to make a major decision. Will you scale the company so it can grow and flourish without you being there, or are you going to be content only reaching that level of success you can achieve when the business is dependent upon you to a large extent? If you truly want to build systematic wealth, you are going to have to invest your time, focus and money into the creation of duplicable processes and the development of a quality management team. What's the point of investing hours and hours into the recruitment and training of key personnel and creation of systems designed to scale if you aren't actually willing to start working on the business and not in the business?

What are your F7 Goals?

Faith	_____	Fitness	_____
Family	_____	Friendship	_____
Finances	_____	Fun	_____
		Focus	_____

Years ago I had the pleasure of working with a medical practice that helped men who were suffering from issues related to low testosterone levels in their bodies. The doctor was a quality hardworking dude who was pouring in up to 70 hours per week, every week. He had seen spikes in his business from time to time over the years as they hired "a talented

> "You don't get paid for the hour. You get paid for the value you bring to the hour."
>
> **-Jim Rohn**
> **(Bestselling author and world-renowned motivational speaker)**

internet marketer" or a "good sales lady." However, when these employees inevitably left to pursue other job opportunities, the business would hop right back into the financial toilet again. When the doctor called me, I took him through the 29-Point Business Evaluation. After investing the 10 minutes needed to fill out the evaluation, it was clear why he was so frustrated. The doctor was doing nearly everything right, except he had never gone to the trouble to document their inbound call scripts, their search engine marketing practices, nor to set up single source customer relationship management software (CRM). It took him and his team about 60 days (working 1 to 2 hours per week on the business while spending the other 65 hours per week working in the business) to implement the systems. However, he began seeing a DRAMATIC AND LIFE-CHANGING IMPACT within the first week of executing his new systems.

The team now knew that their calls were being recorded for quality assurance and they knew that their paychecks were tied to their performance and overall conversion rates. The team knew what and when they needed to execute their daily search engine marketing tasks and the doctor noticed that his customer database of repeat customers was growing slowly and steadily every day.

Do you want to guess what happened just 12 months after he implemented these systems? This doctor grew his medical practice by nearly 400% and was able to reduce his hours spent working in the clinic to just 35 hours per week (down from 70 hours per week). Today his business is booming and yet it is no longer time consuming. Because of the growth of the clinic, he has been able to hire another doctor to meet with patients and he simply checks in – about one hour per day - to verify that all of the daily checklists are being completed.

My friend, your goal should ultimately be to build a business system that is so solid that the business does not actually need you. When you reach the point in your business career when you can spend your entire day away from the business and no one texts you, calls you or e-mails you for help, you will know that you have made it. To create this time freedom, you are going to need to create tight systems and business processes. Now it's almost time to roll up our sleeves and get it done. However, what might be the hardest part of this process is for you to realize that this might be the first time in your career when just working harder will not produce the systematic solutions you are looking for to create both the time and financial freedom you seek. In fact, your intense work ethic may actually be part of the problem. THE SYSTEMS MUST WORK WITHOUT YOU. I repeat, THE SYSTEMS MUST WORK WITHOUT YOU. Before we start, we need to figure out where you currently are. Take a moment to download all of the proven templates and systems at www.ThriveTimeShow.com/TreasureTrove.

> "Nature cannot be tricked or cheated. She will give up to you the object of your struggles only after you have paid her price."
>
>
> **-Napoleon Hill**
> **(Best-selling author of** *Think & Grow Rich***)**

The time will never be right. You must act now!

$2,100,000 — 2022
$1,900,000 — 2021
$912,000 — 2019
$788,000 — 2018
$400,000 — 2017

Foreseeable Milestones

If you were in my shoes (you would be wearing brown size thirteen Johnston & Murphy dress shoes), after working with thousands of companies you would see that nearly every business goes and grows through a very predictable pathway. At first, the business struggles to survive and make a profit in the crowd of capitalism. The founder of the business consumes every possible form of energy drink known to man while attempting to become the world's best marketer, accountant, manager, and public relations wizard. If the owner keeps his or her

> "Our goals can only be reached through a vehicle of a plan, in which we must fervently believe, and upon which we must vigorously act. There is no other route to success."

> **-Pablo Picasso**
> (Renowned painter, sculptor, ceramicist, stage designer, and playwright)

sanity while creating enough profit to sustain the business, the owner then begins to build a successful business that is dependent upon him for everything. No systems are in place, but the profitability is consistent and so the owner (I'm sure not you) is typically not open to advice or feedback because he has finally started to develop some traction after the doubters and sideline theorists said it couldn't be done.

Eventually the owner begins to realize that she is getting a little older and that she is going to have to build a duplicable and systematic approach to generating consistent profits or she isn't ever going to get out of the office again. Once the owner COMMITS TO SYSTEMATIZING THE BUSINESS IN A DUPLICABLE WAY THAT ALLOWS HER TO CONSISTENTLY CREATE A PROFIT BY ADDING VALUE TO HER IDEAL AND LIKELY BUYERS, that's usually when great things start happening. The business begins producing profits while she is on vacation with her family or in the backyard attempting to find her five-year-old daughter's shoe

(which I currently spend half of my life doing. With five kids, I'm very aware that the stores sell kid's shoes in pairs, yet they are always losing one. I basically needed to achieve both financial and time freedom just so that I would have enough time to find shoes and buy shoes when I can't find them). My friend, I want to ask you, why do you want to build and grow a business?

START WITH A DAILY ORGANIZED PLAN OR YOU WILL FIND YOURSELF LIVING IN A VAN.

"MOST ENTREPRENEURS ARE MERELY TECHNICIANS WITH AN ENTREPRENEURIAL SEIZURE. MOST ENTREPRENEURS FAIL BECAUSE THEY ARE WORKING IN THEIR BUSINESS RATHER THAN ON THEIR BUSINESS."
- MICHAEL GERBER

"Basketball is just something else to do, another facet of life. I'm going to be a success at whatever I choose because of my preparation. By the time the game starts, the outcome has been decided. I never think about having a bad game because I have prepared."

- David Robinson
(Thrive15.com Partners / Mentor, NBA Hall of Basketball Player, former NBA MVP, 2-time Olympic Gold medal winner, 2-time NBA Championship winner, founder of the Carver Academy charter schools and the co-founder of the $250 million Admiral Capital Group)

"The top excuse people use for not achieving their goals is that they didn't have time. You do have the time. If you will simply say 'no' to the people and activities not related to making your business grow."

- Clay Clark

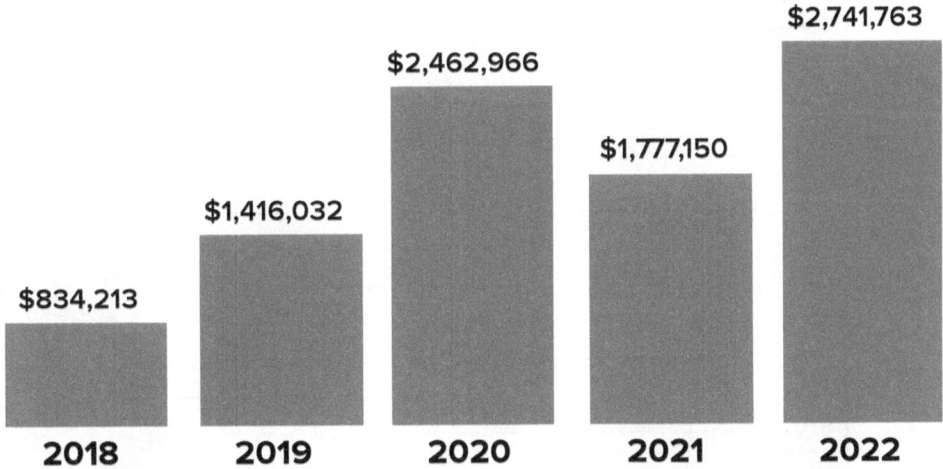

Year	Amount
2018	$834,213
2019	$1,416,032
2020	$2,462,966
2021	$1,777,150
2022	$2,741,763

Christina Nemes & Jeff
Owner / Founder
www.CapeCodAutoBodyandDetailing.co

"What are the problems you can solve for your ideal and likely buyers?"
- Clay Clark

WHAT PROBLEMS CAN YOU SOLVE FOR YOUR IDEAL AND LIKELY BUYERS?

Bottom line: the first step you must take to start a successful business is to solve real problems that real humans have in exchange for real money. If you already have customers because you are already solving problems for real humans, I STRONGLY encourage you to make a list of all of the problems that your IDEAL AND LIKELY BUYERS have and what products and services you could offer to them to help provide them solutions:

Problem	Solution
_____	_____
_____	_____
_____	_____
_____	_____
_____	_____
_____	_____
_____	_____
_____	_____
_____	_____
_____	_____
_____	_____
_____	_____

RUSH TO REVENUE
Money Cures
All Problems

Chapter 4

The Practical Steps of Turning Your Dreams Into Reality

Alright, now I need your permission to GET INTENSE HERE FOR A SECOND and I need for you to UNDERLINE AND HIGHLIGHT THESE WORDS. Nobody cares about your success more than you and in most cases, even at all. I care and you care, and potentially you have a spouse, partner, or friend who really cares, but NOBODY IS GOING TO CARE ABOUT YOUR BUSINESS MORE THAN YOU. When it's time for your first all-nighter, most people are not going to be with you cheering and helping you along. My friend, if you are going to go down this path of turning your dreams into reality, I know the way and our entire team of Thrive15.com Mentors (visit them at www.Thrive15.com/mentors) know the way, and you can refer to this book, come to a workshop, or give us a call if you ever get stuck, but you must keep moving. You must COMMIT TO TAKING MASSIVE ACTION. My friend, here is an outline of the process that you will be going through.

"Here's to the crazy ones, the misfits, the rebels, the troublemakers, the round pegs in the square holes... the ones who see things differently — they're not fond of rules... You can quote them, disagree with them, glorify or vilify them, but the only thing you can't do is ignore them because they change things... they push the human race forward, and while some may see them as the crazy ones, we see genius, because the ones who are crazy enough to think that they can change the world, are the ones who do."

-Steve Jobs
(Co-founder of Apple, founder of NeXT, and the former CEO who turned around PIXAR)

"To Create like the Creator you have to work six days and rest on the seventh."

Stage 1

Giving Birth – You are going to need to formalize your business plan, raise the capital you need, create your logo, create your website, create your initial marketing materials and go out there to see if the world is willing to pay you for the solutions you provide. You think you know whom your ideal and likely buyers are, but you aren't exactly sure. YOU JUST WANT TO FIGURE OUT IF THE HUMAN RACE AND THE MARKETPLACE IS WILLING TO BUY YOUR PRODUCT OR SERVICE AT A PRICE THAT WILL ALLOW YOU TO ACHIEVE FINANCIAL PROSPERITY. During this phase you are going to work countless hours as you try to encourage yourself, fight off doubters, and tell your inner "I'm-scared-out-of-my-mind-that-I'm-an-idiot-if-this-fails" to shut up. If you are crazy enough to go out there and start a business, this shall be your life for a while. However, with our help, you can get through this phase much more quickly.

It's About Time to Form That Limited Liability Company

After you have sold 15 services or products, you will want to form an LLC to insure that you do not lose everything you have personally saved up when you get sued for the first time. To simplify and demystify the process for you (because people tend to fear what they do not know), here are the steps necessary to form an LLC.

1. Accept emotionally that you will get sued at some point (which is the main reason you need to form an LLC in the first place).

2. Find an attorney to help you form an LLC. Attempting to form an LLC by yourself is dumb and will negate the entire purpose of forming an LLC when you get sued for the first time and discover that your LLC cannot protect you because it was filed incorrectly.

3. Select the business name for your LLC. The name of your LLC must be in compliance with the rules of your state's LLC rules and regulations.

4. Write your articles of incorporation.

5. Create an operating agreement.

6. Publish a notice in the states that require it.

7. Get the appropriate licenses and permits.

NOTE:
NONE OF THIS
MATTERS IF YOU
ARE NOT SELLING
SOMETHING!

Stage 2

Raising a Baby Business – At this point, you want to make sure you do not drop the ball so you can deliver a consistent and quality product to your ideal and likely buyers. You spend most of your time in this stage scrambling around answering the phone, training your cousin to make deliveries, trying to convince your mom to answer the phone, and hoping that your minivan that you have converted into the mobile company headquarters doesn't explode after it passes 200,000 miles on the odometer. You are irritated that your first non-family employee broke the handle on the driver-side door and broke the knob on the radio, but you don't have the money or the time to fix either of those. During this time, you must begin formulating your inbound and outbound order taking and deal closing scripts. You must document the steps you have to take to produce your product. You must create an employee handbook, organize your files and develop a naming system for your computer files that makes sense. You're trying to get all of this done while taking your kids to soccer and figuring out what kind of checklist you need to make to get your public bathroom to stop smelling like the rotting remains of a roadkill animal. During this time in your business, you must figure out what works and what doesn't and make the time to transform your findings into checklists, systems, processes, scripts and templates. I know that this phase sounds overwhelming, but as a Thriver, you will have access to hundreds of downloadable and customizable checklists, tools, templates and systems. Visit www.Thrive15.com/TreasureTrove to explore this treasure trove of best-practice documents. It will take you just seconds to download what has taken me and my team over 20 years to collect.

Stage 3

The Bipolar Teenager – If you've ever raised a teenager, been around a teenager, or were a teenager, then you will know what I'm talking about. It is during this time that you are just trying to get everybody to CALM DOWN AND STOP LOSING THEIR FREAKING MINDS!!! Just like teenagers who are overloaded with hormones and freaking out at their bodies that are changing so rapidly, they don't even recognize themselves in the mirror. When you get to this point in your business you are going to be acting a little nuts. One moment you are PUMPED and you KNOW THAT THIS WILL BE THE BEST YEAR EVER; the next moment you are convinced that THE ENTIRE UNIVERSE HATES YOU AND YOU ARE NEVER GOING TO GET OVER THAT COLD. Exhausted, you press on because you financially cannot afford to stop now. You are tired of being tired and you are irritated when your team members tell you how tired they are BECAUSE YOU HAVE BEEN UP SINCE TWO IN THE MORNING AND YOU HAVEN'T TAKEN A FREAKING DAY OFF IN FOUR YEARS. Because you are so emotional at this point, I'm encouraging you to mellow out and begin to F.O.C.U.S. (Focus On Core tasks Until Success) on creating six systems as soon as possible.

System 1 – Define Your Three-Legged Marketing Stool - You must figure out the three most profitable ways to reach your ideal and likely buyers.

 System 2 – Learn to Dominate Internet Marketing - Sometimes I hate to be the guy who has to point out to Doctors, Attorneys, Bakers, Dentists, Neurologists, Roofers, Real Estate Agents, Hair Stylists, Carpet Cleaners, Appliance Sellers, Retailers, and everybody else... THE INTERNET IS STARTING TO CATCH ON. In all sincerity, people use their smartphone for everything so you are just DUMB if you don't know what you are doing on the Internet when it comes to building your website, social media marketing, targeting your ideal and likely buyers, and closing deals.

 System 3 – The ABC Sales Machine – You must define specifically how your ABC (Always Be Closing) Sales Machine works if you are not the one personally closing the deals.

 System 4 - Define Your Product and Service Delivery Systems - You must refine and document your systems to the point that an honest moron could deliver your products and services.

 System 5 - Accounting Systems - You must invest the time needed to define your break-even point, your profit per customer, your lifetime customer value, when your taxes are due, and what the heck is going on with your numbers. If you fail to do this, you will lose.

 System 6 - Hiring, Managing, and Training People - As long as your business is based on Planet Earth, you are going to have to manage people. Finding, inspiring, training, and holding people accountable has proven to be almost impossible to do without following time-tested best-practice management systems. Good news, we will teach you how to do this.

My friend, these six systems comprise the foundation of every successful business so you must learn how to master these six systems. Once you master them, you will be like the Yoda of business (except I hope you don't choose to live alone in a swamp after achieving your success).

Stage 4

The Adult – As an adult, you and I know that we are "supposed to act like adults" and generally we do, but occasionally we lose our minds. This is where most people get stuck. My friend, you cannot get stuck here. MOST ENTREPRENEURS GET STUCK HERE BECAUSE THEY ARE THE ONES WHO RUN EVERY ASPECT OF THE DAILY BUSINESS OPERATIONS. THEY DRUM UP ALL OF THE HUGE SALES DEALS AND THEY MUST MAKE EVERY KEY DECISION. Unless we can learn to raise other adults by teaching our employee children how to develop, we will get stuck here. You must learn to train people who can train people; you must learn how to grow your team into the mature adults you need them to be.

Stage 5

The Adult with Grey Hair – As an adult, we can either be like Jabba the Hutt in his prime or like Richard Gere in his prime. Both are considered to be movie stars and both are males, however that is where the similarities end. When Richard started getting that grey hair, he owned it. He had that look that said, "I could be your dad or I could be dating Julia Roberts, but either way I'm a wise guy because I somehow figured out how to win in this game of life." The goal at this stage of your business development is to be wise and to be viewed as a source of wisdom for your team, whom you keep busy executing your duplicable processes and systems. At this phase in the business game, your focus needs to be on delegating and growing your people.

Stage 6

The Bruce Wayne – Once you have successfully trained your people how to train people and have installed all of the systems needed for your business to run effectively and efficiently without you, it's time for you to actually step out and focus on incrementally improving your business processes and systems, strategically coaching up your leaders to take your business to the next level. You need to be working on your business and not in your business at this point so you can focus on other more important things like "running the city." This is the stage of business that business superheroes reach. I once spent the majority of an afternoon with Thrive15.com CEO, Doctor Robert Zoellner, as he attempted to bring balance to his fish aquarium because he had recently acquired an exotic fish (the only one of its kind in Oklahoma) that the other fish inside the fish tank were trying to eat. Dr. Zoellner spent hours researching what could be done to bring balance back to this ecosystem. It was incredible. Wouldn't it be nice to be able to spend your day trying to solve the problems inside your aquarium rather than trying to find the quarters that may have fallen behind your car's seats so that you can pay for some gas? Have you ever noticed how few hours Bruce Wayne seems to be working? Now I've never spent any time with Batman, but it seems as though Wayne Enterprises is doing pretty well without him.

Stage 7

The Business Mogul – At this stage of the business, you should start to view your team members truly as partners and your goal is to constantly make sure that your top people are focused on their highest and best use at all times. By now, you should have coached your people up to be the leaders needed to help your company dominate the marketplace. Your team should all work in concert with you to help you refine, build, and create the duplicable business systems that you are going to need to truly scale your business.

Stage 8

Drop the Mic – In my first business (in my former life as the founder of www.DJConnection.com), I worked as an entertainer. As an entertainer, you go into every event with the mindset that you want to take each event to the next level and you want the audience to leave the event stunned and wanting more because you've taken them to a place they've never gone before. When you have rocked a show or speaking event at this level, you simply "drop the mic" with nothing left to say. You've dominated, everyone is cheering, and you walk off stage. As an entertainer I've had the pleasure of doing this dozens of times, and as an entrepreneur I've been able to do this a few times. My friend, you know that you have arrived and that your business has reached the "Drop the Mic" level once your business is:

» Dependent on processes and systems and not people.

» Stable with a competitive and goal-achieving leadership team in place.

» Secure with powerful "guardrails" or controls in place that keep your team accountable on a daily basis for taking the action steps required to produce predictable success.

» Flushed with clients who come to your business for the products and services they want and not to you specifically as the owner.

Once you have taken your business to this level, it's now the appropriate time to contemplate and create an exit strategy. My friend, this does not mean that you have to sell the business; it just means that you are no longer personally required to GRIND INTENSELY FOR THE BUSINESS TO THRIVE. At this level you can choose to be actively involved in the business or not because you have developed six main exit strategies:

1. You can exponentially grow the business into different territories, states, or countries. *Example: I've helped many medical doctors do this. Essentially, they know how to deliver the products and services they offer so we refined their marketing systems, lead conversion systems, accounting systems, and quality control systems to the point that it just made sense for them to open up multiple locations.*

2. You can own the business passively while only being involved in the daily operations and strategic decisions for four hours per week or less. *Example: This is the relationship I have currently with several of my business ventures. I've built the brands by intensely focusing on building all of the scalable systems needed for them to succeed and now I simply follow up an average of three hours per week maximum to confirm things are running as they should.*

3. You have built such a strong business model that you could sell the business if you wanted to. *Example: The DJConnection.com systems worked, and worked well. People knew the systems worked and constantly approached me about buying the business from me. Eventually, I agreed to sell. I did the same thing with a company called "Party Perfect" that I systematized and sold to Party Pro. On a smaller level, I also did this with a professional video production company I started.*

4. You have developed such a systematic and turnkey business model that you could franchise the business. Example: One of the clients I have had the pleasure to work with over the years is a company called Oxi Fresh Carpet Cleaning (www.OxiFresh.com). The founder of the company, Jonathan Barnett, is a business partner of mine with the Elephant in the Room Men's Grooming Lounge. Since opening up his first Oxi Fresh Carpet Cleaning franchise, he has literally sold hundreds of franchises. At www.EITRLounge.com, we now have 5 locations.

5. You have the option to license the business. *Example: Many professional sports teams and brands know that their systems and brand recognition are so powerful that companies will literally pay millions just for the right to use their brands. Think about the New York Yankees. People pay millions for the right to put their logo on their apparel that they then sell. Think about the glasses manufacturer, Luxottica. Have you ever purchased a pair of Nike, Eddie Bauer, or Gucci glasses? Luxottica pays these brands millions for the right to use their brand name on the prescription glasses frames that they produce.*

6. You could bring on a massive infusion of outside venture capital or private equity and take the business all over the world quickly with millions to invest in scaling what works. *Example: The ladies who started SoulCycle, Elizabeth Cutler and Julie Rice, built a business model that worked and that people loved. They had a massive goal to help revolutionize the fitness industry and they clearly proved that their business model was viable. Wealthy investors, including the quasi-famous billionaire and real estate guru Stephen M. Ross and his company Related, own the health club chain Equinox and acquired a majority share of SoulCycle in 2011.*

Checking in to Make Sure that You Are Learning Something...

My friend, now that we've have thoroughly gone over all eight stages of a successful business' development, it's important that you take a moment to "marinate," as Paul Pressey would say (the Thrive15.com Mentor and former coach of the Orlando Magic, Golden State Warriors, San Antonio Spurs, Boston Celtics, and Los Angeles Lakers). Right now, get out a pen and underline which one of the following statements best describes you so that you can know at what level of business development you and your business are today.

Stage 1 – You are super excited about your new idea, but you are still trying to raise the capital, refine that business plan, and you are getting ready to start that new business.

Stage 2 – You are trying to show the world that you are not crazy by actually selling that product or service that you have been obsessing about. You are hustling to close some deals and actually deliver on what you promise. You don't sleep much, but you are excited. Like when you are in love for the first time and you keep meeting your girlfriend for 3-hour make out sessions behind the classroom center on the campus of Oral Roberts University. (I'm sorry I just got super personal there. I'll make sure that doesn't happen again until the next page.)

Stage 3 – Your business model is actually quasi-sustainable. You are able to consistently close deals and deliver on what you promise, but it does take a lot out of you to make it happen. At this point, you are your company's top salesperson, service /product provider, and accountant. At the end of the day, the company begins and ends with you.

Stage 4 – Your company is doing well and you are gaining traction and new business quickly, but you have not yet developed any other leaders or top-level managers. You realize that you need quality people to turn your big vision into reality and you've recently realized that you need to become a developer of people if you are ever going to develop your idea and take it to the NEXT LEVEL. You are spending massive amounts of hours per week attempting to improve both your business process and your leadership / management team.

Stage 5 – The team you have views you as a source of wisdom. Your business is absolutely beginning to produce big revenues and you are excited about it. You have now developed at least three leaders and managers who are capable of running the daily operations of your business.

Stage 6 – You no longer must work in the daily operations of your business, and you are beginning to make large amounts of money while no longer exchanging your time for money. You could spend massive amounts of time pursuing your non-business-related hobbies and passions, but you desire to take your business to the next level.

Stage 7 – You have developed a team of hard-working strategic leaders and are confident they could do your job as well as you do it, or better. You are very comfortable with where you are financially, but you have begun to see the vision of your company expanding regionally, nationally, and even internationally.

Stage 8 – Your business model is now so well-refined that it may make sense to license the business, franchise the business, sell the business or bring in an infusion of venture capital and private equity. You want to positively impact the world and now you are looking for a way to scale your vision to get it out to the rest of the planet.

"Face reality as it is, not as it was or as you wish it to be."

-Jack Welch
(The legendary former CEO of GE who grew the company by 4,000% during his tenure)

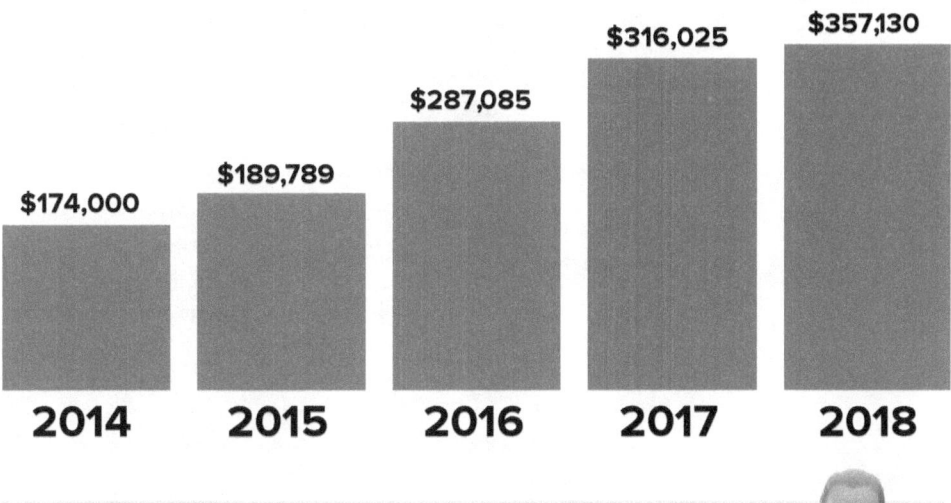

$174,000 — 2014
$189,789 — 2015
$287,085 — 2016
$316,025 — 2017
$357,130 — 2018

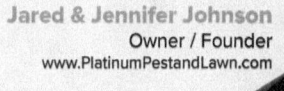

Jared & Jennifer Johnson
Owner / Founder
www.PlatinumPestandLawn.com

"We've met some of the biggest CEOs in the world, guys that run Fortune 500 companies and Clay has 100 times the backbone of the toughest person that you will see. The guy doesn't stop. He will never EVER back down."

-Eric Trump

(Executive Vice President of The Trump Organization Eric Trump who is responsible for managing the TRUMP business empire and the thousands of incredible employees who work together to make the TRUMP organization great. Eric is the proud husband to Lara Trump, a tireless advocate of St. Jude Children's Hospital, and an unapologetic 2nd amendment advocate who happens to be a great shot and Eric Trump is the son of America's real President, President Donald J. Trump.)

"It's important to celebrate the small victories that you achieve in route to achieving your big goals. In fact, back in the day I made our yellow page representative stop and pose for a photo after we achieved my goal of having the biggest advertisement for entertainers in the phone book."

- Clay Clark
(The former U.S. SBA Entrepreneur of the Year, the father of 5 kids and the owner of 9 businesses)

IT'S NOT ABOUT HOW MUCH YOU MAKE.
ITS ABOUT HOW MUCH YOU KEEP.
-CLAY CLARK

Phase 2

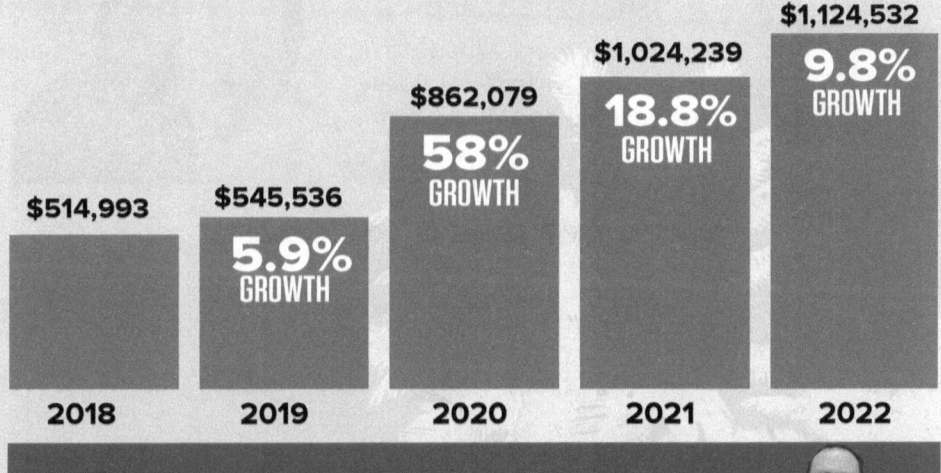

2018	2019	2020	2021	2022
$514,993	$545,536	$862,079	$1,024,239	$1,124,532
	5.9% GROWTH	58% GROWTH	18.8% GROWTH	9.8% GROWTH

MINI MALL

Jason Lett
Owner / Founder
www.LakeMartinCubed.com

"Overall for the year we
are up 15% over last year."

- Jason Lett
Owner, Lake Martin Mini Mall

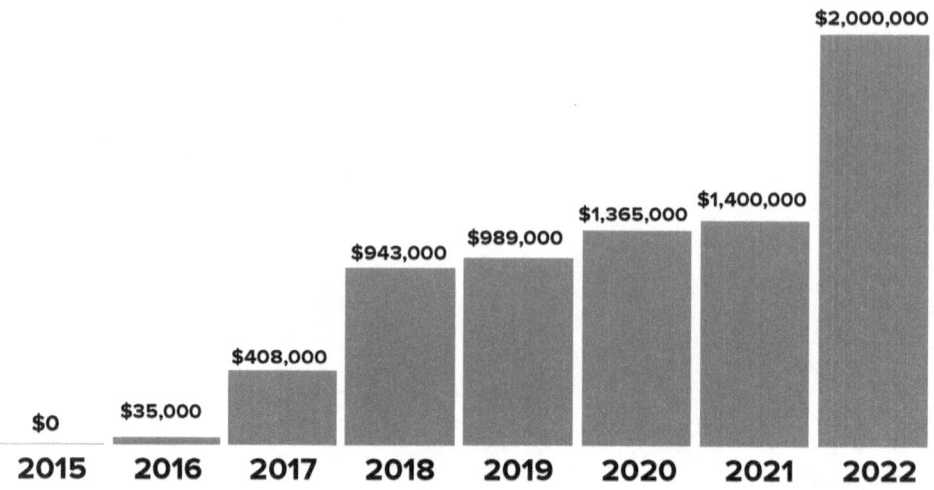

**Thomas Crosson &
Gretchen Mikulich**
Owner / Founder
www.FullPackageMedia.com

"WHAT IS THE PURPOSE OF YOUR BUSINESS?"

YOUR BUSINESS EXISTS TO SOLVE PROBLEMS
FOR YOU AND YOUR CUSTOMERS.
- CLAY CLARK
FOUNDER OF THRIVE15

Chapter 5

Create a Duplicable Business Model Based Upon the Foundations of a Duplicable Process, a Winning Team, and Well-Defined Guardrails

Consider this: If you had millions of dollars to invest and SHOCKINGLY, your goal was to make a good return on your investment, which of the following would you rather invest in? Would you rather invest in a company that is stable, scalable, and profitable, or would you rather invest in a business that is entirely dependent on the owner and key team members, where no systems are recorded, and where tons of gross revenue is generated but no profits are actually created?

Having worked with thousands of companies over the years, I can tell you from first-hand experience that most business people build systems that are dependent on key people who know all of the passwords, who have all of the skills and who could actually kill the company simply by deciding to move on. This is not a good thing.

My friend, when you build a business that is dependent upon documented processes, checklists, and systems, you eliminate the necessity of hiring geniuses. When you have good systems in place, you can actually just focus on hiring honest and diligent people (which are semi-hard to find). Creating these systems allows you to hire for character and not for skill; this is where you want to be. When you decide to build your business around processes, checklists, controls and systems, you make it much easier to find key employees to fill key positions and DRAMATICALLY EASIER to grow your business exponentially.

Most people deep down crave to have structure and systems in place to guide them, especially at work. By diligently working to install the systems, checklists, and processes for each position within your company, you will make it EXPONENTIALLY EASIER to hire new people. I realize that most people (including me) are very visual so we have provided proven checklists, systems, and processes for you at www.ThriveTimeShow.com/TreasureTrove.

What the Heck Is a System? Systems Are Really the Skeleton of Any Successful Business

My friend, I realize the word "systems" is very cyborg-like and may come across as sounding very mechanical, so I am going to dial in with some details for you. A system is a step-by-step process or

> "Checklists seem able to defend anyone, even the experienced, against failure in many more tasks than we realized."
>
> *-Atul Gawande*

(Bestselling author of *The Checklist Manifesto* and the Professor of Surgery at Harvard Medical School)

checklist that has been created to systematically produce predictable, satisfactory results for your ideal and likely buyers. A system has been typed up and saved into a location that is quickly accessible by your team members who need to use this system on a daily basis to minimize errors and avoid results that are less that satisfactory.

When referencing checklists, I am talking about a specific list of items that your company will hold your team accountable for delivering to each of your clients. These lists need to cover nearly every aspect of your business from the smallest tasks to the most complex. These checklists need to cover the processes that you will use to edit videos, clean bathrooms, train your staff, code websites, provide haircuts, fly airplanes, maintain vehicles, onboard employees, manage the finances of the business and beyond. If you expect anyone on your team to do anything on a consistent and repeatable basis, you must create a checklist and follow-up loop for this.

To begin creating your first checklist and download sample best-practice checklists visit: www.ThriveTimeShow.com/TreasureTrove

My friend, you and I need to create systems for every repeatable process involved in the daily operations of our businesses. You need to create systems for the automatic e-mails you are going to send out to your new leads and prospective clients. You need to create systems for what managers are going to say in a hiring interview. You need to create systems for how the phone is going to be answered. I cannot stress this enough, THE BUSINESS SYSTEMS THAT YOU CREATE MUST INCLUDE EVERY PIECE OF COMPANY SPECIFIC KNOWLEDGE THAT YOU AND YOUR COMPANY HAVE. THIS INFORMATION CANNOT BE TRAPPED WITHIN THE MIND OF AN INDIVIDUAL MEMBER OF YOUR COMPANY.

> "(Without a checklist) the volume and complexity of what we know has exceeded our individual ability to deliver its benefits correctly, safely, or reliably. Knowledge has both saved us and burdened us."

> *-Atul Gawande*
> (The bestselling author of *The Checklist Manifesto*, a surgeon and a professor in the Department of Health Policy and Management at the Harvard T.H. Chan School of Public Health)

You may be one of those humans who likes to say, "Well, it's really hard for me to document our systems because every customer is different." If you keep saying that, your business will never scale. Once upon a time, I was explaining to my very successful uncle Clynt how it was impossible to teach adult men who had no entertainment and disk jockey experience how to become successful DJs. He explained to me that if I believed that, then my company would never grow. He said it is entirely possible to duplicate nearly any process if you are detailed enough and fully committed to training. Seven years after that conversation, I had built such a duplicable system for DJing that I am 100% confident that I could teach you or any other coachable human with integrity how to become very successful as a corporate and wedding entertainer.

If you create systems the right way, they will make life much easier for you and your company and it will become very easy to produce predictably happy clients. As you begin to introduce these systems to your team, you must know your team will initially push back and fight against the idea of systemizing every aspect of their job.

They will start to worry that they can now be "easily replaced" as a result of these systems. However, you must point out to them that great business systems are not in place to allow for the replacement of people; they are in place to enable your team to consistently wow clients, and even allow members of your team to occasionally take a day off without a nuclear meltdown occurring at your business. Imagine that!

Notable Quotable:

"Better IS possible. It does not take genius, It takes diligence. It takes moral clarity. It takes ingenuity. And above all, it takes a willingness to try."

-Atul Gawande
(Bestselling author of *Checklist Manifesto* and an American surgeon, write and public researcher. He also has worked with the Harvard Medical School as their Professor of Surgery)

"Whether you think you can, or think you can't – you're right."

-Henry Ford
(The self-made millionaire and founder of the Ford Motor Company)

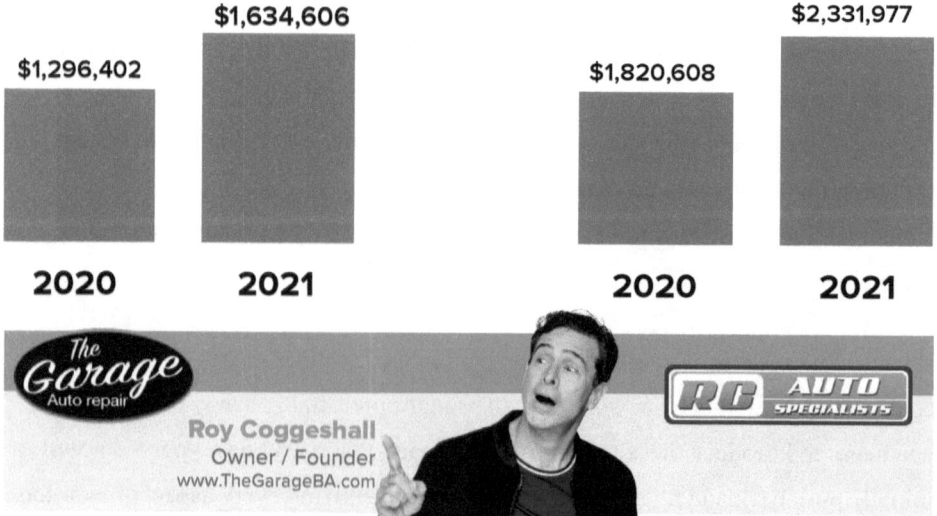

"We don't like checklists. They can be painstaking. They're not much fun. But I don't think the issue here is mere laziness. There's something deeper, more visceral going on when people walk away not only from saving lives, but from making money. It somehow feels beneath us to use a checklist, an embarrassment. It runs counter to deeply held beliefs about how the truly great among us—those we aspire to be—handle situations of high stakes and complexity. The truly great are daring. They improvise. They do not have protocols and checklists. Maybe our idea of heroism needs updating."

-Atul Gawande
(The bestselling author of *The Checklist Manifesto***, a surgeon and a professor of surgery at Harvard Medical School)**

The Three Levels of All Successful Business Systems

My friend, I have worked with thousands of successful companies and I want to clearly lay this out so that we don't have a bunch of pushback later. Every successful and duplicable business that I have ever coached or observed has three levels of systems that support it.

» **Layer 1** – The processes and checklists layer

» **Layer 2** – The presentation layer

» **Layer 3** – The "this is why we do it" layer

The Processes Layer

The processes layer basically is all about the "check-this-box" and "do-that-thing" systems. It's all about the processes that your team must follow to produce the given result your company has promised customers. As an example, my super wife has some incredible recipes for creating some incredible organic and fruit-based smoothies that my kids love. The two times I followed her recipes and made the smoothies, the kids loved them. However, the other 994 times I have produced smoothies without using her recipes, my kids acted like a bee stung their tongues and they still talk about how terrible those smoothies were. There is a specific and right way to do things and a wrong way to do things. To quote the R&B pop artist who has now become a pastor, Montell Jordan, "This is how we do it." My friend, you have to document the super moves that you have developed that actually work.

"Acronyms Seriously Suck: There is a creeping tendency to use made up acronyms at SpaceX. Excessive use of made up acronyms is a significant impediment to communication and keeping communication good as we grow is incredibly important. Individually, a few acronyms here and there may not seem so bad, but if a thousand people are making these up, over time the result will be a huge glossary that we have to issue to new employees. No one can actually remember all these acronyms and people don't want to seem dumb in a meeting, so they just sit there in ignorance. This is particularly tough on new employees. That needs to stop immediately or I will take drastic action—I have given enough warnings over the years. Unless an acronym is approved by me, it should not enter the SpaceX glossary. If there is an existing acronym that cannot reasonably be justified, it should be eliminated, as I have requested in the past."

-Elon Musk
(An e-mail he sent to his team in May of 2010)
A Man whose life I do not endorse and currently the world's wealthiest man.

The Presentation Layer

The presentation layer is all about presenting your systems in a way that an honest human with a functioning brain can follow. You won't believe how many times I have gone into a business to help them and found their checklists so filled with jargon that no one has any idea what the crap is going on. In one specific situation I recall, I went into a cosmetic surgeon's office and found he had created jargon for every aspect of his business. Everything was BVD, ACT, MVP, etc. After spending a day with his team, I realized that all of the jargon had been created by a man who no longer worked at his office. The owner didn't even know what the jargon stood for. The staff just checked the boxes on the checklists every day because they thought that would keep them from getting in trouble. It was absolute jackassery (from the root word "jackass"). You must present your systems and checklists in a way that your team WILL ACTUALLY IMPLEMENT AND EXECUTE ON A DAILY BASIS. If you don't do this, it's going to be a disaster.

Think about Jiffy Lube or McDonald's. They have a created repeatable systems

"Good checklists, on the other hand are precise. They are efficient, to the point, and easy to use even in the most difficult situations. They do not try to spell out everything--a checklist cannot fly a plane. Instead, they provide reminders of only the most critical and important steps--the ones that even the highly skilled professional using them could miss. Good checklists are, above all, practical."

-Atul Gawande
(The bestselling author of *The Checklist Manifesto***, a surgeon and a professor of surgery at Harvard Medical School)**

"Good management consists of getting the people on your team to execute their daily action items with a spirit of excellence, delivered with enthusiasm."

-Clay Clark
(Founder of the ThriveTime Show podcast and the ReAwaken America Tour)

so simple that I think even my small brain could execute them. When you go into Jiffy Lube they simply click from screen to screen and say, *"Sir, your manufacturer recommends that you change your air filter every 'x' number of miles. Sir, your windshield wipers look as though they are worn. Sir, it looks as though your air coolant is low, however we can top that off for $4.00 today if you would like."*

I mean no disrespect when I say this, but those dudes get me for $176 every time I come in for the $19 oil change. I love it. They have built a very effective presentation layer at Jiffy Lube. Go there and you will see what I'm talking about.

This is why Steve Jobs absolutely nailed it with the iPad, the iPod, and the iPhone. He recognized that people were not rejecting technology enhancements designed to make their life easier and more efficient; they were rejecting the format in which the technology was being delivered. He and his team watched humans interact with technology, and they developed the iPod as a device that a non-nerd would love to use (with all due respect to the nerds reading this). He and his team focused on developing products that would be easy to use by almost anybody. You didn't have to know code or how to be a computer hacker to use the products they developed. My six-year-old daughter, Scarlett, has figured out how to text her Grandma and we have never had a conversation, training, or an all-day workshop to show her how. The design of smartphones is so intuitive that she just figured it out.

"Simple can be harder than complex: You have to work hard to get your thinking clean to make it simple. But it's worth it in the end because once you get there, you can move mountains."

-Steve Jobs
(Co-founder of Apple and the former CEO of Pixar)

As you are designing your presentation layer, you must keep your consumer and your team members in mind. Watch them use the systems you create and be 100% COMMITTED TO CREATING A REPEATABLE PROCESS THAT WORKS; do not get emotional about whether your presentation is right or not. If your team can't figure out your systems, you must keep redesigning them until anybody who is diligent and honest can figure them out.

My friend, if you want to nail this, you must go through the time consuming hassle of actually watching your team try to use the systems you created. If they can't figure it out, that means your system is too complex. Who is old enough to remember the original Apple computers? You had to actually load in a floppy disk and type in lines of code to get that computer to do anything. It was painful and so the majority of the planet rejected them. Now that operating a computer has become a much more simplified task, everyone is using one. Remember that the entire reason you are creating systems is to establish a scalable way to add value to your customers and make COPIOUS AMOUNTS OF MONEY FOR YOU.

The "This-Is-Why-We-Do-It" Layer

Writing about this layer irritates even me because I am a "shut-the-heck-up-and-put-your-head-down-to-get-the-job-done" kind of worker. Growing up without anything, I've always viewed every job (since I became enlightened after reading Napoleon Hill's Think and Grow Rich) as a blessing and a gift, not as an obligation. I do speaking events all of the time where the event planner asks me to do something that I don't want to do and I do it. Do you know why? Because they are paying me $14,000. However, we are now at a point in world history where the reason behind "why I am supposed to do this or that" now matters a lot to many people. Thus, even though I don't personally like this layer, I am telling you right now that this layer really does matter to many employees and potential team members. You and I must go out of our way to explain to team members why they are doing what they are doing.

Companies like Tom's Shoes, Warby Parker, and Whole Foods Market are winning for many reasons, but one of the main reasons is because they are connecting with their team members on a deep and emotional level. Many of the people who work for Tom's Shoes really do buy into the vision of the company and they come to work motivated every day because of it. Tony Hsieh has assembled an army of people

"Branding through customer service over the years, the number one driver of our growth at Zappos has been repeat customers and word of mouth. Our philosophy has been to take most of the money we would have spent on paid advertising and invest it into customer service and the customer experience instead, letting our customers do the marketing for us through word of mouth."

-Tony Hsieh
(CEO of Zappos and the bestselling author of *Delivering Happiness: A Path to Profits, Passion, and Purpose***)**

in Las Vegas working with his Zappos company who are obsessed about offering the best customer service on the planet. You and I must be able to inspire this same level of motivation from our teams and the only way to do it is to share with them why you are doing what you are doing. You must invest the time to explain to them why they need to follow your company's checklists and systems and once they connect with the sincerity of your purpose, most of them will want to come to work with you.

To make your life 2% better, I have included here 47 different ways you can present your process and systems to make them easier to digest for your team members.

47 Ways to Present Your Process & Systems

1. Checklists
2. Step-by-Step Videos That Your Employees Will Actually Watch
3. Customized Worksheets
4. One Sheet
5. Call Scripts
6. Documented Company Guidelines
7. Customer Relationship Management Software
8. Written Guidelines
9. Menu Pricing

10. Pricing Lists

11. Employee Handbooks

12. Training Mastery Checklists

13. Step-by-Step Instructions

14. Spreadsheets with Built-In Formulas

15. Pre-Approved Logos and Photography

16. Pre-Approved Videography Samples and Clips

17. Pre-Approved Audio Samples and Clips

18. File Naming System

19. File Nomenclature Rules (How You Name Things)

20. Pre-Vetted Vendor Lists

21. Standardized Product Numbers

22. Standardized Equipment Numbers

23. Custom-Coded Software to Automate Processes

24. Written Company Policies

25. Written Company Mission Statement

26. Written Company Values Statement

27. Frequently Asked Questions Document

28. Written Company Policies

29. Templates of Online Marketing Materials

30. Templates of Offline Marketing Materials

31. Templates of Legal Agreements

32. Templates of Sales Contracts

33. Delivery Timetables

34. Job Descriptions

35. Project Management Tools / Company-Wide To-Do List Management Systems

36. Visual Product / System Diagrams

37. Budgeting Templates

38. Automated Data Backups

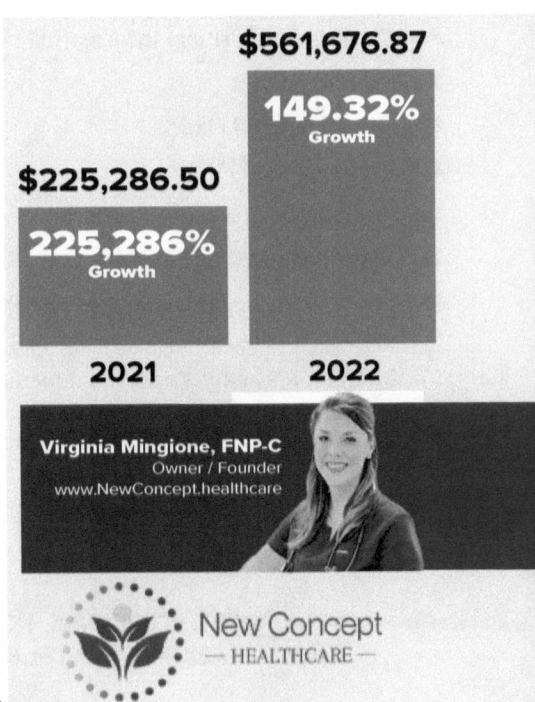

39. Databases of Critical Information

40. Tracking Sheet

41. Organizational Charts

42. Pre-Approved Forms

43. Pre-Approved Vendor Contacts

44. Master Marketing Calendar

45. Pre-Written Legal Documents for Predictable Issues (Employee Non-Compete Violations, etc.)

46. Monthly / Weekly Reporting Documents

47. Search Engine Optimization Content Production Templates

My friend, at the end of the day, quality people really do want to do a good job at work. If the diligent people on your team find your systems and checklists to be easy to use and pragmatic, they are usually going to want to follow them. However, if your systems are too complex to understand, your team members may begin improvising in an attempt to consistently meet your expectations without getting confused. They may resort to making their own "short version" of your systems, which is not good.

Before we move on, I want to provide more clarity on this idea. Diligent people want to do a good job and will try to implement your systems. Thus, it is important that you listen to their feedback. Lazy people will try not to implement your systems and it is important that you do not listen to their feedback.

Building One Checklist at a Time

As a man who has been self-employed for over 20 years and who has worked with thousands of clients, I have vast experience when it comes to seeing and personally doing what you shouldn't do. DO NOT TAKE A MONTH OFF FROM YOUR BUSINESS AND SPEND EVERY WAKING HOUR MAKING SYSTEMS, PROCESSES, AND CHECKLISTS.

"Discipline is the bridge between goals and accomplishment."

-Jim Rohn
(Bestselling author and renowned motivational speaker)

The absolute best way to create all of your systems is to create them as you see the need for them. Every time you see a member of your team doing a repeatable task and you notice it's not being done right or it is consuming copious amounts of his or her time, create a checklist to scale that system or job. Every time you see someone on your team creating excellent products and services that far surpass the quality

"Systems permit ordinary people to achieve extraordinary results predictably."

-*Michael Gerber*
(Bestselling author of the E-Myth book series)

of the average team member, take the time to document the method, processes, and steps they are taking to create this exceptional level of service or product. However always keep in mind, creating documents that no one does or ever will use is not a good use of your time.

You must come to embrace a NEW MINDSET FOR YOUR BUSINESS. Both you and others in your business must begin creating a culture that is reliant upon DISCIPLINED, ACCURATE, AND DETAILED CHECKLISTS THAT ARE ALWAYS BEING UPDATED TO IMPROVE YOUR COMPANY AND GUARANTEE THE BEST OVERALL VALUE FOR YOUR CUSTOMERS.

Building your business systems is not an event, it's an ongoing process. Think of building your business systems as more similar to brushing your teeth than to getting married. Unless you are a real sick freak, you are going to want to brush your teeth twice per day on an ongoing basis to maintain your oral hygiene. On the flip side, unless you are a real sick freak, I don't recommend that you attempt to get married twice per day on an ongoing basis. (I don't recommend you get married twice per day, ever.) When you first start building your business systems, they are going to be very simple and incomplete. However, as you update these systems week-by-week, they will become the solid foundation upon which your company is built.

Alright, now let's talk about the humans you are hiring.

Building the A-Team

I realize that up to this point we have focused much of our time on discussing building systems, but later in this book we will get very specific about how to recruit, hire, inspire, and retain top talent. But for right now, I just want to clarify that you

"We will hire someone with less experience, less education, and less expertise, than someone who has more of those things and has a rotten attitude. Because we can train people. We can teach people how to lead. We can teach people how to provide customer service. But we can't change their DNA."

-Herb Kelleher
(The co-founder and former CEO of Southwest Airlines)

will not make copious amounts of profit just because you have incredible business systems. To build a success-driven, healthy, and growing business, you are going to need systems and a great company culture. When you have a great company culture in place, it will help reinforce your company's values and will ensure that your business is a positive place for customers to shop and for your employees to work. Don't get overwhelmed. Throughout this book, I will teach you the best-practice and proven systems that will show you specifically and systematically how to grow and develop a winning company culture.

Installing the Guardrails

As your business team climbs up Mount Awesome, it's very important that nobody on your team falls off the side of the mountain on the way to the top. To prevent your team members from falling off the mountain to their certain death, you must develop systems called GUARDRAILS. Guardrails are created to keep any one member of your team from ever being able to make a MASSIVELY COSTLY MISTAKE due to negligence, idiocy, carelessness, or just plain "JACKASSERY."

A very practical example of a guardrail would be making sure members of your sales team are not responsible for both calculating and paying themselves commissions. Another example of a good guardrail would be making sure that the person who makes your daily or weekly bank deposits is not the same person who reconciles the account balances and bank statements. Years ago I worked with a doctor who hired a man whose entire job was to "handle all of the finances for the business." This man would deposit 95% of the money the business brought in and take 5% of the money for himself. Without exaggeration, this man deposited well over $500,000 of money within a year while embezzling around $25,000 for himself. To make matters worse, this man was also allowed to use the company credit card as he saw fit without any oversight. Within a year, he had charged over $10,000 on personal purchases before he was caught.

> "My #1 job here at Apple is to make sure that the top 100 people are A+ players. And everything else will take care of itself."
>
>
> **-Steve Jobs**
> (Co-founder of Apple and the former CEO of Pixar)

How was he eventually caught, you ask? When I was hired to improve the business systems for this doctor, I began setting up guardrails. When I insisted the same person not both deposit the money and reconcile the statements, this guy lost his mind. He pushed back, he attacked me, and asked repeatedly, "Why doesn't this guy trust me?!" I calmly pointed out that we were simply setting up best-practice systems to ensure that no one person could make a catastrophic error that could kill the company and that these systems would take the pressure off of him, placing the pressure on the systems themselves, instead. Within two weeks, the man submitted his resignation - just before we collected enough information to press charges.

This is a true story and unfortunately, it is a story that is repeated every day all over the world of business because companies have not installed the proper guardrails to hold people accountable for being both honest and accurate. You must install daily key performance indicator reporting systems within your business to keep your team focused and on target.

You may be wondering how you can possibly delegate more and more of the daily tasks of your business without completely losing control. Unless you just started your business yesterday, you have probably already witnessed firsthand the dangers associated with delegating key aspects of your business to a person on your team who absolutely screws up and drops the ball. My friend, I want you to circle this and highlight this and do whatever you need to do remember this statement: YOU WANT TO BUILD AND INSTALL SELF-REGULATING SYSTEMS INTO YOUR BUSINESS THAT ALLOW ETHICAL AND DILIGENT PEOPLE TO GET THEIR JOB DONE RIGHT WITHOUT EVERYTHING HAVING TO GO THROUGH YOU FIRST.

You must grasp that no systems will work well without ethical and diligent people executing them. Don't build great systems and then delegate to dishonest idiots. You must build great systems that you then delegate to HONEST and DILIGENT PEOPLE.

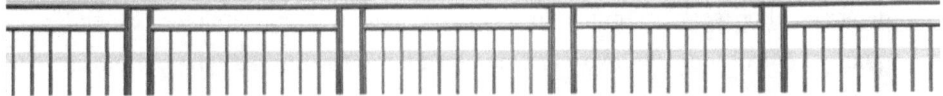

8 Examples of Effective Guardrail Business Systems

1. **Systems that provide transparency within your organization.**
    Think of the UPS package tracking system. This system allows both customers and employees of UPS to see where a package is and when it was last touched. This holds employees accountable and lets customers see what is going on. Think about the glass walls that many high-end restaurants around the world have installed so that customers can see their food being prepared right in front of them. Both of these systems hold employees accountable and provide transparency for all.

2. **Dashboards that show the daily activity and results of each employee.**
    Creating dashboards that allow everyone within your organization to see the daily activity and results being delivered by each member of your team holds everyone accountable and again creates a culture of transparency.

Download an example of a Sales Team Management Dashboard at www.ThriveTimeShow.com/TreasureTrove

3. **Checklists.**

Checklists that require the signatures of both the person completing the task and the manager who is holding everyone accountable for doing their jobs correctly and accurately give you a single resource to know exactly who was responsible. Download a best-practice Sample Checklist at www.ThriveTimeShow.com/TreasureTrove

4. **Fixed Expense and Variable Expense Budgets.**

These spreadsheets allow you and your team to see where additional money is being spent that is not within the constraints of the pre-agreed financial boundaries. Download a sample Fixed Expense and Variable Expense Budget at www.ThriveTimeShow.com/TreasureTrove

5. **Scorecards and Scoreboards.** Creating charts that show everyone within the department or work group the performance, statistics, conversion rates, and quality control scores of everyone involved helps to eliminate finger pointing and shows everyone who the top performers really are.

6. **Standardized and Compliant Contracts.**

If you are going to engage in the same type of transaction over and over again, it makes sense to operate with a standardized contract. Over the years I have worked in commercial real estate, photography, entertainment, speaking, consulting, membership-based medical care, and other fields. I have sample downloadables for all of these contracts available for you at www.ThriveTimeShow.com/TreasureTrove

7. **Official Policies and Procedures.** Clearly communicating in advance what your company's process is for handling complaints, refunds, mistakes, and customer service issues, will save management a ton of time putting out small fires and you will empower your team to make good decisions.

Years ago, I worked with a retail business in which thousands of transactions took place per week. Less than 2% of the customers were ever upset, but you could almost guarantee that the owner was going to be called and asked how to handle nearly 40 customer service issues per week (2,000 transactions x 2% = 40 customer service issues). When I sat down with the owner to discuss his business, we analyzed where he was spending most of his time and he explained that it was impossible for him to get anything done because he was dealing with a customer service issue nearly every hour of the day (which was nearly true, as his business was open over 50 hours per week).

We agreed that he would be OK if his front line team (the staff that interacts with the customers) was empowered to give up to a 100% refund to any customer who was dissatisfied. When they installed the L.A.S.T. (Listen Answer Satisfy Trust) system for dealing with customer complaints, guess what happened? The staff was able to deal with nearly 38 out of 40 issues per week directly and customers were able to get an immediate solution to their problems. Because the members of his team were instructed to fill out L.A.S.T. forms and bring them to the weekly management meeting, the owner was still in the know about customer service issues. This small changed allowed the man to get his life back and become a proactive business owner once again. BOOM!

Download the L.A.S.T. Customer Complaint Template at www.ThriveTimeShow.com/TreasureTrove

Download an example of a Policy for Handling Customer Complaints at www.ThriveTimeShow.com/TreasureTrove

Automated Backups. You would not believe how many business owners I have met who have lost every digital file at once because the entire brain of the company, including all critical company files, were saved on someone's personal computer. My friend, you must install a system that automatically backs up every digital file daily. I highly recommend that you use the following two vendors for this:

www.DropBox.com – This is one of my favorite companies. These people allow you to access any file from anywhere any time. I have developed a file nomenclature for clients, which is just a naming system, that is a game-changer for many businesses. I highly recommend you implement it now so that you no longer have to waste time hunting for mission critical files and passwords.

To watch the training we have created for correct file naming, visit www.ThriveTimeShow.com/TreasureTrove

If you build these GUARDRAILS the right way, you are going to create a system that safeguards your business systems, which will dramatically decrease the number of decisions you need to make a daily basis. This will take the lid off of your company's growth and will dramatically improve your mental health. I am not kidding when I say that installing these GUARDRAILS to reduce the number of decisions you have to make every day will actually help improve your Life.

To make your life 2% easier and to help solidify my claim that this is the best business book ever written, I'm providing you with a massive list of the best-practice business GUARDRAILS you and your company need to have in place, along with accompanying templates for many. These documents are provided to help you establish the baseline level of quality and detail you need to provide in your company. Get ready for a FIREHOSE OF KNOWLEDGE.

SYSTEMATIC SALES CHECKLIST

1. Create an inbound sales script.

2. Create an outbound sales script.

3. Create pre-written sales emails.

4. Create pre-written sales texts.

5. Create sales one sheet.

6. Create pre-written sales / presentation book.

7. Create pre-written presentation script.

8. Create sales **FAQ** sheet related to the questions asked by your ideal and likely buyers.

9. Create sales manual.

10. Print, review, and post deal wheel method at every sales station.

11. Create a documented sales workflow using a white-board.

12. Create a lead tracker spreadsheet.

DAILY SALES KEY PERFORMANCE INDICATORS

1. How many outbound calls were made?

2. How many appointments were made?

3. How many deals were closed?

4. Why did people say no?

Base Sales KPI's on the super star sales person, not the average in the group.

Keep team accountable to KPI's with short, daily standing meetings.

"You don't have to be a doctor to build a sales focused culture. However, you do need a PHD: Pig-Headed Discipline."

CLAY CLARK
Co-Host of the ThriveTime Business Coach Radio Show and member of the Forbes Coaches Council

Standardized Sales One Sheet-

Download at www.ThriveTimeShow.com/TreasureTrove

Standardized Sales Brochure -

Download at www.ThriveTimeShow.com/TreasureTrove

Standardized Sales Concessions for Negotiations -

Download at www.ThriveTimeShow.com/TreasureTrove

Standardized Pre-Approval Letter (for the mortgage industry) -

Download at www.ThriveTimeShow.com/TreasureTrove

Regulated and Limited Access to Company Database of Current and Past Clients –

Download at www.ThriveTimeShow.com/TreasureTrove

Automated Drip Email System -

Download at www.ThriveTimeShow.com/TreasureTrove

Automated Customer Surveys -

Download at www.ThriveTimeShow.com/TreasureTrove

Preferred Vendor Recommendations List -

Download at www.ThriveTimeShow.com/TreasureTrove

Refund Policy -

Download at www.ThriveTimeShow.com/TreasureTrove

Press Release Template -

Download at www.ThriveTimeShow.com/TreasureTrove

PR Kit -

Download at www.ThriveTimeShow.com/TreasureTrove

Time-Off Request Policy -

Download at www.ThriveTimeShow.com/TreasureTrove

Dress-Code Policy -

Download at www.ThriveTimeShow.com/TreasureTrove

Point System for Employee Write-Ups -

Download at www.ThriveTimeShow.com/TreasureTrove

"A popular concept of quality in manufacturing is the importance of "doing things right the first time." But customers of service organizations often allow one mistake. Some organizations are very good at delivering service as long as nothing goes wrong. Others organize for and thrive on service emergencies. Outstanding service organizations do both by giving frontline employees the latitude to effect recovery. Southwest Airlines maintains a policy of allowing frontline employees to do whatever they feel comfortable doing in order to satisfy customers. Xerox authorizes frontline service employees to replace up to $250,000 worth of equipment if customers are not getting results."

-Heskett, Sasser, Schlesinger, etc.
**(Authors of "Putting the Profit Chain to Work"
in the Harvard Business Review)**

Cross-Selling Checklist -
Download at www.ThriveTimeShow.com/TreasureTrove

Pre-Approved On-Hold Music -
Download at www.ThriveTimeShow.com/TreasureTrove

New Customer On-Boarding WOW Checklist -
Download at www.ThriveTimeShow.com/TreasureTrove

Once you have built these systems, the natural temptation is to sit back and not make any updates. But if you actually take this approach, you are going to end up with a business model that is as viable in the current marketplace as Blockbuster Video (with all due respect to Wayne Huizenga). With the entertainment company I founded (www.DJConnection.com) I used to be the king of Yellow Page advertising. I literally purchased the largest Yellow Page ads they sold and then all the sudden, out of nowhere came this thing called Google. One of my employees pointed out that I might want to look at building a website for our company and I remember thinking that he was out of his mind. I was so content with the results I was getting that I was no longer open to feedback from the marketplace. I finally pulled my head out of my rectum three years before the Yellow Pages completely died off as a viable advertising platform. Today, I would strongly discourage you from investing heavily in Yellow Page advertising.

Fun Fact:

Wayne Huizenga is an American entrepreneur who has been involved in the founding of three Fortune 500 companies. He has also owned three top tier professional sports franchises and is the man who grew Blockbuster from just a few stores in 1987 to become the nation's largest movie rental chain in 1994.

Unlocking Your Company's Fast and Sustainable Growth Potential by Listening to Your Customers

Years ago I had an opportunity to work with a dentist who had heard me speak at a business conference in Florida. I was speaking about the importance of listening to your current customers to make sure you were not missing out on any low-hanging fruit or obvious upselling opportunities that would meet the needs of your current customers. I asked

"My young daughter asked me for career advice. I told her, "Go into sales. Pick a profession that feels that selling is a sleezy activity, below its professional standards. Study that profession with the idea that you'll make your money selling. There will be little competition and your colleagues will be delighted to pay you handsomely, even more than they earn themselves."

-Jerry Vass
(Bestselling author of Soft Selling in a Hard World**)**

everyone in the audience to rate on a scale of 1 to 10 the effectiveness of their current systemic and checklist driven upselling processes. This man came up to me after my talk and told me that he was one hundred percent certain that he could dramatically increase his sales if he just knew how to create upselling systems for his business.

We started the process by simply having his two front desk team members call each and every one of his current and former patients to ask them what other dental related services they had paid for during the past year. As each patient answered, the responses were added into a spreadsheet. After getting in contact with over 500 of his former and current patients, we discovered that nearly 30% of them over the past five years had paid for teeth whitening, the (braceless) Invisalign teeth straightening system, or cosmetic veneers. We discovered that many of his patients did not know that he routinely provided cosmetic dentistry solutions, including veneers, to patients. We also discovered that practically none of his patients knew that he and his office could provide long-term financing solutions through their partnership with a third-party medical financing company called CareCredit.

When I sat down and shared our findings with the dentist, you could see in his eyes that his mind was about ready to explode at the thought of how much business (low-hanging fruit) he was letting slip through the cracks each year. His current patients were going to other dental offices because they simply did not know that he provided the services and financing options they were seeking. After the dentist emotionally recovered from the dropping of this bombshell, he decided to implement the use of a check-out checklist with which his team would educate every single patient about the services they offered and the financing options each patient had available to them. By simply doing this, he was able to increase sales by nearly 35%.

My friend, if you have not asked your customers what other services they are looking for that relate to the products and services your company has the capacity to offer, you are potentially missing out on thousands and thousands of dollars of sales and in many cases, you might be missing out on millions of dollars of sales. I have worked with funeral homes, basketball training facilities, wedding-related service providers, hotels, and businesses in nearly every kind of industry you can think of, and I have found that in almost every single case, most companies are not systematically cross-selling and up-selling in such a way that every single customer knows about every single product and service that you offer every single time. This must happen or you are leaving tons of money on the table.

Identify Your Ideal and Likely Buyers.
Find Their Needs and Sell Them Solutions

In order for you to have massive success, you must take the time to sit down and clearly identify who your ideal and likely buyers truly are. You can't simply say that every human with a pulse who lives within a certain distance of your business is an ideal and likely customer. Take the time to fill out the Ideal and Likely Buyer Identification Worksheet that we have provided for you at www.ThriveTimeShow. com/TreasureTrove and begin focusing on marketing to these people exclusively.

Fill out the Ideal and Likely Buyer Identification Worksheet at www.ThriveTimeShow.com/TreasureTrove

I once sat down with an insurance salesman to help him identify who his ideal and likely buyers truly were. After investing approximately 30 minutes, we both discovered that his ideal and likely buyers were only people who had a credit score of 700 or above, who were consistently employed, owned a home, and were married with children. The insurance brand that he represented always quoted insanely high insurance rates to people who had low credit scores and who were not married. He discovered that the time he invested in meeting with his non-ideal and non-likely buyers was often a complete waste of time and almost never fruitful. When he met with non-ideal and non-likely buyers, the rates he was allowed to quote were insanely high compared to what these non-ideal and non-likely buyers were willing or able to pay. Once my client was able to clearly identify who his ideal and likely buyers truly were, he was able to make smart decisions that impacted nearly every aspect of his ongoing marketing campaign. Immediately he knew the networking groups he needed to stop attending, and he knew the ongoing advertising campaigns he needed to stop funding.

. . . .

DESCRIBE YOUR IDEAL AND LIKELY BUYER

Write down a description of who your ideal and likely buyers are:

1. Men or Women or Both? _____

2. Average Age? _____

3. Average Income Level? _____

4. Geographical Location? _____

5. Places They Go? _____

6. Schools Their Kids Attend? _____

7. Search Terms They Type Into Search Engines? _____

8. Shared Fears? _____

9. Shared Goals? _____

10. Shared Hobbies and Interests? _____

11. Shared Problems? _____

12. Sports Their Kids Play _____

13. Stores They Shop At? _____

14. Types of Cars They Drive? _____

15. Proven Ad, Landing Page, and Set Budget _____

Learn more about my deep dive into the world of commercial real estate by visiting: http://www.kjrh.com/news/local-news/new-downtown-entertainment-district-coming-to-tulsa

If you run a business that sells products and services to other businesses, you can quickly put together a profile of your ideal and likely buyers by identifying the following:

» The gender of your ideal and likely buyers _____

» The age of your ideal and likely buyers _____

» The publications that your ideal and likely buyers consume (trade journals, magazines, blogs, podcasts, etc.) _____

» The industry or industries that your target market is involved in

_____

» The number of employees who work for your average ideal and likely buyer

_____

» The geographic locations of your ideal and likely buyers _____

» The job title of your ideal and likely buyers _____

» The connections, networks, and key industry influencers who interact with your ideal and likely buyers _____

» The social circle of your ideal and likely buyers _____

» The schools the children of your ideal and likely buyers attend

_____

If you run a business that sells products and services direct to consumers, you can quickly put together a profile of your ideal and likely buyers by identifying the following:

» The gender of your ideal and likely buyers _____

» The age of your ideal and likely buyers _____

» The publications that your ideal and likely buyers consume (trade journals, magazines, blogs, podcasts, etc.) _____

» The hobbies of your ideal and likely buyers _____

» The stores and online retailers routinely visited by your ideal and likely buyers

» The net worth of your ideal and likely buyers _____

> "It's not sufficient that I succeed; everyone else must fail."

-Larry Ellison
(The billionaire CEO of Oracle who you may not agree with, but who you may be competing with)

» The value of the home of your ideal and likely buyers _____

» The geographic locations of your ideal and likely buyers _____

» The job title of your ideal and likely buyers _____

» The connections, networks and key industry influencers who interact with your ideal and likely buyers _____

» The social circle of your ideal and likely buyers _____

» The schools the children of your ideal and likely buyers attend _____

While building your ideal and likely buyers profile, there is no time to focus on being politically correct. Your number one priority must be to create a laser focus for your marketing efforts and campaigns. You don't want to waste a single dollar marketing to the wrong crowd of people.

Identify Your Main Competitors and Then Take the Food Out of Their Mouths

You need to clearly know whom your competition is, or they are going to beat the crap out of you in the marketplace. Why waste time trying to reinvent the wheel when you may already have a competitor out there who can point you and your marketing efforts in the right direction? Take advantage of what their mistakes and successes can teach you.

You want to take the time to complete what I call The Ultimate Competitor Analysis or you could call it T.U.C.A. if you want to make sure no one understands what you are talking about.:

Who are your competitors?

» What top four competitors are already profitably selling to your ideal and likely buyers? _____

» Which indirect competitors do your ideal and likely buyers turn to in order to get the products and services they need outside of your direct competitors? _____

» How did your top four competitors acquire your ideal and likely buyers?
_____

» What are the strengths of your top four competitors? _____

» What are the weaknesses of your top four competitors? _____

» What opportunities exist to beat the crap out of your top four competitors?
_____

» What are the threats your top four competitors face? _____

» What are the reasons you dislike your top four competitors (if you don't have any, that's OK; but I doubt that's the case)? _____

» Why are you motivated to beat the crap out of your top four competitors?
_____

» What about your top four competitors' websites are better than yours?
_____

» What about your top four competitors' marketing materials is better than yours?
_____

» What niches in the market are not currently being dominated by your competition (best price, best cheerleader, really friendly, best customer service, easiest to use, easiest to order, best tasting, most interactive, most customized, or best experience)? _____

» Who is going to mystery shop (code for spying) your top four competitors?
_____

» What is your marketing plan to beat your top four competitors (in two sentences or less)?
_____

» What is your plan to offer a better product and service experience for your ideal and likely buyers than is currently being offered by your top four competitors? _____

> "Buy or bury the competition."
>
>
> **-Jack Welch**
> (Former CEO of GE who many consider to be the best CEO of his time)

I once coached a Dallas-area-based attorney who reached out to me after reading an article I wrote on Entrepreneur.com. He was absolutely being killed by another attorney in the marketplace. When I asked him who his biggest competitor was, he responded with the typical dumb statement entrepreneurs initially make, "Well, my biggest competition is myself."

Just like him, I also once had the physical flexibility needed to shove my entire cranium up my rectum, so I understood where he was coming from. I pointed out that he might feel like that, but he was absolutely being crushed by multiple competitors, with one in particular just killing him. To help my client figure out why he was being killed by his competition, I led him through answering the questions listed in this section. We hired some people (you could call them spies) to enlist the services of his competition. We quickly realized how his competition was getting his business and out-performing him in nearly every way. Within 60 days, we developed a strategic plan to beat the living daylights out of his competition and within 12 months, we were doing just that. You may think that I'm a little dramatic when I say, "killing the competition" and "spying on your enemies," but I promise you that if you are not spying on your competition, they are going to take your lunch, take your customers, and take half of the potential income that could be coming to you.

My friend, Netflix and Amazon absolutely destroyed Blockbuster Video by redefining the way people rent movies. iTunes came into the industry and devastated the CD manufacturing business. Uber is taking massive quantities of business away from taxi drivers. Airbnb is decimating the hotel industry in many cities. Henry Ford showed up with his Model T and single-handedly blew up the horse and carriage industry. I took my wife away from a dude she was dating at the time (true story and I still feel very proud of this achievement). My friend, you can turn your life into the reality you want to see.

 MY WIFE, VANESSA

"Face reality as it is, not as it was or as you wish it to be."

 *-Jack Welch*
(Arguably the most successful CEO of his era as the CEO of GE who grew the company 4000% during his tenure)

Most businesses that I have worked with over the years have had no clue about the evil Darth Vaders and outside trends that are coming to destroy their business models, their means of supporting their families, and fulfilling their dreams. Unless you want to get hit by the bus of an industry destroyer, you at least need to know what is going on and who those major disrupters are so that you can pivot your business model, if needed. When Jack Welch took over as the CEO of General Electric, they had not grown much at all in the past decade and the company had become stagnant. Overseas companies and the cheap labor they had access to were beginning to produce toasters and refrigerators that they would sell at low costs GE could not match. Rather than allowing the company to die a slow death from outside competition, Jack Welch completely switched the company's focus. He abruptly pulled the company out of industries he felt that they could not be competitive in and moved them into industries and markets that he thought they could dominate. Before he retired from GE, the company had grown by 4000% and had become a leader in jet engine production, medical equipment, financing, and the world of television (Jack Welch and GE purchased NBC in 1986).

To prevent yourself from being run over by an industry-destroying bus, take the time to answer the following questions:

» What are the four biggest industry-destroying buses that are headed your way?
» What will you have to do if these industry-destroying buses collide with you and your business?

Now that you have a good understanding of how you stack up versus the competition, it's very important to formalize your observations into a visual tool that you can use to help you beat the living daylights of your competition.

YOU MUST MARKET WITH THE SUBTLETY OF A MISSILE

"IN A CROWDED MARKETPLACE, FITTING IN IS FAILING. IN A BUSY MARKETPLACE, NOT STANDING OUT IS THE SAME AS BEING INVISIBLE."
– SETH GODIN

Find the Market's Need and Fill It in a Memorable and Differentiated Way

My friend, you must figure out what market need you can fill in a memorable and differentiated way. Imagine that you own a sporting goods store and you are competing against Walmart, who is your next-door neighbor in the adjoining shopping center. How would you beat Walmart? First off, you can't beat them on pricing for popular sporting goods items. Walmart is a notoriously aggressive negotiator who buys in such volume that you wouldn't stand a chance. So you're not going to beat them on price. However, you could beat them in the way the founder and late, great entrepreneur Sam Walton once suggested in his own book, Made in America. To beat Walmart, you would have to make sure that your sporting goods store focused on providing a wide variety of specialty sporting goods items not carried by Walmart. In addition, to providing some of the same sporting goods items carried by Walmart. You would have to make sure that you provide Trader Joe's-, Disney-, and Nordstrom-level customer service. If you do those things, you could actually compete with Walmart and beat them in this particular niche. For you to win in the game of business, you must find your niche.

If you are stuck attempting to find your niche, simply determine where you can win in the marketplace. Don't devote your life to an unwinnable war. If you still can't figure out your niche, come to one of my conferences and I will help you personally to find:

» Your company's biggest strengths

» Your competition's biggest weakness

» Your target market's needs

» Your core competency (the product or service your company can scalably provide)

Once you find the need in the market that you can fill better than anyone else in the world, you will become known for this. Think about the following brands. Ample examples that your brain can handle.

» **Chipotle**
This company was founded by Steve Ells who focused on providing quality and completely organic ingredients he could find. He focused the experience inside each Chipotle around simple, high quality ingredients and simple industrial decor. Steve did not focus on providing the best-priced burritos and fresh Mexican food, he focused on providing the highest quality burritos on the market. He grew the business to 16 locations before the McDonald's corporation offered to purchase the majority of the company from him.

» **Zappos**
This company was founded by Nick Swinmurn who focused on building the world's first major online shoe retailer with a focus on offering free returns, a huge selection of shoes and incredibly high levels of customer service. In 1999, Nick reached out to Tony Hsieh to help him scale his concept. Tony joined Zappos

as their new CEO in 2000 when the company did approximately $1.6 million in sales. By 2009, Zappos revenues had reached $1 billion.

» **Airbnb**

This company was started in October of 2007 in San Francisco by Brian Chesky and Joe Gebbia. They focused on offering short-term living quarters for people who would rather stay at someone's residence or home instead of a hotel. By 2010, there were 15 people working from Chesky and Gebbia's loft apartment (their home office). The company continued gaining traction and then in November 2010, they raised $7.2 million from Greylock Partners and Sequoia Capital, having booked 80% of their total 700,000 bookings in just the past six months.

» **Starbucks**

Howard Schultz joined the existing company called Starbucks with a vision to create a "third place" for people who appreciate coffee and want to gather with others to connect and enjoy coffee. He focused on making sure that Starbucks customers came there as much for the experience as they did for the coffee itself. To create this experience, he insisted on incorporating beautiful decor, smells, and ambiance into every Starbucks location. He made sure that the people who made the coffee were referred to as baristas and that even the sizes of the coffee and lattes being offered were referred to with value-adding nomenclature. Starbucks doesn't offer small, medium, and large coffees like everyone else. They offer tall, grande, and venti.

"Make sure that everybody in your [company] comes to work every day trying to find a better way. You have to absolutely look outside, inside, [and] know that somebody is doing it better than you and you've got to drive that into every person in your organization. 'There is a better way of doing this, damn it, find it!' You may be number one, but you're only number one for as long as the snapshot [in time] and somebody is always shooting at you. So this is a drive that people have to come with."

-*Jack Welch*
(The legendary former CEO of General Electric)

My friend, in order to win in the game of business, you must "be the first or second best in something." You must find a niche that you can absolutely dominate and then you can start finding more ways to solve the problems of the ideal and likely buyers in that niche. If you are stumped and you don't know what niche you can fill, I recommend finding 15 ideal and likely buyers and asking them all the same question:

"As it relates to industry, what company first comes to mind when you think of _____ (your unique niche)?"

If every human you talk to keeps immediately mentioning Zappos or Starbucks, you may need to rethink your unique niche and value proposition. You must find a way to generate a product by offering products and services that your ideal and likely buyers want in a way that is currently not being served by your competition.

Branding 101

I view branding as simply the perception that the world has about you and your business. "Branding is simply a perception, and perception that will match reality over time. Sometimes your brand will be ahead, other times it will be behind. But your brand is simply what people think about your company and the products and services you offer.

Your brand is simply what people think about when they think about your company and the only way to brand (sear) that idea into the brains of your ideal and likely buyers is to focus on the results you provide your customers and the emotional connection you want your ideal and likely buyers to have with your products. Once you know what your brand is and who your ideal and likely buyers are, it is very important that you brand your company properly by consistently doing the following two things right:

» Always have your ideal and likely buyers in mind when you do any marketing. Ask yourself what message will resonate most with them.

» Never do any branding or marketing that will cause your ideal and likely buyers to lose trust in you and your brand.

Mentally marinate on the following four examples of great branding at work. When most people think of the following brands, what do they think about?

Apple

1. It works.

2. It's designed with function and style in mind.

3. It is innovative and different.

Whole Foods Market

1. They are focused on quality.

2. They are focused on healthy and organic products.

3. They provide great customer service.

Southwest Airlines

1. They are fun.

2. They have consistently low fares.

3. They won't hit you with any hidden fees.

Disney

1. It's a magical and happy place for families.

2. It offers good clean fun.

3. It is epic and everything about it is always done on a grand scale.

> "The number of new customers we've had is up 411% over last year."
>
> *-Jared & Jennifer Johnson*
> (Owners, Platinum Pest)

> "My Conversion Percentage Went From 32% to 69% in 2 Months."
>
> *-Placid Ajoku*
> (Owner, Built Phoenix Strong)

Alright, now we need to take a moment to think about your company. What do people think about when they think of your brand? This is typically where it gets hard for many business owners who are focused on trying to do everything from consensus. The Walt Disney Company has decided over and over to focus on providing a good clean environment where families can enjoy their experience.

Undoubtedly at some point, someone associated with the company probably found a niche they could dominate if they moved slightly away from that focus. Southwest Airlines is focused on providing low fares but without a doubt, at some point somebody within the company probably suggested they could make a quick profit if they would hit the customer up with a few extra fees. Apple was the love of Steve Jobs' life, but he was actually fired from the company in part for deepening the brand. Once he was fired, the company shifted to offer a ton of products loaded with features customers did not want. They had to bring Jobs back to fix the brand before it went under. After Howard Schultz left Starbucks, they began to experience an avalanche of problems and their legendary customer service began to slide into mediocrity. The company struggled and Schultz eventually chose to come out of retirement to right the ship and get the company's customer service back where it needed to be.

Now it's time for you to roll up your sleeves and get to work. Start defining how your business will provide a memorable experience for your customers that is consistent with the emotions you want them to feel. To turn your ideas into a visual that can keep your company focused, take a moment to define the overall experience, the sights, the sounds, the smells, the interactions, and the emotions you want your customers to have when engaging with your brand. Do this by filling out the Branding Experience Worksheet found at: www.ThriveTimeShow.com/ TreasureTrove.

In order to turn your Branding Experience Worksheet into reality, you are going to need to create detailed checklists for each aspect of your branding experience with a quality control / accountability loop to ensure that the "brand promise" you make to your customers is never compromised. To improve the quality of your life by 2%, we have made an example Checklist for Implementing the Branding Experience available at: www.ThriveTimeShow.com/TreasureTrove.

The Customer Will Only Pay for Experience They Want

Now before you start getting "too mystic" about those elements of the branding experience you want the customer to enjoy, please understand that the customer is the boss. You must allow the customer and their emotional and practical needs to dictate how you brand your business. If you open up a quick oil change and car maintenance business and your daughter is obsessed with princesses, you may decide to brand your business based upon her love of princesses. You may be in for a rude awakening when you have bad reception from your customers. Perhaps your customers will appreciate the fact that your team of technicians is wearing pink and the "Nutcracker Suite" is playing overhead at all times. However, if they don't understand how the theme works in conjunction with the products and services you are offering, you cannot be offended or completely unwilling to accept feedback from the customer. You must provide a product, service and brand that your ideal and likely buyers love.

"There is only one boss. The customer. And he can fire everybody in the company from the chairman on down, simply by spending his money somewhere else."

-Sam Walton
(American businessman and entrepreneur best known for founding the retailers Walmart and Sam's Club)

One famous example of a brand no longer meeting the customer's needs is Harley Davidson. In 1969, Harley Davidson was purchased by American Machine and Foundry. When AMF bought the company, they streamlined production, decreased the size of the workforce and attempted to build expensive motorcycles designed to compete with the Japanese high performance motorcycles. Owners of Harleys revolted and hated the look, the quiet sound, the feel and overall direction that the company was headed. The company nearly went bankrupt and AMF ended up selling it to a group of 13 investors led famously by Willie G. Davidson and Vaughn Beals. The new owners refocused Harley on producing loud and massive motorcycles. By the time they introduced the "Fat Boy" motorcycle to the market in 1990, Harley Davidson was once again the leader in the heavyweight motorcycle category. Remember, give the customers what they want and they will happily pay for it.

"PUT ALL OF YOUR EGGS IN ONE BASKET, AND WATCH THAT BASKET."
- ANDREW CARNEGIE
SELF-MADE STEEL TYCOON AND PHILANTHROPIST

SUPER MOVES FOR ENHANCING YOUR BRANDING

1. Create a website that is better than your competition.

2. Create a logo that is better than your competition.

3. Create a one sheet that clearly shows the value between you and the competition.

4. Create print materials that are better than your competition.

5. Create a marketing video that succinctly explains what problems you solve, who you are, and why people should buy from you.

6. Create signage that will wow your ideal and likely buyers.

7. Make sure that everything that your customers see or experience is first-class and intentional.

8. Create Google My Business account: business.google.com.

9. Get Google reviews.

10. Gather testimonial videos from your happy clients.

11. Have your team wear memorable uniforms.

12. Create a story video.

"If you give someone a present, and you give it to them in a Tiffany box, it's likely that they'll believe that the gift has higher perceived value than if you gave it to them in no box or a box of less prestige. That's not because the receiver of the gift is a fool. But instead, because we live in a culture in which we gift wrap everything — our politicians, our corporate heads, our movie and TV stars, and even our toilet paper."

MICHAEL LEVINE
Thrive15.com mentor and the man who has been the PR consultant for Michael Jackson, Prince, Nike, Pizza Hut, Nancy Kerrigan, and many other celebrities and large brands

Ample Example

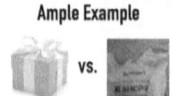

VS.

From the list below, circle which marketing vehicles that you think are most likely to carry your marketing message effectively to your ideal and likely buyers:

Adwords

Amazon.com

Automobile Wraps

Billboard Advertising

Blog Based Advertising

Business Development / Partnership Deals

Buying Your Competition / Mergers and Acquisition

Celebrity Endorsement

Cold Call Marketing

Door to Door Sales

Dream 100

Email Marketing

Facebook Advertising

Flyers

Google Maps

Google Reviews

Google Shopping

Magazine Advertising

Mall / Shopping Center Traffic

Mass Mailers

Mass Texting (Twilio)

Mass Voicemails (Slybroadcast)

Mass Emails (AWeber, Constant Contact)

Networking Intentionally (Set number of meetings per month and specific organizations)

Newspaper Advertising

Outdoor Signage

Pandora.com Radio Advertising

Pay Per Click - Search Engine Marketing / Advertising

Pop-Up Shop

Public Relations
- Celebrity Tie-In Strategy
- Expert Strategy
- Giveback Strategy
- National News Tie-In Strategy
- Shock and Awe Strategy

Radio Advertising

Referral Based Advertising

Retargeting Online ads (See SEO Conversion checklist)

Search Engine Optimization (See next pages for details)

Sign-Based Marketing

Sign-Flipper Marketing

Social Media Advertising

Speech Based Marketing

Spotify Advertising

Targeted Online ads

Television Advertising

Text Marketing

Trade Show Advertising

Valpak Advertising

Yelp Reviews

YouTube Advertising

Bias Alert... But Still True

ThriveTime Show sponsors make more money than they spend on advertising.

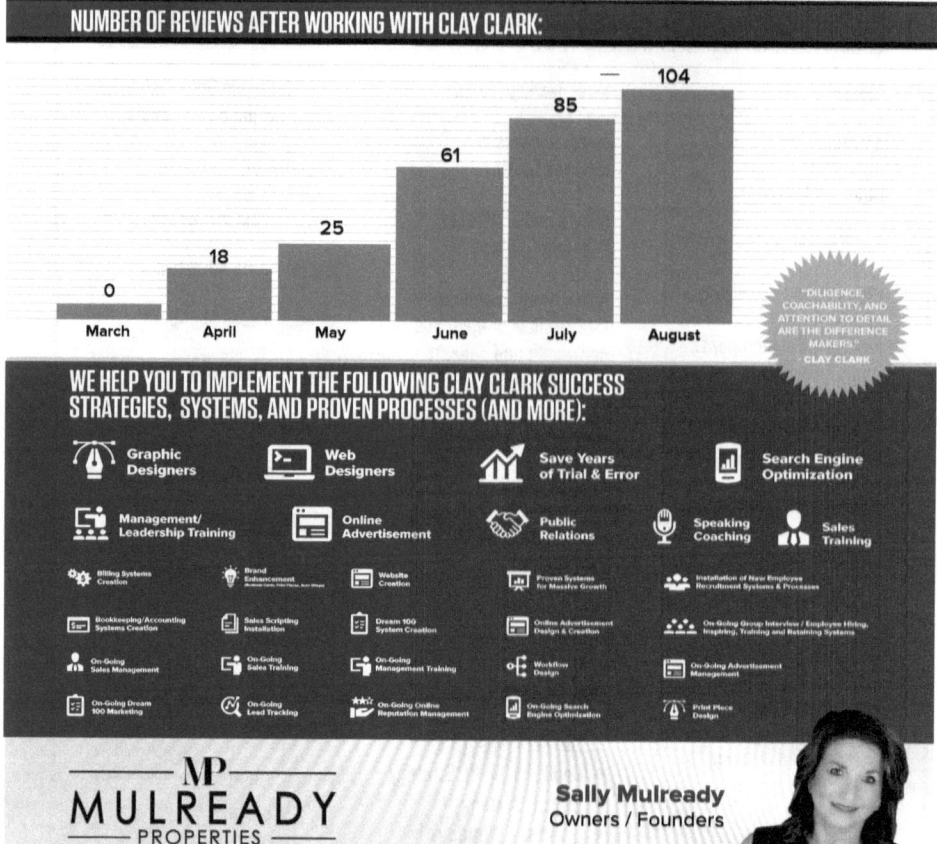

NUMBER OF REVIEWS AFTER WORKING WITH CLAY CLARK:

March	April	May	June	July	August
0	18	25	61	85	104

"DILIGENCE, COACHABILITY, AND ATTENTION TO DETAIL ARE THE DIFFERENCE MAKERS."
- CLAY CLARK

WE HELP YOU TO IMPLEMENT THE FOLLOWING CLAY CLARK SUCCESS STRATEGIES, SYSTEMS, AND PROVEN PROCESSES (AND MORE):

- Graphic Designers
- Web Designers
- Save Years of Trial & Error
- Search Engine Optimization
- Management/ Leadership Training
- Online Advertisement
- Public Relations
- Speaking Coaching
- Sales Training

- Billing Systems Creation
- Brand Enhancement
- Website Creation
- Proven Systems for Massive Growth
- Installation of New Employee Recruitment Systems & Processes
- Bookkeeping/Accounting Systems Creation
- Sales Scripting Installation
- Dream 100 System Creation
- Online Advertisement Design & Creation
- On-Going Group Interview / Employee Hiring, Inspiring, Training and Retaining Systems
- On-Going Sales Management
- On-Going Sales Training
- On-Going Management Training
- Workflow Design
- On-Going Advertisement Management
- On-Going Dream 100 Marketing
- On-Going Lead Tracking
- On-Going Online Reputation Management
- On-Going Search Engine Optimization
- Print Piece Design

MP MULREADY PROPERTIES

Sally Mulready
Owners / Founders

Phase 3

SET S.M.A.R.T. GOALS ONLY. (SPECIFIC, MEASURABLE, ACTIONABLE, REALISTIC, AND TIME-SENSITIVE)

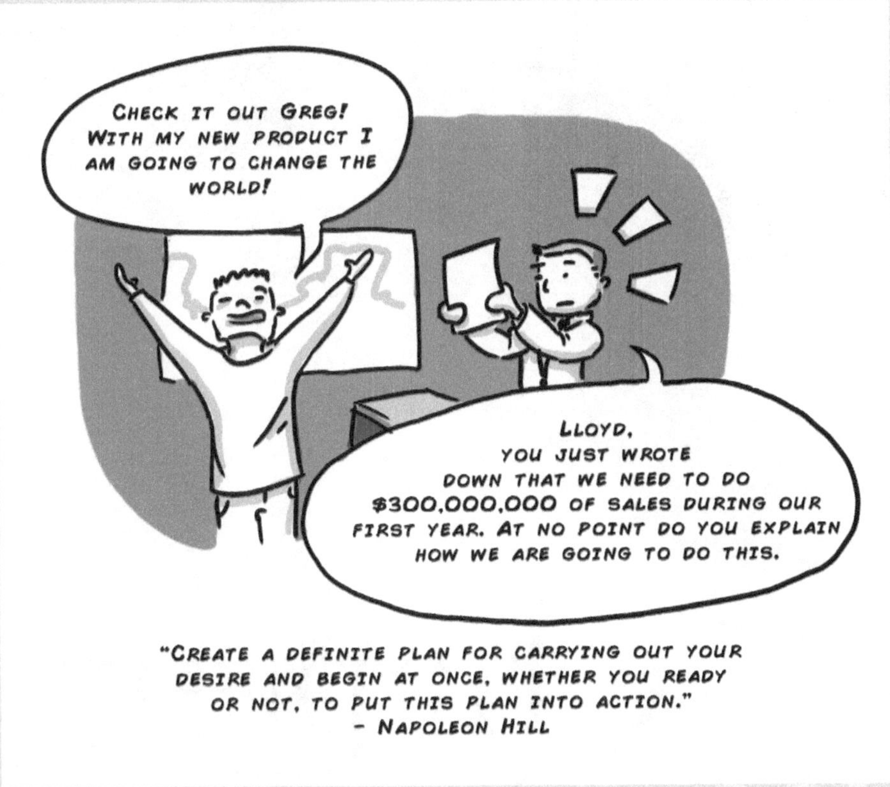

> CHECK IT OUT GREG! WITH MY NEW PRODUCT I AM GOING TO CHANGE THE WORLD!

> LLOYD, YOU JUST WROTE DOWN THAT WE NEED TO DO $300,000,000 OF SALES DURING OUR FIRST YEAR. AT NO POINT DO YOU EXPLAIN HOW WE ARE GOING TO DO THIS.

"CREATE A DEFINITE PLAN FOR CARRYING OUT YOUR DESIRE AND BEGIN AT ONCE, WHETHER YOU READY OR NOT, TO PUT THIS PLAN INTO ACTION."
— NAPOLEON HILL

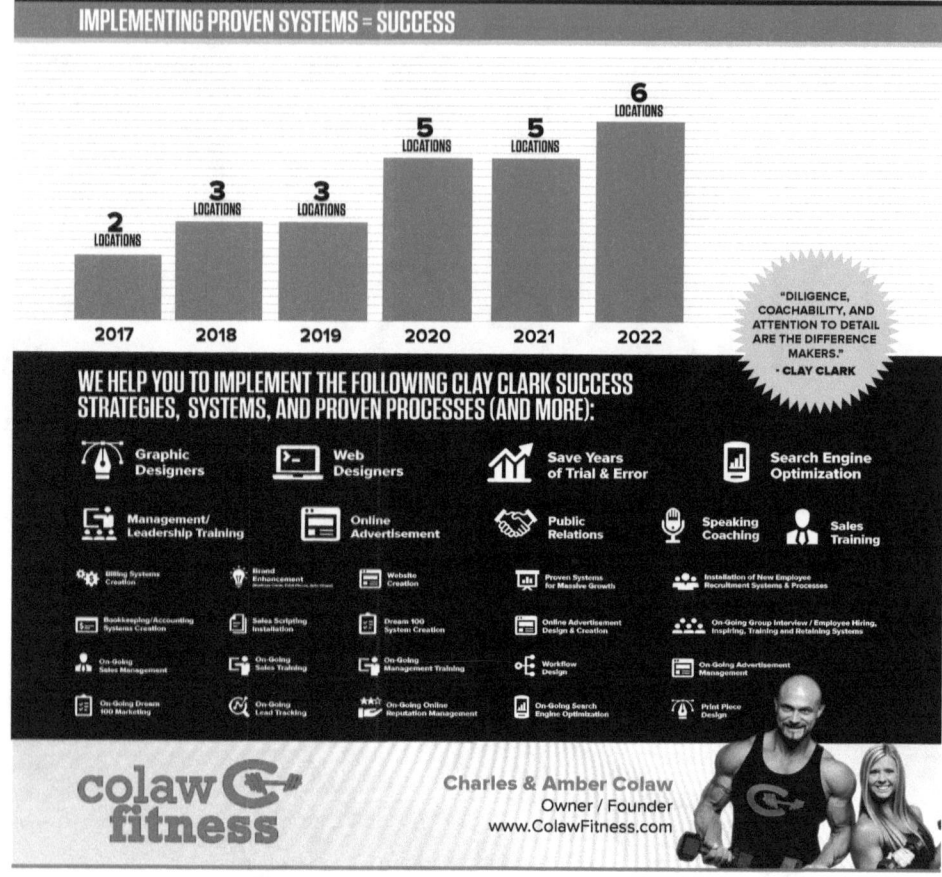

Chapter 6

Taking the Limiters Off of Your Growth

Alright, now that we have determined what our ideal and likely buyers want, hopefully they are starting to buy our products and services from us often enough for us to be able to make a profit (although at this point, it's probably a small one). Now it's time to teach you how to quickly identify and eliminate barriers, limiting beliefs, and systems that are causing your business to become stuck or to grow at a very slow annual growth rate. After working with thousands of companies, the Thrive15.com Mentors and I can all confidently say that you will never do this if you do not consistently schedule a specific time in your calendar to intentionally compare the direction your company is actually going versus the direction you had planned for the company to go.

> "Drifting, without aim or purpose, is the first cause of failure."
>
>
>
> *-Napoleon Hill*
> **(Bestselling author of** *Think & Grow Rich***)**

Schedule a weekly, one hour or 90-minute recurring meeting where you look at big wins of the week, the status of your team's key performance indicators, any big issues or burning fires that need to be solved, any low hanging fruit that your sales team needs to focus on, following up on the status of action items from last week, and assigning action items for the following week. To help insure that your weekly meetings have a concrete and definitive agenda, we have provided the Perfect Weekly Meeting Agenda Template[64] at www.Thrive15.com/ThePerfectWeeklyMeetingAgendaTemplate.

The items to be covered during each Perfect Weekly Meeting include:

» Big wins of the week _____

» The vision of your company / why your business exists _____

» What problems are your ideal and likely buyers willing to pay to solve?
  _____

» The status of key performance indicators (quantifiable sales numbers and key performance metrics) _____

» Biggest limiting factors _____

» Burning fires _____

» Low hanging sales fruit _____

» Follow-up action items (did everyone get their assignments done?)

_____

» Assign action items (who, what, when?) _____

Your commitment to follow this agenda each week will keep your company from ever drifting too far away from your core customers, your core vision, your core brand and your core values. However, there is much in the way of practical action steps that must be taken after these meetings if your company is going to succeed and truly grow quickly. First up is the area of HR... ahh... human resources. From my experience coaching companies all over the planet, I believe this is perhaps the single most challenging aspect of running a business, once you have figured out how to consistently produce and sell a product or service that the marketplace wants. Without quality and well-trained people in place, your business systems and visions will eventually die. However, do not get overwhelmed by the "BIG IDEA" of hiring people. To improve the quality of your life by 3%, I have broken up the entire human resources system into four segments:

1. Recruit

2. Hire

3. Inspire

4. Fire Those You Cannot Inspire and Who Cannot Do What Is Required

Step 1: Recruit

Let's start with the recruiting aspect of the business. You must view the human resources aspect of your business as the LIFEBLOOD OF YOUR BUSINESS. Without quality people, nothing will get done and thus, you must focus on recruiting. When I say focus, I mean to F.O.C.U.S. This stands for "focus on core tasks until success." My friend, you cannot ever take the pedal off of the metal when it comes to recruiting. So how do you do this? First off, you must create a winning job post that generates inquiries.[65] Nobody wants to work in a dead-end job with no career opportunities, no ongoing education, and no potential for benefits and bonuses and no one wants to work in a negative or no-culture business for an absent and uninspiring boss. However, this is exactly what most job posts describe. If you are going to post a job opportunity on Craigslist, Monster, Indeed, or other third party source, you are going to be spending money to do so – don't waste it. Your job posts must be inspiring and must resonate with highly motivated people who are looking for a career and not just a job. Visit www.ThriveTimeShow.com/TreasureTrove to find a sample job post that is both practical and inspiring.

The statistics show us that most people hate or strongly dislike their jobs so you must offer an alternative to these workplaces most people do not like.

Mystic Statistic:
"Less than one-third (31.5%) of U.S. workers were engaged in their jobs in 2014."

Amy Adkins, author of "Majority of U.S. Employees Not Engaged Despite Gains in 2014," Gallup, January 28, 2015

Schedule a Time to Post Your Weekly Job Posts

If you do not schedule a specific time to post your job posts, you won't do it. You will get busy or you will forget. Do not let this happen to you. Block out time in your schedule right now for posting job opportunities. You must also determine what job posting boards or third-party sites you are going to post on. From my experience working with neurologists, dentists, photographers, limo drivers, and nearly every other industry under the sun, Craigslist is the most effective and lowest cost platform on which to post your available jobs. However, I would strongly recommend that you post on Monster.com, Indeed.com and Craigslist.com simultaneously. I would budget for it and I would never stop.[67]

"Kelleher believes that hiring employees who have the right attitude is so important that the hiring process takes on a "patina of spirituality." In addition, he believes that anyone who looks at things solely in terms of factors that can easily be quantified is missing the heart of business, which is people."

-Heskett, Sasser, et al.
(Authors of "Putting the Profit Chain to Work" in the Harvard Business Review)

Block Off Weekly Times for New Recruit Interviews

I'm busy and you're busy, but you and I must block off time to conduct weekly interviews to find people who will best represent our company. I love scheduling group interviews because it saves time and allows me to see how candidates compare with each other in a literal side-by-side comparison. A tryout of sorts. If you don't want to do group interviews, then you are going to have to block out many hours throughout your week to interview potential candidates who might or might not show up on time or at all for their interviews. Because I realize that 40% of potential candidates don't have the mental capacity or the diligence needed to actually show up on time for their

"I don't know whether it was Calvin Coolidge or Bianca Jagger who said — they're both thin, that's why I get them confused — 'the business of business is business.' We've always said, 'The business of business is people.'"

-Herb Kelleher
(The co-founder and former CEO of Southwest Airlines)

initial interviews, I love the group interview format. When someone responds to a job post, our team schedules them for an interview without even reading their resume first. We don't tell them the format of the interview - group or individual - we just tell them that we can interview them at this specific time on this specific date. To download an example of the email we send out to potential candidates to invite them for an interview, go to: www.ThriveTimeShow.com/TreasureTrove.

Conduct Your Interviews with Both Passion and Purpose While Following an Agenda

During an interview, so many business owners spend massive quantities of time going on and on about their company and their vision while the candidates sit quietly, scanning the room for a blunt object with which they can respectfully bash in their skull to stop the boredom. Candidates begin to feel as though the person interviewing them has no game plan or agenda, because they don't. To make matters worse, most companies delegate the recruitment and interviewing process to "the new guy" or the person on your staff who hasn't quite found his place within your company culture. This is terrible.

My friend, the person conducting the interviews must look sharp and must be a confidence-inspiring powerhouse who can follow the perfect interview agenda every time; an agenda which includes:

» Clarifying the goals of the company
» Clarifying the goals of the candidate
» Clarifying the expectations of the job
» Clarify the compensation of the job
» Clarifying the career path of the job
» Answering any questions
» Clarifying the next steps for the applicants

To download the Perfect Interview Agenda, go to:
www.ThriveTimeShow/TreasureTrove.

To watch a training video on how to properly conduct a group interview, visit:
www.ThriveTimeShow/TreasureTrove.

What Are You Looking for in a Potential New Hire?

When you are interviewing candidates, you are looking for what the legendary CEO Jack Welch calls the "4 E's."

» **Energy** – Does the candidate have the energy to bring enthusiasm to the workplace every day?

» **Energize** – Does the candidate have the ability to energize those around him or her?

» **Edge** – Does the candidate have the edge needed to make the tough decisions?

» **Execute** – Does the candidate have the ability to execute and actually get their job done?

» **BONUS** – I have also found that it is extremely important that you search for candidates who are coachable.

Deep Thoughts:

Schedule Time for Candidates You Like to Shadow Your Team Before Calling References

If you like a few of the candidates you interviewed, that is great; however, statistics show that person you like may not impress you so much once they start doing the

"85% of job applicants lie on resumes."

-Inc. Magazine

> ## "75% of employees steal from the workplace and that must do so repeatedly."
>
> *-U.S. Chamber of Commerce*

job. CBS News featured an article written by Rich Russakoff and Mary Goodman called "Employee Theft: Are You Blind to It?" This article revealed that the U.S. Chamber of Commerce estimates that 75% of employees steal from the workplace and that most do so repeatedly. CNBC also published a disturbing article written by Cindy Perman titled, "Employees Behaving Badly: Vampires and Gossips," stating that 43% of human resources managers said the number one reason a new employee didn't work out was because he or she couldn't accept feedback. My friend, the sad fact is that most people you interview will not work out. You want to find out who will not work out as soon as possible, before investing the time and money needed to pay for formal background checks and verify references.

Mystic Statistic
"The average cost of a bad hiring decision can equal 30% of the individual's first-year potential earnings."

US Department of Labor

The Shadowing Process Almost Always Confirms or Denies Job Candidates within the First Four Hours

Now I am going to explain how the shadowing process works. After you conduct enough group or individual interviews to lose a little faith in humanity, you may also have found a few people whom you believe might be the "perfect fit." The next step is to schedule them to shadow you or one of your top performers at the workplace. The candidate should be instructed to dress in appropriate work attire and act as if they already have the job. Explain to them that this process is designed so that both you and they can see if this opportunity is a great fit for you both.

During this shadowing process, approximately 50% of the candidates you initially liked will show themselves to be crazy, dishonest, drunk, or uncoachable. The other half will show themselves to be hireable. This is why we complete the shadowing process before checking references and investing in professional background checks.

Background Checks and References

Once you have found a candidate you really like, it is now time to conduct a professional background check and call their references. I can't explain to you how important this is. I recommend using GoodHire.com because they have low cost options, they have an easy-access online portal, and you can purchase one background check at a time. Visit www.GoodHire.com to check the backgrounds of potential candidates

· ·

Mystic Statistic

"The U.S. Chamber of Commerce estimates that 75% of employees steal from the workplace and that most do so repeatedly."

"Employee Theft: Are You Blind to It?" – Rich Russakoff and Mary Goodman – CBSNews / MoneyWatch

Fun Fact:
"78% of the men interviewed had cheated on their current partner."
The Washington Post

 ## The Boring Stuff Matters Most

"I have learned from both my own successes and failures and those of many others that it's the boring stuff that matters the most. Startup success is not a consequence of good genes or being in the right place at the right time. Startup success can be engineered by following the right process, which means it can be learned, which means it can be taught."

ERIC RIES
Best-selling author of the Lean Startup and former consultant at Kleiner Perkins

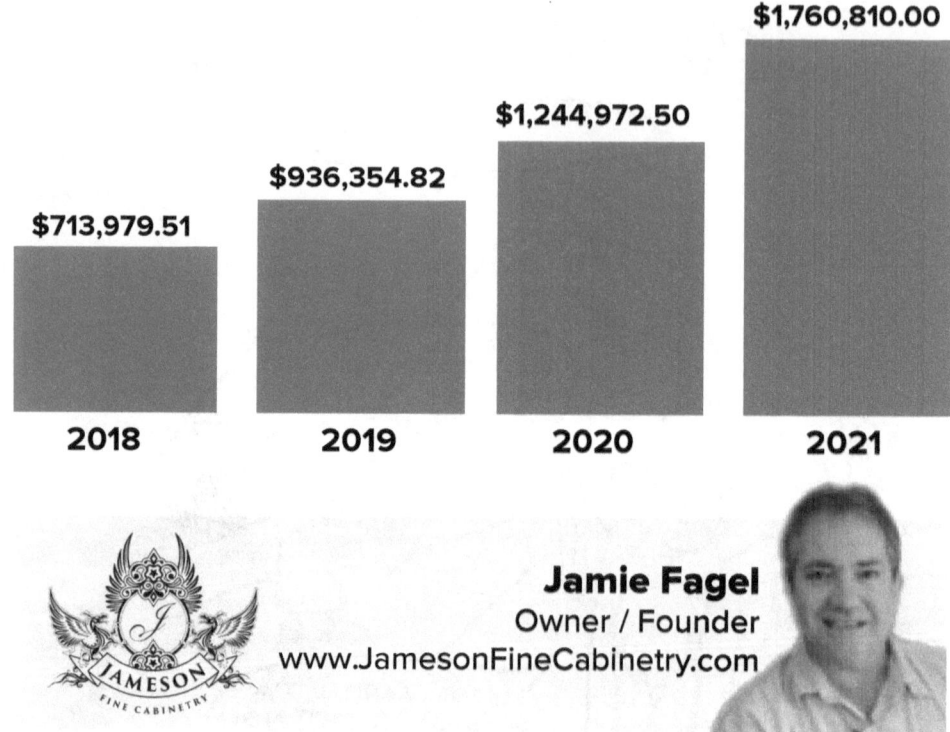

Chapter 7

Step 2: Hire

Once you have selected the candidate you believe is going to be the best fit, you'll want to hire this person as soon as possible. When you bring a new person onto your team, it is very important that you use a formal, new employee Onboarding Checklist,[73] an Employee Handbook,[74] and a Job Skills Mastery Checklist.[75]

To access templates for all of these documents, visit: www.ThriveTimeShow.com/TreasureTrove

You must be very intentional about your new employee's experience their first 72 hours on the job. Having worked with thousands of companies, I can say that most employers have terrible, uninspiring and disorganized onboarding processes. My friend, these first 72 hours will absolutely make or break an employee's relationship with your company. Forbes featured an article written by Carmine Gallo titled, "70% of Your Employees Hate Their Jobs." This article referenced a Gallup survey that showed that 71% of workers hate their jobs. The majority of the employees' dislike for their jobs stems from a general dislike of their boss. My friend, in order to successfully hire and retain employees, you must embrace the fact that in today's world, management is truly mentorship. You must inspire those you hire or they will not want to do what is required.

"When you are in a key leadership position you must be an inspirational leader and not just a personality free administrator if you want to get the results which are possible with a team of inspired employees."

Clay Clark
(Father of five kids and founder of several multi-million dollar businesses)

"MAKE A PLACE FOR EVERYTHING."
-CLAY CLARK

Action Items:

1. Buy a White Board.

2. Create a Linear Workflow.

3. Put Your Goals on Your White Board.

4. Write Down the Number of Sales Per Day You Need to Achieve Your Financial Goals.

5. Write Down the Number of No's You Need Per Day to Achieve Your Goals.

MAKE YOUR PRIORITIES SCARED

"EAT THE BIGGEST FROG FIRST"
-BRIAN TRACY

(BEST-SELLING AUTHOR AND LEGENDARY SALES TRAINER)

Chapter 8

Step 3: Inspire

This part of the hiring process can really wear you out if you are not intentional about inspiring your teammates and if you approach the management of your people without a plan. When you manage people, you must understand that most humans behave in a fairly predictable way and that for the majority of people, their emotional state controls two thirds of the actions they take on a daily basis. The bestselling author of Emotional Intelligence, psychologist Daniel Goleman, once said, *"If your emotional abilities aren't in hand, if you don't have self-awareness, if you are not able to manage your distressing emotions, if you can't have empathy and have effective relationships, then no matter how smart you are, you are not going to get very far."*

This quote used to make my brain explode because I'm old school. If I'm paying you to do something, I personally believe that you should do it and be happy to do it because you are being paid.

Create a list of all of your employees.

Label all employees as either A, B or C players (talk to your coach if you get stuck).

Block out time to train up your team members on a weekly basis.

Work with your coach to develop job descriptions for all of the positions within your business.

Schedule time into your schedule for your weekly group interviews (go over this concept with your coach).

Every week: Launch hiring advertisements (On Craigslist, Monster.com and Indeed. com) to promote job openings before they are open. This way you are not stuck dealing with dysfunctional employees.

Commit to firing / replacing the bottom 10% of your employee roster if they show themselves to be unwilling to improve.

Let team members know that you are focused on the growth of the company and their personal growth. Then begin kicking, hugging, documenting and pruning as needed.

However, I discovered that in order to effectively manage people, you must have both a carrot and a stick that you are offering to employees for nearly every aspect of their job. In short, merit-based pay makes the slackers go away.

Schedule Daily Time for Accountability

At the Elephant in the Room (one of the businesses I own), we do this every morning. Each morning, the store manager huddles up the team for 15 minutes to go over the following items:

» Big wins and positive stories from yesterday

» Burning fires or issues that need to be resolved

» The game plan for the day

These morning huddles keep everyone connected, everyone inspired, and any small fires from spreading. My friend, you must work very hard to develop a culture of excellence, positivity and proactivity or your business will struggle.

When will you schedule time for daily accountability?

_____

_____

_____

_____

> "CHERISH YOUR VISIONS AND YOUR DREAMS AS
> THEY ARE THE CHILDREN OF YOUR SOUL, THE
> BLUEPRINTS OF YOUR ULTIMATE ACHIEVEMENTS."
> – NAPOLEON HILL
> BEST-SELLING AUTHOR OF "THINK AND GROW RICH"

FROM STARTUP TO SUPER SUCCESS

$561,676.87

149.32%
Growth

$225,286.50

225,286%
Growth

$0

| 2020 | 2021 | 2022 |

New Concept
— HEALTHCARE —

Virginia Mingione, FNP-C
Owner / Founder
www.NewConcept.healthcare

You will Create Enemies if You are Honest

"You have enemies? Good. That means you've stood up for something sometime in your life."

WINSTON CHURCHILL
The Prime Minister of the United Kingdom from 1940 to 1945 who lead the British in their fight against Adolf Hitler and Nazi Germany. He also led the country from 1951 to 1955. Churchill was an officer in the British Army, a non-academic historian, a writer (as Winston S. Churchill), and an artist. He won the Nobel Prize in Literature in 1953 for his overall, lifetime body of work.

Chapter 9

Step 4: Fire Those You Cannot Inspire and Who Cannot Do What Is Required

If you can't inspire someone or if they just do not fit into the company culture, you must fire them quickly. When people think about Zappos, they think about a great company culture where everyone is happy, yet their CEO bluntly said, "I fire those who don't fit our company culture." Elon Musk, a man whose life I do not endorse and currently the wealthiest man alive once said, "One lesson I learned [at PayPal] is to fire people faster. That sounds awful, but I think if somebody is not working out, it's best to part ways sooner rather than later. It's a mistake to try too hard to make something work that really couldn't work."

I can keep giving you quotes from super successful people all day, but ultimately you must accept that it is important to quickly part ways when a team member shows they cannot be inspired and cannot do what is required. The longer you take, the tougher it gets and the more hurtful it is for the person being fired. However, because of various labor laws and for ethical reasons, I wouldn't recommend just hauling off and firing somebody unless you have given them some type of previous warning known as a "write-up."

Deep Thoughts

"Fire people who will not do their jobs even and especially if they are family."

-Clay Clark
(Founder of Thrive15.com, former U.S. SBA Entrepreneur of the Year, host of the Thrive Time Show and America's #1 Business Coach)

Write-Up Often and Fire Bad Hires Quickly

When an employee's job performance is poor, there are really two possible explanations for what is going on. Either the employee doesn't know what to do or they are simply choosing not to do it. If the employee is choosing not to do what they know they are supposed to do, write them up. We have made a sample Employee Write-Up Form available for you at www.ThriveTimeShow.com/TreasureTrove To make sure everyone is on the same page, you should also use a point system that accompanies your Write-Up Policy. Essentially, if someone is late to work, they get this many points, and if they choose not to do their job, they get this many points. If they are caught stealing, they get this many points. If they don't show up to work, they get this many points. Whenever they reach a certain point total, they will be fired. When you take the time to set up a system like this, you take the emotion out of everything and you make the firing of someone a clear-cut issue. We have provided a sample Employee Write-Up Point System Document at www.ThriveTimeShow.com/TreasureTrove. If you would like additional training on the proper way to fire employees, watch the Thrive15.com CEO's training video on how to properly fire an employee at www.ThriveTimeShow.com/TreasureTrove

"People don't care how much you know until they know how much you care."

-Theodore Roosevelt

(American statesman, author, explorer, soldier, naturalist, and reformer who served as the 26th president of the United States)

Don't Life Coach Unless You Are a Life Coach

If your employees can't stay sober, drug-free, and focused on doing the task that you assign them, fire them as soon as possible or you will spend your life coaching adults which means that you are a life coach.

The Compensation Game

Having worked with thousands of employers all over the world, I can tell you that one of the most frustrating aspects of building a team is developing a fair compensation package. Most entrepreneurs will buy into either an A or B approach to compensation. "Option A" involves paying people as little as possible to do their jobs while "Option B" involves paying an employee whatever they ask in order to attract and keep the most talented people around. After years of first-hand experience and case study-driven research, I have found that neither option is the best.

Here is the best way to develop a fair compensation plan:

1. Cast a vision that is both inspiring and motivating to potential employees. People will rarely commit to staying in a workplace for very long if there is no clear and inspired vision for where the company is headed.

2. Determine what your candidates' life and career goals are. Show them how a job in your organization can help them gain the skills and develop the connections they need to achieve their career goals.

"Face reality as it is, not as it was or as you wish it to be."

-Jack Welch
(Arguably the most successful CEO of his era as the CEO of GE who grew the company 4000% during his tenure)

3. Determine what the job market would currently pay someone with the skill sets you're looking to employ. It's important that you aren't flying blind so when it is time, you can make a job offer that makes sense financially to both parties.

4. Determine what an employee's key interests and passions are as they relate to ongoing projects in your workplace. If you can offer a candidate an opportunity to work on projects that really interest them, this can go a long way toward creating a win-win employee / employer relationship.

5. Determine what small details and benefits would greatly improve a prospective employee's quality of life. Years ago, I worked with a doctor who paid his office manager's day care fee and to have her deposits and dry cleaning picked up and dropped off so she could work the needed hours without feeling overwhelmed. I have personally provided employees with a car that they desperately needed or with housing until they could find a more permanent residence.

6. Determine what stretch goals and bonuses you can offer. If you can clearly explain to an employee that if they help your company achieve a particular goal then they will receive a specific reward, this often motivates people.

7. Explore the option of giving an employee equity once they have helped the company achieve certain goals. I would not offer this to just anyone, but it's important that you consider this an option for qualified and key employees if you and the candidate cannot 100% agree on the compensation level.

8. Establish how the employee can earn freedom and autonomy over many aspects of their workday and projects. Some employees really want to be able to dress how they want and want the option to wear headphones while working. Although this may not fit your current culture, this may be a great incentive to help you land your next key hire.

9. Determine the actual amount of cash that you can sustainably afford to pay. It's important that you know how much you can offer and that this number is clear in your head.

10. To download the Checklist for Developing a Fair Compensation Plan for a Candidate, visit: www.ThriveTimeShow.com/TreasureTrove.

You Must Inspire Those That You Hire

Most people really need to know that the projects they are working on matter and are making a positive impact. Your company will succeed if you find a way to profitably solve the problems of your ideal and likely buyers. More often than not, your employees will succeed if you are able to establish a connection that helps them see how their role in the company actually helps your customers and company alike.

When you are able to show people how their work matters, honest and diligent team members will work with a sense of purpose. One great way to do this is to engage your team in the improvement of the products and services you offer. I highly recommend that you create a platform for your team to share ideas they may have to improve your company. I have found that you must take three steps to make this system work effectively.

1. Create an inbox into which your team members can either email or physically place their money-saving and profit-increasing ideas.

"Your work is going to fill a large part of your life, and the only way to be truly satisfied is to do what you believe is great work. And the only way to do great work is to love what you do. If you haven't found it yet, keep looking. Don't settle. As with all matters of the heart, you'll know when you find it."

-Steve Jobs
(Co-founder of Apple and legendary former CEO of Pixar)

2. Explain to your team members that any ideas they submit that result in the company saving $500 per six months will result in a $500 bonus for the team member who suggested the idea. Explain to your team members that any ideas that result in the company making more than $500 of additional profits per six months will net a $500 bonus for the team member who suggested the idea. Incentivizing your team to think like owners has been proven to work well in countless industries. In fact in the book, *Nuts!* Southwest Airline's Crazy Recipe for Business and Personal Success written by Kevin and Jackie Freiberg, multiple examples are given that show this system working to save Southwest Airlines millions of dollars.

> "Good business leaders create a vision, articulate the vision, passionately own the vision, and relentlessly drive it to completion."
>
>
> *-Jack Welch*
> (CEO who grew GE by 4000% during his tenure)

3. Announce a weekly or monthly time when you will discuss the ideas that you believe have the most immediate applicability and potential to be executed so that your teammates will know that you are actually listening to their suggestions.

Remember that you must find ways to engage your team mentally and emotionally in the execution of your company's mission or you will create a culture that encourages drifters, gossips, and poor performers. I'm sure that lack of employee engagement does not plague your business, but Gallup statistics published on April 13th of 2016 reveal that only 34.1% of U.S. employees are engaged in the workplace. Stop and think for a moment how much it is costing you and your business to not have your employees engaged in work.

Mystic Statistic:

An article written by Cheryl Conner and published in Forbes titled, "Wasting Time At Work: The Epidemic Continues," showed that 89% of people surveyed admit to wasting time at work.

http://www.forbes.com/sites/cherylsnappconner/2015/07/31/wasting-time-at-work-the-epidemic-continues/#238be2653ac1

As an employer, that statistic irritates the heck out of me; but there are things you can do to engage your employees in the workplace and now it's up to you to do them.

In Order for Your Team to Succeed You Must Become an Effective Executive

You can take the time to read the countless books that have been written on leadership and what it means to be an effective executive. However, because this is the best business book in the history of the world, I have distilled for you the core roles that you as an executive must be able to deliver on.

> "Nothing will work unless you do. Stop calling in sick, stop making excuses. Stop being a weakass and start showing up to work everyday and following through on your homework."
> -*Clay Clark*

F.O.C.U.S. | Keep Your Team Focused On Core Tasks Until Success

The co-founder of Apple and legendary former CEO of Pixar, Steve Jobs, once said it best when he commented, "People think focus means saying yes to the thing you've got to focus on. But that's not what it means at all. It means saying no to the hundred other good ideas that there are. You have to pick carefully. I'm actually as proud of the things we haven't done as the things I have done. Innovation is saying no to 1,000 things."

My friend, to be an effective executive, you must keep your team focused on your mission, your values, and your ideal and likely buyers. To help you and your company maintain its core focus, we have developed a worksheet titled, The Effective Executive: Maintaining Focus on Your Mission, Your Values, and Your Ideal and Likely Buyers (Download at www.ThriveTimeShow.com/TreasureTrove). Take a moment to fill out this form and print it. Tape it on the wall next to your desk. Tape it on your bathroom mirror. Place it everywhere that you and everyone else can see it so your company does not lose its focus.

The 8 Specific Super Moves for Keeping Your Company's Vision Out Front

Super Move #1 – Put your company's vision and mission statement in writing and place it somewhere where everyone can see it. If this document gets too long, no one will read it. Keep it short and simple.

Super Move #2 – Repeat your company's mission statement over and over and over again until you almost can't stand to say it one more time; then don't stop saying it. You must constantly clarify the vision with your team because over time, most teams tend to drift at the first sign of adversity. You must bring up your company's mission when formally speaking, when having a casual conversation with teammates and when self-talking.

Super Move #3 – Share testimonials. Any time you can share with your team a company success story or a testimonial from one of your ideal and likely customers who was happy using your products and services, you must do it.

> "If you have no major purpose, you are drifting toward certain failure."
>
>
>
> **-Napoleon Hill**
> (Bestselling author and advisor to Woodrow Wilson and Franklin Delano Roosevelt)

Super Move #4 – Add your company's mission statement to all internal and external memos, newsletters, and forms of communication. You want every human working in your office to know what your company's mission is. This will ensure that your mission can motivate them to make good decisions on a daily basis. Then they will keep your vision, your mission, and your ideal and likely buyers in mind.

Super Move #5 – Publicly praise members of the team who wow your ideal and likely buyers and who achieve results that help your company move closer to turning the vision into reality.

Super Move #6 – Fire people who don't believe in your company's mission and big vision. At Thrive15.com, we are obsessed with ongoing education and the pursuit of excellence in both business and life. Our entire mission is to "mentor millions" and anyone who is working on our team who does not understand or get fired up emotionally about this is viewed as an enemy and resource-sucking leech. As soon as I identify these people and can replace them, I always do.

Super Move #7 – Repeatedly clarify how each team member's job and daily tasks help the company achieve its mission and help your ideal and likely buyers.

Super Move #8 – Create a Core Values Document for your team that clearly expresses the values you expect your team to live up to as you pursue the achievement of your company's mission. The mission explains why you are doing something, but the values explain how you will go about achieving this mission.

"A culture of discipline is not a principle of business; it is a principle of greatness."

-Jim Collins
(Bestselling author of books *Good to Great, Built to Last,* **and** *Great by Choice)*

To download the Core Values Document, visit: www.ThriveTimeShow.com/TreasureTrove.

"GREAT SPIRITS HAVE ALWAYS ENCOUNTERED VIOLENT OPPOSITION FROM MEDIOCRE MINDS."
– ALBERT EINSTEIN
DEVELOPER OF THE GENERAL THEORY OF RELATIVITY

Note: I drove a 1984 Chevy brown conversion van that was missing a door for years because it was paid for and because I didn't buy things I can't afford to impress people I don't know.

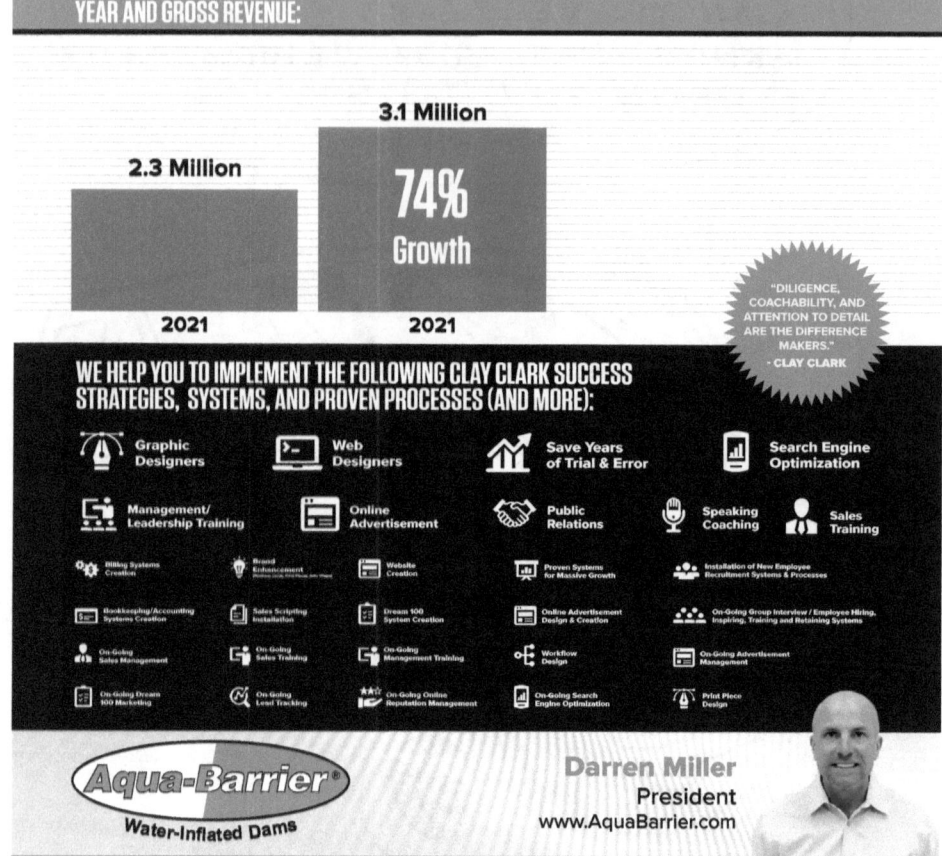

Chapter 10

Holding Your Team Accountable

At the end of the day, your company must consistently wow your ideal and likely buyers in a scalable way or you will not be able to earn enough revenue to turn your big dreams into reality. You must hold your team members accountable to completing their daily tasks whether they feel like it or not. As a consumer, when we go to Disney World, we don't care whose birthday it is, who is sick, who is tired, or who simply forgot to do their job this morning. We expect Disney World to be incredible because we are spending a boatload of hard-earned cash to take our families there. As a consumer, when we go to In-N-Out Burger, we don't care who is running late, who is going through a divorce, who has a headache, or who feels that working at In-N-Out may not be their life's purpose. We expect In-N-Out Burger to provide great customer service and great tasting food because we have decided to spend the money we have earned at their establishment. For some reason in the world of small business, this concept is not always understood.

I could write an entire book about all the stupid and weak-sauce excuses I have heard over the years from small business owners who have tried to explain to me why their team members did not deliver the level of service that they promised. We all make mistakes from time to time, but you must hold your team members accountable.

> "Customers will hold you to a high standard. If you want to achieve true excellence, raise that bar even higher for yourself, your colleagues, and your team."
>
>  *- Clay Clark*

Mystic Statistic:
Thirty-eight percent of U.S. employees called in sick to work during the last year, even though they felt fine.

www.careerbuilder.com

Top-ten most memorable claims (false reasons for calling in sick) reported by the employers surveyed:

1. Employee said his grandmother poisoned him with ham.

2. Worker claimed to be stuck under the bed.

3. Employee said he broke an arm while trying to grab a falling sandwich.

4. Worker claimed the universe was telling him to take a day off.

5. Employee said his wife learned he was cheating — so he had to recover his belongings from a dumpster.

6. Worker said she poked herself in the eye while combing her hair.

7. Employee said his wife put all his underwear in the washer.

8. Worker said the meal he prepared for work potluck turned out badly.

9. Employee said she was going to the beach because a doctor said she needed more vitamin D.

10. Worker said her cat was stuck inside the dashboard of her car.

Kevin McCoy, "Study finds absurd excuses for calling in sick to work," USA Today, October 16, 2015, http://www.usatoday.com/story/money/business/2015/10/16/study-finds-absurd-excuses-calling-sick-work/74044732/

"Strong managers who make tough decisions to cut jobs provide the only true job security in today's world. Weak managers are the problem. Weak managers destroy jobs."

-Jack Welch
(CEO who grew GE by 4000% during his tenure)

The best businesses in the world are comprised of management and employees who hold themselves accountable to take 100% responsibility for their individual roles and responsibilities within a company. Far too often, business people (not you, but other people) let their people get away with half-assing tasks, partially filling out checklists, missing deadlines, organizing items improperly, showing up late, overall missing the mark, and making costly mistakes that could easily be prevented if management was tough enough to hold people accountable.

Once you have gone through the growing pains associated with creating an office culture where people are held accountable, you will begin to win more and you will find that the level of drama within your office will decrease dramatically. However, this culture of discipline and rigor must start with you and your chosen management team.

Create a Culture of Accountability

If you are not 100% obsessed with delivering on every promise you have made to your customers, then your entire workforce will quickly learn through observation that they really won't be held accountable either. To make your life 2% easier, I have provided 10 proven methods to creature a company culture of accountability.

1. Assign every task in writing as you conclude all meetings. By assigning tasks in the meetings, you are creating transparency and patterning the behavior you want the leaders you are developing to emulate. When you end a meeting you need to say, "Okay, so Team America, here is quick recap of the action items that each person is taking." Then go on to list out specific action items for each team member with corresponding deadlines for completion.

   For an example of what a completed agenda with action items looks like, visit: www.ThriveTimeShow.com/TreasureTrove.

2. Follow-up on all assigned action items during each meeting. Meetings where the entire team is gathered are great times to follow up on assigned tasks and action steps. I love to give my team members autonomy and let them work

without my Darth-Vader-esque presence constantly looming over them. Giving your team members one week to fully accomplish their tasks allows them to set their priorities and work at their own pace. However, when someone does not complete an action item that they committed to, be prepared to get INTENSE.

3. Follow-up on all assigned action items while working off the assumption that these items were not completed in an accurate and timely manner. This is simply a safeguard to protect your brain from exploding when you find that tasks have been left incomplete. It's dangerous to assume your people are being effective and 100% honest with you.

It's very important that you invest the time to circle back with the members of your team who were assigned specific action steps. You must set the standard in this regard. When you complete a task, it's very important to tell the members of your team to complete action items of their own that you have assigned them. If you do miss a deadline, be up front with your team members, "Team America, I have yet to get the task completed, however I am grinding through it and action items 1, 2 and 3 should be done by April 24th."

Mystic Statistic:
The U.S. Chamber of Commerce estimates that 75% of employees steal from the workplace and that most do so repeatedly.
Rich Russakoff and Mary Goodman, "Employee Theft: Are You Blind to It?" CBS News, July 14, 2011, http://www.cbsnews.com/news/employee-theft-are-you-blind-to-it/

4. Be prompt all of the time. As business leaders when we are on time, our team will feel as though we truly value them and that we are an honest and accountable person. When we are constantly late, our team members will believe that we don't care about them because we are holding them to a higher standard than we hold ourselves accountable for. My friend, you and I must come to grips with the fact that our time is not more valuable than our team member's time.

5. Work on improving your reputation and credibility every day. Unfortunately, it takes months and months for you and I to establish ourselves as a source of wisdom, honesty, credibility, and accountability for our teams, but it takes just moments to lose all credibility. You and I must hold ourselves accountable to perform at a higher level and meet a higher standard.

6. It is very important that you are candid about what you cannot get done or do not need to get done. You do not want the people on your team to lose respect for you as a leader simply because you did not have the courage to speak up and say that you do not have the time needed to get an action item done or that the action item is simply not a priority based upon the other items on your to-do list. Often a member of your team will suggest a bad or unexecutable idea during a meeting that they will somehow try to assign to you. If you know that the idea is a bad idea, then state openly that you will not do it.

> "Don't let any person's lack of preparation create an emergency for you. Time is your most valuable asset. Don't let people waste it."
> - *Clay Clark*

Story Time:
Years ago, a member of our team suggested that it would mean a lot if the ownership and leadership of our company (me and Doctor Zoellner) would personally call every customer and thank them for using our products and services after every purchase. This employee then went on to state that it would mean even more to our customers if the ownership and leadership of our company were willing to invest the time to personally update our company Pinterest account every day to be more "authentic." Although this idea might have merit for many small business owners, I am a man with 38 chickens, five kids, nine businesses, and a father with ALS. I don't have the time to complete those tasks on an ongoing basis and even if I did, I am 100% sure that those tasks would not allow me to put my skills and talents to their highest and best

use. Thus, I told the person during the meeting, "I'm not going to do that." I knew that the employee who made the suggestion did not have the personal level of diligence to complete the work either, based on her flaky and half-baked history of getting things done. Thus, when she volunteered to do the work herself, I said, "You already have a lot on your plate and I would like to see you consistently complete the items you've already been assigned - for 90 days in a row now - before I'll have the confidence to give you something else to manage on top of your current workload." I said this because I value a culture of accountability.

· ·

7.   Take responsibility for your mistakes. When you make a mistake, you must own it. Although you need to focus on holding yourself accountable to a higher standard, you still are a member of the human race and you will mess up from time to time. It's important that you take 100% ownership of the mistakes you make as opposed to simply skipping over that agenda item or making dishonest excuses. Although it is hard to do, you must publicly take responsibility for your mistakes.

"It will take you decades to build a reputation and a few quick minutes to ruin it. If you think about that, you will act differently."
-*Clay Clark*

· ·

8.   Make sure that the ball does not get dropped as a result of poor communication or handoffs between team members. My friend, at the very second that an action item is dreamed up and discussed, you must specifically assign the action item to a person who will be responsible for getting the action item done accurately and by the deadline. Someone on your team must clearly own each action item.

When you assign an action item to a member of your team, you must make declarative and clear statements such as, "Greg, you need to get the video edited by Thursday at 1:00 PM. Sarah, you will then need to quality control the video and have it up on the website in time for the 5:00 PM news. Is everyone clear about this?"

To begin using the Time Management System and Delegation Station developed by Thrive15.com Mentor Lee Cockerell (the man who once managed and effectively delegated to over 40,000 team members when acting as the Executive Vice President of Operations for Walt Disney World resort), visit www.ThriveTimeShow.com/TreasureTrove.

9. Never delegate an action item to a group of people. An individual on your team must solely be held accountable for the successful execution of every action item. Too often in meetings people say, "Susan and I will have this knocked out by Tuesday." Then when the Tuesday executive meeting rolls around, Susan says, "I thought Josh was going to handle it," while Josh says, "Oh, I was waiting for Sarah to clarify what needed to be done."

10. Don't allow vague and non-action items that sound like action items to be assigned to members of your team. Constantly, I see businesses delegate tasks like, "Discuss the possible options and do research by Wednesday." Because the action items are so vague, when the follow-up happens and management asks the question, "Steve, did you discuss all of the possible options and do the research," Steve says, "Yes, I did." Yet in reality, nothing was accomplished; Steve didn't do any work and another week has passed. Your action items must call for tangible and measurable results: "By Wednesday, Steve, I need you to have created a spreadsheet showcasing all of the available options that we have for installing a new metal roof. I want side-by-side comparisons of the pros and cons of each option and I need to know the bottom line all-in costs of each option, including installation. Steve, do you have any questions?"

As a person who has had to learn how to become an effective delegator in order to effectively grow my wallet, watching people assign action items that are not actually action items causes me to literally experience high-levels of stress and anxiety.

"If you have an important point to make, don't try to be subtle or clever. Use a pile driver. Hit the point once. Then come back and hit it again. Then hit it a third time - a tremendous whack."

-*Winston Churchill*
(former Prime Minister of the United Kingdom who stood up to Adolf Hitler)

Four Effective Tools for Effective Team Accountability Management

1. **Require Everyone to Use the Same System**

   Today there are many time management systems out there. I sincerely believe that the system Thrive15.com developed in conjunction with Lee Cockerell is the best because I believe that Disney World is the best resort in the world. If this system is good enough for the man who managed Walt Disney World, I believe it's good enough for me. However, at the end of the day, it's super important that everyone on your team use the same system so they can be physically and digitally on the same page and project management platform. When I go into work with businesses that need help growing, I often find that no one knows what they are supposed to be doing. When I am asked to audit an employee's performance, 95% of the time employees will say, "Oh, I didn't know Kim even wanted me to handle that. I thought she was handling that."

Ample Example:
Many moons ago, I sat down with the owner of an electrical company who wanted to hire me to help him dramatically increase the number of online leads he was getting for his commercial and residential electrical company. As I went through each one of his online marketing and Internet advertising systems, my team and I discovered something that was TERRIBLE yet GREAT at the same time. Can you guess what it was? Oh yes! Nobody had been checking the inbox the leads were being sent to for over seven months. This client literally had over 1,200 inbound leads sitting there in his inbox. Over one thousand people had reached out for a quote and not a single person on his team was responding to them. Why was this?

Were those leads not being checked because each member of the team was a bad person? No. Were the leads not being checked because everyone was too busy? No. The leads were not being checked because each member of the team was using a different time management and project management system, so there was no single source they could refer to, to ensure that all responsibilities were covered. One person was using the Slack Project Management System, one team member was using Basecamp, and yet another person was using the Yellow-Notepad-and-Huge-Sharpie-Marker method. The problem was that everybody was using his or her own system.

2. Assign Key Performance Indicators and Follow-Up

Bestselling author Gino Wickman wrote a masterful book entitled *Traction: Get a Grip on Your Business* in which he describes at great length the importance of using Key Performance Indicators. These are also often referred to as KPIs by people who like to make life more confusing by using abbreviations to save syllables while speaking, thus adding hours to their work schedule as they constantly have to explain to new people what all of their jargon means.

At the end of the day, key performance indicators are the measurable deliverables and the quantitative metrics that you will hold each member of your team accountable for achieving. By giving your team specific and actionable key performance indicators, you ensure that your team is focused on what matters and on what is truly the highest and best use of their time. The metrics also give you, as the leader, the data that you need to know what is actually going on in your business.

These numbers will help you accurately predict whether your team is going to achieve their goals or not. By holding your team accountable for tracking their daily key performance indicators, you can keep your finger on the pulse of the business without having to be there with each member of your team, holding them accountable during every moment of their workday.

Download the template and an example of an effective Key Performance Indicator Dashboard by visiting - www.ThriveTimeShow.com/TreasureTrove.

 Story Time:

I worked with a bridal business years ago that was experiencing almost zero success with their online marketing efforts. When I met with the three members of the online marketing team, things got a little intense at first because all of the team members refused to allow me to quantify their work performance. However, the owner was serious about changing her life and moving beyond just barely surviving, so she told her employees that compliance was mandatory. One by one, I met with them and determined that the following was supposed to be happening:

1. One (one-thousand word) blog post was supposed to be written every business day (25 per month).

2. Five (one-thousand word) articles were supposed to be written every business day (125 per month).

3. Two social media updates were supposed to be happening every business day (50 per month).

4. Two online ads were supposed to be measured each morning for effectiveness. All inbound Internet leads were supposed to be called, texted, and emailed every day until they were reached.

5. One customer review was to be gathered every business day on Facebook or Google's review service (25 reviews per month).

As I invested the time to meet with each person, they assured me that they were "doing their best" and that it "wasn't possible to do any more." When the data was finally collected, I discovered that the following was actually happening:

1. One (one-thousand word) blog post was not being written every business day (two per month were actually being posted).

2. Five (one-thousand word) articles were not being written every business day (four per month were actually being posted).

3. Two social media updates were not happening every business day (three per month were actually happening).

4. Online ads had never been measured for effectiveness (resulting in wasted money everywhere as the advertisements were actually taking visitors to a landing page that hadn't even been set up yet).

5. *Inbound Internet leads were not being called, texted, and emailed every business day until they were reached (leads were being called once per week at the very maximum).*

6. *A total of one customer review had been gathered from Facebook or Google's review service.*

By simply going into this business and teaching the business owner the importance of scheduling a specific daily follow-up time with her team members, we were able to change this person's life. The owner was able to go from the bottom of Google's search engine results to the top within 60 days. Without exaggeration, the owner of the business was able to grow her gross revenue by over 40% within just two months. When are you going to schedule a follow-up with your people?

• •

To create your weekly Effective Management, Follow-up, and Training Calendar, visit: www.ThriveTimeShow.com/TreasureTrove.

The reason why the system was not working in that bridal business was because nobody was following up, EVER. The owner was blindly trusting each team member as they guided her off of the financial cliff. Do not let this happen to you. You must focus on clearly defining the key performance indicators for every member of your team and holding them accountable by scheduling a set time for regular follow-ups. This is the only way to ensure that your business avoids this struggle.

My friend, you must picture the key performance indicators as being like the dials on your grill (I love grilling). When you are grilling a certain type of meat, you should be able to turn up the heat to get the sear you want. However, when you are grilling steak and shrimp kebabs, you want to slow-cook those babies. This is your business and just like with your grill, you need to have the dials in place to be able to apply the measured heat necessary to achieve the desired results.

It's not important that you measure every activity that every member of your team is doing every day (unless you are an obsessive Major League Baseball fan, which I used to be as a kid). However, it is important that you take the time to measure the most important key performance indicators in each area of your business. When you tightly measure key performance indicators, you are then able to focus more of your time on the fewer and more important action items that must be accomplished to generate the biggest reward for your company.

I do not want to provide you with a technological justification failing to hold your team accountable for the completion of their daily key performance indicators. In a perfect world where leprechauns ride unicorns and where your budget allows you to do so, you would ideally set up systems in which key performance indicators are either scored by each member of your team or tabulated through automation. This will allow you to have accurate feedback that is updated on a weekly, daily, or even real-time basis.

Mentally marinate on this example. Let's say that you are a solid basketball player and you are playing against another solid player in a competitive game of basketball. Although each of you is over the age of 30, you both care about the outcome of the game because you have a bet riding on it. Before you began, you said, "Listen Justin, I am going to beat you and when I do, you are going to have to buy me the steak of my choice!"

Justin said, "Dude, there is no way in the world that you are going to beat me. I'm younger than you and I'm in better shape."

You then said, "Listen, I've got old man moves bro. I've got the scoop shot, sky hook, and the power pump fake. You are going down!"

During intense situations like this where winning matters, what do we do? We keep score! And why do we keep score? Because watching and playing socialist basketball is stupid. When you are running an efficient and profitable business, you need to empower each member of your team by holding him or her accountable to the daily

achievement of one or two daily key performance indicators. You must hold your teammates accountable to meeting their daily goals. When they fail to meet their daily goals, you must give them feedback, coaching, and pushing. When they achieve their daily goals, you must give them praise, bonuses, or both.

> "What gets measured gets done."
>
> **-Gino Wickman**
> (Author of bestselling
> book *Traction: Get a Grip on Your Business*)

When you are formulating these daily key performance indicators, you must make them super easy to understand. Your daily key performance indicators should be measurable. Such as number of memberships sold per day, number of calls made per day, or percentage of times that customers are successfully cross-sold or upsold. It's very important that each member of your team understands their daily key performance indicators and how their achievement or failure to achieve their daily goals affects the business and their teammates.

Key Performance Indicator Pitfalls

1. In the real world, I constantly see business owners making three demoralizing and key Performance indicator-destroying decisions.

2. They assign somebody 27 key performance indicators and expect them to stay on top of all of them. This creates a situation in which your team spends their whole day keeping score, leaving no time to actually do anything.

3. They assign absolutely zero key performance indicators to the people who work within the company. This creates a workplace in which people have no accountability.

4. They fail to follow-up on the key performance indicators they have assigned. My friend, if you travel to a space and time where people just magically do what they are supposed to do without any supervision, please tell me about this place because I would like to travel there and start to hire those people.

Mystic Statistic:

"24% [of employees] are "actively disengaged," indicating they are unhappy and unproductive at work and liable to spread negativity to coworkers."

Steve Crabtree, "Worldwide, 13% of Employees Are Engaged at Work," Gallup, October 8, 2013. http://www.gallup.com/poll/165269/worldwide-employees-engaged-work.aspx

Implementing key performance indicators should not be complicated or require a committee. Just simply ask yourself, "What are the two most important repetitive action items that we should measure and focus on improving to make the biggest positive impact on our business?"

> Anybody with a mind knows socialism has failed everywhere, every time.

Time to Make It Visual

Now that you are familiar with the concept, it's time for us to actually go through the effort of defining the two daily key performance indicators for each position within your company that you want to measure. To access the Assigning Game-Changing Key Performance Indicators Worksheet Template, visit: www.ThriveTimeShow.com/TreasureTrove.

It doesn't really matter what medium you use to post these key performance indicators, what matters is that you actually do post them in a massive way as soon as possible. If you and your people can't see the goals in black and white, it will be very hard to manage for achievement of these key performance indicators.

Schedule Daily Standing Team Accountability Meetings

Over time, almost anything begins to drift or fall apart if it is not properly managed. Your team is no exception. I highly recommend that you hold Daily Standing Meetings to keep teammates accountable, assign the daily action items of the day, celebrate wins, and continue establishing your culture of accountability.

To make your life 2% easier, we have attached an outline for Daily Standing Meetings to Hold Your Team Accountable at: www.ThriveTimeShow.com/TreasureTrove.

It is so CRITICAL that you make these meetings a priority because if you do not your team will begin to drift, miss deadlines, break commitments, and become something less than excellent. Obviously, this is not going to be good enough for your customers or for your wallet. You must get into the habit of having this daily meeting so you and your team can stay focused on the proactive tasks that will grow and expand your business. So much of our day can get filled up with reactive customer service issues, reactive legal battles, and reactive human resources issues (like when Karl calls in sick for the 17th time). You must hold your team accountable during these daily meetings or you will default to the mediocrity that naturally occurs when businesses are not intentional about growth related activities.

To keep your Daily Standing Team Accountability Meetings from becoming a mindless waste of time, I highly recommend that you implement the following super moves.

Super Move #1 – Keep these meetings short, to the point, and candid.

Super Move #2 – Make sure this meeting is a standing meeting (literally, stand up) and not one that features bagels, muffins, coffee, and a bunch of moving parts.

Super Move #3 – Start these meetings on time, every time. Don't keep your team waiting on the dude who comes to work looking like he took a shower on the walk to the front door.

Super Move #4 – Constantly bring up your team's big goal, your ideal and likely buyers, and why both you and the company are committed to helping your customers get what they want.

Super Move #5 – Bring energy to these meetings. Nobody wants to work for a low-energy sloth.

"What's measured improves."

-Peter Drucker
(Austrian-born American management consultant, educator, and author)

Super Move #6 – Publicly praise the members of your team who are getting things done and privately chastise the members of your team who consistently fail to reach their daily key performance indicator goals.

Super Move #7 – Have the members of your team prepare a short end of the week appraisal of what they got done and what they did not.

Super Move #8 – Have the members of your team publicly share if they accomplished their tasks or not. It's amazing to me, but the power of positive peer pressure really does help keep many team members focused and on task.

Management Today Is Mentorship

If you truly desire to turn your business into a duplicable and scalable cash-producing and value-adding machine that is capable of working without you, then you will need to develop your management and leadership team. In most cases, delegating leadership of your management team will be the very last step in creating a company that can truly run without your daily hands-on involvement.

Where Have All the Good People Gone?

We now live in a world that is abundant with opportunities everywhere if we just know where to look. Unfortunately, we also live in a world where the average American was not raised in a stable home by stable parents who invested the time and effort needed to teach their kids the importance of having a solid work ethic, developing an actual skill that the business world appreciates, and establishing the daily practice of refining our faith, family, financial, fitness and friendship goals. Moral boundaries and a solid work ethic are simply no longer present in the average new hire. This creates both challenges and opportunities for employers.

Mystic Statistics:
More than half of all youths incarcerated in the U.S. lived in one-parent families as a child.

20 million children are growing up either without a father or mother in the United States.

www.fathers.com

On the negative side of things, many employees today do not have the moral boundaries, the communication skills, the business skills, or the work ethic needed to be successful in the workplace when they show up for their first day of work. Looking at the bright side however, those companies that do invest in the mentorship of their people and development of a solid company culture will stand out from the pack. Many employees view companies that have a commitment to personal development and upbeat culture as beacon of hope and light within the job market.

Mystic Statistic:
"64 percent of millennials would rather make $40K a year at a job they love than $100K a year at a job they think is boring."
Peter Economy, "11 Interesting Hiring Statistics You Should Know," Inc. Magazine, May 5, 2015. http://www.inc.com/peter-economy/19-interesting-hiring-statistics-you-should-know.html

10 Super Moves to Develop Your Management Team

Super Move #1 – You want to staff your biggest weakness. Humans all have different gifting, strengths and skills. As a business owner, you want to be self-aware enough to recognize what your biggest limiting factor and biggest weakness is as a boss and you want to hire someone who can come in an immediately fill in the gaps where your skills are lacking. When you begin to bring in management talent and company leadership, you must view these hires as needle-moving, game-changing investments in your company's future.

Story Time:

Years ago, I was brought in as a consultant to work with a mortgage company that had a virtual lid (maximum) on the number of sales the company could do on a monthly basis. When I sat down with the owner, I discovered that the entire process of drumming up sales leads and processing the actual loans (dealing with the mountain of paperwork and forms) was locked inside the head of just one person – the owner. Over a 60-day window of time, I helped him turn his entire process into a duplicable system capable of running without him. However, he kept bringing up the idea that if the system was as good as it was supposed to be, then he had no need for an operations manager.

After hammering him with example after example of companies that became stuck because their owners shared this mentality, I finally was able to get him to see the light and hire an office manager who was obsessed with details, follow-up, and accuracy. This one hire changed this business owner's life. Within 90 days of hiring this person, all of his systems were being executed on a daily basis. This allowed the owner to invest time in developing more strategic relationships with sources of funding and realtors within the community. Long story short, the business boomed as a result of the owner's decision to hire and fully commit to training his office manager.

> "Only the paranoid survive."

> *-Andy Grove*
> (Founding member and former CEO of Intel)

Super Move #2 – Be prepared to replace members of your management team as your business outgrows their ambition, drive, and skills. In the process of growing a typical company by 50%, only 50% of the management team will make it through the transition. Some of your existing team members will have a growth mindset and will be moldable. However, at least 50% of managers typically push back hard and say things such as, "Well this is how we used to do it," or "If it is not broken, why are we trying to fix it?" Additionally, some members of your team might need to be moved to different positions within your company if they simply choose to not keep up.

Super Move #3 – You must make sure that you invest in providing your management team with the documented systems and processes that you want them to manage.[105] Too often I see businesses make a key hire and then begin to give them a series of verbal commands, oral traditions and non-written general platitudes that they call "systems." I vividly recall the look on these new hires' faces as they say to themselves, "What the crap are they talking about? Doesn't anyone know where the passwords are saved?"

> "The success you will achieve in life is relative to the number of uncomfortable conversations you are willing to have."
> *-Clay Clark*

Super Move #4 – When you do the hard things first, your life will get easier and your business will grow. Letting people go is always tough to do, but you must be 100% committed to your big vision and your big goals. No matter the cost. You must be committed to the health of your organization and to the rapid growth of your business in a scalable way. People who refuse to get on board with your vision of creating a duplicable business, that is capable of producing consistent value for your customers and profits for your team, must be let go.

Super Move #5 – You must develop yourself so you can be a sincere source of wisdom for your management team. Many business owners hire talented people and then they start running around like they're reenacting Justin Bieber's notorious trip to Brazil. Don't hire quality people and then begin acting like a jackass.

Super Move #6 – Don't hire people who are less skilled than you, just so your ego will not be impacted. Your goal is to hire people who are more talented than you in their given focus area.

Super Move #7 – Delegate generously to members of your team who consistently produce great results and who show a commitment to excellence and a growth mindset. However, fire negative, dishonest, and incompetent people as soon as possible. Hiring really good people is hard to do, but once you do hire really good people, your life will get a lot easier if you will just get out of their way and let them do their job.

Super Move #8 – Delegate, but do not abdicate. ALMOST 100% OF THE BUSINESS OWNERS I HAVE EVER COACHED, SPOKEN TO, OR EVEN JUST MET GET THIS WRONG. According to Webster and his magical dictionary, the word delegate means, "to entrust to another or to assign responsibility or authority" (Merriam-Webster Online Dictionary, s.v. "delegate"). According to Webster, the word abdicate means, "to fail to do what is required (a duty or responsibility)" (Merriam-Webster Online Dictionary, s.v. "abdicate"). Too often I see business owners throw the keys to the

> "Throughout my career I've learned to fire people faster. If it's not working out it's better to move in quickly than to spend your time trying to make it work when it will never work."
> *-Clay Clark*

company to their newest hire and completely remove themselves from the aspects of running the business. This is not healthy and THIS WILL KILL YOUR CULTURE, YOUR BUSINESS, YOUR GROWTH, AND YOUR VISION. You simply cannot ever completely lose sight of what is going on inside of your business and within each department. In order to grow a duplicable and scalable business that has the capacity to run without you, you must focus on holding people accountable to get their jobs done by using key performance indicators, weekly meetings, mystery shoppers, call recording, and by having an overall conspiracy theory mindset that somebody within your company is always trying to screw you.

> "Remembering that you are going to die is the best way I know to avoid the trap of thinking you have something to lose. You are already naked. There is no reason not to follow your heart."

> *-Steve Jobs*
> (Co-founder of Apple and former CEO and founder of Pixar)

Super Move #9 – Commit to getting weekly updates from your management team. Every week, you must hold your management team accountable for the achievement of their daily key performance indicators. If their items don't get done, you must determine if they didn't know what to do or if they simply chose not to do their jobs effectively. If someone did not know what to do, then you owe it to them to coach, train, and offer better clarity to them beginning NOW. However, people who choose to not do their jobs consistently must be fired.

Super Move #10 – Invest your personal time into people who are worth the investment. If a key member of your management team is in the hospital, invest in that relationship and check in on them. If a key member of your management team is going through a rough spot in their marriage and they reach out for help or advice, listen to them and show them that you care.

"You have to be responsible when you're running an organization, and firing people who are your friends is part of that responsibility."

-Ben Horowitz

(Self-made billionaire, the co-founder of Opsware which was acquired by Hewlett-Packard for $1.6 billion in cash, and the co-founder of Andreesen Horowitz venture capital firm)

In 1995, Ben Horowitz joined Marc Andreessen at Netscape as one of Netscape's first product managers. He was rapidly promoted to Vice President and General Manager and was responsible for much of the Netscape Server product line, including 300+ people and $100M+ in revenue. After Netscape was acquired by AOL in 1998, Horowitz served as Vice President of AOL's eCommerce Division.

"People don't care how much you know until they know how much you care."

-Theodore Roosevelt

(The 26th President of the United States)

Born a sickly child with debilitating asthma, Theodore Roosevelt successfully overcame his health problems by embracing a strenuous lifestyle. He integrated his exuberant personality, vast range of interests, and world-famous achievements into a "cowboy" persona defined by robust masculinity. He served as the 26th President of the United States from 1901 to 1909.

MOST PEOPLE WILL NOT THANK YOU FOR
HOLDING THEM ACCOUNTABLE.

LORD,
DO NOT HOLD THIS
SIN AGAINST THEM.

THEN HE FELL ON HIS KNEES AND CRIED OUT,
"LORD, DO NOT HOLD THIS SIN AGAINST THEM."
WHEN HE HAD SAID THIS, HE FELL ASLEEP.
ACTS 7:60

Once you have invested the time and money into building world-class business systems, you need to take the following 5 action steps or they will not work:

1. Trust but verify everything and everybody
2. Always create a followup loop
3. Hire consistant Mystery Shoppers
4. Create a pipeline of inbound new people
5. Fire when ready

MAKE IT REPEATABLE

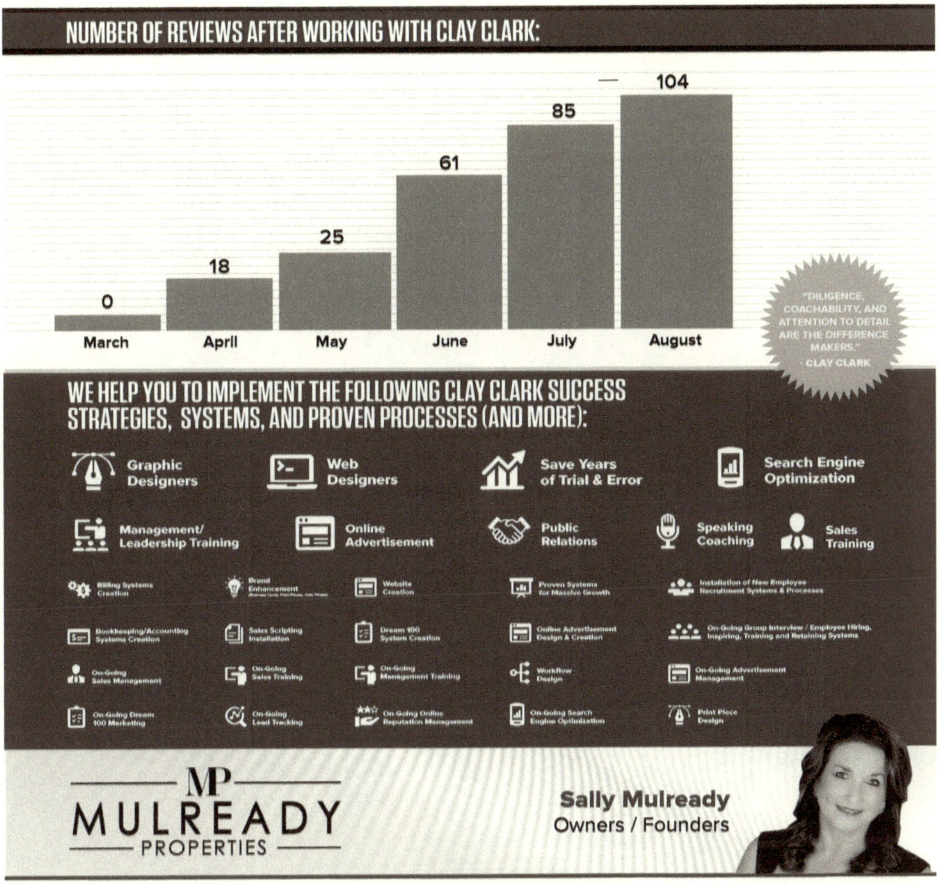

NUMBER OF REVIEWS AFTER WORKING WITH CLAY CLARK:

March	April	May	June	July	August
0	18	25	61	85	104

"DILIGENCE, COACHABILITY, AND ATTENTION TO DETAIL ARE THE DIFFERENCE MAKERS."
- CLAY CLARK

WE HELP YOU TO IMPLEMENT THE FOLLOWING CLAY CLARK SUCCESS STRATEGIES, SYSTEMS, AND PROVEN PROCESSES (AND MORE):

- Graphic Designers
- Web Designers
- Save Years of Trial & Error
- Search Engine Optimization
- Management/ Leadership Training
- Online Advertisement
- Public Relations
- Speaking Coaching
- Sales Training
- Billing Systems Creation
- Brand Enhancement
- Website Creation
- Proven Systems for Massive Growth
- Installation of New Employee Recruitment Systems & Processes
- Bookkeeping/Accounting Systems Creation
- Sales Scripting Installation
- Dream 100 System Creation
- Online Advertisement Design & Creation
- On-Going Group Interview / Employee Hiring, Inspiring, Training and Retaining Systems
- On-Going Sales Management
- On-Going Sales Training
- On-Going Management Training
- Workflow Design
- On-Going Advertisement Management
- On-Going Dream 100 Marketing
- On-Going Lead Tracking
- On-Going Online Reputation Management
- On-Going Search Engine Optimization
- Print Piece Design

MP MULREADY PROPERTIES

Sally Mulready
Owners / Founders

YOU CANNOT SKIP PUTTING IN THE WORK.

"ONE OF THE PENALTIES OF LEADERSHIP IS THE NECESSITY OF WILLINGNESS UPON THE PART OF THE LEADER TO DO MORE THAN HE REQUIRES OF HIS FOLLOWERS."
- NAPOLEON HILL

Chapter 11

Identify and Destroy Your Business' Biggest Limiting Membrane

In every business, there are limiting membranes that are causing your business to become stagnant. As the owner of the business, you must always be asking yourself what is the single largest factor capping the growth of your business? What is that thing that if you just could get your hands on it, fix it, or move it out of the way, would be a game-changer for your business? Who is that critical hire we need to take our business to the next level almost immediately? My friend, you must DEEP DIVE into asking yourself these questions with great intensity.

Once you have identified your biggest limiting factor, you must now list out a minimum of 10 possible solutions to eliminate this problem.

· ·

 Story Time:
I was hired to work with yet another mortgage company, and this particular company was based in Miami, Florida. When they flew me out to speak to their group, they put me up in the beautiful art deco Hotel Victor located right next to the beach at 1114 Ocean Drive in Miami, Florida.

When I arrived at the hotel, I was bombarded with handshakes and pleasantries from attendees of the workshop who had all descended upon the Hotel Victor to learn how to take their businesses to the next level. I met some really sharp people and I could tell that this group was going to be a great group to work with.

During the actual workshop, I asked the event attendees to rate their overall satisfaction with the level of excellence they were achieving in 29 different areas, just like I do with other groups all over the country. I asked the group to rate their organization in all 29 areas on a scale of 1 to 10, with 10 being the highest. After everyone had privately turned in their worksheets, something became very clear. These people were terrible at online marketing with almost no search engine optimization-related leads being generated at all. However, the team had built a systematic and very tight lead conversion system, service delivery workflow system, and had thousands of happy customers. Basically, they were closing deals with almost every prospect they met, they just were not getting enough prospects into the pipeline. Can you guess what we focused on during the entirety of the weekend workshop?

· ·

If you want to download the 29-Point Biggest Limiting Membrane Identification Worksheet, visit: www.ThriveTimeShow.com/TreasureTrove.

After completing the evaluations with their top leadership team, the head of the company pulled me aside privately and said, "Our search engine marketing sucks and I want to spend every second of our weekend workshop focused on improving our Internet marketing systems and plans. Let's get it done."

After he and I spoke, he announced to the group that they were going to be focusing the entire weekend on improving the company's Internet marketing, search engine marketing, targeting ads, and retargeting ads. The two dozen leaders in attendance all began clapping their hands and we rolled up our sleeves and got to work installing the key performance indicators, systems, checklists, metrics, and game plan needed to dominate online marketing.

After you have determined your biggest limiting factor, it is very important that you push both you and your team to identify many possible solutions to destroy the limiting membrane that is holding your company back. Try to develop at least five possible solutions for each of your company's biggest limiting membranes. After you have done this, you want to ask yourself which of these ideas is a game-changer and which of these potential solutions is effective and quickly doable.

Once you have identified the effective and quickly doable items, you must assign who is going to take action, when they need to have it done, and what resources they need to get the job done.

Now as for those game changers, we are not going to forget about them. Game changers have the ability to do just that; they can change the game and take your company, your income, and your life to the next level. However, game changers typically take a ton of time to implement and they also have the potential to blow up and not ever come to fruition because of the complexity of the deals and how massive an opportunity it may be. Thus, you are going to want to assign weekly action items focused on executing the game changer,[114] but not at the expense of missing out on the immediate wins and quick successes that could easily be produced by knocking out a few of the quickly doable items.

> "Often any decision, even the wrong decision is better than no decision"
>
>
> -*Ben Horowitz*
> (Self-made billionaire and co-founder of both Opsware and Hewlett Packard)

Opportunity Cost 101

If you'll pardon me, I'm going to go a little farther into the world of entrepreneurship than most people are comfortable with. Here's the scoop. On Planet Earth, we all only have 24 hours per day at our disposal. Entrepreneurs tend to be very aware of this fact, while the majority of people in the world are not aware of this concept, judging by their actions. Effective entrepreneurs grasp the reality that they only have a finite amount of time to turn their dreams into reality, but yet they have an unlimited number of choices and ideas. If you are going to become an effective entrepreneur, YOU MUST BECOME OBSESSED WITH BEING THE MOST EFFECTIVE MANAGER OF TIME ON THE PLANET. You must become very good at gathering all the facts and repeatedly saying no to good, average, or terrible things so that you can stay focused on the action items that have the opportunity to produce the most fruit for both you and your organization.

It is very important that you realize that time is your most valuable resource. You must constantly evaluate your focus to remain committed to things that make the highest and best use of your limited time. Occasionally you may want to schedule a leadership retreat with your team or step away from the daily battle yourself to really analyze

"People think focus means saying yes to the thing you've got to focus on. But that's not what it means at all. It means saying no to the hundred other good ideas that there are. You have to pick carefully. I'm actually as proud of the things we haven't done as the things I have done. Innovation is saying no to 1,000 things."

-Steve Jobs
(Co-founder of Apple and the former CEO of Pixar)

where your company is headed and if you are truly directing the company in a way that will offer the most value to your customers and ensure the most profits for you.

As for right now, I want to help you get some big wins and have the data you need to make small or even large changes in direction, if need be. Take a moment and answer the following questions right here in your book.

1. People – Do you like the people you are working with, or are you just settling for the people you've already hired?

_____

2. Marketing – Who are truly your ideal and likely buyers?

_____

3. Marketing – What is the best place to most effectively reach your ideal and likely buyers?

_____

4. Marketing – How good are your marketing materials when compared to your top competition?

_____

5. Service Quality – Which of your competitors are doing what you do better than you?

_____

6. Service Quality – Is your product or service truly the best in the world?

_____

7. Service Quality – What systematic quality control problems do you repeatedly struggle with?

_____

LOOK AT YOUR BRAND AS IT IS, AND NOT HOW YOU WISH IT TO BE.

"FACE REALITY AS IT IS, NOT AS IT WAS OR AS YOU WISH IT TO BE."
— JACK WELCH

"The art of leading comes down to one thing: facing reality, and then acting decisively and quickly on that reality."

-Jack Welch

(The former CEO of GE who grew the company by over 4000% during his tenure)

8. Product / Service – Are you making a product that you are proud to make and that really solves a problem in a way that wows your ideal and likely buyers?

    _____

9. Product / Service – Which products should you be promoting that produce the highest amount of value for your customers and the most profit for you?

    _____

10. Product / Service – Which of the products and services that you offer pays you the highest profit margin?

    _____

11. Product / Service – Which products should you eliminate and stop selling altogether because they aren't profitable, aren't worth your time or aren't the right fit for your company for some other reason?

    _____

12. Pricing – How much are your competitors charging for the similar products and services that you offer?

_____

13. Pricing – How much more could you charge your customers without taking advantage of them?

_____

14. Pricing – How much profit do you generate per customer?

_____

"You've found market price when buyers complain, but still pay."

-Paul Graham
(Co-founder of the Y-Combinator business incubator famous for helping to launch Reddit, Airbnb, Dropbox, and Weebly)

LOCK YOURSELF INTO THE WAGE CAGE.

"SOME PEOPLE DIE AT 25 AND AREN'T BURIED UNTIL 75."
- BENJAMIN FRANKLIN
FOUNDING FATHER OF THE USA

15. Pricing – How many customers do you need to have this year to fund the achievement of your financial goals at your current pricing structure?

_____

16. Pricing – What does it cost your customer to not have the products and services that you offer?

_____

17. Pricing – What type of long-term financing offers could you offer your customers that would allow you to close more deals now?

_____

"Value is not equated with low prices. Goods and services of high value may carry high or low prices. In fact, customer needs are so different that they are often willing to pay greatly differing prices for a given service, depending on its importance at a given time and place. Because price is only one element of value, it can be influenced as well by the ease of accessing a service. That is, by making a service easier to acquire, it can be made less sensitive to price, thus enhancing margins and profits."

Service Profit Chain **(Harvard Case Study) - James L. Heskett, Thomas O. Jones, Gary W. Loveman, W. Earl Sasser, Jr., Leonard A. Schlesinger**

18. Pricing – If the demand for your products and services exceeds your ability to produce, how will you use this to your advantage when pricing your products and services?

_____

19. Pricing – Why do you charge what you charge? Are you charging what you charge now simply because some strong-willed person who no longer works for you suggested it or because of some other reason that does not make sense?

_____

• •

 Fun Fact:
"(Steve) Case (AOL Founder) says that he doesn't remember the total amount spent on the discs specifically, but says that in the early 1990s, AOL's goal was to spend 10 percent of lifetime revenue to get a new subscriber. He says that since the average subscriber life was around 25 months, revenue was about $350 off of each of these users. So he guesses they probably spent about $35 per user on things such as these discs."

"How Much Did It Cost AOL To Send Us Those CDs In The 90s? 'A Lot!,' Says Steve Case"
– MG Siegler in Tech Crunch

• •

20. Sales – What is the best way to get your product out to the masses (direct selling, retail presence, Internet marketing, affiliate marketing, etc.)? (Example – Remember when AOL mailed CDs to almost every adult human in America?)

_____

21. Sales – Should you build a call center team of telesales professionals to help you market your product?

_____

22. Sales – Should you use strategic partners to help distribute your product to your ideal and likely buyers? *(Example: Dell computers came pre-loaded with Microsoft Products)*

_____

23. Sales – What is your most effective sales strategy or process that you should focus on turning into a duplicable system?

_____

24. Sales – What are ineffective sales strategies that you should stop pursuing?

_____

KNOWLEDGE WITHOUT APPLICATION IS MEANINGLESS

"DON'T LET SCHOOLING INTERFERE WITH YOUR EDUCATION."
– MARK TWAIN

Fun Fact:
Diageo agreed to split any profits with Sean "Diddy" Combs and if the company ever sold Ciroc, he'd be entitled to a share of the proceeds. The rationale: Why not? The brand wasn't selling, and Diddy was always known for having a flair for marketing. In 2007, sleepy Ciroc was moving cases at a rate of 60,000 per six months, or 120,000 per year. In 2009, Diddy's second year with the brand, Ciroc moved 400,000 cases. This year Ciroc is on pace to sell more than one million cases. The boom was fueled in large part by Diddy's diligent shilling—on billboards, in lyrics, on Twitter and even through a self-proclaimed nickname, "Ciroc Obama."

Zach O'Malley Greenburg, "Why Diddy Will Be Hip-Hop's First Billionaire," Forbes, March 16, 2011, http://www.forbes.com/sites/zackomalleygreenburg/2011/03/16/why-diddy-will-be-hip-hops-first-billionaire/#60e6867d6d00

25. Sales – What celebrity could I team up with to dramatically increase my sales now? (Example: George Foreman was very successful as the face of the George Foreman Lean Mean Fat-Reducing Grilling Machine. In addition, Cîroc [a brand of vodka made in France and distributed by the multi-national alcoholic beverage maker, Diageo] elected to team up with the famous rapper and producer, Sean "Diddy" Combs and since that time, the company has soared in value.)

26. Systems – If you did not have an emotional tie to the way you are currently doing things, how would you do things differently?

27. Human Resources – Which member of your team needs to go?

28. Human Resources – What position in your company needs a key hire right now?

_____

29. Human Resources – What core competencies, skills and capabilities will your company need to have one year from now?

_____

30. Competition – What competitor is coming to kill us and take our business?

_____

31. Competition – What competitor has taken or is beginning to take your market share?

_____

32. Competition – What competitor should you have a team spying on, investigating, mystery shopping and using every legal method possible to study what they are doing and what is working for them before they come and destroy your business?

_____

"I have been up against tough competition all my life. I wouldn't know how to get along without it."

- Walt Disney

(An American entrepreneur, animator, voice actor and film producer. A pioneer of the American animation industry, he introduced several developments in the production of cartoons. As a film producer, Disney holds the record for most Academy Awards earned by an individual, having won twenty-two Oscars from 59 nominations.)

"Every time you make the hard, correct decision you become a bit more courageous, and every time you make the easy, wrong decision you become a bit more cowardly. If you are CEO, these choices will lead to a courageous or cowardly company."

-Ben Horowitz
(Self-made billionaire and co-founder of both Opsware and Hewlett Packard)

DON'T WASTE YOUR TIMES TRYING TO BUILD A BUSINESS THAT CAN'T WORK

Getting Stuff Done with Quarterly Execution Plans

Alright, I know we've discussed a lot up to this point. I hope that your brain has not yet exploded as we've defined who our ideal and likely buyers are, what niche we are focused on, the importance of systems, and the importance of working on your business and not just in your business. Now we need to actually start executing your big vision to turn your plans into reality.

Let's Get Simple

My friend, your ability to turn your dreams and ideas into reality is going to come down to your ability to direct your daily calendar and your team's calendar towards the achievement of your quarterly goals while continuing to deal with the daily challenges involved in running a business. Having a quarterly focus is ideal, as it breaks down your big-vision action items and stretch goals into manageable pieces. A quarterly outlook provides a long enough period of time for you to get large quantities of work done, bringing you closer to the achievement of your big, hairy, audacious goals.

> "Simple can be harder than complex. You have to work hard to get your thinking clean to make it simple."
>
>
>
> **-Steve Jobs**
> (The guy who co-founded Apple and the former CEO of Pixar who helped launch the first completely computer animated box office hit, *Toy Story*)

Break Down Your Big Goals into Rolling Daily Actionable Items (To-Do Lists) for Your Team

This step is where the magic really begins to happen. If nothing gets scheduled, nothing will get done. If massive goals are not broken up into specific step-by-step action items, then nothing will get done, either. You and your leadership team must become proficient at breaking down big goals into small daily action steps. So that I don't leave you with only a vague understanding of this HUGELY IMPORTANT

"Rarely do we find men who willingly engage in hard, solid thinking. There is an almost universal quest for easy answers and half-baked solutions. Nothing pains some people more than having to think."

-Martin Luther King, Jr.
(An American Baptist Minister best known for his role in leading the civil rights movement in the United States based on his non-violent Christian beliefs)

CONCEPT, I am going to give you a little peek into the behind-the-scenes work that happened when my team and I opened up Elephant in the Room Store #2 at 91st and Yale in Tulsa, Oklahoma.

• •

 Story Time:
The big goal was to get Store #2 into the profit zone within 90 days of opening, and we did it. This is a partial look at the marketing to-do list that made it happen.

»Elephant in the Room – Michael design Valpak mailer (see Clay for verbiage) – Due Monday – 7/29

»Elephant in the Room – Michael design targeted online ads (see Clay for verbiage) – Due Monday – 7/29

»Elephant in the Room – Michael design landing page (see Clay for verbiage) – Due Monday – 7/29

»Elephant in the Room – Tonya reach out to Valpak to determine the cost of mailing 30,000 men who live within three miles of the 91st and Yale Location 2. Only mail to homes worth more than $300,000 – Due Monday – 7/29

»Elephant in the Room – Jonathan – Write press release announcing dollar give-back to the Tulsa Boys Home for every haircut we provide – Due Monday – 7/29

»Elephant in the Room – Jonathan set up Twilio account to mass text entire database of clients about new location (see Clay for verbiage) – Due Monday – 7/29

»Elephant in the Room – Jonathan create mass email to be sent out via Constant Contact to every client in our database (see Clay for verbiage) – Due Monday – 7/29

»Elephant in the Room – Jonathan design online targeting ad demographic – Due Monday – 7/29

» Elephant in the Room – Devin populate the Twilio database with customer information – Due Monday – 7/29

» Elephant in the Room – Devin populate the Constant Contact database with customer information – Due Monday – 7/29

» Elephant in the Room – Clay proof Valpak mailer – Due Monday – 8/1

» Elephant in the Room – Clay proof targeted online ads – Due Monday – 8/1

» Elephant in the Room – Clay proof landing page – Due Monday – 8/1

» Elephant in the Room – Clay proof Valpak costs for mailing 30,000 men who live within three miles of the 91st and Yale Location 2. Only mail to homes worth more than $300,000– Due Monday – 8/1

» Elephant in the Room – Clay proof press release announcing dollar give back to the Tulsa Boys Home for every haircut we provide – Due Monday – 8/1

» Elephant in the Room – Clay proof Twilio account to mass text entire database of clients about new location – Due Monday – 8/1

» Elephant in the Room – Clay proof mass email to be sent out via Constant Contact to every client in our database – Due Monday – 8/1

» Elephant in the Room – Clay proof online targeting ad demographic– Due Monday – 8/1

» Elephant in the Room – Clay proof the Twilio database with customer information – Due Monday – 8/1

» Elephant in the Room – Clay proof the Constant Contact database with customer information – Due Monday – 8/1

• •

As you can intuitively sense, most people don't like this part. Everyone likes to make money but nobody really seems to enjoy sitting down and creating a linear and detailed plan to turn the goal of getting Store #2 into the profit zone within 90 days into small achievable actionable items. Disorganized entrepreneurs tend to have a rude awakening when they discover that the most successful entrepreneurs are the ones who are the most organized and well planned. At this point, somebody usually says to me, "But I thought if I just believed it and was motivated enough, that money would just jump into my wallet from the Law of Attraction."

"In the absence of processes that can guide people, experienced people need to lead. But in established companies where much of the guidance to employees is provided by processes, and is less dependent upon managers with detailed, hands-on experience, then it makes sense to hire or promote someone who needs to learn from experience."

- *Clayton M. Christensen, author of How Will You Measure Your Life?*

(An American Baptist Minister best known for his role in leading the civil rights movement in the United States based on his non-violent Christian beliefs)

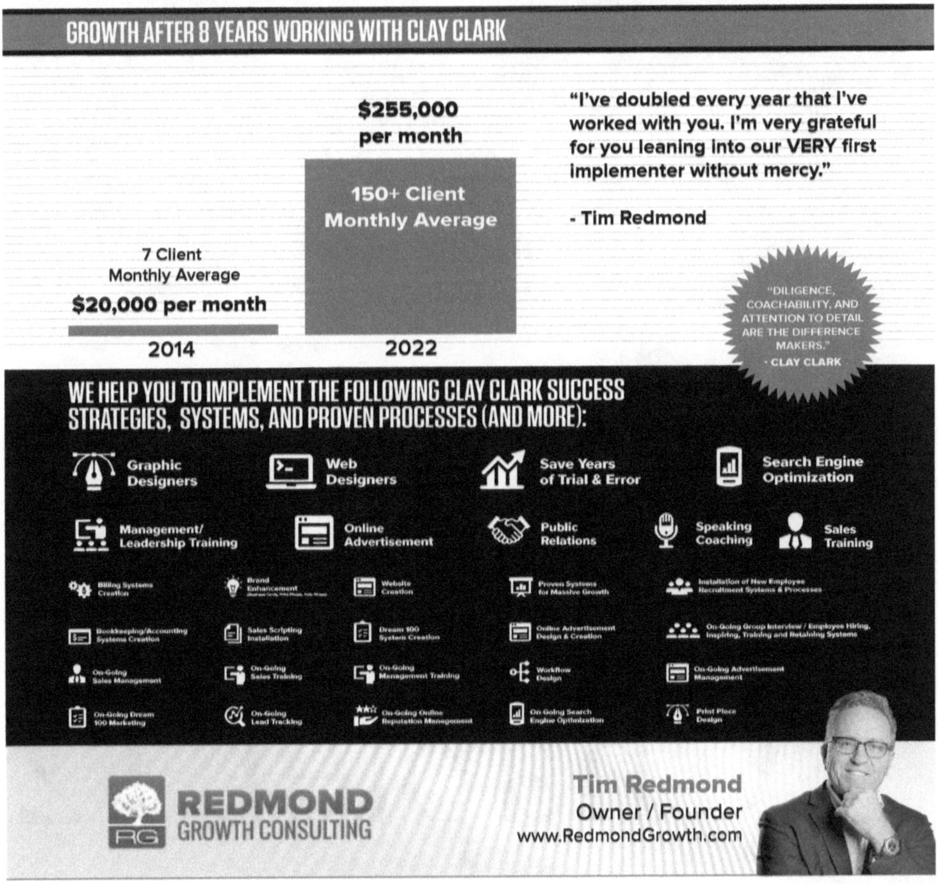

GROWTH AFTER 8 YEARS WORKING WITH CLAY CLARK

$255,000 per month

150+ Client Monthly Average

"I've doubled every year that I've worked with you. I'm very grateful for you leaning into our VERY first implementer without mercy."

- Tim Redmond

7 Client Monthly Average
$20,000 per month

2014   2022

"DILIGENCE, COACHABILITY, AND ATTENTION TO DETAIL ARE THE DIFFERENCE MAKERS."
- CLAY CLARK

WE HELP YOU TO IMPLEMENT THE FOLLOWING CLAY CLARK SUCCESS STRATEGIES, SYSTEMS, AND PROVEN PROCESSES (AND MORE):

- Graphic Designers
- Web Designers
- Save Years of Trial & Error
- Search Engine Optimization
- Management/ Leadership Training
- Online Advertisement
- Public Relations
- Speaking Coaching
- Sales Training
- Billing Systems Creation
- Brand Enhancement
- Website Creation
- Proven Systems for Massive Growth
- Installation of New Employee Recruitment Systems & Processes
- Bookkeeping/Accounting Systems Creation
- Sales Scripting Installation
- Dream 100 System Creation
- Online Advertisement Design & Creation
- On-Going Group Interview / Employee Hiring, Inspiring, Training and Retaining Systems
- On-Going Sales Management
- On-Going Sales Tracking
- On-Going Management Training
- Workflow Design
- On-Going Advertisement Management
- On-Going Dream 100 Marketing
- On-Going Lead Tracking
- On-Going Online Reputation Management
- On-Going Search Engine Optimization
- Print Place Design

REDMOND GROWTH CONSULTING

Tim Redmond
Owner / Founder
www.RedmondGrowth.com

Chapter 12

Booming Business Foundational Principle #1
Setting Up the Sales Machine

My friend, as you know, you can have the most incredible business model on the planet, but if you do not have leads, you are not going to sell anything. If you don't sell anything, you are going to end up living with your mom and sleeping on a beanbag in the basement (not that there is anything wrong with that).

You must find a duplicable, memorable and compelling way to get in front of your ideal and likely buyers that will produce sales and income for your business. It is this part of the business that really, really gets me fired up.

When I talk about sales, I am referring to every activity and every action step that you take to turn the pitches and offers you make to your customers into selling opportunities. You can deliver your sales pitches and your offers in an endless number of ways including:

» Deploying a team of well-trained sales people to go business-to-business and door-to-door to sell the products and services you produce.

» Setting up a call center where your team of trained sales people dial and smile until they sell something to another human.

» Setting up online advertisements and online sales conversion funnels that take the payment from the customer without you ever having to speak to your prospects.

» Setting up a local retail store where you sell the products and services you offer when speaking face-to-face with consumers.

» Creating direct response mailers that earn the interest of your ideal and likely buyers by conveying a compelling piece of information in a way that gets the attention of your target market.

When I talk about marketing, I'm referring to action steps you can execute on an ongoing basis to get you in front of your ideal and likely buyers. The marketing game is all about getting in front of those beautiful ideal and likely buyers under the most favorable conditions possible. If you participate in nude, door-to-door megaphone marketing, you would definitely get a few of your ideal and likely buyers to open their doors, but you would also likely not sell anything before you were hauled off to jail. Those are not favorable conditions, my friend.

Fun Fact:
My average client grew by 104% last year and I document all client success stories at www.ThriveTimeShow.com. if my clients can be super-successful. Why can't you?

Marketing is how you brand your business into the brains and hearts of your ideal and likely buyers. You invest in marketing because marketing is what produces sales leads. You invest in marketing because you want leads who are ready to do business and who already have a favorable impression of you and your business. This will ensure your selling processes can easily convert these people into happy clients who are confident about buying from you time and time again.

I know people have a fear of selling, but growing up without money, I have a much bigger fear of not having money. Regardless of the reason why most soon-to-be-unemployed entrepreneurs avoid the topic of sales, they do. The majority of entrepreneurs really hate this aspect of entrepreneurship so they'd better start to love eating ramen noodles (the cheapest food known to modern man). Struggling entrepreneurs are afraid of selling the products and services they create to their family and friends. They are worried about self-promotion and they hesitate to engage in the aggressive marketing needed to actually sell something to another human. This might be you right now, but you need to understand this big concept. Once you have created a product you are confident people will love, your focus as the founder (owner, leader, etc.) must be on selling, then selling, and after that, selling some more. If you are not obsessed with sales, your business will not make it and it will die.

My friend, your number one focus must be on sales until your business has grown to the point that you can afford to hire a sales super talent whom you can delegate effectively to without experiencing a massive dip in sales numbers. When you start up a business, you have to make sure that the sales deals get closed, which is why you

"To me, job titles don't matter. Everyone is in sales. It's the only way we stay in business."

-Harvey Mackay
(Best-selling author of seven New York Times bestselling books, including three #1 bestsellers)

"Hire sales people who are really smart problem solvers, but lack courage, hunger, and competitiveness, and your company will go out of business."

-Ben Horowitz
(Self-made billionaire and founder of Opsware, which he sold to Hewlett-Packard for $1.6 billion cash. He is a high technology entrepreneur and co-founder and general partner along with Marc Andreessen of the venture capital firm, Andreessen Horowitz)

"I'd be like, alright, I don't know anything about sales. So I would search for sales on Amazon, get the three top-rated books and just go at it."

-Drew Houston
(Founder of Dropbox.com, an online backup and storage service; according to Forbes magazine, he's now worth over one billion dollars)

are going to need to be the person who meets with the clients and closes deals. Once you refine your system that actually closes deals, then you want to shift your focus into creating duplicable processes that will allow other members of your team to sell and sell well, without your direct involvement in each deal.

. . . .

 Fun Fact:
I hate going out to eat and actually just hate going out in general, as I have created an office environment that has everything I need for maximized effectiveness and a man-cave / home-office at my home that strongly resembles a speakeasy. In addition, my wife and I have developed our home (what we call Camp Clark and Chicken Palace) into what we believe to be paradise on earth. We have five kids, 38 chickens, six ducks, two Great Pyrenees dogs and everything else we want, so I really dislike ever going anywhere but my house or the office.

However, back in the day when I was starting www.DJConnection.com, I told my team that I was willing to meet with any potential bride, groom, or party planner anywhere and at any time as long as they were a sincerely interested prospect. I did this for exactly four years until we reached profitability. I didn't like it, but I did what I had to do.

. . . .

My friend, for every Booming Business Foundational Principle, I am going to provide you with specific and actionable items you must get done for your business to succeed. Although I am going to DEEP DIVE into these Booming Business Foundational Principles (like Jacques Cousteau) later in this book, I want to briefly provide you with an outline of these principles now to warm you up mentally.

The 21 Core Tasks of Your Marketing / Sales Team

Determine your company's overall MARKETING / SALES TEAM SYSTEMS SCORE in the following 21 areas by rating your business on a scale of 1 to 10 with 10 being the highest. This scoring system can be found at www.ThriveTimeShow.com/TreasureTrove.

1. Clearly define who your ideal and likely buyers are_____

2. Clearly define the needs and wants of your ideal and likely buyers_____

3. Clarify the unique value proposition that your business is going to offer (how do you uniquely solve problems for your ideal and likely buyers).

4. Specifically determine your no-brainer offer (an offer that the customer almost never refuses because it makes so much sense).

5. Determine how you are going to generate leads.

6. Determine how you are going to convert leads into paying customers.

7. Determine the easiest and most likely three ways to close deals now.

8. Determine how your brand will be different than the competition.

9. Determine how your brand can better meet the needs of your ideal and likely buyers. _____

10. Write a duplicable inbound sales script._____

11. Write a duplicable outbound script._____

12. Write a duplicable auto-responder e-mail._____

13. Write a duplicable drip e-mail campaign._____

14. Create sales one sheet to be used to present to your ideal and likely buyers._____

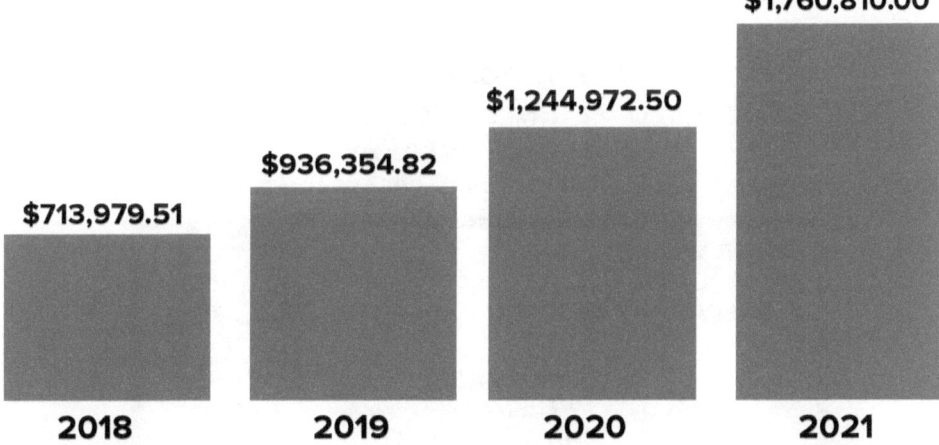

Jamie Fagel
Owner / Founder
www.JamesonFineCabinetry.com

15. Create a presentation script.

16. Create a Frequently Asked Questions and common objections script for overcoming objections.

17. Determine key performance indicators and metrics to which each sales person will be held accountable.

18. Create a system for measuring the success or failure of your print and off-line advertising.

19. Create a system to measure the conversion success of your website.

20. Create a system for measuring the effectiveness of your online advertisements.

21. Create a system for tracking where each and every deal comes from (advertising sources, word of mouth, etc.)

To download best-practice and examples of each of the items listed above, visit: www.ThriveTimeShow.com/TreasureTrove.

"BE LIKE A POSTAGE STAMP.
STICK TO IT UNTIL YOU GET THERE."
-HARVEY MACKAY
ENTREPRENEUR, MOTIVATIONAL SPEAKER AND AUTHOR

DETER MEND
MEDIOCRITY PL.
NOWHERE, UTAH

CLAY CLARK
777 SUCCESS AVE.
74119 TULSA, OK

REVENUE GROWTH AFTER WORKING WITH CLAY CLARK:

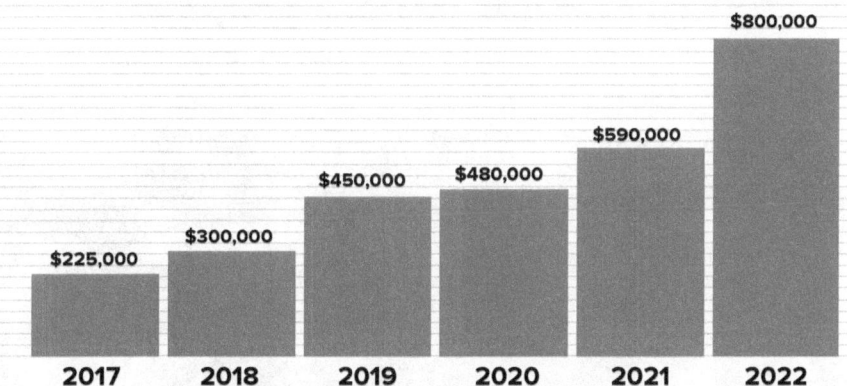

$225,000 — 2017
$300,000 — 2018
$450,000 — 2019
$480,000 — 2020
$590,000 — 2021
$800,000 — 2022

Luke Owens
Owner / Founder
www.TheHubGym.com

Chapter 13

Booming Business Foundational Principle #2
Executing Your Daily Operations

"Every time I read a management or self-help book, I find myself saying, 'That's fine, but that wasn't really the hard thing about the situation.' The hard thing isn't setting a big, hairy, audacious goal. The hard thing is laying people off when you miss the big goal. The hard thing isn't hiring great people. The hard thing is when those 'great people' develop a sense of entitlement and start demanding unreasonable things. The hard thing isn't setting up an organizational chart. The hard thing is getting people to communicate within the organization that you just designed. The hard thing isn't dreaming big. The hard thing is waking up in the middle of the night in a cold sweat when the dream turns into a nightmare."

-*Ben Horowitz, author of The Hard Thing About Hard Things: Building a Business When There Are No Easy Answers*
(Self-made billionaire and founder of Opsware, which he sold to Hewlett-Packard for $1.6 billion cash. He is a high technology entrepreneur and co-founder and general partner along with Marc Andreessen of the venture capital firm, Andreessen Horowitz)

It seems that most of the entrepreneurs I know who can consistently and successfully sell something tend to really struggle when it comes to executing their daily operations. Having consulted with many clients in the home remodeling and contracting industry, this seems to have reached an almost epidemic level within that industry. The contractors who can sell well have no problem picking up the business, but they do not have the systems in place or the will needed to actually get a project done on time and at budget. It's amazing how common it is for a contractor to begin using money from one project to finance another project because they have no concept of what things are going to cost, how to manage their staff, how to hire people, and how to effectively delegate work.

Your Ability to Effectively Execute Your Daily Operations Is Critical to Your Success

Daily operations is the part of your organization that actually produces and delivers the products and services your business sells. It is super important that you create a duplicable workflow that allows your operations team to deliver the products and services promised by your marketing and sales team. I realize that in many small businesses, YOU are both the marketing / sales team AND the operations department; regardless, you must deliver on your promises in a documented and scalable way. The operations department of your business also exists to carry out the behind-the-scenes and administrative aspects of your business.

I don't care how great your product or service is, no business will survive and flourish without having a detailed and organized operations backbone keeping everything together. If you are one of those highly motivated people who has the pig-headed discipline needed to go out there and actually sell something, you are going to show up on rip-off report websites, third-party customer complaint websites, and at the top of Google searches for all of the wrong reasons if you cannot deliver on the promises you make to customers.

I know it seems nuts, but I can tell you countless stories of business people who totally destroyed their businesses because they did not have systems in place to insure that their company delivered on the promises made to their ideal and likely buyers. When you irritate enough customers by over-promising and under-delivering, life can become very difficult.

TRAINING CHECKLIST / PROCESS CREATION

1. You Tell them
2. You Show Them
3. They Show You
4. They Demonstrate Mastery

Story Time:

Life before systems was not pleasant for me and I still feel occasional discomfort when I walk into a certain Barnes & Noble. Picture this. The year was 2002, I was 21 years old and I was selling as many deals as I wanted. www.DJConnection.com was the talk of the town in the event entertainment and wedding industries arena and because I personally DJ'd, handled the sales, maintained the equipment, trained the DJs, met with the customers and handled the accounting, things were rocking. I was focused, committed and simply unwilling to compromise. As things grew, I began delegating responsibilities without having the discipline needed to first create systems, checklists, processes, and workflows. I delegated the training of our DJs to a guy who didn't care about the business like I did and who didn't have any systems to use as a reference, a standard, a best-practice or a guardrail. Thus, we started destroying people's weddings one by one for a good three weeks in a row before I started hearing the feedback and immediately began both training the DJs again and creating training systems, checklists and processes.

Unfortunately, I really screwed up the wedding of the lady who managed the Barnes & Noble in Tulsa because I did not properly train the man who was training our DJs. The DJ went to her wedding and played the wrong song for her first dance, forgot to play her requests and changed the agenda for her entire wedding on the fly because he thought it would go better if he did it his way. If you haven't figured this out by now, I'm an avid reader. But now, every time I would go into that Barnes & Noble, I would try to avoid eye contact with this lady. One time I did have to checkout at her register and I attempted to apologize. Some seven years after the incident occurred, she was still upset about it and gave me yet another piece of her mind and essentially told me that I was a horrible person for ruining her wedding. She said all this while I was at the bookstore being accompanied by my five-year-old daughter. Now nearly 15 years since that incident, I think that she really should have told me "You ruined my wedding because you didn't have the discipline needed to build systems, file naming systems, checklists, processes, and workflows that were scalable and would have allowed an idiot to run those systems! Go make a system, you jerk!"

"I try to build businesses that are so scalable and so repeatable that an idiot can run it because eventually and idiot will."

-Clay Clark

The 12 Core Tasks of Your Operations Team and Systems

Determine your company's overall OPERATIONS TEAM SYSTEMS SCORE in the following 12 areas by rating your business on a scale of 1 to 10 with 10 being the highest. This scoring system can be found at www.ThriveTimeShow.com/TreasureTrove.

1. Delivers on the promises made by your marketing and sales team.

2. Creates a linear workflow that clearly documents the steps that your teammates need to take turn a customer's order into a customer's product or service and a customer's thank you as a result of you wowing them.

3. Provides office space for your team.

4. Provides a phone system for your team that is capable of recording calls.

5. Provides a universal place for your team to save digital files.

6. Provides a universal nomenclature system for your team to save files so that you can always find digital documents.

7. Provides the tools, resources, and equipment your staff needs to do the job right.

8. Provides the website(s) needed for your company to make a great first impression for your ideal and likely buyers.

9. Provides a quality customer service experience for your customers.

10. Provides a system WOW and high-promoter-causing interaction for every customer.

"If your business depends on you, you don't own a business—you have a job. And it's the worst job in the world because you're working for a lunatic!"
-*Michael Gerber*
(The best-selling author of the E-Myth book series.)

11. Systemic purchasing controls in place.

12. Systemic cost controls in place.

13. To download templates of the Tasks of Your Operations Team and Systems, visit: www.ThriveTimeShow.com/TreasureTrove.

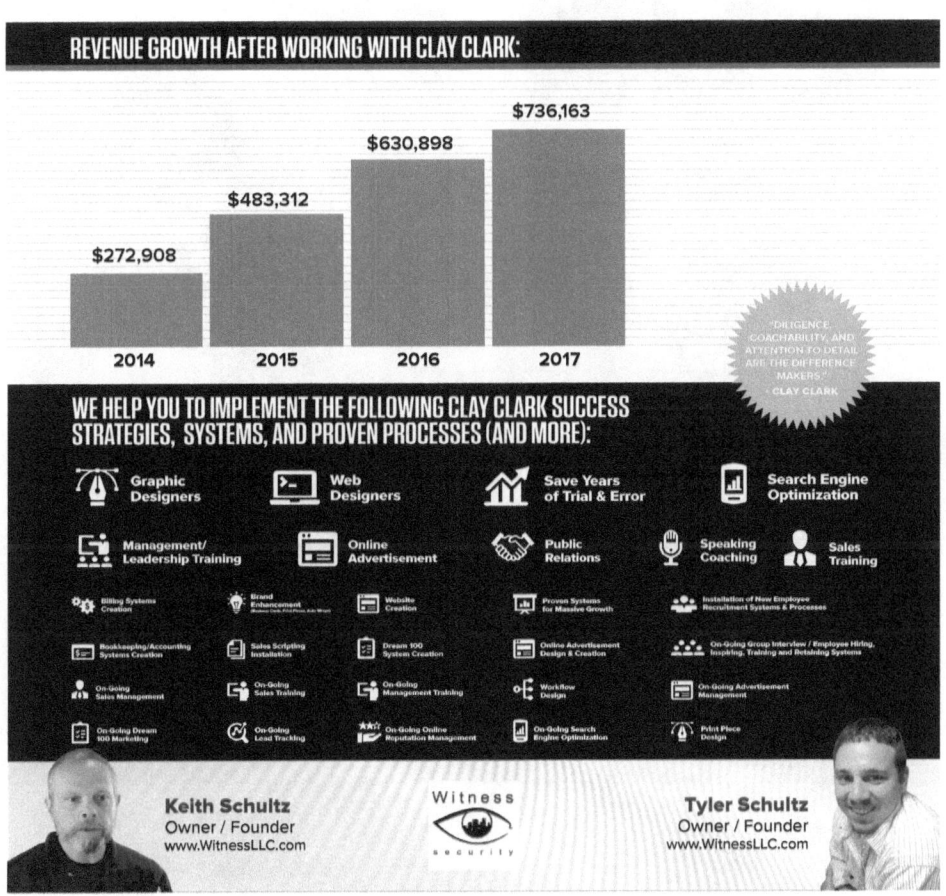

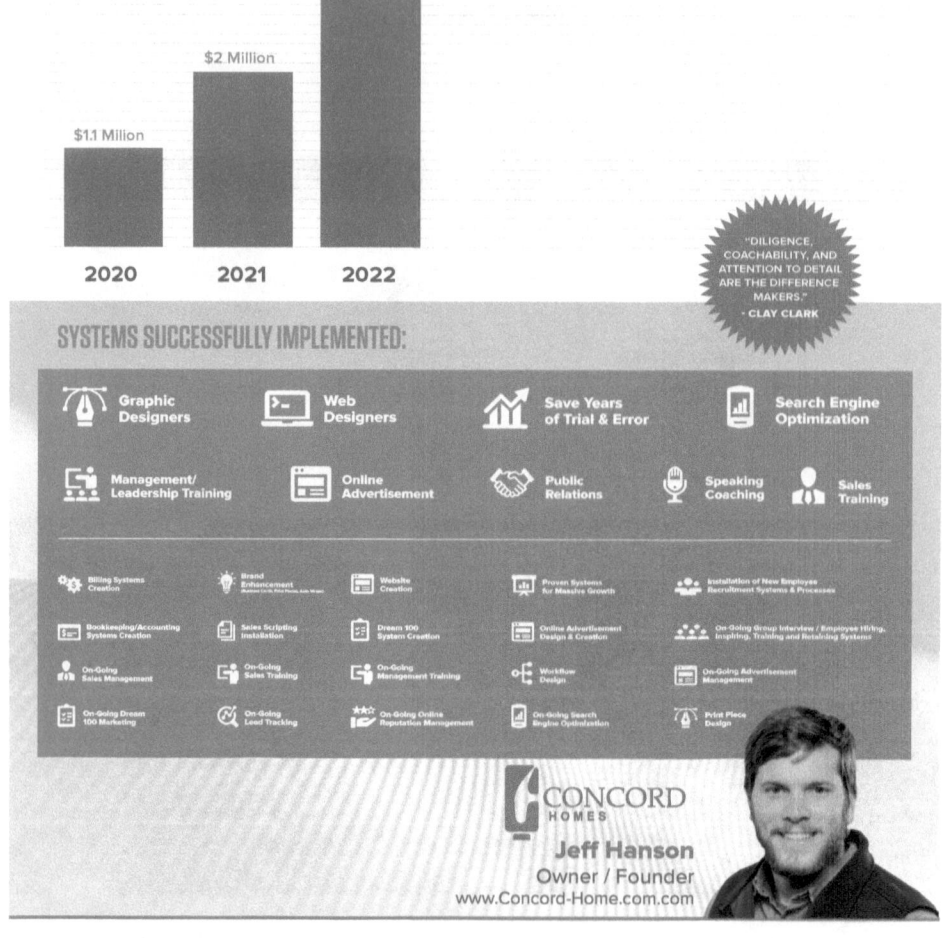

Chapter 14

Booming Business Foundational Principle #3
Accounting and Finance

This foundational principle is very important to the success of your business venture because people such as you and I need to exchange currency, money, coin, or Bitcoin for the products and services we both need and want. At the end of the month if we don't have any money left, we lose the business game. Game over. The accounting and finance aspect of your business requires an investment of time so you can maintain a proactive perspective and overall approach to the handling of the money end of your business. YOU SHOULD VIEW THE ACCOUNTING AND FINANCE ASPECT OF YOUR BUSINESS AS A COMPASS AND NOT A REAR VIEW MIRROR.

This area of your business includes everything related to filing with the government, tracking money, collecting money, distributing money, paying your team, and strategically directing the cash flow of money both in and out of your business. This aspect of your business should include processes for the following areas of your business. How do you stack up?

The 13 Core Tasks of Your Accounting and Finance Team and Systems

Determine your company's overall ACCOUNTING AND FINANCE TEAM SYSTEMS SCORE by rating your business in the following 13 areas on a scale of 1 to 10 with 10 being the highest. This scoring system can be found at www.ThriveTimeShow.com/TreasureTrove.

1. A system is in place to verify that your team members are paid on time.

2. A system is in place to verify that your team members are paid accurately.

3. A system is in place to verify that your vendors are paid on time.

4. A system is in place to verify that your investors are paid on time.

5. A system is in place to verify that all incoming deposits are placed into the company bank accounts.

6. A system is in place to verify your weekly account balance.

7. A system is in place to verify how much in tax is owed weekly.

8. A system is in place to verify the accuracy of your profit and loss statement.

9. A system is in place for cross-referencing your weekly budget against your weekly expenses.

10. A system is in place for managing your potential risk and insurance needs.

11. A system is in place for cash flow management.

12. A system is in place for tax filing and planning.

13. A system is in place to communicate with investors to keep them updated.

To download templates of the Tasks of Your Accounting and Finance Team and Systems, visit: www.ThriveTimeShow.com/TreasureTrove

"Being excellent is different. Which is why so few people are used to an environment where excellence is expected."
-*Clay Clark*

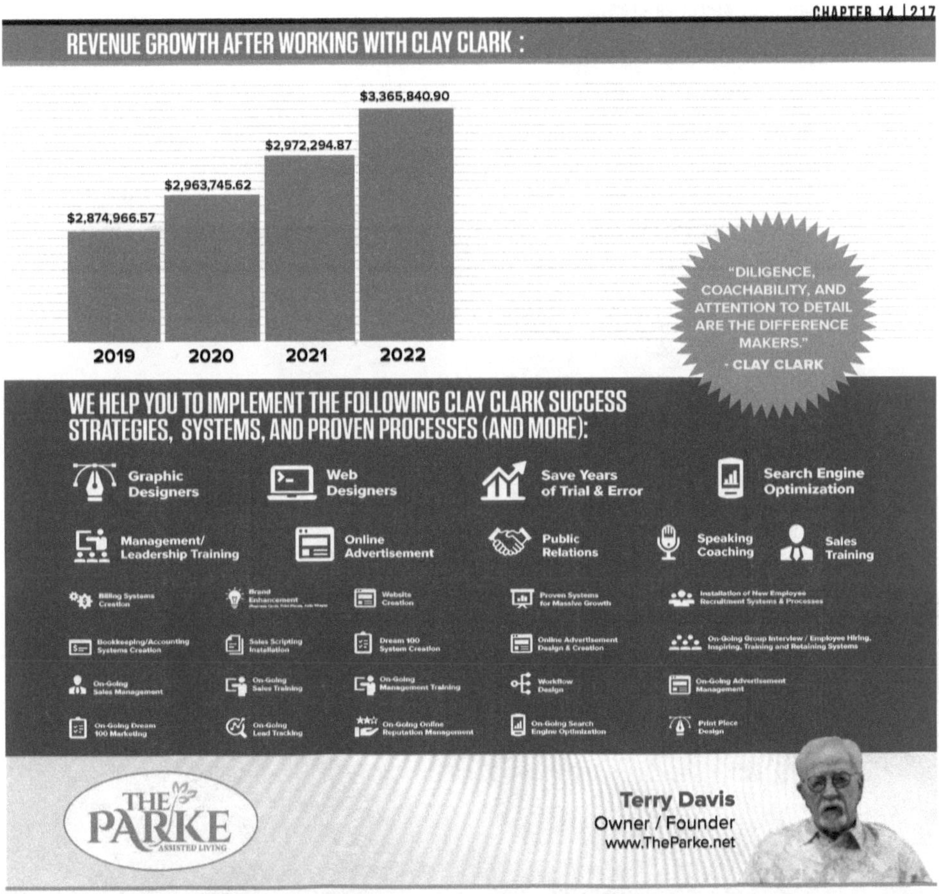

REVENUE GROWTH AFTER WORKING WITH CLAY CLARK :

2019	$2,874,966.57
2020	$2,963,745.62
2021	$2,972,294.87
2022	$3,365,840.90

"DILIGENCE, COACHABILITY, AND ATTENTION TO DETAIL ARE THE DIFFERENCE MAKERS."
- CLAY CLARK

WE HELP YOU TO IMPLEMENT THE FOLLOWING CLAY CLARK SUCCESS STRATEGIES, SYSTEMS, AND PROVEN PROCESSES (AND MORE):

- Graphic Designers
- Web Designers
- Save Years of Trial & Error
- Search Engine Optimization
- Management/ Leadership Training
- Online Advertisement
- Public Relations
- Speaking Coaching
- Sales Training
- Billing Systems Creation
- Brand Enhancement
- Website Creation
- Proven Systems for Massive Growth
- Installation of New Employee Recruitment Systems & Processes
- Bookkeeping/Accounting Systems Creation
- Sales Scripting Installation
- Dream 100 System Creation
- Online Advertisement Design & Creation
- On-Going Group Interview / Employee Hiring, Inspiring, Training and Retaining Systems
- On-Going Sales Management
- On-Going Sales Training
- On-Going Management Training
- Workflow Design
- On-Going Advertisement Management
- On-Going Dream 100 Marketing
- On-Going Lead Tracking
- On-Going Online Reputation Management
- On-Going Search Engine Optimization
- Print Piece Design

THE PARKE
ASSISTED LIVING

Terry Davis
Owner / Founder
www.TheParke.net

"ENTREPRENEURS SOLVE THE WORLD'S PROBLEMS AND UNAPOLOGETICALLY MAKE MONEY DOING IT."
- CLAY CLARK

REVENUE GROWTH AFTER WORKING WITH CLAY CLARK:

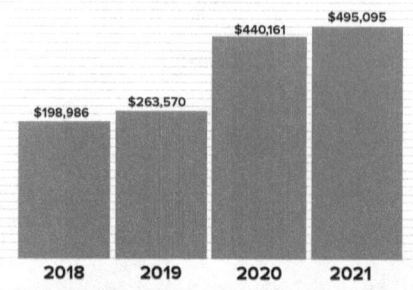

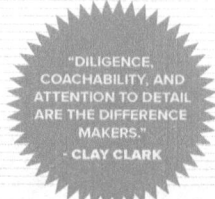

"DILIGENCE, COACHABILITY, AND ATTENTION TO DETAIL ARE THE DIFFERENCE MAKERS."
- CLAY CLARK

2018	2019	2020	2021
$198,986	$263,570	$440,161	$495,095

WE HELP YOU TO IMPLEMENT THE FOLLOWING CLAY CLARK SUCCESS STRATEGIES, SYSTEMS, AND PROVEN PROCESSES (AND MORE):

CANNON CONCRETE PUMPS
582-PUMP

Charles Ulrich
Owner / Founder
www.CannonPumps.com

Chapter 15

Booming Business Foundational Principle #4
Human Resources Team

"I've built a lot of my success off finding these truly gifted people and not settling for B- and C-players, but really going for the A-players...I found that when you get enough A-players together, when you go through the incredible work to find five of these A-players, they really like working with each other. Because they've never had a chance to do that before. And they don't want to work with B- and C-players and so it becomes self-policing and they only want to hire more A-players. And so you build up these pockets of A-players, and it propagates."

-Steve Jobs
(The co-founder of Apple and the legendary former CEO of Pixar who led the company to massive commercial success and critical acclaim)

It's super important that you build an A-level team and this Booming Business Foundational Principle encompasses everything you need to know to recruit, interview, hire, on-board, train, assess, pay, inspire, and even fire members of your team. This area of focus includes employee procedures, process, manuals, documents, and the legal aspects of hiring and working with employees.

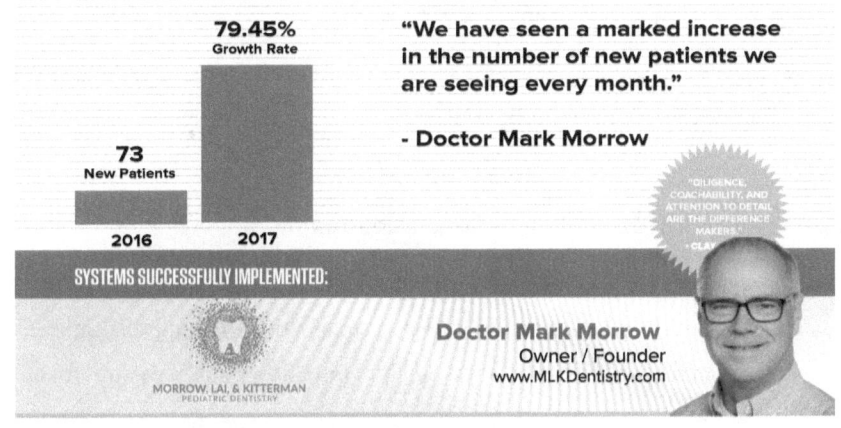

79.45%
Growth Rate

73
New Patients

2016   2017

"We have seen a marked increase in the number of new patients we are seeing every month."

- Doctor Mark Morrow

SYSTEMS SUCCESSFULLY IMPLEMENTED:

Doctor Mark Morrow
Owner / Founder
www.MLKDentistry.com

MORROW, LAI, & KITTERMAN
PEDIATRIC DENTISTRY

"I've built a lot of my success off finding these truly gifted "MANAGING STRICTLY BY NUMBERS IS LIKE PAINTING BY NUMBERS. Some things that you want to encourage will be quantifiable, and some will not. If you report on the quantitative goals and ignore the qualitative ones, you won't get the qualitative goals, which may be the most important ones. Management purely by numbers is sort of like painting by numbers—it's strictly for amateurs."

-Ben Horowitz, author of The Hard Thing About Hard Things:
Building a Business When There Are No Easy Answers
(Self-made billionaire and founder of Opsware, which he sold to Hewlett-Packard for $1.6 billion cash. He is a high technology entrepreneur and co-founder and general partner along with Marc Andreessen of the venture capital firm, Andreessen Horowitz)

To grow a business, at some point you are going to need to recruit employees who are diligent, talented, and coachable. At the end of the day, your company's strongest limiter and overall throttle on your growth will directly relate to your ability to recruit, hire, on-board, assimilate and coach diligent, talented and coachable people. If you don't master the art of hiring, inspiring, training, and firing employees, you are going to "end of up living in a van down by the river" or at the very least, trapped inside a business vehicle from which you cannot escape without your business collapsing in the vacuum of your exit.

"You are going to end up living in a van down by the river."
-Chris Farley
(Chris said this while playing a fictitious motivational speaker by the name of Matt Foley during a Saturday Night Live sketch comedy)

The 22 Core Tasks of Your Human Resources Team

Determine your company's overall HUMAN RESOURCES SCORE[179] by rating your business on a scale of 1 to 10 in the following 22 areas with 10 being the highest. This scoring system can be found at www.ThriveTimeShow.com/TreasureTrove.

1. A description is in place of your ideal job candidate

2. You know what job-posting platforms your company is willing to invest in (Monster.com, Craigslist, Indeed, etc.)

3. You have an initial contact email for your first contact with a prospective employee.

4. A script is in place for your initial phone contact with a prospective employee.

5. An effective job interview outline / script is in place

6. An effective job shadowing process has been developed

7. An onboarding checklist is in place, including a list of all documents needed

8. A non-compete agreement has been created

9. A team compensation plan has been developed

10. A team benefits plan has been developed

11. Staff evaluation forms have been created

12. Weekly standing team huddle meeting are scheduled

13. A detailed employee handbook has been created

14. A well-defined employee onboarding process is in place

15. A skill mastery checklist document has been created

16. A consistent employee training program is in place

17. A formal employee write-up policy is in place

18. An employee point system for disciplinary actions is in place

19. A consistent employee evaluation checklist has been created

20. A quick exit process for staff who must be fired has been developed

21. An organizational chart has been created

22. A company values document has been created

To download templates of the 22 Core Tasks of Your Human Resources Team, visit: www.ThriveTimeShow.com/TreasureTrove.

"Without candor, everyone saved face, and business lumbered along. The status quo was accepted. Fake behavior was just a day at the office. And people with initiative, gumption, and guts were labeled troublesome—or worse...Now for the really bad news. Even though candor is vital to winning, it is hard and time-consuming to instill in any group, no matter what size...To get candor, you reward it, praise it, and talk about it. You make public heroes out of people who demonstrate it. Most of all, you yourself demonstrate it in an exuberant and even exaggerated way—even when you're not the boss."

JACK WELCH
Arguably the most successful CEO in the history of American business. The former CEO of GE.

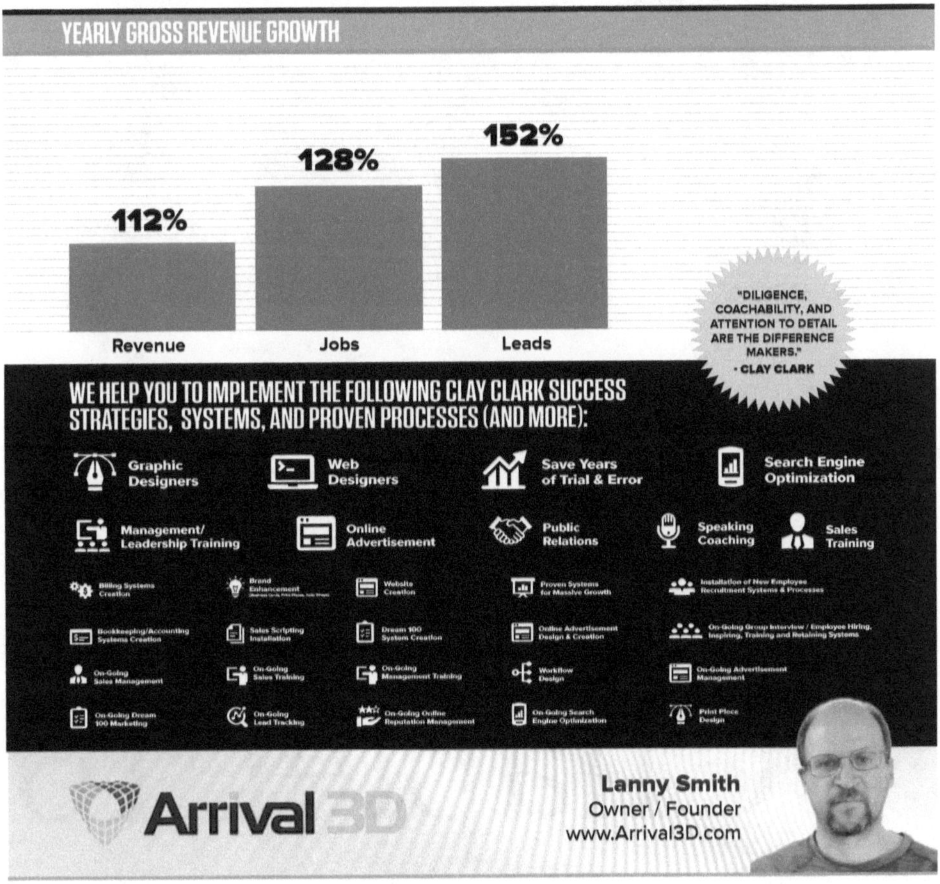

YEARLY GROSS REVENUE GROWTH

112% Revenue

128% Jobs

152% Leads

"DILIGENCE, COACHABILITY, AND ATTENTION TO DETAIL ARE THE DIFFERENCE MAKERS."
· CLAY CLARK

WE HELP YOU TO IMPLEMENT THE FOLLOWING CLAY CLARK SUCCESS STRATEGIES, SYSTEMS, AND PROVEN PROCESSES (AND MORE):

- Graphic Designers
- Web Designers
- Save Years of Trial & Error
- Search Engine Optimization
- Management/ Leadership Training
- Online Advertisement
- Public Relations
- Speaking Coaching
- Sales Training

- Billing Systems Creation
- Brand Enhancement
- Website Creation
- Proven Systems for Massive Growth
- Installation of New Employee Recruitment Systems & Processes

- Bookkeeping/Accounting Systems Creation
- Sales Scripting Installation
- Dream 100 System Creation
- Online Advertisement Design & Creation
- On-Going Group Interview / Employee Hiring, Inspiring, Training and Retaining Systems

- On-Going Sales Management
- On-Going Sales Training
- On-Going Management Training
- Workflow Design
- On-Going Advertisement Management

- On-Going Dream 100 Marketing
- On-Going Lead Tracking
- On-Going Online Reputation Management
- On-Going Search Engine Optimization
- Print Piece Design

Arrival 3D

Lanny Smith
Owner / Founder
www.Arrival3D.com

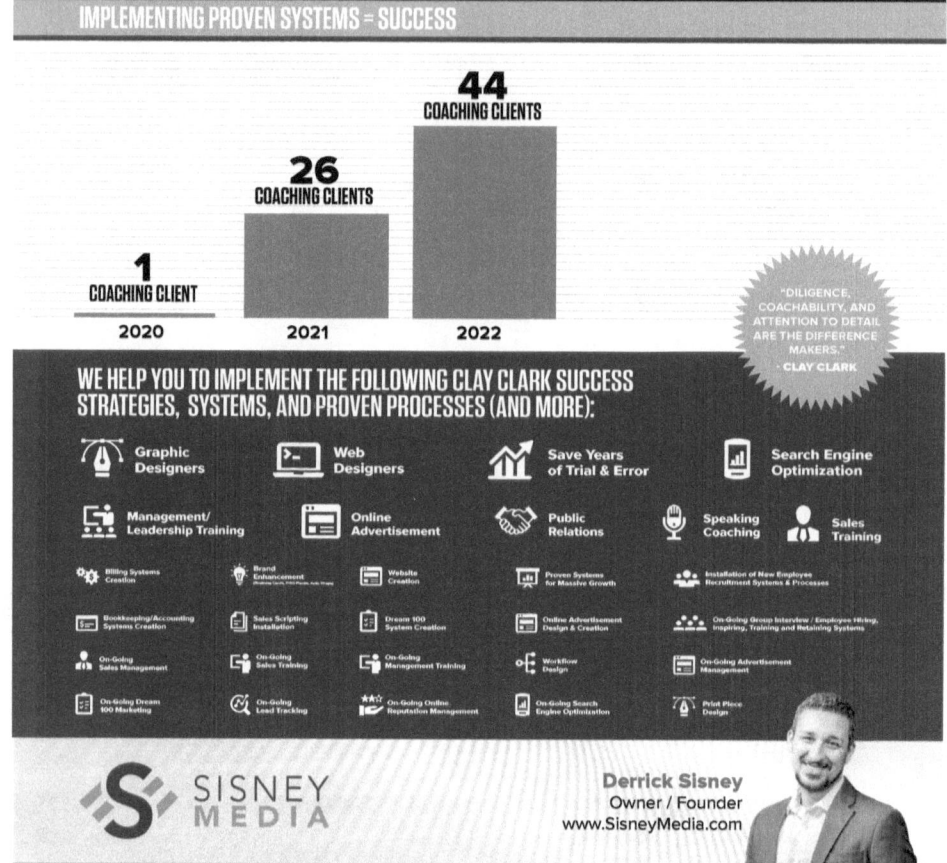

Chapter 16

Booming Business Foundational Principle #5
Management and Leadership Team

The last business foundational principle I'm going to cover in this book concerns the area of your management and leadership team. The vision and overall direction the company is headed must be clearly set in this area. Undoubtedly, this will be the last area of your business that you decide to delegate because this business is your baby and you have been sacrificing massive quantities of time and money to build it. Once you build a business that is growing year after year because of the scalable systems that both you and your team have built, it is certainly attractive to potential buyers. But why would you want to sell your business? Some owners want to sell and some do not. The main truth I want to sear into your cranium is that when you build a duplicable business system, you can work as little or as much as you want. You can stay committed to growing your business until the very last day of your life or you can retire and "drop the mic."

I decided to sell www.DJConnection.com years ago because doing so would allow me to achieve all of my financial goals and because I've never really had an aspiration to become a DJ. I became a DJ because I knew that I could start and grow a successful entertainment company, based upon my experience as a young middle school student. Growing up with very limited financial means, my goal was always to make copious amounts of money so that I could do whatever the heck I wanted. Today, my goal is to mentor millions of people like you who need to know what they need to do to start and grow a successful company; these people are willing to put in the work, they just don't know where to start.

Who Says the Goal of Life is to Retire?

There are many great business leaders who opted to stay connected to their business until the end of their days.

» **Walt Disney** – Up until the day of his death in 1967, Walt Disney stayed active in producing Disney Films. He never did retire.

» **Sam Walton** – Sam Walton was the chairman of Walmart until the day of his death. He briefly retired for two years, but he missed the company so much that he came back.

» **Steve Jobs** – Steve Jobs worked until August 24, 2011, when he physically was no longer able work due to a terminal illness. He died less than 45 days later on October 5, 2011.

» **Michael Jordan** – "I'm my own worst enemy. I drove myself so much that I'm still living with some of those drives. I'm living with that. I don't know how to get rid of it. I don't know if I could. And here I am, still connected to the game."

» **Harrison Ford** – "I think retirement's for old people. I'm still in the business, thank you. I have a young child of nine years old, and I want to live as long as I can to see him grow up. I'm enjoying my life and I want to stick around for as long as I can." (The 73-year old man who played the role of Indiana Jones and just played Han Solo in the most recent installment of the Star Wars movie series, Star Wars: The Force Awakens).

Business owners who win and are successful over the long term focus on training, empowering, and coaching up the people who will eventually take over when they are ready to move on. Successful business owners focus on creating a company culture of excellence that will help their organization thrive regardless of whether the founder is still involved in the day to day. Those business owners who train, empower, and coach for the future then have a choice to stay on because they want to remain involved in the company or they can move on, knowing that the company's future success is not dependent on their presence.

· ·

 Fun Fact:
When the CEO of Zappos, Tony Hsieh, decided to allow Amazon to become the only shareholder of Zappos stock, he did so with confidence knowing that Zappos would continue to operate in the same way and with the same culture that had made them so successful in the past. He was so confident of this fact that he wrote the following e-mail that he sent to all Zappos employees to announce the deal with Amazon.com.

· ·

Tony Hsieh Email

Date: Wed, 22 Jul 2009

From: Tony Hsieh (CEO - Zappos.com)

To: All Zappos Employees

Subject: Zappos and Amazon

THIS GUY

"If you pick the right people and give
them the opportunity to spread their
wings and put compensation as a carrier
behind it you almost don't have to
manage them."

JACK WELCH
*Former CEO of GE, who many argue is the most
successful CEO in the history of American business*

75% OF EMPLOYEES STEAL

Unfortunately, according to the study the U.S. Chamber did in
conjunction with CBS News, they found that over 75% of employees steal
from the workplace and most do so repeatedly. In fact, Gallup showed
70% of U.S. workers not engaged at work. Forbes has reported that the
number of people who admit to wasting time at work every day has now
reached a whopping 89%.

http://www.cbsnews.com/news/employee-theft-are-you-blind-to-it/

If you can't find, hire, inspire, and train good people, nothing will
work. The good news is that Doctor Zoellner now employs 8
optometrists and EpicPhotos.com is now able to find and train over
40 photographers per week who can go out there and deliver award-
winning photography.

THE PURPLE COW CHECKLIST

1. What is your Unique Service Offering?
   (Elephant in the Room Experience)

2. What is your Unique Product Offering?
   (DrZoellner.com)

3. Describe your Unique Decor:
   (Rainforest Cafe, Krispy Kreme)

4. Describe your Unique Music / Ambiance:
   (Victoria Secret, Howl at the Moon, H&M)

5. Describe your Unique Experience:
   (Wholefoods, Samples Everywhere)

6. Describe your Unique Smell:
   (Starbucks, Auntie Ann's Pretzels, Godiva)

7. Describe your Unique Branding
   (Chick-Fil-A, Purple Cow, Harley, Starbucks)

8. Give Back:
   (Tom's Shoes: Buy a pair, give a pair!)

9. Deep Empathy:
   (What does our ideal and likely buyer want: West Jet Christmas Miracle)

10. Experience:
    (Early Southwest Airlines Uniforms, Dick's Last Resort & Bar, Howling at the Moon)

CREATE YOUR NO BRAINER TODAY

Determine a sustainable giveback program (like Toms Shoes, Warby Parker, Starbucks, etc.).

Create a NO-BRAINER OFFER that your competition isn't willing to do (an offer so good that your ideal and likely buyers almost can't say no).

Examples of NO-BRAINER OFFERS:

1. Buy One Get One Free

2. $1.00 First Purchase

3. Freemium

4. Try It Before You Buy It

5. Money Back Guarantee

6. Samples

7. Deep Discounts

8. Endorsement from a World-Class Celebrity (George Foreman endorsed the Lean Mean Fat-Reducing Grilling Machine and sold over 100 million units. His endorsement deal involved him getting paid a percentage of the sales instead of amount of money up upfront).

Ample Examples:

Elephant In The Room – $1.00 first haircut

Dr. Robert Zoellner and Associates – $99 first eye exam and pair of stylish glasses

Tylenol – Maximum Strength

EXAMPLES OF WORLD'S BEST LOGOS

Deep Thoughts

"After working with many businesses. When people can't sell a lot they end up writing poetry, quoting Bob Dylan, living in a park in downtown Denver and smoking pot."

CLAY CLARK
A man-bear-pig who tricked a queen into marrying him.

Deep Thoughts:

"I have worked with many businesses who get stuck in the 'logo stage' of business. If you get stuck on the 'logo stage', your company will never grow and you will start living in a van down by the river."

CLAY CLARK
Business Coach, ThriveTime Show, & RGC

HOW TO SET UP GOOGLE MAPS

1. Login to business.google.com

2. Register your address and check the box "service customers at their location" (this hides your physical address)

3. Get the postcard from Google (about 5 days) and enter the code

4. Name your business with business name and keyword you want to rank for. ie. Bob's Gym of Tulsa Gyms

5. Get reviews

6. Get reviews

7. Get some more reviews

8. When you are finished with the last step, get a drink of water and get more reviews

9. Never ever stop getting reviews

BONUS FUN FACT

According to Forbes, 88% of consumers read reviews before buying.

Behold... the Clark 5 (our kids) pictured above. Success is not about the acquisition of stuff. Success is about being able to have both the time freedom and financial freedom needed to be able to pursue your dreams and visions. Success is about having enough financial resources to be able to spend your time when and where you want to.

THE NUMBERS YOU NEED TO KNOW

Determine how much money your business needs to produce per year to fund the pursuit of your F7 Goals (faith, family, friendship, fitness, finance, focus, and fun):

_____

Determine how much money your business needs to produce per month to fund the pursuit of your F7 Goals (faith, family, friendship, fitness, finance, focus, and fun):

_____

Break Even Formula:

Fixed Costs / Sales Price – Variable Costs = Break Even Point

Determine how much money your business needs to produce per week to fund the pursuit of your F7 Goals (faith, family, friendship, fitness, finance, focus, focus, and fun):

_____

The F7 Life
DESIGN THE LIFE YOU WANT OR LIVE THE LIFE YOU DON'T WANT BY DEFAULT.

Psalm 118:24

"This is the day that the Lord has made.
We will rejoice and be glad in it."

F7

What are Your F7 Goals?

Focus Goals — When?_____

Fun Goals — When?_____

Finance Goals — When?_____

Fitness Goals — When?_____

Friendship Goals — When?_____

Family Goals — When?_____

Faith Goals — When?_____

"Control your destiny or someone else will."

JACK WELCH
Former CEO of GE who grew the company by 4,000% during his tenure as CEW

What is your biggest limiting factor?

What questions do you have?

OPTIMIZE YOUR LIFESTYLE

Write Down a List of the Activities That You Are Going to Stop Doing:

_____

_____

_____

_____

_____

OPTIMIZE THE PEOPLE IN YOUR LIFE

Write Down a List of the People You Will No Longer Spend Time With:

_____

_____

_____

_____

_____

DON'T FOCUS ON THESE ITEMS IF YOU WANT TO SUCCEED.

1. Likes

2. Clicks

3. Funnels

4. Impressions

5. Products "They don't want you to know about."

6. Viral Social Media Marketing Plans

7. Pop-Up Get-Rich-Quick Schemes

8. Subscription-Based Education Programs

9. Ideas

10. Movements / Causes

11. Products that have not been proven to work:

12. Certifications for training / coaching

The 11 Core Tasks that You Have as a Leader of a Thriving Business

Determine your company's overall LEADERSHIP SCORE by rating your business in the following 11 areas on a scale of 1 to 10 with 10 being the highest. This scoring system can be found at www.Thrive15.com/TreasureTrove.

1. Communicate with your entire team and cast the vision and mission for the company's future.

2. Help your team create duplicable processes and systems capable of working without you.

3. Refine your brand (what people think of when they think of your company).

4. Create written values that will keep the company operating with an insistence on excellence now and in the future.

5. Refine who your ideal and likely buyers are and are not, so that your company knows who it is making its products and services for.

6. Create guardrails and rules that will keep your company in check even if you get abducted by aliens, are on vacation or simply decide to sell the business.

7. Identify the biggest threats that your business faces in the short term.

8. Identify the biggest threats that your business faces over the next five years.

9. Identify the potential for strategic partnership relationships (such as Amazon. com teaming up with Zappos).

10. Develop your successor.

11. Weed your cultural garden, identifying the weeds (bad employees) that need to be pulled and the flowers (key employees) that need to be planted.

Download templates of the 11 Core Tasks You Have as a Leader at: www.ThriveTimeShow.com/TreasureTrove.

Determine the Overall Score of Your Business

It is very important that you go through the exercise of determining the overall score for your company IMMEDIATELY. You cannot know what you need to do to move into a place where you can achieve both financial and time freedoms until you first know where you are right now. If you are sincerely passionate about moving from where you are to where you want to be, you need an honest, objective and reliable evaluation of the current state of your business. We've provided the tools for you at Thrive15.com to get that evaluation.

"A healthy company culture encourages people to share bad news. A company that discusses its problems freely and openly can quickly solve them. A company that covers up its problems frustrates everyone involved."

-Ben Horowitz
(Self-made billionaire, the co-founder of Opsware which was acquired by Hewlett-Packard for $1.6 billion cash. The co-founder of Andreesen Horowitz)

"What is trust? I could give you a dictionary definition, but you know it when you feel it. Trust happens when leaders are transparent, candid, and keep their word. It's that simple. Your people should always know where they stand in terms of their performance. They have to know how the business is doing. And sometimes the news is not good—such as imminent layoffs—and any normal person would rather avoid delivering it. But you have to fight the impulse to pad or diminish hard messages or you'll pay with your team's confidence and energy."

-Jack Welch, author of Winning
(Bestselling author and arguably the most effective modern day executive in American history, having grown GE by over 4000% during his tenure)

If you are just starting a business or attempting to grow your business systematically for the first time, it is more than likely that your scores are not going to be very great at this point. This does not mean that you are weird, this means that you are normal and that you have room for specific and detailed improvement. Most owners I have met over the years have no idea where they are, where they are going or how to get there and so they end up just reading endless numbers of motivational success and self-improvement books in between attending motivational seminars. This is not you. You are focused on achieving success and you are willing to invest both the time and money needed to turn your business dreams into reality.

You will quickly increase your scores in each area once you commit yourself to following the path called, "Guaranteed Success on Thrive15.com." When you are first starting a business, the most critical Booming Business Foundational Principles you must diligently observe are both the Marketing / Sales and the Executing Your Daily Operations Foundational Principles. If you are reading this right now and your score in the area of Marketing / Sales is dangerously low, you must commit yourself to

"I went to Google, typed in San Francisco chauffeur or San Francisco limousine, I just filled out an excel sheet and I just started dialing for dollars, right? First ten guys I called, three of them hung up before I got a few words out, a few of them would listen for like 45 seconds and then hung up, and three of them said 'I'm interested, let's meet.' And if you're cold calling and three out of ten say 'let's meet', you've got something."

-Travis Kalanick
(Founder of Uber)

improving your systems for generating leads, closing deals, and bringing in business. However, you must also be committed to simultaneously creating the best systems, checklists and processes available to help you Execute Your Daily Operations. I cannot force you to do this, but I highly recommend that you HOLD YOURSELF ACCOUNTABLE FOR EVALUATING ALL FIVE OF YOUR BOOMING BUSINESS FOUNDATIONAL PRINCIPLES EVERY QUARTER.

Now that we have an overall understanding of the systems we must build in order to create a business that is capable of producing the time and financial freedom you desire, we must now get to work implementing the specific improvements in each aspect of our business to produce sustainable growth quickly.

Deep Thoughts

"Wishful thinking won't help. You must learn to see life as it is and not how you wish it to be if you ever want to improve."

-Clay Clark
(Founder of ThriveTimeShow.com, former U.S. Small Business Administration Entrepreneur of the Year, host of the *Thrivetime Show* podcast, and America's #1 Business Coach)

"We are up over 100% since implementing Clay Clark's Systems."

-Josh Spurrell
Owner, Spurrell CPA

Chapter 17

Booming Business Foundational Principle #1
Setting Up the Sales Machine

"An empowered organization is one in which individuals have the knowledge, skill, desire, and opportunity to personally succeed in a way that leads to collective organizational success."

-*Stephen Covey*
(Bestselling author of *The 7 Habits of Highly Effective People*)

In order for a business to grow at a scale that outpaces the owner's individual ability to prospect and personally close deals, the business must develop a system to find an ongoing supply of sales leads that it is then able to convert into paying customers. Just last week, I was sitting down with a business owner who was explaining to me in great detail his personal, incredible ability to both drum up sales leads and close deals. The problem is that he is celebrating the very activity that has him trapped inside his business. You must develop the processes, systems, guardrails, and put in place a team capable of generating more deals and leads than you could ever personally produce if you want to create the time and financial freedom many entrepreneurs seek. You will never build a sales system capable of working without you if you are not intentional about it.

· ·

Mystic Statistic:
"Today's small business owner works an average of 52 hours per week, with fifty-seven percent working at least six days a week, and more than twenty percent working all seven."

Wells Fargo & Gallup, "More Than Half of Small Business Owners Work at Least Six-Day Weeks, Still Find Time for Personal Life," PRNewswire, August 09, 2005. http://www. prnewswire.com/news-releases/wells-fargogallup-more-than-half-of-small-business-owners-work-at-least-six-day-weeks-still-find-time-for-personal-life-54729812.html

· ·

Sales Pipeline Problems Checklist

In order to help you identify the biggest limiting factors related to your sales pipeline, I want you to take a moment to honestly and candidly rate your business on the following areas on a scale of 1 to 10 with 10 being the highest.

—— Ability to consistently produce a steady volume of leads (as opposed to having a ton of leads one month and then zero leads the next month)

—— Step-by-step lead management and organization system your company uses

—— Follow-up system to consistently follow-up with all inbound generated leads

—— Follow-up system to consistently follow-up with all outbound generated leads

—— Internal lead scoring and rating system to identify which leads are the most important and mostly likely deals to close and which leads are the least important and least likely to close

—— Inquiry source and lead-generation track efforts to determine which lead sources are the most effective

—— Lead generation system to produce a consistent number of leads each month at a predictable cost per acquisition/per lead

—— Scalable lead generation processes to generate leads that are not dependent upon the super talents of one team member

—— Current cost paid per lead

—— Quality of the inbound leads your team receives

—— Company's ability to generate leads via search engine optimization

—— Company's ability to generate leads from social media

—— Company's ability to generate leads via online retargeted advertising

—— Company's ability to generate quality leads from e-mail marketing

—— Company's ability to generate quality leads from cold-call and call center-based marketing

—— Company's ability to generate quality leads from tradeshows

—— Company's ability to generate quality leads via print media

—— Company's ability to generate quality leads via public relations

—— Company's ability to generate quality leads from walk-in traffic

—— Company's ability to generate quality leads from sign-flipper generated walk-in traffic

— Company's ability to generate leads via referrals from your current customers

— Company's ability to generate leads from networking

— Company's ability to formulate quality lead generating ideas and actually execute them

— Company's ability to generate quality leads via the mailing of individual print pieces to your ideal and likely buyers

— Company's ability to generate quality leads via television advertising

— Company's ability to generate quality leads via radio advertising

— Company's ability to generate quality leads via online radio (Pandora, IHeartRadio, etc.)

— Company's ability to generate quality leads via guest podcast appearances (members of your team being featured as guests on successful podcasts such as www.EOFire.com)

— Company's ability to generate quality leads via ad spots on podcasts enjoyed and listened to by your ideal and likely buyers

— Company's ability to generate quality leads via guest blog appearances (members of your team being featured as guests on successful blogs such as www.HuffingtonPost.com, www.LifeHacker.com, www.TechCrunch.com, etc.)

— Company's ability to generate leads via mass mailers where multiple coupons and print pieces are packaged in one envelope such as Valpak or RSVP

— Company's ability to produce leads from executing an effective face-to-face representative-based marketing game plan (example: pharmaceutical sales representatives generating referrals from doctors)

— Company's ability to generate sales outside of the individual talents of one team member (Example: Think about the devastating impact Justin Timberlake's departure from N' Sync had on the group.)

• •

 Fun Fact:
With Justin Timberlake acting as the group's lead singer the boy band's (N' Sync) first three albums sold over 30 million copies. After leaving N' Sync, Timberlake's album "The 20/20 Experience" was the biggest selling album of 2013 according to Billboard, with a total of 2.43 million copies sold. The rest of the group since Justin's departure...not so much.

• •

Take a moment to look at how you honestly rated your company's ability to generate quality leads using the lead producing activities listed above. In order to build a consistently successful and stable business, you must find three affordable ways to produce leads on an on-going basis. Why three? For the same reason that you don't want to sit on a bar stool that has only one stable leg; you do not want to create a business model that generates leads using only one viable and consistently successful avenue of generating business. Look at the list again and circle the marketing avenues you feel would best resonate with your ideal and likely buyers.

> "No other trade or profession has more opportunity for one to rise from poverty to great wealth than that of salesman."
>
>  *-Og Mandino*
> **(Bestselling author of The Greatest Salesman in the World)**

Now that you have identified which marketing avenues you believe would best resonate with your ideal and likely buyers, you must commit to creating and mastering a step-by-step system that an honest and diligent person with very little or no experience could implement with 10 hours or less of training. If your system is too complex for you to train the members of your team in a step-by-step and linear fashion, your system is not good enough and must be reworked until it scales (works without you). To make your life 2% easier, we have created the following list of Thrive15.com trainings that will teach you how to massively succeed in each marketing avenue you choose.

All of these tools are available to www.ThriveTimeShow.com/TreasureTrove

» Step-by-step lead management and organization system creation

» Inbound sales lead system creation

» Outbound sales lead system creation

» Internal lead scoring and rating system creation

» Inquiry source and lead generation tracking system creation

» Measuring the true costs associated with generating a consistent amount of leads each month

» Scalable lead generation process creation that is not dependent on sales superstars

» Determining the overall quality of the inbound leads that your team receives

» Generating leads via search engine optimization

» Generating leads via social media

» Generating leads via online retargeted advertising

» Generating quality leads from e-mail marketing

» Generating quality leads from cold-call and call center-based marketing

» Generating quality leads from tradeshows

» Generating quality leads via print media

IF IT'S NOT A WIN-WIN THE RELATIONSHIP HAS TO END

MR. LEECH I FEEL LIKE YOU AND I ARE BECOMING BEST FRIENDS.

"ONLY ENGAGE IN MUTUALLY BENEFICIAL
RELATIONSHIPS."
- CLAY CLARK

» Generating quality leads via public relations -

» Generating quality leads from walk-in traffic -

» Generating quality leads from sign-flipper generated walk-in traffic -

» Generating leads via referrals from your current customers -

» Generating leads from networking -

» Generating quality lead generating ideas and actually executing them -

» Generating quality leads via the mailing of individual print pieces delivered to your ideal and likely buyers

» Generating quality leads via television advertising -

» Generating quality leads via radio advertising -

» Generating quality leads via online radio -

» Generating quality leads via guest podcast appearances -

» Generating quality leads via ad spots on podcasts enjoyed and listened to by your ideal and likely buyers

"The faster you run high quality experiments, the more likely you'll find scalable, effective growth tactics. Determining the success of a customer acquisition idea is dependent on an effective tracking and reporting system, so don't start testing until your tracking/reporting system has been implemented."

-Gabriel Weinberg
(Bestselling author of *Traction: A Startup Guide to Getting Customers***)**

» Generating quality leads via guest blog appearances -

» Generating leads via the mailing of mass mailers where multiple coupons and print pieces are packaged into one envelope such as Valpak or RSVP:

» Generating leads from executing an effective face-to-face representative-based marketing game plan

Having worked with hundreds of small and medium-sized businesses over the years, I can tell you that it is all-too-common for a business to be stuck in the cycle of feast or famine. The average business owner is guilty of spending all his energy focusing on delivering the products and services he just sold, only to discover that his pipeline is now completely dry and the business is going to die if he doesn't stop everything and immediately begin focusing on selling again. My friend, if this is you, you must get out of this cycle.

The good news is that this entire feast and famine is going to stop right here and now because you are going to do the following six activities as soon as possible.

1. Create a customer database:
    Watch the video at - www.ThriveTimeShow.com/TreasureTrove

2. Create an annual marketing calendar: Watch the video at
    – www.ThriveTimeShow.com/TreasureTrove

3. Create a step-by-step sales system for the three marketing systems you are committed to mastering:
    Watch the video at – www.ThriveTimeShow.com/TreasureTrove

4. Determine the daily metrics you will hold your sales team accountable for producing: Watch the video at – www.ThriveTimeShow.com/TreasureTrove

5.   Create an inbound sales tracking system to determine which advertisement, marketing and sales activities are producing the most fruit for your business: Watch the video at – www.ThriveTimeShow.com/TreasureTrove

6.   Once you have built a sales process, commit to training your salespeople and managing the sales and marketing systems (instead of actually working in the sales process): Watch the video at – www.ThriveTimeShow.com/TreasureTrove

> "Almost every failed startup has a product.
> What failed startups don't have are enough customers."
>
> **-Gabriel Weinberg**
> **(Bestselling author of** *Traction: A Startup Guide to Getting Customers*)

You Must Document the System that Works

Once you have gone to the trouble to identify the best sales and marketing systems to attract your ideal and likely buyers, you're not finished. You must go the extra mile and create duplicable sales systems that will help anyone who is honest and diligent to both produce and close sales leads. When you build systems that are stuck in your head and not documented on paper, you really set yourself up for failure. If a successful member of your team gets upset, gets hurt, or decides to move on to greener pastures and no one has any idea what they were doing that worked, you find yourself in a very dangerous spot. You also can't easily tweak or improve a system that is 100% verbal and not recorded anywhere in a linear fashion.

8 Steps for Creating an Effective Documented Sales System

1. Identify and document which three marketing systems work best to generate both leads and actual sales.

2. Determine which marketing and sales system is far-and-away the most effective lead-generating activity. Ask yourself, if you had to only use one system to market your business, which system would you use.

3. Create the step-by-step processes involved in executing the marketing system

> "To succeed consistently, good managers need to be skilled not just in choosing, training, and motivating the right people for the right job, but in choosing, building, and preparing the right organization for the job as well."
>
>  **-Clayton Christensen**
> (Harvard Business School professor and bestselling author of *The Innovator's Dilemma: When New Technologies Cause Great Firms to Fail*)

4. Buy a huge white board or sheets of white paper and a massive amount of tape (scotch tape, masking tape, etc.)

5. Post in a highly visible place your giant white sheet of paper or a chalkboard or a massive white board.

6. Write out all of the steps of your sales process on that paper or chalkboard or white board.

7. Adjust the description and the steps of your sales process until you have developed a perfect strategy that actually works best for you.

8. Once you have created the perfect system, take a picture of the written steps and produce a PDF image that you can easily distribute to your sales people to accurately execute the steps involved in your sales process.

Create a Sales Tracking System to Measure the Effectiveness of Each System

The most important aspect of this process is to make sure that you are collecting and measuring accurate and actionable data that can tell you objectively which of your sales and marketing systems are working the best and which ones need to be refined or blown up. Based on my experience as a consultant, I would estimate that approximately 75% of the businesses I analyze are wasting nearly all of their marketing dollars on strategies that simply do not work. In many small and mid-sized companies, the ownership is committed to ineffective marketing strategies merely because of fear of breaking tradition or because they have not invested the time and resources needed to determine what marketing avenues are in fact working.

> "You need the kind of objectivity that makes you forget everything you've heard; clear the table, and do a factual study like a scientist would."
>
> **-Steve Wozniak**
> (Co-founder of Apple)

Create a Usable Process and System that Honest and Diligent Team Members Will Be Able to Use

Once you have a created and documented the step-by-step process that has proven to produce results for your team, you must create the checklists, scripts, and systems that they will use to execute the process. Unfortunately, I have found that most owners of small to medium-sized businesses can be divided into two groups (both of which are stuck):

Group A – These business owners have never taken the time to document any of the systems, tactics and processes they use on a daily basis, thus they struggle with teaching these systems to anybody else and are trapped inside of their business.

Group B – These businesses owners have actually invested the time to document their systems, tactics and processes, but they lack the intensity, drive, accountability, force of will and leadership skills needed to insure that their team actually understands and implements the systems they have created.

My friend, you must commit to documenting the systems that work and then hold your team accountable for implementing those systems, regardless of the level of push back you get from those who miss the old and dysfunctional way of doing things.

> "People judge you by your performance, so focus on the outcome. Be a yardstick of quality. Some people aren't used to an environment where excellence is expected."
>
> **-Steve Jobs**
> (Co-founder of Apple and the former CEO of Pixar)

 Fun Fact:
Because the company was not able to deliver the excellent level of customer service that Howard Schultz demanded when he returned to the role of CEO and Chairman of Starbucks, in February 2008, he famously closed 7,100 stores nationwide for three hours to retrain 135,000 in-store employees and people who oversaw the stores.

"Starbucks to Close All U.S. Stores for Training," NBCNews.com, February 26, 2008. http://www.nbcnews.com/id/23351151/ns/business-us_business/t/starbucks-close-all-us-stores-training/#.V3vYhY5qb1w

Don't worry about whether your team (who will probably not work with you in three years anyway) accuses you of being maniacally focused on implementing a level of systemization they say is proof of your "anal retentiveness." You must focus on creating systems that honest and diligent members of your team will be able to use. If the complexity of your systems is too intense, even honest and diligent members will not be able to use them, EVEN THOUGH THEY WANT TO. Remember, complexity will not scale well.

Definition Magician:
The term "anal retentive," or "anal" in its shortened version, is often used to describe a person who pays an incredible amount of attention to detail to the point that it annoys others. In Freudian psychology, the anal stage follows the oral stage of infant or early-childhood development. I believe that Freud was mentally ill based upon the experiments he conducted on his own family and that is all the further I am willing to go with this definition.

As I discussed earlier, every business system that you build really has two parts. The first part involves the painstaking process of developing, testing, measuring, and documenting a system that works. The second part involves the painstaking process of creating a checklist or tool that your team can actually use to implement the system. Personally, I don't care whether your people want to use the system or not, I just care that they can use it and that the system you have created is capable of generating success based upon my RULE OF THE 3 Ps.

Clay's Rule of the 3 Ps:

Rule #1 – Product – In order for a business to be sustainable and successful, it must be able to create an insanely popular product or service that people love and that you love to share with your ideal and likely buyers.

"Pay attention to design. We made the buttons on the screen look so good you'll want to lick them. Design is not just what it looks like and feels like. Design is how it works."

-Steve Jobs
(Co-founder of Apple and the former CEO of Pixar)

"The secret of happiness is minimizing the amount of time you spent with people you don't choose to be with. This is just math!"

-Phil Libin
(The CEO of Evernote)

Rule #2 – People – People are excited about and willing to be a part of businesses that are made up of individuals they genuinely like. If you sincerely hate the people you are forced to work with every day, no amount of money will ever be able to replace the amount of time you wasted being with people you do not like.

Rule #3 – Profit – In order for a business to be viable over the long term, it must create a consistent and predictable profit for its owners and investors.

"Profit in business comes from repeat customers, customers that boast about your project or service, and that bring friends with them."

-W. Edwards Deming
(Leading business consultant and bestselling author of his time. Many historians credit Deming for playing a big part in helping Japan become an industrialized nation after World War II)a

Create the Best Way to Enable Your Team Members to Use Your Proven Marketing System

Humans are very visual. Therefore, unless you are hiring and managing aliens, your systems must be very visual as well. Unlike the world of academia where the goal is to see who can remember the most crap for the test before everyone begins memorizing for the next test, in the world of business, everything is exactly opposite. In the world of business, memorization could not be less important. What you are looking to do is create an actual one-page – a quick cheat sheet or checklist your team can use to guide them each time they attempt to execute your proven system.

"Good checklists, on the other hand are precise. They are efficient, to the point, and easy to use even in the most difficult situations. They do not try to spell out everything--a checklist cannot fly a plane. Instead, they provide reminders of only the most critical and important steps--the ones that even the highly skilled professional using them could miss. Good checklists are, above all, practical."

-Atul Gawande
(Bestselling author of *Checklist Manifesto* and an American surgeon, write and public researcher. He also has worked with the Harvard Medical School as their Professor of Surgery)

A Checklist for Making Sure that Your System Is High Quality:

1. Download an example of a world-class checklist right now at www.ThriveTimeShow.com/TreasureTrove.

2. Your checklist / system is free of industry or business related jargon that a new hire cannot possibly know.

3. Your checklist / system explains the step-by-step proven process involved in producing the desired income you want to produce.

4. You have tested your checklist on multiple humans who are both honest and diligent and they have been able to produce the desired results while using your checklist.

Specific Items that May Need to Be Included in Your System:

1. An instruction document with text explaining in detail how to do any given task

2. Screen shots of the computer screens that members of your team may be seeing as they execute your checklist

3. A video training that shows a member of your team executing the task perfectly

4. Photos, pictures, or drawings showing visually what you're trying to accomplish

5. Examples of a perfectly executed task

6. Template documents your team can fill out

The Entrepreneurial System Creation Success Cycle

My friend, you must never get out of the entrepreneur success cycle. The cycle is comprised of the following steps:

1. Define

2. Act

3. Measure

4. Refine

> "Progress comes not only in great leaps but also from hundreds of small steps."
>
>  **-Walter Isaacson**
> (The famous author whom Steve Jobs personally asked to help him write his famous autobiography entitled, *Steve Jobs*)

As an entrepreneur, you must constantly define the outcome you want to see. Act before you have everything figured out, measure the results, and refine the process until it is perfected. If you ever feel as though you are not up to this task, you must sell your business or delegate the running of your business to somebody who is up to this never-ending task.

You must pay close attention to the outcomes you are experiencing as a result of your team's lead creation efforts so that you can spot the best ways to enhance and improve your sales systems. I don't care whether we are talking about measuring the results of a sales script, a sales video, an auto-responder email, a podcast, a TV commercial, a mailer, a text marketing campaign or any other type of marketing and lead generation activity under the sun, YOU MUST INVEST THE TIME TO MEASURE THE RESULTS YOU ARE GETTING ON A DAILY BASIS. I highly recommend that you track the results daily and that your team commits to pivoting, nuancing, and updating your lead generation systems on a weekly basis, as dictated by the results you are seeing.

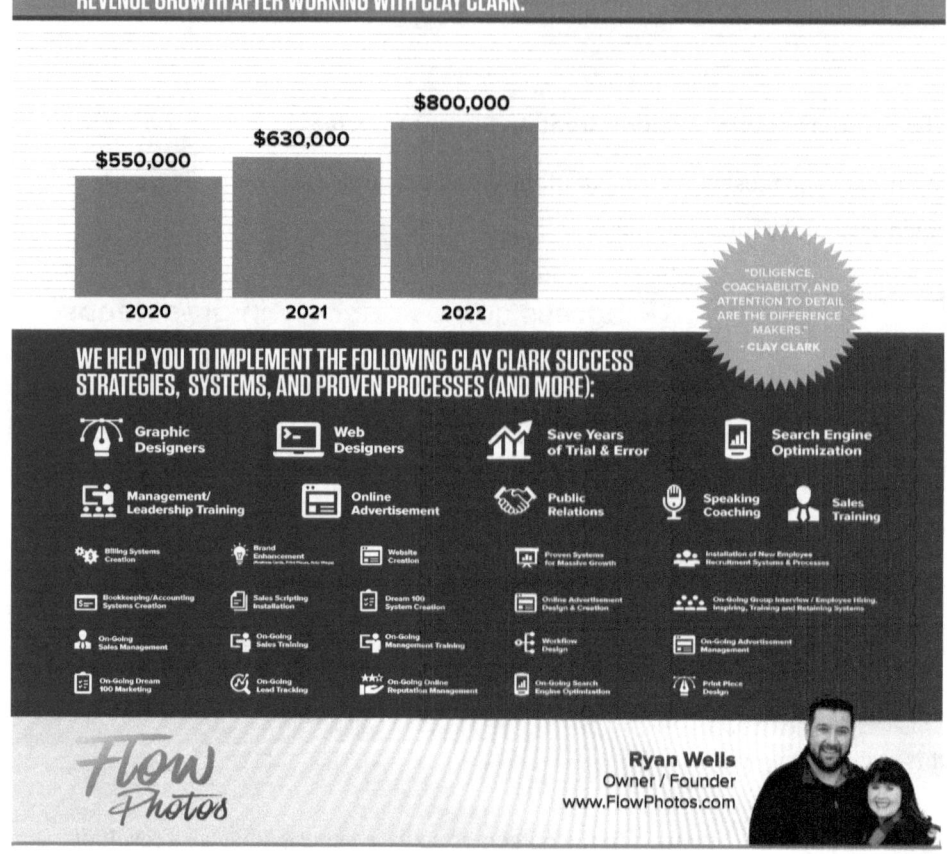

Chapter 18

Creating Marketing and Sales Guardrails

It is very important you install three different marketing guardrails to ensure that sales processes you are attempting to implement, but that may not be working, don't lead you too far astray. To improve your quality life by 2% and to help you join the top 1% of income earners, I have listed here the five most important marketing guardrails so you don't lose your shirt while attempting to earn copious amounts of profit.

Sales and Marketing Guardrail #1: Create a Marketing Calendar for the Next 90 Days

You must create a quarterly (90-day) lead generating marketing calendar for your organization. On each day of the week, you need to clarify what you are going to be doing. Here is an example:

February 1

1. Post Monday Evening Customer Testimonial to LinkedIn, Facebook, and Twitter

2. Call 400 former customers to seek referrals

3. Email 400 former customers to thank them for their business

4. Place road signage and balloons in front of store

5. Set out internal signage promoting Valentine's Special

February 2

1. Post Ground Hog Day Product Special Video to LinkedIn, Facebook, and Twitter

2. Text 400 former customers to thank them for their business

3. Place road signage and balloons in front of store

> "Create a definite plan for carrying out your desire and begin at once, whether you're ready or not, to put this plan into action."

-Napoleon Hill
(Bestselling author of *Think & Grow Rich* and the former personal apprentice of the late, great, self-made millionaire Andrew Carnegie)

4. Mail 400 former customers flyers promoting the Valentine's Special

5. Set out internal signage promoting Valentine's Special

It is very important that your marketing calendar is highly visual so that you can hold yourself and your teammates accountable for the execution of the system. This calendar will also help ensure that your marketing intentions do not become marketing wishes that are never acted upon.

The discipline of creating a visual marketing calendar will also force you to think proactively instead of reactively. When you think proactively, you can avoid scheduling conflicts, address the logistics and procure the items you need to have on hand in order to properly execute your marketing visions and see real results.

To view a powerful training on how to create a Marketing Calendar visit: www.ThriveTimeShow.com/TreasureTrove

Sales and Marketing Guardrail #2: Create Uniform Marketing Materials

My friend, as you begin to build a duplicable business model, getting the details right the first time will save you precious time that you simply cannot afford to waste as the number of both successes and issues that you will experience on a daily basis increases exponentially. Right now, before your world gets super crazy with thousands and thousands of daily customers, you will want to standardize the following marketing items:

1. Standardized Logo

2. Standardized Brand Colors

3. Standardized Brand Slogan

4. Standardized Envelopes

5. Standardized Uniforms (if applicable)

6. Standardized Brochures

7. Standardized One Sheets

8. Standardized Trifolds

9. Standardized Pricing

10. Standardized E-Mail Signature

11. Standardized Tradeshow Display

12. Standardized Lead Sheets

13. Standardized Sales Scripts

14. Standardized Pre-Written Emails

15. Standardized Sales Presentation

16. Standardized Web Pages

17. Standardized Valpak Ads

18. Standardized Mass Mailers

19. Standardized Point of Purchase Signage

20. Standardized Digital Menu Boards

"[The ThriveTimeShow 2-Day Business Conference] is exceptional – filled, brimming with passionate entrepreneurs."

-Michael Levine
(PR consultant for Michael Jackson, Prince, Nike, Pizza Hut and more)

BUY LOW, SELL HIGH

"WHEN IT COMES TO INVESTING, SIMPLY ATTEMPT TO BE FEARFUL WHEN OTHERS ARE GREEDY, AND BE GREEDY WHEN OTHERS ARE FEARFUL."
- WARREN BUFFET

21. Standardized Menus

22. Standardized Targeting Ads

23. Standardized Retargeting Ads

24. Standardized Landing Pages

25. Standardized Marketing Videos

26. If it's related to marketing, make it standardized

"Details matter, it's worth waiting to get it right."

-Steve Jobs
(Co-founder of Apple and the former CEO of Pixar)

People will judge the value of the products and services you sell based upon the appearance of your brand, so you must work to get it right. With that being said, don't freak out if you have just come to the conclusion that every aspect of your branding is terrible. Just start today, standardizing everything and getting it right the first time you touch it. Don't make something terrible now that you have to come back and fix later. Get into the cultural discipline of "excellence or nothing" when it comes to your marketing materials.

"If you don't have time to do it right, when will you have time to do it over?"

-John Wooden

(Arguably the most successful basketball coach in history and the man who led his UCLA men's basketball team to an astounding 10 NCAA national championships during a 12-year period of time as a result of having a maniacal focus on the small details, even down to the way his players tied their shoes)

Sales and Marketing Guardrail #3: Create an Executable Marketing Tracking Wall

You must begin tracking your cost per lead like you never have before. You must know the following four marketing measurements for your business or your marketing efforts will sooner or later prove to be unmanageable.

Marketing Measurement #1 – What are you paying per lead? If you spent $2,500 for a chance to speak at an industry trade event and then you paid another $1,500 for hotel and travel expenses and another $1,000 on marketing materials to be used at the tradeshow, you just spent $5,000 on marketing. If expending all these resources resulted in five leads, then you just paid $1,000 per confirmed lead. That's a very expensive lead, unless you are selling a product or service that produces a profit of more than $10,000 per year, per customer. When you know your numbers, you can make logical decisions and compare what is working versus what is not working.

Marketing Measurement #2 – What are you paying per confirmed deal? It is absolutely vital that you know this number because if you did spend $5,000 to generate a total of five leads and you only ended up closing one deal, you just spent $5,000 per deal, which again is super expensive unless you are selling a product or service that generates an annual profit of $10,000 per year, per customer. I keep using this scenario because I work with one business that literally has numbers that look like this and they are very successful. They send out their representatives to give talks at industry tradeshows and if they only book one deal, they believe the entire investment of both time and money was worth it. However, they have to book that one deal per event or their boss loses his mind every time. The level of intensity that these people put into their follow-up systems is amazing and that is why they are successful. They never come back from an event saying, "Well, at least we got our name out there." The only companies that come back from tradeshows saying "Well, at least we got our name out there," are companies that will be out of business soon. When you know how much money you are spending on actually closing a deal, you can quickly determine which marketing strategies you should blow up and which ones you should continue refining.

Marketing Measurement #3 – You must know what the overall "Return on Investment" is per marketing dollar that you actually spent. If you spent $5,000 to market at a tradeshow but you ended up bringing in $10,000 of income as a result of your team's marketing efforts, then you have doubled your money. If you could double your money every day, you would be making more money (slightly more money than the folks who own the casino that is closest to you).

• •

 Fun Fact:
"Looking at MGM Resorts, it operates 15 owned resorts in the U.S. The company offers more than 22,000 slots and 1,000 gaming tables in the region (excluding the slots and tables in JVs). Like other casino operators, MGM has also seen similar growth over the past few years with revenues increasing from $2.48 billion in 2010 to $2.60 billion in 2013."

Trefis Team, "Trends In The Casino Industry -- A Shift From The Las Vegas Strip To East Asia," Forbes, January 7, 2015. http://www.forbes.com/sites/greatspeculations/2015/01/07/trends-in-the-casino-industry-a-shift-from-the-las-vegas-strip-to-east-asia/#57ea70306e3c

• •

Marketing Measurement #4 – You must keep and manage all of your leads within stable customer relationship management software often referred to as a CRM system. Don't freak out as we get 2% nerdier than typically healthy. Don't over think this. If your team gathers five qualified leads at the tradeshow, that is great and you will want to store this information somewhere. If your team closes one actual deal, that is great and you will want to store this information somewhere. If your team gathers 15 leads that are currently unqualified but could become qualified leads in six months, that is great and you will want to store their contact information somewhere. YOU MUST SAVE THE CONTACT INFORMATION FOR THE POTENTIAL LEADS, QUALIFIED LEADS AND ACTUAL IDEAL AND LIKELY BUYERS IF YOU ARE GOING TO GROW A SCALABLE AND VALUABLE COMPANY.

There are many quality and low-cost CRM solutions on the market today.

When starting out in business, it is totally okay to use a spreadsheet, sheets of paper and post-it notes to sell something. However, after you sell one hundred somethings, you need to begin maintaining the organization (also known as data integrity) of your customer database. Specifically, I recommend that your CRM solutions allows you to manage the following 14 pieces of information:

1.   The Prospect / Customer's First Name

2.   The Prospect / Customer's Last Name

3.   The Prospect / Customer's Email Address

4.   The Prospect / Customer's Personal Phone Number

5.   The Prospect / Customer's Characteristics (decision maker, manager, assistant, etc.)

6.   The Prospect / Customer's Mailing Address

7.   The Prospect / Customer's Industry (characteristics of the type of business)

8.   The Prospect / Customer's Ranking (apostle, loyalist, mercenary, hostage or terrorist)

9.   The Prospect / Customer's Inquiry Source (how they heard of your business)

10. The Prospect / Customer's Purchase History (they have purchased X at Y amount in the past or they considered buying X at Y amount)

11. The Prospect / Customer's Hot Button (why the customer is considering buying from you)

12. The Prospect / Customer's Pain Points (why the customer should buy from you, what problems they will have if they don't buy from you)

13. The Prospect / Customer's Memorable Qualities (they play what instrument, have how many kids, etc.)

14. The Prospect / Customer's Likelihood to Buy on a Scale of 1 to 10 (with 10 being the highest)

Fishing in the Lake with a Net | Find the Lowest Cost and Effective Tactics to Create More Sales Now

Having grown up in the city, at one time I did not understand why the rural people in Minnesota go fishing. We moved to Minnesota when I was in seventh grade and a school friend by the name of Aaron asked me to go fishing. I said yes, and being naturally competitive and totally unaware of the fact that most people go fishing for relaxation and conversation purposes, I brought a net. After fishing with poles for a few hours, we decided to dock the boat and grab some lunch. When everyone else went inside to grab lunch, I went back out onto the dock and I put out a net. The snow and ice had just finished melting so you could literally see the fish swimming around. Quickly, I snatched a dozen fish or so in my net. When my friends came back outside, they looked at me as though I had a disease or had committed a horrible crime against humanity. One dude said, "Man the limit is three fish per person. You can't use a net to catch!"

Proud of my ingenuity, I shared with him that one could actually catch 20 fish quite easily by using a net. What is the point of this story? The point of this story is that in the world of business, many entrepreneurs are not actually fishing for sales; they simply want to hang out at networking events to have something fun to do during the day. However, when you are trying to quickly build a scalable and duplicable business model that has the potential to create both the economic and time freedom that I've been talking about, you don't have time to screw around fishing with a pole. You need to be fishing with a net.

Many entrepreneurs get excited about busyness. I'm passionate about making a profitable business, not perpetual busyness. The "why" is the only real difference between busyness and business, both literally and figuratively. Why are you in business? Are you in business to be busy 24/7 or to make money 24/7 while creating a product or service that you are proud of while working with people you like? LET'S GO ACTUALLY SELL SOME STUFF!

I realize that right now we are talking about how to generate leads, but I want to make sure that you do not make the same costly mistake that most business owners tend to make. Just because you are focused on generating new leads, does not mean that you must focus your entire marketing campaign on discovering brand new sales prospects with whom you've never had any previous connections. In fact, 95% of the time when I've been brought in to help grow a business, I've found that the big money and fast growth is achieved by focusing on methodically and systemically adding more value to your previous and current customers. To help you sell more to existing and previous customers, I have put together a list of Six Super Moves that have been proven to work time and time again.

> ## "You can't build a reputation on what you are going to do."
>
>
>
> **-Henry Ford**
> **(An American Industrialist, the founder of the Ford Motor Company and the man who is often credited as being the inventor of the modern assembly line concept)**

"Hire sales people who are really smart problem solvers, but lack courage, hunger and competitiveness, and your company will go out of business."

- Ben Horowitz

(Pictured left. He co-founded and served as president and chief executive officer of the enterprise software company Opsware, which Hewlett-Packard acquired for $1.6 billion in cash in July 2007.)

"ACTION IS THE REAL MEASURE OF INTELLIGENCE."
– NAPOLEON HILL
BEST-SELLING SUCCESS AUTHOR OF "THINK AND GROW RICH"

1. When will your daily meta-time be?

   _____

2. Where will your daily meta-time take place?

   _____

3. What do you need to have with you to make this time the most productive it can be? (computer, pen, pad of paper, stapler, 3 monitors, etc.)

   _____

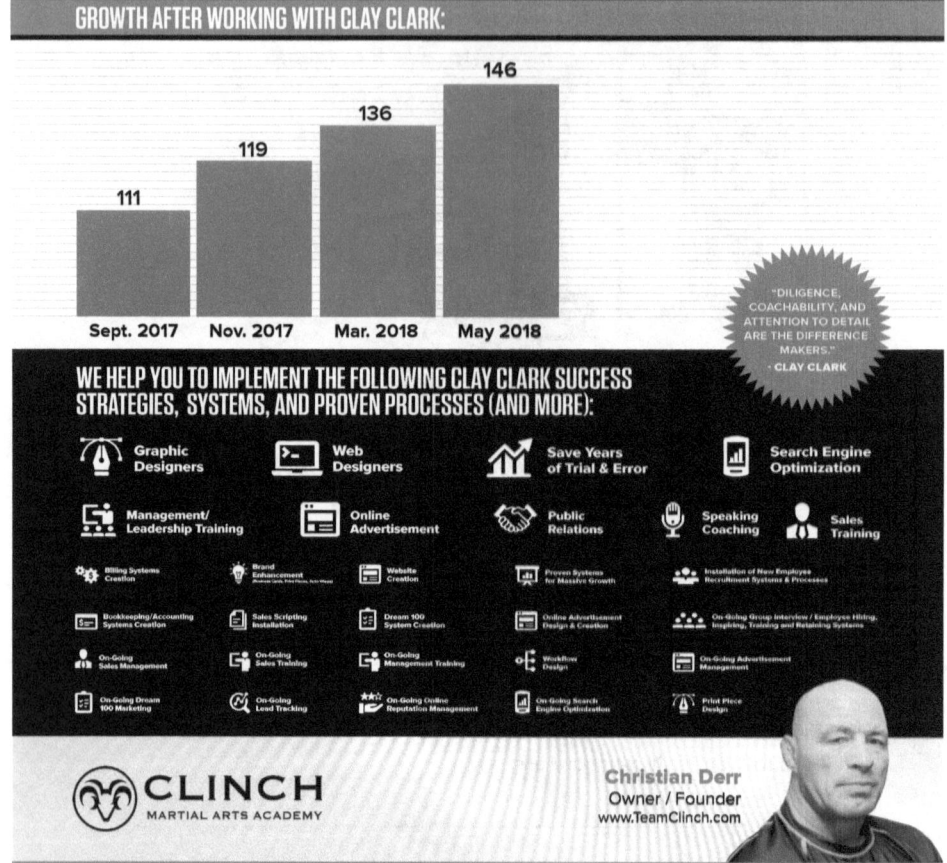

Chapter 19

6 SUPER MOVES TO SELL MORE TO EXISTING AND PREVIOUS CUSTOMERS

Super Move #1: Add the Adroll Retargeting Pixel to Your Website

Adroll is a company founded in San Francisco in 2007 by Adam Berke, Peter Krivkovich and Valentino Volonghi. They designed a product that allows you to create online ads that will follow previous visitors of your website around the Internet to other websites they visit. This technology allows your company to achieve the almighty "TOA" (top of mind awareness) that you need to keep your products and services in the minds of the previous visitors to your website.

For an in depth and specific video training on how to install the Adroll Retargeting Pixel on your website, visit: www.ThriveTimeShow.com/TreasureTrove

Super Move #2: Implement the WUPHF

In the seventh season and 135th episode of the American comedy TV series, The Office, the character known as Ryan convinces Michael, Stanley, Darryl, and Pam to fund his new startup called www.WUPHF.com. His technology was supposed to allow users to reach their ideal and likely buyers by sending them a call, fax, voice mail, Facebook message, and a text all at the same time.

Although WUPHF technology does not actually exist, I would schedule a monthly or quarterly time to text, e-mail, call, mass mail, and send a voice mail to all of your previous and current customers. In effect, WUPHF them.

1. The best programs for texting your current and former customers are either ZipWhip.com or Twilio.com.

a. For training on how to set up ZipWhip.com to work for you and your business, watch this training at www.ThriveTimeShow.com/TreasureTrove

b. For training on how to set up Twilio to work for your business, visit: www.ThriveTimeShow.com/TreasureTrove

2. Some of the best programs for mass e-mailing your current and former customers are MailChimp.com or ConstantContact.com.

3. To learn about the best way to call your former and existing customers to let them know about the services and solutions you and your company can offer them, I highly recommend that you attend an in-person ThriveTimeShow workshop.

4. There are many high quality mass-mailing companies around the country that we have worked with over the years to handle the bulk-mailing needs of my clients and my own businesses. I have had the most success over the years with the folks at The UPS Store and a small bulk mailing service called Flanagin's Bulk Mail Service (www.MyBulkMail.com).

5. The best program to simultaneously send all of your current and former customers a voice mail is www.SlyBroadcast.com.

Super Move #3: Create an Intentional and Scripted Referral Generating System

Most established business owners of small to medium-sized businesses tell me that most of their business comes from word-of-mouth referrals, which is a good thing. However, the word-of-mouth referrals they're describing depend solely on the customer touting the business, without any prompting from the business owner. Basically, these business owners are putting the health of their referral system into the hands of someone with no stake in their company.

To take back control of your referral system and make word-of-mouth consistently work for you, you must be the catalyst driving the referrals that come from your existing customers.

To help you install a specific system that has been proven to work, we have created a step-by-step training on How to Generate Referrals in a Systemic Way Without Irritating Your Loyal Former Customers. Watch this training at: www.ThriveTimeShow.com/TreasureTrove

Super Move #4: The Resuscitation of Your Customer Nation

If you've been in business for years and you've focused on doing business the right way by adding value to your former customers, then I would highly recommend creating a systemic previous customer reactivation game plan. This involves mailing, calling, texting, emailing and voice mailing your former customers to invite them to check out the 2.0 version of your business. Don't get overwhelmed at the thought of doing this. To reactivate your previous customer database, you only need to take 10 quick and simple steps:

1. Compile a database of your former customers.

2. Detail the reasons why you are reaching out to your former customers and what is in it for them. Why should your customer want to do business with you now when they decided to stop using you in the past? What has changed?

3. Design the reactivation request. You want to first reestablish rapport with your former customers and then you want to make sure that your call to action is very clear. Are you inviting them to an open house? Are you inviting them to take advantage of a new special?

4.   Design a bulk mailer that you will physically mail to your former customers.

5.   Create a call script for the calls your team will make to your former customers.

6.   Create a mass text for the text message your team will send out to your former customers.

7.   Create a mass email for the emails your team will send out to your former customers.

8.   Design a voicemail that you will send out to all of your former customers.

9.   Block out the time needed to execute this game plan.

10. After you have executed the game plan, make sure that you measure the effectiveness of this campaign and make adjustments so the next campaign will be even more effective.

Super Move #5: Wow and Retain Your Existing Customers by Focusing on Increasing Your Net Promoter Score

Although it never feels good, over the long haul it is very normal and healthy to see a few customers leave you as they find a better fit with your competitor (whose business you hope implodes). However, it is critical that you focus on keeping your client attrition to an absolute minimum because the costs associated with getting a new customer are dramatically higher than the costs associated with keeping an existing customer. Think about all the work and that costs that you and your team have to put into marketing to, attracting, wooing, and selling every new customer. Trust me on this, it's much cheaper to wow and keep existing customers happy than it is to attract new ones.

"Be miserable. Or motivate yourself. Whatever has to be done, it's always your choice."

-Wayne Dyer

(Bestselling author of *Your Erroneous Zones*, **which sold over 35 million copies)**

Mystic Statistic:

Attracting new customers will cost your company five times more than keeping an existing customer.

Alex Lawrence, "Five Customer Retention Tips for Entrepreneurs," Forbes, November 1, 2012. http://www.forbes.com/sites/alexlawrence/2012/11/01/five-customer-retention-tips-for-entrepreneurs/#7c1af4b817b0

Unless your business is a funeral home, a wedding entertainment service (like the business I originally founded, www.DJConnection.com), or a business that is completely focused on the "buy from us once" business model, it is very important for you to schedule three hours per month to analyze how effectively your business retains new customers. After you have completed this analysis, you will then want to look at your workflow map (the diagram of your entire service and product delivery process) to determine how you can systematically improve your systems to retain a higher number of your ideal and likely buyers. Since it's important to know what you are going to need to measure before you begin, here is the list.

» On a scale of 1 to 10 with 10 being the highest, how likely is the customer to refer another client to your business? _____

» If the customer does not a give you a 9 or 10 rating as it relates to their likelihood of referring others to your business, ask them why. _____

» How many months does the average client stay with your service?_____

» How many customers come back and buy from you two times, three times and beyond? _____

"The service-profit chain establishes relationships between profitability, customer loyalty, and employee satisfaction, loyalty, and productivity. The links in the chain (which should be regarded as propositions) are as follows: Profit and growth are stimulated primarily by customer loyalty. Loyalty is a direct result of customer satisfaction. Satisfaction is largely influenced by the value of services provided to customers. Value is created by satisfied, loyal, and productive employees. Employee satisfaction, in turn, results primarily from high-quality support services and policies that enable employees to deliver results to customers."

-James L Heskett, Thomas O. Jones, Gary W. Loveman, W. Earl Sasser, Jr. and Leonard A. Schlesinger

("Putting the Service-Profit Chain to Work" – Harvard Business Review – July-August 2008 Issue)

» How many referrals does the average customer send to your business?

» A Harvard Business School professor by the name of Frederick F. Reichheld developed a system called the Net Promoter Score, which many top business owners believe is truly the "one number you need to grow." Reichheld states:

"Loyalty is the willingness of someone—a customer, an employee, a friend—to make an investment or personal sacrifice in order to strengthen a relationship. For a customer, that can mean sticking with a supplier who treats him well and gives him good value in the long term even if the supplier does not offer the best price in a particular transaction. Consequently, customer loyalty is about much more than repeat purchases... True loyalty clearly affects profitability. While regular customers aren't always profitable, their choice to stick with a product or service typically reduces a company's customer acquisition costs. Loyalty also drives top-line growth."

- James L Heskett, Thomas O. Jones, Gary W. Loveman, W. Earl Sasser, Jr. and Leonard A. Schlesinger, "Putting the Service-Profit Chain to Work" – Harvard Business Review – July-August 2008 Issue

» Survey your customer on a scale of 1 to 10, with 10 being the highest, "How likely are you to refer a friend or family member to our business?"

» All responders who come back with a 9 or 10 are "promoters."

» All responders who come back with a 7 or 8 are neutral.

» All responders who come back with 1 through 6 are "detractors."

» Calculate the percentage of "promoters"

» Calculate the percentage of "detractors"

» % Of "promoters" minus % of "detractors" equals Net Promoter Score

Customer Wow Systems

My friend, don't get overwhelmed with this concept of retaining and wowing your customers. To begin wowing your customers now, you simply must begin implementing the following proven quality control systems:

1. **Hire mystery shoppers.** Pay people who are ideal and likely buyers to act as customers and make sure that the rest of your team is completely clueless about their involvement in the mystery shopper program. Ask these mystery shoppers to provide you with the brutally honest feedback that you need. How long did they have to wait on hold? How many days did they have to wait for a returned call? Was the service or product delivered on time? Was the pricing transparent and honest? How does your website stack up against the competition? Make a list of 10 questions that you want your mystery shoppers to answer each time that they shop your business and BOOM, you are off to the races!

2. **Survey your existing customers.** Make sure that you ask your ideal and likely buyers on a scale of 1 to 10 with 10 being the highest, how likely they are to refer another client to your business. If the customer does not give you a 9 or 10 rating, ask them why they didn't. Ask them to be candid in their reply.

3. **Install a merit-based pay system.** When you pay people based on the quality of results they generate and not just based upon the number of hours they work, your entire culture will begin to change. Top companies such as Southwest Airlines, UPS, QuikTrip, and Starbucks have installed merit-based pay programs within their cultures to hold people accountable. What is the reward for members of your staff who successfully do their work and complete their daily tasks and checklists? What is the penalty for members of your staff who choose not to do their work and complete their daily tasks on time? How do you know who is doing their work correctly and who is not?

4. **Install a wow moment into the workflow design of your company.** Although this may sound difficult to do, it is really not. Once I discovered the importance of this, I began implementing this wow moment into the workflow of every business that will allow me to. Let me give you an example. Years ago, I managed the cold calling campaigns for several universities to help them bring in donations from alumni. Working with the athletic departments of a couple of these schools, we were able to send surprise gifts of t-shirts, sweatshirts, and various pieces of athletic apparel to donors who chose to donate more than $150. We donated items that were currently in stock in the athletic department so there was no additional outlay of cash, but as the gifts began arriving to the homes of our unsuspecting donors, the "thank you calls" began flooding in to the university. People who had already donated $150 to the school were now creating a "positive buzz" by telling other alumni about how nice their unexpected gift was and about how professional our team was. This created a very positive word-of-mouth buzz and it only cost us the shipping and handling

involved in sending out the unsold inventory that the school truly wasn't sure what to do with any way.

At the Elephant in the Room, we offer each man who comes in for a haircut a complimentary beverage or adult beverage of their choice and it never fails to wow the unsuspecting customer. This simple act of providing a complimentary beverage always creates positive word of mouth and more referrals from our ideal and likely buyers to other ideal and likely buyers. Southwest Airlines has become legendary for encouraging their flight attendants to have fun with passengers as they make their federally-mandated in flight safety announcements. My friend, it should not cost you boatloads of money to implement a wow moment into your workflow design, but it will cost you millions if you fail to do so.

> "The only path to profitable growth may lie in a company's ability to get its loyal customers to become, in effect, its marketing department."
>
>  *- James L Heskett,*
>
> *Thomas O. Jones, Gary W. Loveman, W. Earl Sasser, Jr. and Leonard A. Schlesinger,*
> ("Putting the Service-Profit Chain to Work" –Harvard Business Review – July-August 2008 Issue)

5.   **Install a rewards program for your customers.** We all know people who faithfully buy their coffee from Starbucks each morning using their rewards card because soon they will rack up enough points for a free treat. We all know of people (maybe it's you) who diligently and consistently only book flights on one airline using only one credit card to rack up as many points as possible, even when the logistics of doing so are tough, because they want to earn those points to take "that free trip to Hawaii." Top companies understand how effective rewards programs are at building customer loyalty, but most small and medium-sized businesses are so busy putting out the fires of the day that they miss this opportunity altogether.

For a powerful training video that you can use to show your staff How to Wow and Retain Your Existing Customers by Focusing on Increasing Your Net Promoter Score, visit: www.ThriveTimeShow.com/TreasureTrove

Super Move # 6 - Implement a Checklist-Driven Cross-Selling and Upselling Program ASAP

Years ago I had an opportunity to work with several struggling wedding facilities and in each case, implementing this Checklist-Driven Cross-Selling and Upselling Program saved the day. The best example of a company that has this down pat is Jiffy Lube. Every time I go in for my $19.99 Jiffy Lube oil service and leave with a $182.43 bill, I smile as I think of their mastery of this area even as I crying inside thinking about how they just upsold me nine times more services than I had expected to buy. Going into Jiffy Lube just creates a tornado of emotions for me. Here are the moves that work for Checklist-Driven Cross-Selling (it's beautiful):

1. Create a checklist of all the related products and services that your company can currently offer to your ideal and likely buyers.

2. Add all of the related products and services that your company could potentially provide to your ideal and likely buyers.

3. Create a list of questions that you want to ask every time you meet with a customer to introduce the additional products and services you can provide. Phrase the questions in such a way that you're offering solutions but not in a high-pressure way.

Again, Jiffy Lube offers a perfect example of this. The dude at Jiffy Lube always says, *"Now Mr. Clark, the manufacturer recommends that you replace your air filter about every x number of miles and it appears to be about time. Did you*

want me to take care of that today or did you want me to leave it until next time? Mr. Clark, it looks as though your wiper blades are a little worn. Did you want to go ahead and replace those or are you good to go? Mr. Clark, your manufacturer recommends that you replace your transmission fluid every x number of miles and it looks as though it's time to replace that fluid. Did you want me to handle that for you today or did you want to wait until next time?"

> "For business-to-consumer companies, you need to have a constant touch system to keep the relationship strong."
>
>  **-Chet Holmes**
> (Bestselling author and the former business partner of Warren Buffet's business partner, Charlie Munger)

This system is honestly so good, it gets me excited even as I write about it. People joke about McDonald's saying that if you don't get your degree you are going to spend your day saying, "Do you want me to super-size that for you?" Actually, that kind of checklist-driven cross-selling and upselling program has produced billions of additional dollars of revenue for McDonald's. It blows my mind.

Here are some ideas to stimulate your brain and the creation of your cross-selling system.

» What are some services and products that you could package together in a premium package for your clients who choose to upgrade?

» What are additional problems and needs that your customer has that your products and services satisfy? I once went to a restaurant in Tampa, Florida, after a speaking event. The owner of that restaurant shared with me that the introduction of jet ski upgrades, tiki torch upgrades, live music upgrades, beach fire pit upgrades, and premium ocean view upgrades (on the roof of his building) not only saved his business, but helped his business thrive.

» What services and products can you begin offering your clients that will take their experience to the next level?

» If the top 5% of your ideal and likely buyers had no pricing concerns or barriers, what products and services could you offer them that would provide them with the elite level of service they would gladly pay for? I once worked with a female sports coach who was charging the average athlete a membership fee of $150 per person for group sports training. Before we talked, she had approximately 140 students. After we talked, she felt as though about eight of the parents would be willing to pay $1,750 per month for more personalized training sessions and a one-on-one coaching experience. She was right. She signed up four parents the first week she offered the package and increased her profit from just over $7,000 per month to nearly $13,000 per month simply by offering a premium package that she believed 5% of her ideal and likely buyers were willing to pay for.

» What trusted service providers could you work with to establish a pay-for-play referral program? For example, on Southwest.com, you and I can buy airplane tickets, rent a car, and book a hotel. Last time I checked, Southwest Airlines had not acquired 50 hotel chains and five national car rental companies, yet they still offer these services on their website. How? Southwest Airlines has entered into win-win relationships with service providers that offer related services and products Southwest's ideal and likely buyers need. Are you tracking with me? I'm getting myself pumped up here.

» What is the perfect amount of time after the initial purchase to introduce the additional products and services that your company provides? Is it at the time of the initial purchase? Is it two months after the purchase? I once worked with a mortgage company and after doing my research, I asked the owner if his experience confirmed the statistic that the average American family refinances their home or moves every three years. He told me that based on his experience, this was true. We created a series of letters that we mailed out to his former customers at six-month intervals and it worked like magic. This lending company that formerly did approximately 18 deals per month was now doing nearly 40 deals per month as a result of this little magic move.

» What is your current customer repeat buying cycle? How often do your customers rebuy and how can you stay in their minds to convince them to buy more often? I once worked with a family recreation and skating facility and we were able to increase the number of skaters coming to this facility by nearly 100 people per week by simply installing a membership model and a drip-marketing campaign (e-mail, text, and calling) to let people know about our upcoming events.

"About 3 percent of potential buyers at any given time are buying now. 7 percent of the population is open to the idea of buying. The remaining 90 percent fall into one of three equal categories. The top third are "not thinking about it." The next third are "think they're not interested."

-*Chet Holmes*
(Author of the best-selling book, the Ultimate Sales Machine)

Chapter 20

Converting Leads into Actual Sales 101

When working with a business to help them grow quickly, I often find that their marketing team is already doing a great job, but their sales team is just brutal when it comes to closing deals (or vice versa). At the end of the day, it's the marketing team's job to produce leads and it's the sales team's job to close deals. These two groups must both be functioning at full capacity.

It doesn't matter what kind of business model you have, your sales team must close deals. Your company needs to have a system in place that everyone can trust to produce consistent paying deals. I'll teach you the specific mechanics of how to build this system, but I want to first intensely look at the system that you already have in place. Currently, you may have a system that only resides inside your brain, but if it works, let's analyze it.

THE SALES SYSTEM ANALYSIS

On a scale of 1 to 10 with 10 being the highest, I want you to rate yourself on the following statements:

—— You have a concise way of explaining your product and service to your ideal and likely buyers.

—— You have sales copy in place that emotionally connects with your ideal and likely buyers, supplying them with verifiable facts that support your claim that your company makes regarding your products and services.

—— You have a step-by-step and well-defined sales system in place.

—— You have a step-by-step and well-defined sales system that is written out and visual.

—— You are not the only salesperson in your business capable of closing deals.

—— You do not close more than 10% of your company's deals yourself.

"I would rather earn 1% on hundreds of people's efforts than 100% of my own work."

-Clay Clark

· ·

 Fun Fact:
At the time of John D. Rockefeller's death he was worth $1.4 billion dollars. Adjusted for inflation today, he would have been worth $ 23,358,891,429.51. The devaluation of your currency since President Richard Nixon's alarmingly stupid decision to move America off the gold standard in 1971 can be calculated by visiting the website www.WestEgg.com or by visiting www.BLS.gov.

· ·

— You have a scalable system in place that allows you to properly follow-up with all the inbound leads you are currently receiving.

— You have a sales system that is not trapped inside the brain of your top sales person only.

— You accurately track where all inbound leads come from.

— You have sales scripting in place for all inbound leads.

— You have sales scripting in place for all outbound leads.

— You have a written and scalable face-to-face sales presentation system.

— You have a systematic cross-selling and upselling checklist in place that you use every time.

— You have standardized all sales contracts and agreements.

— You have standardized sales brochures in place.

— You have standardized sales one-sheets in place.

— You have equipped your team with industry statistics, customer case studies, testimonies, provable facts and verifiable data to support the claims they are making on behalf of the company.

— You have recorded video testimonials available to show to your ideal and likely buyers.

— You have created a pricing sheet that clearly shows the prices, price ranges and pricing boundaries that your sales people must quote within.

— You have scheduled weekly ongoing sales training for your sales team that actually takes place and is effective.

— You record your calls for quality assurance.

— You have a linear diagram of your sales process that you can easily refine over time.

— You are aware of your conversion rate.

— You are aware of your cost per lead.

— You are aware of your cost per paid customer.

— You know how many deals each sales representative needs to generate each month to pay for herself.

— You know how many deals you need to close per month to achieve your financial goals.

— You know how many deals you need to close per month to break even and pay all the bills.

— You have a solid lead organization system in place for sorting and accurately keeping track of your hot leads, your cold leads, your upcoming appointments and your missed appointments.

— You have a well-organized follow-up system in place for systematically converting the ideal and likely buyers of the future who are currently in your pipeline.

— You have a solid e-mail drip-marketing campaign in place that will be sent to your ideal and likely buyers during the months and weeks after their contact with you.

To take this assessment online, visit: www.ThriveTimeShow.com/TreasureTrove.

"The only essential thing is growth. Everything else we associate with startups follows from growth."

- Gabriel Weinberg

(Bestselling author of Traction: A Startup Guide to Getting Customers)

There are a total of 310 points that you could have scored on the evaluation above. If your score was less than 275, YOU REALLY NEED TO FOCUS ON IMPROVING YOUR SALES SYSTEM as quickly as possible. Massive sales can cure a lot of problems and remove massive amounts of financial stress from your entire team. Then you can come back and knock out creating the rest of the systems with a large bank account and the confidence that comes with it.

Deep Thoughts

"If you cant sell, your business will fail regardless of how passionate you are about your vision, purpose, product, or service."

-Clay Clark

(Founder of Thrive15.com and former U.S. Small Business Administration Entrepreneur of the Year)

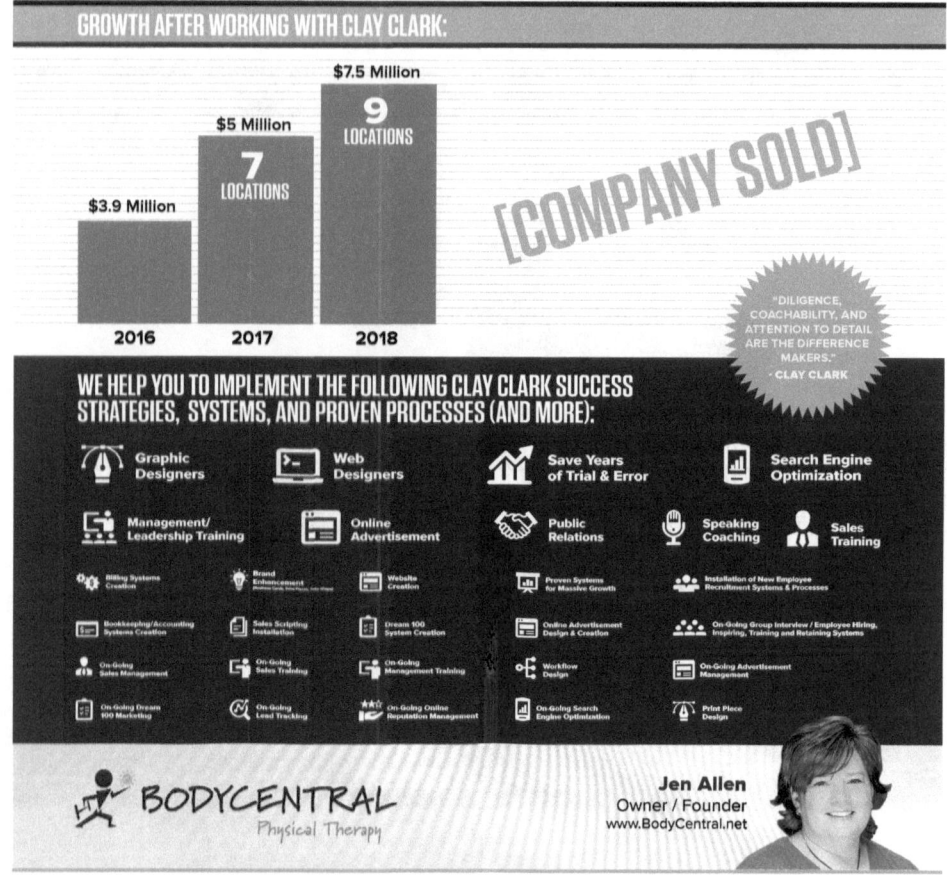

Chapter 21

The 7 Ninja Moves to Building an Effective Sales System Now

Unless you were drunk or lying when you took the Sales System Analysis, you are probably slightly overwhelmed or at least dissatisfied with your overall score. Don't stress out about this, as it's very hard to fix a problem that you did not even know existed. However, now that you do know of your company's weaknesses, you must go through the painstaking process of actually fixing these problems or "opportunities for growth," as the optimist would put it. DON'T FREAK OUT. We'll get it done together.

The starting point where we need to focus is on converting ideal and likely buyers who are prospects into actual paying customers and closed deals. Here is the super plan to get this done.

1. You must draw out your current sales system process and workflow on a white board. You might be asking, "Why the heck do I need to buy a white board? Can't I just use an APP on my phone?" The answer is NO. This system must be SUPER VISUAL.

2. Make each part of your sales system into a square that connects to another square moving from left to right. Chinese Thrivers, calm down about the left to right thing. I don't speak Mandarin yet, but if you keep building those man-made islands, maybe we'll all eventually be speaking Mandarin.

3. Create an area on the whiteboard to track each part (square) of your sales workflow process. The goal here is to figure out where in the sales workflow process your potential deals are blowing up. Are they blowing up when you first speak to the ideal and likely buyer? Are they blowing up when those buyers come for their appointment? Are they blowing up when you go for the close? Where are your potential deals blowing up?

. . . .

Ample Example:

Just this year I worked with a business in the fitness space who had a huge amount of website traffic. In fact, this owner had almost 15 inbound leads flooding into his e-mail inbox each week and approximately 20 inbound sales calls from ideal and likely buyers who were trying to schedule their first consultation and their free 2-week trial period.

After we created the detailed workflow chart for his business, it was quickly discovered that he was having no problem generating leads. He also was having no problem converting leads once they came out for their free 2-week trial. Looking at the workflow sales process on the board, it became clear that we had a people problem and not a system problem. We discovered that the team member who was supposed to be answering all inbound calls and responding to all inquiries within 12 hours had actually put his phone on silent permanently and had set up some ridiculous automated call routing system. This person was only responding to inbound leads via e-mail.

Once we fired this slug and replaced him with a hungry lady who really valued the job, our sales numbers grew exponentially. The company went from having three conversions per week to having nearly 11 per week. The profound levels of "jackassery" (my word, but feel free to use it) that were impacting our sales system would have never been discovered if we had not looked at the system from a very linear and non-emotional perspective.

. . . .

4. Focus on each area of your sales process system one at a time. Don't attempt to fix the entire system in one night. Just look for the biggest limiting factor then fix it, dealing with the factors one at a time.

. . . .

Ample Example:

I once worked with a bakery and discovered that the business owner was getting 15+ appointments per week from her website, inbound leads and referrals, yet her gross revenue was less than $6,000 per week. After examining her entire workflow, I discovered that the owner's closing percentage was AWFUL. This person was only closing 1 out of 15 set appointments. By simply moving her into a position where she could thrive (making the cakes) and moving a honey-badger (deal closing focused person) into the position of sales, the bakery was able to close nearly 7 deals per week at nearly $1,200 per wedding cake, on top of the additional $6,000 per week that they were already generating. Never underestimate the likelihood of having a human problem. I have found that once you build the proper systems, 9 times out of 10 you simply have non-compliant people messing up the systems.

. . . .

"RIGHT PERSON, WRONG SEAT...This person has been promoted to a seat that is too big, has outgrown a seat that is too small...Generally, this person is where he or she is because he or she has been around a long time, you like him or her, and he or she is a great addition to the team. Until now."

-Gino Wickman
(Bestselling author of *Traction: Get a Grip on Your Business*)

5. Don't move on until you have fixed the problem. Having worked with thousands of entrepreneurs, I have found that many people struggle with focusing on a problem until it is solved and therefore, nothing ever truly gets done. Everything within the business just gets half-done. Focus on the problem with laser intensity until it is no longer a problem. Here are some examples of areas possibly needing a fix

    a. **Fix your sales presentation materials.** You might have third world marketing materials that simply don't inspire confidence in the minds of your ideal and likely buyers.

    b. **Fix your sales presentation.** You might have great marketing materials, but your sales presentation or the person giving the sales presentation might need to change.

    c. **Fix your scripting.** You might have inbound leads coming in all day, but your inbound sales script might be incredibly awful and it might repel ideal and likely buyers.

    d. **Fix your people.** You might have great systems but awful people. Small and medium-sized businesses tend to hold on to bad hires because they operate with a scarcity mentality, which is fueled by the fact that they invest nearly zero time or money into the ongoing recruitment of honest and diligent people.

    e. **Fix your product or service videos.** Your demonstration videos might be awful and in most cases, they are. Recently I sat with a man who has an absolutely brilliant business idea, but his videos were beyond bad. I would have laughed if I didn't want to cry for him. He was doing his best, but he wasn't comparing his video quality to his competition and he wasn't aware of the options that exist for him to have a quality video made at a very affordable price point.

f.   **Fix your product or service photos.** You might have terrible photos that look like your mom took them because your mom actually did take the photos for you because she is a sweet lady. I used to use terrible photography in everything I did because I didn't know how to access the world of great, high-quality photography. Some of the early designs I used are almost comical in their appearance. However, when I consider that they were keeping me poor, it's just not funny.

g.   **Record your gold-standard sales presentation for your team to pattern themselves after.** It's very hard for people to do an excellent job at something if they do not know what an excellent job looks, sounds, or feels like.

· ·

 Ample Example:
Years ago, I went into a commercial paint supplier's call center in Texas and simply asked them who their top sales people were. Everyone agreed that in the call center of 30+ representatives, two people were just dominating in terms of the total amount of sales revenue they were able to bring in each month. We invested the time to record their over-the-phone sales presentations and we quickly discovered that these two women were doing almost the exact same sales presentation, yet it was 180-degrees different from the presentations the other sales representatives were delivering on a daily basis. We quickly created sales scripts that documented the systems, wording, and overall strategy these two successful reps were using, and we agreed to teach it to the two next most successful representatives. After teaching the next two sales representatives the sales moves, they began to nearly replicate the previously unattainable amounts of sales being generated by the top two ladies. This type of training is commonly referred to as "best-practice modeling" or "best-practice duplication."

· ·

The big idea that I want to make sure I am conveying here is that you need to focus on making one actionable improvement to your system at a time. Don't try to reinvent everything in one day. My friend, you must always keep in your mind that it is better to implement fewer ideas that you can actually execute that to try to implement a ton of ideas that never get done.

Fun Fact:
When Steve Jobs returned to take over Apple in 1997, the company was within 60 days of going bankrupt. During the last quarter of 1996, the company's sales had dropped by 30% and Microsoft was beating the heck out of them. In order to save the company, Steve had to get them focused on two major needle-moving activities. First, he needed to infuse the company with capital. He knew that Microsoft's co-founder Bill Gates needed to end the public perception (and reality) caused by the pending federal lawsuits that were threatening to break his company apart, that Microsoft had become a monopoly. Thus, Jobs went for and successfully secured a $150 million investment from Microsoft who could not actually say that they had invested in their own competitors. Second, he needed to get Apple focused on producing "insanely great" products instead of dozens of crappy products. He cut the number of products that Apple was focused on developing by 70%. MOVING FORWARD, JOBS FOCUSED ON THE CREATION OF ONLY FOUR PRODUCTS.

"Deciding what not to do is as important as deciding what to do. It's true for companies, and it's true for products."

 -Steve Jobs
(Co-founder of Apple and former CEO of Pixar)

"Equally important is what 'writing it down' symbolizes... the act implies a commitment, like a handshake, that something will be done. The supervisor, also having taken notes, can then follow up at the next one-on-one."

 -Andy Grove
(Founding team member and the former CEO of Intel)

6. Create a mini-sales system overhaul and delegate effectively. As discussed earlier, when you delegate effectively, you must clearly document what needs to be done, who needs to do it and when it needs to be done. If you do not follow-up it will not get done.

7. Anything that you assign must be tracked and reviewed on a weekly basis or you simply will not get things done. If you find yourself delegating to people who need to be followed up with daily to keep them on track to hit their weekly goals, make a note of it, attempt to coach them, and replace them if they cannot be coached.

"If you're wrong, you will die. But most companies don't die because they are wrong; most die because they don't commit themselves. They fritter away their valuable resources while attempting to make a decision. The greatest danger is in standing still."

-Andy Grove
(Founding team member and the former CEO of Intel)

GROWTH AFTER WORKING WITH CLAY CLARK:

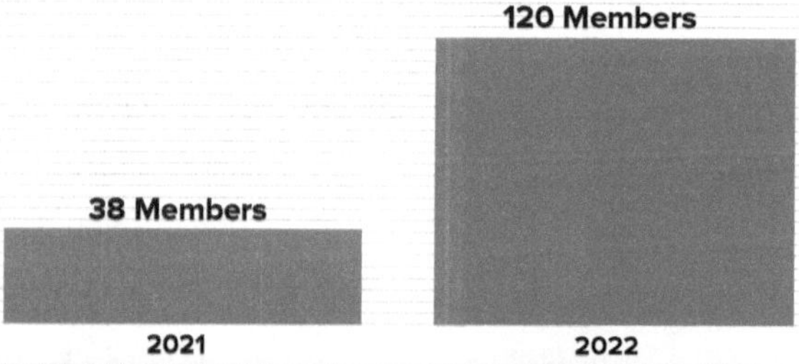

120 Members

38 Members

2021   2022

"DILIGENCE, COACHABILITY, AND ATTENTION TO DETAIL ARE THE DIFFERENCE MAKERS."
- CLAY CLARK

WE HELP YOU TO IMPLEMENT THE FOLLOWING CLAY CLARK SUCCESS STRATEGIES, SYSTEMS, AND PROVEN PROCESSES (AND MORE):

- Graphic Designers
- Web Designers
- Save Years of Trial & Error
- Search Engine Optimization
- Management/ Leadership Training
- Online Advertisement
- Public Relations
- Speaking Coaching
- Sales Training
- Billing Systems Creation
- Brand Enhancement
- Website Creation
- Proven Systems for Massive Growth
- Installation of New Employee Recruitment Systems & Processes
- Bookkeeping/Accounting Systems Creation
- Sales Scripting Installation
- Dream 100 System Creation
- Online Advertisement Design & Creation
- On-Going Group Interview / Employee Hiring, Inspiring, Training and Retaining Systems
- On-Going Sales Management
- On-Going Sales Training
- On-Going Management Training
- Workflow Design
- On-Going Advertisement Management
- On-Going Dream 100 Marketing
- On-Going Lead Tracking
- On-Going Online Reputation Management
- On-Going Search Engine Optimization
- Print Piece Design

Molly & Ronald Frazier
Owner / Founder
www.SchoolOfRespect.com

"Action is the real measure of intelligence."

-*Napoleon Hill*
(Best-selling author of *Think & Grow Rich* and the former apprentice of Andrew Carnegie)

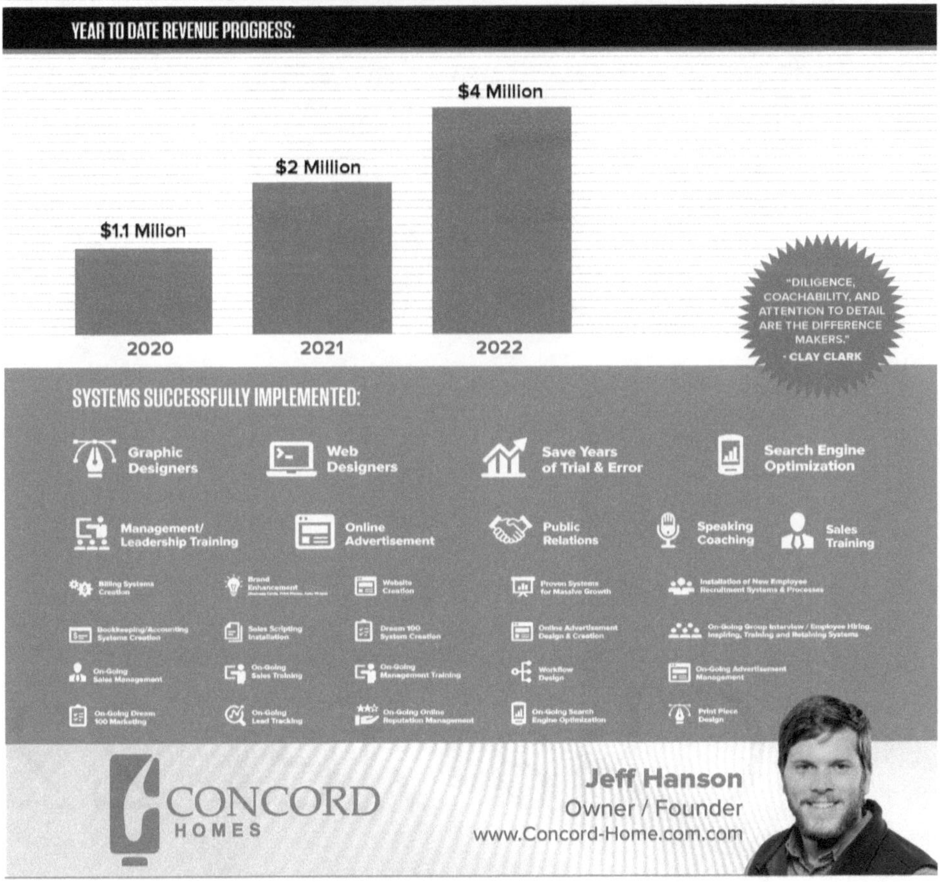

YEAR TO DATE REVENUE PROGRESS:

$4 Million

$2 Million

$1.1 Million

| 2020 | 2021 | 2022 |

"DILIGENCE, COACHABILITY, AND ATTENTION TO DETAIL ARE THE DIFFERENCE MAKERS."
- CLAY CLARK

SYSTEMS SUCCESSFULLY IMPLEMENTED:

- Graphic Designers
- Web Designers
- Save Years of Trial & Error
- Search Engine Optimization
- Management/ Leadership Training
- Online Advertisement
- Public Relations
- Speaking Coaching
- Sales Training
- Billing Systems Creation
- Brand Enhancement
- Website Creation
- Proven Systems for Massive Growth
- Installation of New Employee Recruitment Systems & Processes
- Bookkeeping/Accounting Systems Creation
- Sales Scripting Installation
- Dream 100 System Creation
- Online Advertisement Design & Creation
- On-Going Group Interview / Employee Hiring, Inspiring, Training and Retaining Systems
- On-Going Sales Management
- On-Going Sales Training
- On-Going Management Training
- Workflow Design
- On-Going Advertisement Management
- On-Going Dream 100 Marketing
- On-Going Lead Tracking
- On-Going Online Reputation Management
- On-Going Search Engine Optimization
- Print Piece Design

CONCORD HOMES

Jeff Hanson
Owner / Founder
www.Concord-Home.com.com

Chapter 22

Notable Quotable

"If you learn a profession well and work hard, your future is secure and you will inevitably rise to the top, drive a fast car, and find beautiful people of the opposite sex pursuing you relentlessly. Like so many romantic promises, this is an illusion. What your parents and professors don't tell you is that the closer you get to the top, the better you must know how to sell because everyone at the top sells better. If you are going to the top of your profession you must sell well, too."

-Jerry Vass
(Author of *Soft Selling in a Hard World*)

WHAT SOLUTION WILL YOU PROVIDE THE WORLD IN EXCHANGE FOR THE MONEY YOU SEEK?

1. Invest the time needed to find and solve a problem that consumers have and are willing to pay for.

2. Invest as much time as needed until you find an existing product or service that you could compete within the marketplace in a differentiated way.

What Problems Can You Solve?

_____

_____

_____

_____

_____

_____

With What Product or Service Can You Compete?

_____

_____

_____

_____

_____

_____

Chapter 23

4 Game Changing Moves to Scale Your Ability to Deliver and Produce the Products and Services Desired by Your Ideal and Likely Buyers

As discussed earlier, the Daily Operations Team is responsible for producing and delivering the products and services that your company sells to your ideal and likely buyers. This team's job is to deliver what you committed to when you took payment from the customer. They're in charge of the overall administrative and back-office aspects of your company.

I'm going to teach you 4 GAME CHANGING MOVES that will help you consistently deliver an insanely high amount of value to your ideal and likely buyers as you scale your business.

First, I'm going to provide you with the proven game plan to help you build out your critical business processes and systems. I call these "Guru Systems" because I cannot legally refer to them as "Yoda Systems" without paying George Lucas.

 Fun Fact:
After selling the Star Wars franchise to Disney, George Lucas' net worth stood at approximately $5.1 billion. I'm sure he's spent it all on Yoda figurines since then.

Natalie Robehmed, "Never Invest In A Movie, Says Billionaire Director George Lucas," Forbes, April 17, 2015. http://www.forbes.com/sites/natalierobehmed/2015/04/17/never-invest-in-a-movie-says-george-lucas/#7aa0ab4e459f

Second, I'm going to teach you something that I am passionate about on almost a spiritual level and that is **"Universal File Nomenclature."** This is the system you will use to properly name files so that people quit asking you where something is saved. This is especially important as your business scales and the number of customers and team members you interact with increases exponentially.

Third, I'm going to teach about the horrible blame-game-causing-problem I see in most businesses called the "Fumbled Handoff." Essentially, this is the part of the business where one of your team members blames the other for not completing a project while your customer is made to suffer. Improving the way projects are delegated and handed off will eliminate this problem almost entirely.

Fourth, I'm going to teach you about the awful wealth destroying mental disorder that has taken over the minds of at least 49% of our population called, *"Work-Related Jackassery – The Interactive I-Did-Not-Know-I-Forgot-Or-Was-Not-Properly-Trained-Responsibility-Repelling-Game."*

Let's start with *"Guru Systems."*

Guru Systems

I don't care how motivated you are or how many times you have attended a Tony Robbins coal-walking seminar. Your ability to grow your business exponentially is directly related to your business' capacity to quickly produce duplicable systems.

When you work as hard as you do, you must be able to create replicable systems that you then outline and formalize to

> "An organization's ability to learn, and translate that learning into action rapidly, is the ultimate competitive advantage."

> **-Jack Welch**
> (The former CEO of GE who completely reinvigorated the company and grew it exponentially during his tenure)

reproduce the desired result over and over again. When you do this properly, you will end up with the following items for each of the company's core competencies:

1. Defined outcomes and deliverables

2. Defined workflow and step-by-step processes

3. The checklists, tools, or systems that allow you to actually delegate the completion of the process

4. The checklists, tools, or systems that allow you to measure the quality control aspects of the process

5. A training system to teach the process once it has been properly documented

6. A training video or system that allows you to teach 15 new people per day the systems without an investment of your personal time to teach each person

7. A quiz based upon the training video or system that you have produced that helps you see what the members of your team are or are not learning from your training videos

I realize that for many of the clients I have worked with over the years, this is the part of the discussion where their brain begins to melt and they fall into a boredom-induced coma. However, this is where the magic happens. Just imagine what you would do with your day if you had consistent revenue coming in and you had all the time freedom in the world. If that were the case, what would you be doing? I enjoy running around my backyard chasing my wife, harassing my five kids, feeding ducks, feeding the Great Pyrenees, watching the New England Patriots, reading business case studies of successful companies, writing books like this, and having marital sex.

Alright, with SEX on our minds, let's get to work. I need you to grab that white board yet again. If you are telling me that you can't afford the white board, then sell some crap on Craigslist and cancel your premium TV subscription because we have to get this done.

Step 1 – Grab that dry erase marker and starting writing on the far right side of the board, the Defined Outcomes and Deliverables you are trying to consistently produce and achieve.

Step 2 – Write out all the step-by-step processes needed to create and deliver the core products and services that your company sells to your ideal and likely buyers.

Step 3 – Write out the checklists, tools, or systems that you would need to have in place to fully delegate this system to an honest and diligent person who has never done this task before.

Step 4 – Write out the checklists, tools, and systems that you would need to have in place to fully delegate to a manager who was honest and diligent the quality control aspects of verifying that the systems were executed correctly. How would they know if the products and services were being delivered properly?

Step 5 – Take a picture of the system you have just drawn up on the board and have it turned into a PDF graphic that you can use to train people.

Step 6 – Create a training video of you or a team member who is excellent at performing the task being systematized for use in scaling the training of your staff without you personally having to participate in all trainings moving forward.

> "In God we trust; all others must bring data."
>
> "You can expect what you inspect."
>
> **-W. Edwards Deming**
> (Legendary management expert and bestselling author)

Step 7 – Create a quiz that corresponds with the training video you have produced to verify that learning has taken place. If you trust that your people are watching your videos but do not go the extra mile to verify that they are, you will get frustrated when you discover that WHATEVER YOU INSPECT IS WHAT YOU CAN EXPECT.

After you have built this system (or any system, for that matter), you must invest the time to reflect upon the system you have built and constantly ask yourself:

1. What results are you producing that just do not matter?

2. What results are you producing that really matter?

3. What results are you promising that you are not delivering?

4. What results are your customers asking for that you currently cannot produce or deliver due to your current pipeline?

5. Can you reduce the number of steps required to produce the results that your ideal and likely buyers want?

6. How can you dramatically decrease the number of people needed and yet still consistently deliver high-quality results?

7. How can you dramatically decrease the number of people needed but still improve the results you are currently producing?

8. Can you design or automate a more streamlined process?

9. How can you reduce the costs associated with producing the desired result without decreasing the quality of the product?

10. What easy-to-implement enhancements can you employ to improve the quality of the output you are consistently producing?

11. Would slightly increasing the costs of the products and services you deliver dramatically increase their value or perceived value in the eyes of your customers?

12. How can you increase the value of the products and services you produce to

allow you to charge dramatically more for what you deliver?

13. How can you increase the perceived value of the products and services that you produce by teaming up with a celebrity, improving the quality of the branding, etc.?

. . . .

Fun Fact:

The Armand de Brignac brand of champagne used to be sold in the same $60 price range as Antique Gold. However, since Jay-Z began to endorse the champagne during his music video, "Show Me What You Got," the brand has now increased its retail price to $300 per bottle simply by gaining that endorsement. The story gets a little complicated,but Jay-Z essentially claimed to have no financial involvement in the company until he purchased a controlling interest of the brand in 2014. It was reported by Billboard.com that "Jay-Z had a favorite champagne brand, so he bought it."

Marc Schneider, "Jay Z Had a Favorite Champagne Brand, So He Bought It," Billboard, November 6, 2014. http://www.billboard.com/articles/business/6311831/jay-z-buys-armand-de-brignac-champagne-ace-spades-brand

. . . .

14. Who is your top competitor on the planet who has produced a related system or process that you can study and ultimately reverse engineer to help better your systems?

15. Are there any portions of your system that you could delegate to a reliable company who could frankly do what you do better and at a better price than you could do it?

. . . .

 Ample Example:

At ThriveTimeShow.com, we happily delegate out the transcription of our videos to two companies that do an incredible job when it comes to transcribing content.

. . . .

16. How could you decrease the number of errors that are currently committed using your existing system?

17. How could you make your current system less prone to error?

18. What type of person should ideally be executing these systems?

19. Do you currently have the right people executing your systems?

> "Great vision without great people is irrelevant."
>
> *-Jim Collins*
> **(Bestselling author of *Good to Great* and *Built to Last*)**

After you have asked yourself these tough questions, it's time to get back to your white board and begin to adjust, tweak, remove, erase, and enhance aspects of your system until your system is better, more efficient, of greater value to your customers, less expensive, and more duplicable.

ACTION WITH A PASSION – At ThriveTimeShow.com, we offer powerful online training, in-person group workshops and one-on-one monthly coaching packages. Our entire focus is to help you take your income and your life to the next level, so do not hesitate to e-mail us at info@ThriveTimeShow.com to decide which option is the best for you to take your business to the next level.

REVENUE GROWTH AFTER WORKING WITH CLAY CLARK:

2015	2016	2017	2018	2019	2020	2021	2022
$24K	$161K	$331K	$450K	$611K	$739K	$1.1 Million	$1.8 Million

"DILIGENCE, COACHABILITY, AND ATTENTION TO DETAIL ARE THE DIFFERENCE MAKERS."
- CLAY CLARK

WE HELP YOU TO IMPLEMENT THE FOLLOWING CLAY CLARK SUCCESS STRATEGIES, SYSTEMS, AND PROVEN PROCESSES (AND MORE):

- Graphic Designers
- Web Designers
- Save Years of Trial & Error
- Search Engine Optimization
- Management/ Leadership Training
- Online Advertisement
- Public Relations
- Speaking Coaching
- Sales Training
- Billing Systems Creation
- Brand Enhancement
- Website Creation
- Proven Systems for Massive Growth
- Installation of New Employee Recruitment Systems & Processes
- Bookkeeping/Accounting Systems Creation
- Sales Scripting Installation
- Dream 100 System Creation
- Online Advertisement Design & Creation
- On-Going Group Interview / Employee Hiring, Inspiring, Training and Retaining Systems
- On-Going Sales Management
- On-Going Sales Training
- On-Going Management Training
- Workflow Design
- On-Going Advertisement Management
- On-Going Dream 100 Marketing
- On-Going Lead Tracking
- On-Going Online Reputation Management
- On-Going Search Engine Optimization
- Print Piece Design

White Glove Auto
STYLE. PROTECT. MAINTAIN.

Myron Kirkpatrick
Owner / Founder
www.WhiteGloveAutoTulsa.com

Chapter 24

Universal File Nomenclature

Alright, now it is time to talk about something that nobody wants to talk about because it is detailed. My friend, we are now going to talk about proper nomenclature or the proper naming of things. Almost nobody in the world gets this right and thus people run around confused, frustrated, unproductive, and not knowing how to properly save things or retrieve digital documents quickly. This is bad because like it or not, we're living in the digital age.

Here's a little something from that controversial book, the Bible:

• •

And the whole earth was of one language, and of one speech. 2 And it came to pass, as they journeyed from the east, that they found a plain in the land of Shinar; and they dwelt there. 3 And they said one to another, Go to, let us make brick, and burn them thoroughly. And they had brick for stone, and slime had they for morter. 4 And they said, Go to, let us build us a city and a tower, whose top may reach unto heaven; and let us make us a name, lest we be scattered abroad upon the face of the whole earth. 5 And the Lord came down to see the city and the tower, which the children of men builded. 6 And the Lord said, Behold, the people is one, and they have all one language; and this they begin to do: and now nothing will be restrained from them, which they have imagined to do. 7 Go to, let us go down, and there confound their language, that they may not understand one another's speech. 8 So the Lord scattered them abroad from thence upon the face of all the earth: and they left off to build the city. 9 Therefore is the name of it called Babel; because the Lord did there confound the language of all the earth: and from thence did the Lord scatter them abroad upon the face of all the earth.

-Genesis 11:1-9
The Bible (King James Version)

• •

For those of you who did not appreciate me quoting the Bible to demonstrate the importance of sharing a common organization and communication system within your team, I have put together some quotes from other notable people not referenced in the Bible.

"For every minute spent organizing, an hour is earned."

-Benjamin Franklin

(One of the founding fathers of the United States, a leading author, a printer, a politician, a postmaster, a scientist, an entrepreneur and the diplomat who helped America secure the funding from France that ultimately helped the colonists score a win in the Revolutionary War and gain their independence from the British Empire. A man who had to stay fairly organized.)

• •

"Simplicity is the ultimate sophistication."

-Leonardo DaVinci

(An inventor, painter, sculptor, architect, scientist, poet and a man who had to stay fairly organized)

• •

"Fail to plan. Plan to fail."

-Winston Churchill

(A man who had to stay very organized as the Prime Minister of Great Britain who stood up to the fascist, racist, hate-crazed Nazi leader Adolf Hitler who was hell-bent on taking over the world and killing all of the Jews on the planet)

As I've worked with business owners for more than a decade helping them to establish, grow and scale successful companies, I have found this lack of Universal File Nomenclature is a stumbling block to just about every kind of business and profession. I'm always amazed at the snail's pace at which we are forced to work when we first sit down with a doctor who can't find his passwords and who doesn't know where any of his digital files are saved. I'm always blown away that a multimillion dollar faux-stone creator, a home-builder, a lawyer, a photographer, a landscaper, a pastor, a sports coach, a fitness expert, online retailer, or any other professional sincerely has no universal naming systems in place in their business to organize their digital files. However, once I begin working with a client, I insist that all of the files I create for them follow a very specific naming system. I will teach this system to you now.

No One Will Use Your Systems If No One Can Find Them

Many business owners say, "We definitely have an operations manual and John knows right where it is," or "The reason we aren't currently using the system is because we are going through crisis A, B, and C." The truth is, no one within their company is using the systems because no one can find anything and just searching for files is such a massive time-wasting and anxiety causing experience, even the driven members of the team eventually give up and just begin creating their own systems. This is how company-wide jackassery becomes the norm. Everybody makes up their own systems on the fly until the company is right back to where it started without any systems.

You Know You Have an Effective Universal Nomenclature System When...

You will know that you have created and implemented an effective Universal Nomenclature System when the following statements are true:

1. The cumulative best-practice systems and processes of your business are easy to locate (within 30 seconds by every member of your team).

2. Your business systems are being used on a daily basis to execute the daily core competencies of the business.

3. Your business becomes reliant on systems and processes and not people.

4. Your leadership team can quickly access and edit the core workflow documents of your business.

5. Your files are backed up and easily retrievable.

"I was taking this bus to New York. I realized I'd forgotten my thumb drive. Suddenly I'm powerless. I thought, how long are we going to be doing this? I never want this to happen to me again."

-Drew Houston
(Billionaire and co-founder of Dropbox.com)

HERE IS THE SECRET SAUCE AND THE FIVE STEP SYSTEM FOR CREATING YOUR UNIVERSAL NOMENCLATURE SYSTEM

Step 1 - Save Your Files Using a Backed-Up and Always Accessible Cloud-Based System that You Can Access from Anywhere

Right now, I am accessing and editing this digital file while aboard a Southwest Airlines flight en route to "The Great Bus Station of the Sky," La Guardia Airport (LGA) in New York, New York. I am making edits and updates to this book working on a different computer than the one I started writing the book on. In fact, thus far I have used four different computers and workstations composing "the best business book in the world." I can quickly access the file from any computer anywhere in the world because the file I am working on is saved digitally with our good friends at Dropbox.com. And since I took the time to develop a universal file saving system years ago, I know exactly where to find the file without asking anybody. The file for this book is not saved on a desktop computer somewhere; it's saved in the cloud so I can access it from any location.

Yesterday, I was speaking in the Tourist Capital of the World (Tulsa, Oklahoma), and though I did not have any time blocked off in my schedule for writing, I was able to tell a member of our team to continue proofreading the book. He knew exactly where the file was and how it was saved even without asking me because he is familiar with our universal file saving system. My friend, the vast majority of the things I do find one now.

Cloud-based systems for storing and saving your digital files:

» Dropbox.com

» Google Drive

Regardless of what provider you decide to go with, the provider you choose must be able to provide you and your team with a file storage system that meets the following criteria:

» Your team must be able to access the files from anywhere in the world via their laptops, desktops, tablets and smartphones.

» Your digital documents must be easily searchable and easy for members of your team to locate.

» Your files must be backed up all of the time and every day without you having to think about it.

» Your system must be secure. Although even the IRS, LinkedIn, and countless large organizations have been hacked, you want to make sure that the system you are setting up is as secure as possible.

Step 2 - Establish Your Company's Master Folder Organization Method

Do not form a committee or task force to determine how you will name your files. Just get this done ASAP. You must decide which file naming system is right for you because everyone within your company absolutely must know where all of your digital files are at all times. You will know that your file naming system is working properly after experiencing the first week when nobody in your office asks you, "Hey, where did you save the _____ file?" As you scale your business, you simply cannot spend 30 minutes per day running around telling members of your staff where files are located.

Mystic Statistic:

"It's estimated that a manager loses 1 hour/day to disorder, costing the business up to $4000/year if earning $35,000/year or $8,125/year at $65,000."

"Organizing & Time Management Statistics," SimplyProductive.com. http://www.simplyproductive.com/2012/03/time-management-statistics/

The file naming system rules I have established and use on a daily basis to stay super-organized are as follows:

» **Rule #1** – Assign each aspect / part of your business a different name and number and include that name and number in the file name

» **Rule #2** – End the name of each file with your company's or department's name. If you begin setting up different sub-companies or different departments within your company, you will be glad that you did. To make your life 2% easier, I have included an example of how I would label all of the files if I was ever asked to take over the file organization of David Letterman's company, Worldwide Pants

Ample Example:

1 – Marketing – Worldwide Pants

2 – Sales – Worldwide Pants

3 – Customer Service – Worldwide Pants

4 – Product and Service Delivery – Worldwide Pants

5 – Accounting – Worldwide Pants

6 – Administration – Worldwide Pants

7 – Human Resources – Worldwide Pants

8 – Public Relations – Worldwide Pants

» **Rule #3** – Determine that everything has a place based upon what aspect / part of your business it relates to.

· ·

Ample Example:

1 – Marketing – Worldwide Pants

      Brochures – Worldwide Pants

      Business Cards – Worldwide Pants

      History / Staff Photos – Worldwide Pants

      Landing Pages – Worldwide Pants

      Mailers – Worldwide Pants

      One Sheet – Worldwide Pants

      Photography – Worldwide Pants

      Social Media – Worldwide Pants

      Sponsors – Worldwide Pants

      Tradeshow Booth – Worldwide Pants

      Trifold – Worldwide Pants

      Videos – Worldwide Pants

2 – Sales – Worldwide Pants

      Contracts – Worldwide Pants

      Leads – Worldwide Pants

      E-Mail Templates – Worldwide Pants

      Scripts – Worldwide Pants

      Training Videos – Worldwide Pants

3 – Customer Service – Worldwide Pants

      Customer Ticket Sales Database – Worldwide Pants

      E-Mail Templates – Worldwide Pants

      Scripts – Worldwide Pants

      Swag Items – Worldwide Pants

      Thank You Cards – Worldwide Pants

4 – Product and Service Delivery – Worldwide Pants

Guests – Worldwide Pants

Product Listing – Worldwide Pants

Production Schedule – Worldwide Pants

Show Ideas – Worldwide Pants

Show Intros – Worldwide Pants

Show Outros – Worldwide Pants

5 – Accounting – World Wide Pants

Accounts Receivable – Worldwide Pants

Balance Sheets – Worldwide Pants

Depreciation Schedule – Worldwide Pants

Equipment List – Worldwide Pants

Inventory – Worldwide Pants

Profit and Loss Statements – Worldwide Pants

Tax Filings – Worldwide Pants

6 – Administration – Worldwide Pants

Organizational Chart – Worldwide Pants

Passwords – Worldwide Pants

7 – Human Resources – World Wide Pants

Disciplinary Action – Worldwide Pants

Employee Handbook – Worldwide Pants

Employee Information – Worldwide Pants

Operations Manual – Worldwide Pants

Resumes – Worldwide Pants

Staff Party Plans – Worldwide Pants

Temporary Agency – Worldwide Pants

8 – Public Relations – Worldwide Pants

Press Kit – Worldwide Pants

Press Releases – Worldwide Pants

Talking Points – Worldwide Pants

Step 3 – Hold a 30-Minute Workshop to Teach Each Division of Your Company How the System Works

Everyone on your team must be taught the logic behind your file naming system and shown how to find files within your system or chaos will ensue. Have each member of your team demonstrate his or her mastery of your file naming system before moving on.

Step 4 – Go Through the Terrible Mind-Numbing Process of Renaming All of Your Files NOW

Now it's time for the terrible part. Oh yes. Now it's time to actually rename all of your files and move them into the right location.This process takes most businesses I've worked with over the years 10 hours or more. You will quickly discover that Karl in accounting has been saving super important files on his desktop and that Janice has been saving her files in her Google Drive while Randy can't remember where he saved the passwords. This is going to take some time, but you must insist that all the file saving and reorganization gets done within a one week period of time. Even though it is very important to delegate whenever possible, YOU AS THE OWNER must be very involved in this process and you must OWN IT. The location and security of your digital files is simply too important to delegate to anybody else.

> "Complexity Fails. Simplicity Scales."

You are setting up the file naming system that your company is going to use until the end of time and you must know where everything is being saved and how everything is organized.

Step 5 – Always Label the Newest Version of Every File as the Highest Version Number

As you grow your company, you will find that you are never completely done updating your files and making tweaks to your core documents. Thus, your entire team must be on the same page when it comes to how your organization will name files that have been updated. To enhance your quality of life by 17.3%, I have provided the following example:

 Ample Example:
8 – Public Relations – Worldwide Pants

Press Kit - Worldwide Pants

   Press Kit – Version 1 – Worldwide Pants

Press Kit – Version 2 – Worldwide Pants

   Press Kit – Version 3 – Worldwide Pants

Press Releases – Worldwide Pants

   Press Release Template – Version 1 – Worldwide Pants

   Press Release Template – Version 2 – Worldwide Pants

Talking Points – Worldwide Pants

   Talking Points – Version 1 – Worldwide Pants

      Talking Points – Version 2 – Worldwide Pants

      Talking Points – Version 3 – Worldwide Pants

      Talking Points – Version 4 – Worldwide Pants

      Talking Points – Version 5 – Worldwide Pants

      Talking Points – Version 6 – Worldwide Pants

My friend, you must name the newest update of each file as the highest numbered version because you never know when you are going to want to refer to an older, previous version. If you make a big change to your digital files and something accidentally gets deleted from the new version, you need to be able to quickly go back to the previous version of the file to retrieve what was lost, rather than frantically try to rack your brain to figure out what is missing.

» **YOU MUST BE THE CHAMPION OF FILE NOMENCLATURE** because nobody else in your office is going to care at first.

» **YOU MUST BE THE CHAMPION OF FILE NOMENCLATURE** because being disorganized will make your company move at a snail's pace.

» **YOU MUST BE THE CHAMPION OF FILE NOMENCLATURE** because as you begin to hire more and more people, everyone must know where to find the key files and documents needed to make the company run.

» **YOU MUST BE THE CHAMPION OF FILE NOMENCLATURE** because without a proper file naming and organization system, your company will be much less valuable if you ever attempt to sell it. Imagine trying to explain to a potential buyer of your company that the incredible systems that make your company so successful are not documented anywhere.

The concept of properly naming files cannot be seen as a passing fad. The members of your team must know that henceforth, this is going to be embedded into the very fabric of your business. If you are the type of business owner that decides to begin the process of properly naming your files, but then lacks the intensity needed to actually see the process through (I'm sure you are not), then you will begin to lose all credibility with your team. Your organization must begin to understand on a deep and almost spiritual level how important systems are to the company's overall health and TO YOU. Remember, no one is going to care more about your business and its systems than you.

REVENUE GROWTH AFTER WORKING WITH CLAY CLARK:

5X MORE LEADS

WORKING 5X LESS HOURS

GROWTH FROM $1 MILLION TO $4 MILLION IN REVENUE

"DILIGENCE, COACHABILITY, AND ATTENTION TO DETAIL ARE THE DIFFERENCE MAKERS."
- CLAY CLARK

WE HELP YOU TO IMPLEMENT THE FOLLOWING CLAY CLARK SUCCESS STRATEGIES, SYSTEMS, AND PROVEN PROCESSES (AND MORE):

 Graphic Designers

 Web Designers

 Save Years of Trial & Error

 Search Engine Optimization

Management/ Leadership Training

Online Advertisement

Public Relations

Speaking Coaching

Sales Training

Billing Systems Creation

Brand Enhancement

Website Creation

Proven Systems for Massive Growth

Installation of New Employee Recruitment Systems & Processes

Bookkeeping/Accounting Systems Creation

Sales Scripting Installation

Dream 100 System Creation

Online Advertisement Design & Creation

On-Going Group Interview / Employee Hiring, Inspiring, Training and Retaining Systems

On-Going Sales Management

On-Going Sales Training

On-Going Management Training

Workflow Design

On-Going Advertisement Management

On-Going Dream 100 Marketing

On-Going Lead Tracking

On-Going Online Reputation Management

On-Going Search Engine Optimization

Print Piece Design

 HOLMAN'S CUSTOM CABINETS

Randy Holman
Owner / Founder
www.HolmansCabinets.com

Chapter 25

Stop Dropping the Ball

One of the biggest issues that we see time and time again with companies that are attempting to build a scalable and duplicable business model is their inability to seamlessly pass on aspects of a project from one person to another. For example, in the videography and production company I own:

» **Step 1** – Person A clarifies the needs of the customer

» **Step 2** – Person B schedules the videographer and reserves the equipment

» **Step 3** – Person C loads the videographer out with the appropriate equipment at the appropriate time

» **Step 4** – Person D films the actual event

» **Step 5** – Person C loads the videographer in with the appropriate equipment and uses a checklist to verify that all equipment is returned

» **Step 6** – Person C backs up the digital files and saves them to the server

» **Step 7** – Person D edits the video

» **Step 8** – Person D uploads the final version of the file to Dropbox

» **Step 9** – Person E sends the final video to the customer for final approval

» **Step 10** – Person F uploads and embeds the video onto the website of the client

There are six people and ten steps involved in the proper production of a commercial video for our clients. Thus, six different people have to work together to complete one single project. IF YOU ARE NOT MANIACALLY FOCUSED ON DETAILS AND INSTALLING SYSTEMS THAT WILL KEEP YOUR PEOPLE FROM DROPPING THE BALL, YOUR TEAM WILL BEGIN TO DROP THE BALL. This is even more true as your company begins to grow.

Many business owners push back against me when I begin to train them about the importance of scalability when it comes to delivering their products and services because they are fighting an internal battle against the poverty mindset they have been taught by everyone around them. Everyone around them has told them that quality and quantity are mutually exclusive ideas. My friend, this statement is so important that I am going to write it again in all caps:

EVERYONE AROUND YOU HAS TOLD YOU THAT QUALITY AND QUANTITY ARE MUTUALLY EXCLUSIVE IDEAS... AND THEY ARE WRONG.

If this logic was right, Disney World would have been 50% less magical than Disneyland, and Southwest Airlines flights would be more and more unsafe the bigger the company gets. This is simply not true. You cannot grow in scalable and exponential ways without having duplicable systems in place, thus the BIG COMPANIES actually have HIGHER SAFETY AND QUALITY STANDARDS THAN MOST SMALL BUSINESSES.

Connection Points

Connection points are areas of your business where one person on your team has completed their task and now must hand off the task to another member of your team to complete the project.

Although the founder of Ford Motors, Henry Ford, was famous for first successfully introducing assembly lines into his factories in 1913, this concept of passing off an item to a member of our team who is also working on the project down the line is one that most businesses still struggle with today. That is why I want to teach you how to build systems that will ensure proper connections between members of your team.

To cut down on errors (the actual goal is to eliminate them), the best

> "Being nice to people is just 20% of providing good customer service. The important part is designing systems that allow you to do the job right the first time. All the smiles in the world aren't going to help you if your product or service is not what the customer wants."
>
>  *- James L. Heskett, Thomas O. Jones, Gary W. Loveman, W. Earl Sasser, Jr. and Leonard A. Schlesinger, Service Profit Chain*

businesses take the time to write out scripts, checklists, and workflows that clearly show the steps in their process. Drawing out these workflows on a massive white board will allow you to see where potential connection errors may occur so that you can preemptively design system modifications to prevent those errors.

You must think about this aspect of your business as a pipeline:

» **Step 1** – A team of geologists and geophysicists must first determine, by analyzing seismic data, possible locations of oil and natural gas buried deep under the earth's surface.

» **Step 2** – A team of people working on a drilling rig must auger deep down into the earth's subsurface to find a reservoir of oil.

» **Step 3** – Once the oil has been extracted from the earth, it must be shipped to a refinery.

» **Step 4** – The raw oil must be refined into a usable form.

» **Step 5** – The gas must be shipped to gas stations.

» **Step 6** – The gas must be marketed and sold to customers.

Although the men and women involved in the process may never meet each other as they are geophysicists working on boats, drill deck workers working oil rigs in the middle of the ocean, and truckers hauling the gas from the refinery to a local gas station, they must work together to generate a profit and beat their competition. The goal must be to work as a team to deliver incredible products and services to your ideal and likely buyers while beating the heck out of your competition.

Although the job of hauling gas from the refinery may seem simple to the person buying the gas, it is actually very difficult to organize the great symphony of commerce in a scalable and duplicable way. In the world of business, all your branding efforts, your strategic planning and your good intentions don't matter if your team fails to deliver or if a major oil spill occurs (using the example above). Think about how many millions of people are able to drive their cars and heat their homes because of the quality discovering, drilling, and refining of oil accomplished by British Petroleum. Yet most people today think of oil spills when they think of British Petroleum because of the catastrophic oil spill that occurred on April 20, 2010.

Fun Fact:
On April 20, 2010, the massive Deepwater Horizon oil spill began. After the Deepwater Horizon oil rig sank to the ocean's floor, the oil continued to flow out of the earth and into the Gulf of Mexico for 87 days. Eleven workers went missing and were never found and the coast of Louisiana was devastated by the 4.9 million barrels of oil that spilled into the ocean. Later in November of 2010, the United States settled federal criminal charges as BP agreed to a record-setting $4.525 billion fine.

> "The first thing to say is I'm sorry...We're sorry for the massive disruption it's caused their lives. There's no one who wants this over more than I do. I would like my life back."

-Tony Hayward
(The former CEO of British Petroleum)

Although I am not a British Petroleum apologist, I must say that I can empathize on a very small level with Tony Hayward. When my entertainment company began to grow quickly and I screwed up those weddings, I wasn't trying to destroy the lives of the brides we were working with, I wasn't greedy (I was just trying to earn enough money to cover the cost of living), but I was ignorant about the importance of creating detailed linear systems to greatly reduce the number of errors my team and I would make during critical connection points.

In the world of business, key connection points occur between your marketing and sales teams. Your marketing team has to work very hard to produce leads and they must have the faith that your sales team is going to close the leads that they produce. Key connections occur when your operations and service (or product delivery team) finishes the job and they turn in the documentation to the accounting or billing department whom they trust to collect payment from your customer. Key connections occur between your human relations department and your payroll or accounting department as HR trusts them to pay the members of your team accurately and on time for the work they have provided. You must have detailed and linear workflow that documents your system to make sure that there are efficient connections occurring between your teams all day, every day, without the ball constantly being dropped.

SUPER MOVES FOR CREATING EFFICIENT CONNECTION POINTS

SUPER MOVE #1 – The right information must be gathered. The team that is passing the workload from themselves to the next team must provide the detailed information that is required in a systematic way. When your sales team places the order, they may need to invest a few extra minutes to clearly articulate what was promised to the customer so that the production / fulfillment team can accurately and consistently meet the customer's expectations.

> "The single biggest problem in communication is the illusion that it has taken place."
>
>
>
> *-George Bernard Shaw*
> (The famous Irish playwright who was able to write 60 plays, in part because of the methodical nature with which he worked)

SUPER MOVE #2 – Be clear about who owns each step of the process. It is incredibly important for everyone to know who actually owns each step of the process. In my own office, I fight a constant battle against allowing an ambiguous and unaccountable group of three people to own a step of the process. A person will say, "The three of us will work together and we should have something for you by Monday." I have to passionately fight back and say, "Who specifically is going to own this process and on what specific day will this project be done?" It is incredibly important for everyone to know who owns which step of the process and what step of the process each action item falls within. You must clearly define each step of your workflow and it must be a part of your company culture to declare openly and transparently at which step of the process a project is. You must include all responsible parties in this crucial connection as they acknowledge what step of the process they are in.

. . .

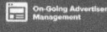
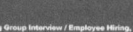

"I HELP REAL BUSINESS OWNERS TO CREATE REAL SUCCESS BY IMPLEMENTING REAL SYSTEMS THAT REALLY WORK. Motivation Is the Emotion You Receive As a Reward of Implementing the Proven Processes, Success Strategies and Best-Practice Systems That Produce Results."

Clay Clark

"8 out of 10 businesses fail within the first 18 months.

Forbes

"90% of Startups fail.

Forbes

YEARLY GROWTH

$1,770,935.94

2020

$2,112,321.02

19.3%
GROWTH

2021

$3,149,141.61

49.1%
GROWTH

2022

"DILIGENCE, COACHABILITY, AND ATTENTION TO DETAIL ARE THE DIFFERENCE MAKERS."
- CLAY CLARK

WE HELP YOU TO IMPLEMENT THE FOLLOWING CLAY CLARK SUCCESS STRATEGIES, SYSTEMS, AND PROVEN PROCESSES (AND MORE):

 Graphic Designers

 Web Designers

 Save Years of Trial & Error

 Search Engine Optimization

 Management/ Leadership Training

 Online Advertisement

 Public Relations

 Speaking Coaching

Sales Training

 Billing Systems Creation

 Brand Enhancement

 Website Creation

 Proven Systems for Massive Growth

Installation of New Employee Recruitment Systems & Processes

 Bookkeeping/Accounting Systems Creation

 Sales Scripting Installation

 Dream 100 System Creation

 Online Advertisement Design & Creation

 On-Going Group Interview / Employee Hiring, Inspiring, Training and Retaining Systems

 On-Going Sales Management

 On-Going Sales Training

 On-Going Management Training

 Workflow Design

On-Going Advertisement Management

 On-Going Dream 100 Marketing

 On-Going Lead Tracking

On-Going Online Reputation Management

On-Going Search Engine Optimization

Print Piece Design

BRIAN T. ARMSTRONG CONSTRUCTION INC.

Brian T Armstrong
Owner / Founder
www.BrianTArmstrongConstructionInc.com

WILL **YOU** BE THE **NEXT SUCCESS STORY?**

Schedule your free consultation with Clay Clark today!
www.thrivetimeshow.com

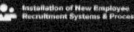

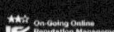
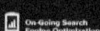

YOUR BUSINESS EXISTS TO SOLVE PROBLEMS
FOR YOU AND YOUR CUSTOMERS.
- CLAY CLARK
FOUNDER OF THRIVE15

You need to break down your customers into four categories, and we've added a fifth:

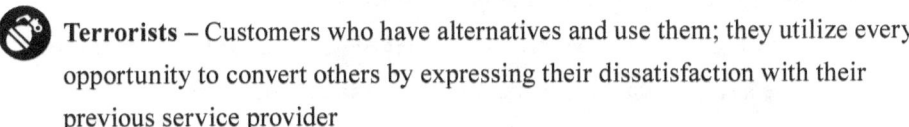

Terrorists – Customers who have alternatives and use them; they utilize every opportunity to convert others by expressing their dissatisfaction with their previous service provider

Hostages – Highly dissatisfied customers who have few or no alternatives

Mercenaries – Customers who may switch service providers in order to obtain a better price, even though they may currently be satisfied

Loyalists – Customers who are highly satisfied but not WOWed enough to virally recommend the product or service

Apostles – Customers who are not only loyal but also are so satisfied that they recommend the service to others.

Here are a few principles and statistics that the authors of the book found that help us understand the importance and value of going above and beyond to ensure the satisfaction of your customers:

» The US Office of Consumer Affairs suggests that satisfied customers for consumer services were likely to tell five other people about their experience (whether or not they were potential customers), while dissatisfied customers were likely to tell eleven other people.

» A 5% increase in customer loyalty can produce profit increases from 25% to 85%.

» Several companies have found that their most loyal customers—the top 20% of total customers—not only provide all the profit for the business but also cover losses incurred in dealing with less loyal customers.

These statistics show the value of building satisfaction among your customers. To build this kind of customer satisfaction, it's necessary to give the employees within your company the resources and latitude to achieve total customer satisfaction. Unfortunately, there will always be a percentage of customers who are "terrorists." I find that these customers tend to inherently hate their current situation in life and are committed to raising hell. YOU MUST PUNT THESE CUSTOMERS. As a business owner, you have a responsibility to achieve customer satisfaction, but you must also protect your employees from these terrorists. Herb Kelleher, CEO of Southwest Airlines, is quoted as saying, *"Something....that is entirely wrong....that has almost achieved a religiousity.... [Is] the customer is always right. That is a betrayal of your people. The customer is not always right."*

Keep this in mind as you are building out the operations systems in your company.

OFFER ANYONE WHO REFUSES TO LIVE UP
TO YOUR BUSINESS STANDARDS A NICE
WARM CUP OF SHUT THE HELL UP.

"EXPECT MORE THAN OTHERS THINK POSSIBLE.
REMEMBER, YOU MUST EXPECT
WHAT YOU ACCEPT."

– CLAY CLARK

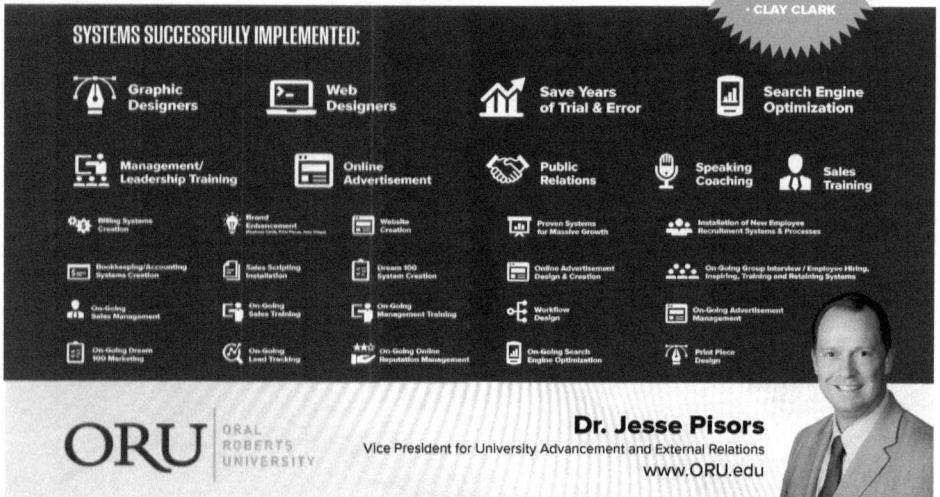

Chapter 26

Booming Business Foundational Principle #3 — Accounting and Finance

During this section of this incredible business book, we are going to be talking about how to effectively handle your cash flow, optimize your profit margins, and finance your company's growth. As you begin to grow your business, you are going to have to become an absolute wizard of financial management. I am willing to fight almost anyone (depending upon how big they are) who believes that they should delegate the financial aspects of their business to someone else. They are wrong.

The Accounting and Financial foundation of your business involves:

» Collections of your accounts receivable

» Tracking of the money that you are owed

» Distribution of the money that you collect

» Reporting of the money that comes in and out of your business

» Billing processes and procedures that you have in place

» Tracking the money that you owe to others (accounts payable)

» Meeting financial reporting requirements of your business

» Preparing profit and loss statements for your business

» Cash flow management of your business

» Money / capital financing of your business

» Risk management aspects of your business

» Financial forecasting of your business

"Beware of little expenses. A small leak will sink a great ship."

-Benjamin Franklin
(A bestselling author, printer, politician, postmaster, scientist, inventor, and the diplomat who convinced France to support and fund the thirteen American colonies in their fight against Great Britain)

Most businesses I work with almost never have any financial management systems in place. If that is true of your business, you should not be beat up for it. I get it. As an early stage entrepreneur, you are absolutely working yourself to the point of

> "Ideas are easy. Implementation is hard."
>
> **-Guy Kawasaki**
> (He was one of the Apple employees who helped to introduce the Macintosh line of computers in 1984)

exhaustion just trying to sell enough stuff to barely survive.

As you start to grow your business, we at ThriveTimeShow.com recommend that you hire an outsourced part-time bookkeeper to work with you to keep your books straight, but we do not recommend that you completely abdicate your responsibilities by assigning all of the accounting duties to some random bookkeeper you just hired. The key is to surround yourself with smart people whom you hold accountable. DON'T EVER TURN OVER YOUR BOOKKEEPING TO AN IN-HOUSE OR OUTSOURCED BOOKKEEPER YOU DO NOT HOLD ACCOUNTABLE.

Once you can afford it, we recommend that you hire a full-time person who will act as both your Chief Financial Officer and your bookkeeper. So what's the big difference between a CFO and a bookkeeper? When you hire someone to act as your CFO, you are hiring somebody who should be able to help you

> "As an entrepreneur, I choose my teachers carefully, very carefully. I am extremely cautious of the people with whom I spend my time and to whom I listen."
>
>  **-Donald Trump**
> (American businessman, politician, television personality, author, and the presumptive nominee of the Republican Party for President of the United States in the 2016 election)

make smart and strategic financial decisions while keeping your books accurate. This CFO / bookkeeper really needs to help you build and manage your financial and accounting systems. I am going to teach you the financial management SUPER MOVES you need to properly manage the financial aspects of your business.

32 SUPER MOVES for Financial Management

SUPER MOVE #1 – You must know your break-even point

I realize that every business is slightly different and the profit margins from item to item or service to service can vary dramatically. However, you must know approximately how many customers you need to have on a weekly basis to cover your total weekly expenses and break even. YOU MUST KNOW THIS. If you don't know this, it becomes very hard to make staffing, financial, and leadership decisions. Most owners I've spoken to are like swimmers swimming in a dense fog only 50 feet from the shore. They have no idea where they are in relation to the shore and if the fog doesn't clear or if someone doesn't show them the way soon, they are either going to drown from exhaustion or they are going to drown because they just gave up, thinking that continuing to struggle is just an exercise in futility.

To download our incredibly helpful break-even point analysis and calculation tool, visit: www.ThriveTimeShow.com/TreasureTrove

Ample Example:
Years ago I was hired to help a dermatologist grow her business. She knew exactly how many customers and upsells she needed per location, per week, to break even. As far as I could tell, every aspect of her business was clearly focused on achieving this goal, which is why she hired me for the specific task of teaching the dermatologists how to systematically upsell 20% of the time. She said, *"We begin to make a really good profit when my team starts upselling to our patients consistently 20% of the time. Our original location upsells at a 25% to 30% average, but I need some help creating a system to do this that isn't reliant upon me constantly coming to close the deal."*

SUPER MOVE #2 – You must know your one-time profit per product or service

It's very important that you know how much profit you actually make per product or service so that you can properly manage your business. When I owned www.DJConnection.com I knew that my team needed to provide entertainment service for eight weddings or events per week just to break even and then after that, I made a profit of approximately $167 per wedding. This knowledge allowed me to approximately determine how many shows we needed to do per week, per month, and per year to achieve my financial freedom and time freedom goals.

SUPER MOVE #3 – You must know much money it costs you to acquire a new customer

In a perfect world, you wouldn't have to spend money on marketing to new customers and word of mouth would organically make your business grow exponentially forever. The reality, however, is that whether you are Nike, McDonald's, Southwest Airlines, or Disney World, you are going to have to invest in consistent advertising to stay in the minds of your ideal and likely buyers. The big question is this. How much money does it cost your company to attract one customer?

Ample Example:
I once worked with this dude who made incredible food so he decided to become a caterer. He did such a good job catering that he decided to start a company to keep up with his word of mouth business. Because he did not know what his break-even point was, how much profit he made per catering gig, and how much money it cost him to acquire a new customer, he was going out of business for the third time when he called me. I wanted to help the man, but I could tell that he was a lost cause when he started saying, *"Things were going good and then the economy tanked and some political changes started happening up at the aquarium where I had that big house account. Next thing you know, the business is falling apart. Every time, I just get bitten by the economy or something I can't control."*

I asked the guy, *"So why did you call me if you truly believe that your businesses just fail and there is nothing you can do about it?"*

He said, *"Well I wanted to see if I could partner with you because it seems as though you are really good at picking the right industries to work in. You've focused on entertainment, photography, public relations, web development, fitness, medical, and other industries that are more stable."*

I'm sure that this guy doesn't hate himself and doesn't want to struggle financially his whole life, but he is going to if he does not take the time to know the numbers, like you are learning to do right now.

SUPER MOVE #4 – You must collect the money you are owed and stop acting like a casual bank

When you go through all the effort to deliver your products and services in a consistent and quality-controlled way, you simply cannot allow yourself to feel bad about collecting the money you are owed. Your customers would not go to the local grocery store and fill up their carts without expecting to pay for those groceries and they shouldn't expect to be able to buy things from you without paying for them, either.

Fun Fact:
According to the U.S. Census Bureau's annual Families and Living Arrangements table package released January 28, 2015, one of five children receives food stamps. The number of children receiving food stamps remains higher than it was before the start of the Great Recession in 2007.

I have noticed a disturbing pattern. For some reason, business owners seem to struggle with the concept of making their customers pay them. It seems as though many business owners are scared to ask their customers to pay them so they just sit back passively waiting to get paid. They just wait passively for their payments to come in without ever directly asking the customers to pay them on time. I've also noticed an even weaker move wherein business owners delegate the collection of their hard-earned money to a passive bookkeeper they have hired. This cannot happen.

 "I HELP REAL BUSINESS OWNERS TO CREATE REAL SUCCESS BY IMPLEMENTING REAL SYSTEMS THAT REALLY WORK.

Motivation Is the Emotion You Receive As a Reward of Implementing the Proven Processes, Success Strategies and Best-Practice Systems That Produce Results."

Clay Clark

"8 out of 10 businesses fail within the first 18 months.

Forbes

"90% of Startups fail.

Forbes

REVENUE GROWTH AFTER WORKING WITH CLAY CLARK:

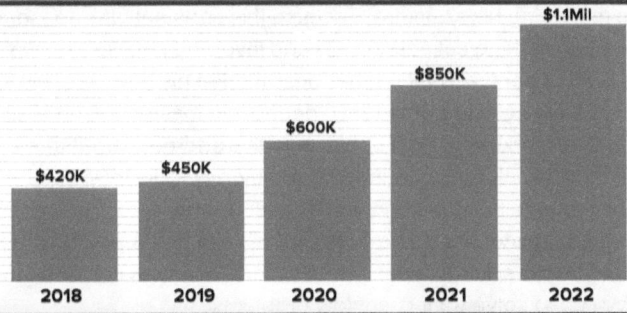

$1.1Mil

$850K

$600K

$450K

$420K

2018   2019   2020   2021   2022

"We've been growing by an average of 40% every year. We can't complain about that."

- Adam Stockdall
(TipTopK9.com - Dallas, Franchise Owner)

"DILIGENCE, COACHABILITY, AND ATTENTION TO DETAIL ARE THE DIFFERENCE MAKERS."
- CLAY CLARK

WE HELP YOU TO IMPLEMENT THE FOLLOWING CLAY CLARK SUCCESS STRATEGIES, SYSTEMS, AND PROVEN PROCESSES (AND MORE):

 Graphic Designers

 Web Designers

 Save Years of Trial & Error

 Search Engine Optimization

 Management/ Leadership Training

 Online Advertisement

 Public Relations

 Speaking Coaching

 Sales Training

 Billing Systems Creation

 Brand Enhancement

 Website Creation

 Proven Systems for Massive Growth

 Installation of New Employee Recruitment Systems & Processes

Bookkeeping/Accounting Systems Creation

Sales Scripting Installation

Dream 100 System Creation

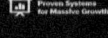 Online Advertisement Design & Creation

On-Going Group Interview / Employee Hiring, Inspiring, Training and Retaining Systems

On-Going Sales Management

On-Going Sales Training

On-Going Management Training

 Workflow Design

 On-Going Advertisement Management

 On-Going Dream 100 Marketing

 On-Going Lead Tracking

 On-Going Online Reputation Management

 On-Going Search Engine Optimization

 Print Piece Design

TIP TOP K9

Adam Stockdall
Franchise Owner
www.TipTopK9.com

WILL **YOU** BE THE NEXT SUCCESS STORY?

Schedule your free consultation with Clay Clark today!
www.thrivetimeshow.com

your clients a percentage up front as a retainer or initial payment and then charge the customer the final balance right as the work, product, or service is being delivered.

Ample Example:

I worked with one particular client, an attorney, who was just getting killed financially. I told him that if I was him, henceforth I would tell the customer what the fees are going to be and require them to pay a 50% retainer before the legal work can begin. The customer would appreciate knowing the estimated total of the legal fees before the project started and the attorney would appreciate no longer having to mail invoices, call about collecting the payments, or even worry about hiring a person responsible for those duties. Don't freak out. This system didn't result in this man firing his assistant. Because this assistant was no longer spending her entire day making collection calls and invoicing people, she was now able to focus 80% of her time helping her boss market his business. My team and I did a deep dive training with her to teach her how to master search engine optimization and online-marketing. I just spoke with this attorney about three weeks ago and he now is making a boatload of money, he works less, and he never has to go after people to collect money, all because he killed the concept of invoicing and collecting later. As a side note, I have used this super move to dramatically help contractors, landscapers, dentists and nearly every kind of company under the sun to solve their cash flow problems.

SUPER MOVE #6 – You must know how much money is owed to you

Just yesterday, we unfortunately had to punt a client because he was behind on his men's grooming membership at the Elephant in the Room. Because the Elephant in the Room business model is a membership-based model, we charge our customers a recurring amount to allow them to enjoy our facility and the services we provide

more often and at a discounted rate. This is a good thing for most men because they never have to wait for service; we keep them on schedule with a recurring appointment to help them maintain their look. Unfortunately, this man kept having his credit card declined but still showed up for his monthly haircuts. Because we keep track of who has paid and who has not paid, we were able to discreetly inform him the next time he came in that we would not be able to cut his hair unless he paid us for last month's haircut and this haircut. He started immediately getting loud and name-calling. Because we track each account, we knew that he had previously attempted to not pay for our service after yelling at a stylist. Armed with this knowledge, we asked him to leave and he did. I'm sure he is writing a bad review about us on Google right now.

Unlike the situation described above, most collections-related issues are a result of having a poor system or no system in place to track what is owed.

SUPER MOVE #7 – If you have to invoice, do it early and often

I really dislike the concept of invoicing because I have found that it can be completely eliminated in about 50% of businesses. If you have to invoice, invoice early and often. When you invoice your customers frequently and early, it establishes the nature of your professional relationship very quickly and it helps you bring in more money faster. If at all possible, don't invoice, but if you have to, invoice early and often.

Download a sample template invoice at www.ThriveTimeShow.com/TreasureTrove.

SUPER MOVE #8 – Give tight deadlines and timelines if you have to move into collections mode

I consistently see situations where business owners allow soul-sucking customers to declare that they will pay after 60 or 90 days. In most cases, the business owner cannot afford to wait this long to be paid and the customer asking for these terms does not have the money to pay the invoice anyway. I would do whatever you must to avoid working with clients who will not pay you for 60 to 90 days. I personally would rather have four smaller accounts that pay on time than to have a massive account that takes 90 days to pay.

Ample Example:
Back in the day, while attending Oral Roberts University as a sophomore, I was asked to leave the school because I wrote and co-produced a parody song about the school president that he did not appreciate as much as I did. In retrospect, it's funny, but I wouldn't advise students to do this as a clever way to market themselves. Years later, I was asked to come in and manage the college's alumni marketing campaign. I worked my tail off and raised a record-setting amount of money for the school. After my third year of running the campaign, I was informed that the school would be moving to a model where they would pay me 60 days after I had completed my work. I punted this client.

SUPER MOVE #9 – Don't be a jerk when attempting to collect payment

When attempting to collect payment, we must keep in mind that everyone has personal challenges from time to time and everyone can make an honest mistake. It's the people who make these mistakes repeatedly that you must worry about. Without even thinking about it, most companies ask their bookkeepers or their accountants to help collect the money that is owed because they are the closest to the situation. However, as a general rule, many of these people lack the people skills necessary to do this job with tact. If they had those people skills, they'd be working in your sales department. I would recommend that you have members of your sales team or your accounting people with the best people skills collect the money so that you do not upset your loyal customers in these delicate situations. I would also insist that you pay your salespeople a commission on the money that is collected (after the money actually comes in, of course).

SUPER MOVE #10 – You must schedule a weekly meeting with your accounting team to go over the key performance indicators

You must schedule a weekly meeting with your accounting team to go over the following information every week:

» How much money is actually in the bank accounts?

» How much money is owed?

» What is the profit amount per customer?

» What is the cost to acquire each customer?

» How many customers do you need to gain at your current expense level to break even?

» What government fees, taxes, licenses, and assorted expenses are due?

SUPER MOVE #11 – Avoid working with the government when possible

Whenever possible, you want to avoid landing the government as a customer because they will wear you out with forms, compliance issues, bidding, and slow payment. Typically, by the time you get paid by the government, you won't even want the money anymore because when they finally send it, you'll be so angry that the sight of their check will send you over the edge.

> "The nine most terrifying words in the English language are, 'I'm from the government and I'm here to help.'"
>
> *-Ronald Reagan*
> **(40th President of the United States)**

I would highly recommend not working for or with the government for the following reasons:

» **It's political.**

I know of one caterer who made millions of dollars by providing food for two families at their secluded ranch. He got the deal because he was able to help a certain political candidate raise a ton of money by hosting events at his banquet facility. The caterer eventually lost that client, and ultimately his entire catering business, because he had become completely dependent upon working with the government and once a candidate fades or leaves office, the business goes with him.

» **The forms.**

Years ago, I did a speaking event for a state government agency that had me fill out a background check form, a 1099 form, an agreement to adhere to their code of conduct form, and five or six other forms before I could send them an invoice. After sending them the invoice and delivering a speech that received a standing ovation, I did not receive a check because I was told "apparently your invoice was lost in our system somehow." These morons took four more months to finally send me a check payable for two times what they owed me. Because I am sometimes an idiot, I called and told them about their error. It then took two more months before I received an accurate final payment. I have yet to have a positive experience working with the government. Furthermore, I have run into hundreds of people over the years who built up their entire business to meet the demands and compliance standards of the federal government, only to have their contracts voided when a president from the opposite political party was elected. If possible, stay away from government contracts.

SUPER MOVE #12 – Collect faster and show favoritism to fast-paying clients

You must insist on creating a culture where you collect the cash that your customers owe you quickly. When you allow customers to go longer and longer without paying you, bad things begin to happen. The debtor gets the upper hand as you start to say, "These people owe me a ton money and I really don't want to upset them and not get paid at all, so I will work with them for one more month." As experience will teach you, the longer you go without getting paid, the lower your chances become of ever getting paid. Also, the longer you let people go without paying you, the higher the fees will be that you have to pay to the collections agencies you finally have to hire to get paid.

SUPER MOVE #13 – Get paid in advance

The quality of your life will improve dramatically once you discover the magic of having your clients pay in advance. If you are not able to collect the total amount due up front, you should at least charge an upfront retainer, enrollment fee, or deposit of some kind. I cannot stress how important it is to create a company culture of getting paid before you actually deliver or fulfill the products or services promised to the customer.

Ample Example:
When I worked at Applebee's, we used to have about one customer per week who would order a massive appetizer, steak, three beers and an incredible dessert before discovering that they had forgotten their wallet. In almost every circumstance, this human (almost always a man) would never come back in to pay us as he'd promised. Although running your business is very different from being a waiter at Applebee's, the same concept applies to a certain extent. In the restaurant business, the profit margin is pretty slim on many of the food items and this one hog-esque customer who came in and ate like a king without paying absolutely killed the profitability of the tables I was working for the next three hours.

It is worth investing two hours to think about how you can get your customers to pay up front in some capacity. One move that we've used in the insurance business

(I have coached hundreds of insurance agents) is to incentivize our ideal and likely buyers to pay up front. We basically lock in the customer's insurance rates for the year and offer them a nice discount if they choose to pay in advance for the entire year. Having consulted numerous customers in the fitness business and the IT consulting business, I have found that about 15% of the customers we asked were willing to pay up front and this is a good thing.

Fun Fact:
The following entrepreneurs struggled through life because they didn't have a degree from a fancy business college (forgive the sarcasm spasms):

 Abraham Lincoln – Despite not having earned the respect of his peers by obtaining a college degree, he went on to become a lawyer and president of the United States. Because he chose to be self-taught, he never stopped learning.

 Amadeo Peter Giannini – Despite not knowing what he was doing because he didn't have a master's degree from a fancy business college, he went on to become the multi-millionaire founder of Bank of America after dropping out of high school.

 Andrew Carnegie – Despite being an elementary school dropout, this man went on to become a billionaire. Amazing, since he couldn't possibly have known what he was doing because he didn't have a college degree.

 Andrew Jackson – This guy went on to become an attorney, a U.S. president, a general, a judge, and a congressman despite being home-schooled and having no formal education at all.

 Anne Beiler – The "Princess of Pretzels" went on to start Auntie Anne's Pretzels and become a millionaire, despite having dropped out of high school. I bet she's disappointed she missed out on the once-in-a-lifetime experiences that so many college graduates with $100,000 of debt enjoy.

 Ansel Adams – I don't know if you are into world-famous photographers or not, but if you are, you know that Ansel Adams became arguably the best photographer in the world despite not graduating from a college of liberal arts. I wonder how he even knew to take the freaking lens cap off of his camera without a college degree.

 Barry Diller – This dude may be a billionaire and Hollywood mogul who founded Fox Broadcasting Company, but I am not impressed with him because he does not have a college degree.

 Benjamin Franklin – This guy might have invented the Franklin stove, lightning rods, bifocals and other assorted inventions while working as a founding father of the United States, but I can tell you that he had a hole in his soul where his degree should be.

Billy Joe (Red) McCombs – Red became a billionaire, but did he have a degree? No. And that is exactly why he doesn't get invited to any of those fancy alumni gatherings, which he would be too busy to attend anyway because he's off counting his money. Seriously, if he started counting the billions of dollars he made by founding Clear Channel media, he would never finish.

 Coco Chanel – She may have a perfume that bears her name, but I am not impressed with her because she doesn't have a degree.

 Colonel Harlan Sanders – This guy dropped out of elementary school and all he knew about was chicken. Sure he made millions, but I didn't truly have respect for him until he finally earned that law degree by correspondence.

 Dave Thomas – Every time I pull into Wendy's to enjoy a delicious snack wrap, I find myself thinking about what a complete waste of talent Dave was. He could have had trillions of dollars if only he had earned a degree and become the head of the Federal Reserve.

 David Geffen – Like a true loser, he dropped out of college after completing only one year. My, his parents must be disappointed. I feel bad just writing about this billionaire founder of Geffen Records and co-founder of DreamWorks.

 David Green – David, oh David. I bet you feel bad about your billions and spend every day living in regret because you do not have a college degree. I know that you took $600 and famously turned that into billions as the founder of Hobby Lobby, but you could have been a good attorney or a bureaucrat or a politician we all could watch argue to an empty room about nothing on C-SPAN.

 David Karp – This guy's last name should be carp, because this bottom feeder obviously will never amount to anything – well, except being the multi-millionaire founder of Tumblr. If he hadn't dropped out of school at age 15, I would respect him more.

 David Neeleman – This guy started a little airline (JetBlue) to compensate for his lack of a degree. I don't even feel safe on the world's most profitable airline because its founder doesn't have a degree.

 David Oreck – David Oreck truly had a career that sucked. This college dropout and multi-millionaire founder of the Oreck vacuum company created vacuums that have sucked the dirt out of carpets for years.

 Debbi Fields – Oh, so sad. Little Debbie, the founder Mrs. Fields Chocolate Chippery, never knew the pride that one could feel upon earning a college degree.

EDITOR'S NOTE: It took Clay three weeks to alphabetize this list of college dropouts because he doesn't have a degree.

 DeWitt Wallace – DeWitt may have founded Reader's Digest, but I'm sure that he couldn't truly enjoy reading in an intelligent way because he never earned his college degree.

 Dustin Moskovitz – Dustin is credited as being one of the founders of that little company called Facebook that only moms, dads, cousins, kids, adults, and humans use. I bet he wishes he had stayed in school at Harvard.

 Frank Lloyd Wright – Frank may have become the most famous architect of all time, but I cannot respect a man who never attended high school.

 Frederick Henry Royce – Ok, so a Rolls-Royce is a symbol of automotive excellence for many people, but this guy had to have been compensating for the fact that he knew nothing about anything because he was an elementary school dropout.

 George Eastman – Perhaps you are not old enough to know about the Kodak brand that used to control the world as part of the Illuminati. How George founded this little company despite dropping out of high school is beyond me. It's so sad.

 H. Wayne Huizenga – Wayne is a beautiful man and founder of WMX Garbage Company, who also helped launch the Blockbuster Video chain. Good for him because without a degree, he was basically screwed.

 Henry Ford – Ok, so I've quoted this guy a few times in the book, but without a college degree, you can bet this billionaire founder of the Ford Motor Company was never respected by his father-in-law.

 Henry J. Kaiser – This multimillionaire and founder of Kaiser Aluminum didn't even graduate from high school. Think about it. Without a diploma, there was no way he could have become one of those pharmaceutical reps who delivers sales presentations and catering to doctors every day in exchange for their allegiance in writing prescriptions for the drugs the rep is peddling.

 Hyman Golden – This guy spent his whole life making drinks and millions. I bet you the founder of Snapple lived a life of regret while endlessly chanting to himself, "Why me? No Degree. Why me? No degree."

 Ingvar Kamprad – I believe IKEA's business model is in jeopardy. Their founder has no degree. The lines of customers are now so long that no one even wants to go there anymore. Oh...and he's dyslexic.

 Isaac Merrit Singer – This sewing machine inventor dropped out of high school because he was spending all his time sewing. I am SEW sorry for him.

 Jack Crawford Taylor – Although this man did serve honorably as a World War II fighter pilot for the Navy, I wonder what he is going to fall back on if his Enterprise Rent-a-Car venture fails.

James Cameron – Avatar...overrated. Titanic...overrated. Winning an Oscar... overrated. But what did you expect from a director, writer, and film guy who dropped out of college?

 Jay Van Andel – A billionaire co-founder of Amway...not impressive without a degree. He does not know the meaning of life.

 Jerry Yang – Who even uses Yahoo anyway, other than the 20% of the world that does? This guy threw it all away and dropped out of a PhD program. I bet you he can't even spell "Yahoo!"

 Jimmy Dean – Food is so simple. You grow it. You eat it. You raise it. You kill it and eat it. How complex could it be if a man was able to start a multi-million dollar company after dropping out of high school at age 16?

 John D. Rockefeller Sr. - So my son and I did name our Great Pyrenees dog after this man, but we wouldn't have named a human after him. Because although Rockefeller became the wealthiest man in the world, he didn't have a degree and I judge him for this.

 John Mackey – The guy who founded Whole Foods Market, the millennial mecca of the great organic panic that has swept our nation, enrolled and dropped out of college six times. Now he's stuck working at a grocery store in a dead-end job.

 John Paul DeJoria – This man is the billionaire co-founder of John Paul Mitchell Systems and dude who also founded Patron Spirits. That's it. That's all he's accomplished. No degree.

 Joyce C. Hall – This man spent his whole life writing apology cards to his family for shaming them by not graduating from college. When he wasn't doing that, he was running that little company he founded called Hallmark.

 Kemmons Wilson – This dude started the Holiday Inn chain after dropping out of high school. But then what? What's he doing now? Well he's not buying huge amounts of college logo apparel and running down to the college football stadium eight Saturdays per year while talking about the good old days with his frat brothers. He doesn't have a degree.

 Kevin Rose – This dude dropped out of college and started a company called Digg.com. I'm not impressed with his millions. I just want to see that degree.

 Kirk Kerkorian – I did see a Boyz II Men concert at the Mirage Resorts that this guy owns. But, I have never stayed at the Mandalay Bay resort that he owns in Las Vegas more than once. It's good that he owns MGM Studios because the closest he'll ever come to a degree is if he makes a movie about himself getting a degree. He dropped out of school in 8th grade.

 Larry Ellison – Larry is the billionaire co-founder of Oracle software company and he is a man who dropped out of two different colleges. Oh, the regret he must feel.

 Leandro Rizzuto – This guy spent his time building Conair and that was it. Now, just because he is billionaire, does he think we should respect even though he does not have a degree?

Leslie Wexner — My wife buys stuff from this person, but I am still not impressed with the fact that this law school dropout started a billion-dollar brand with $5,000.

 Mark Ecko — If you are one of those people who has to define success based upon the success you have, then I supposed Mark Ecko is impressive. This multi-millionaire is the founder of Mark Ecko Enterprises, but he dropped out of college.

 Mary Kay Ash — I feel like Prince should have written a song about the pink Cadillacs that Mary Kay was famous for giving to her top sales reps. But I am not impressed with her because she didn't attend college.

 Michael Dell — He may be the billionaire founder of Dell Computers, but he probably doesn't feel like a billionaire since he never experienced the college joys of drunken music festivals and regrettable one-night stands.

 Milton Hershey — Like I always say, "If you drop out of 4th grade you are going to spend your entire life making chocolate." That is what the founder of Hershey's Milk Chocolate did.

 Rachael Ray — Her happiness and genuine love for people and food makes me mad because without formal culinary arts training, this Food Network cooking show star and food industry entrepreneur is just a sham.

 Ray Kroc — He dropped out of high school, founded McDonald's and spent his whole life saying, "Do you want fries with that?" So sad.

 Richard Branson — So he's the billionaire founder of Virgin Records, Virgin Atlantic Airways, Virgin Mobile, and more. But did he graduate from high school? No. He dropped out of his high school at the age of 16. So sad.

 Richard Schulze — He's the Best Buy founder, but he did not attend college. Doesn't he know that the investment in a college degree is truly the Best Buy you can ever make?

 Rob Kalin — Rob is the founder of Etsy, but who even uses Etsy other than all the humans on earth? This dude flunked out of high school, then he enrolled in art school. He created a fake student ID for MIT so he could take the courses that he wanted. His professors were so impressed by his scam that they actually helped him get into NYU. Rob, you have to get it together.

 Ron Popeil — The dude who is constantly talking about dehydrating your meat and the multimillionaire founder of Ronco did not graduate from college.

 Rush Limbaugh — This guy irritates half of America every day for three hours per day. I believe that this multi-millionaire media maven and radio talk show host would be more liked if he had graduated from a liberal arts college and would have purchased a Prius pre-loaded with bumper stickers.

 Russell Simmons — This guy is co-founder of Def Jam records and the founder of the Russell Simmons Music Group. He's also the founder of Phat Farm fashions and a bestselling author. He didn't graduate from college because he claims to have been too busy introducing rap and hip hop music to the planet.

S. Daniel Abraham – This man founded Slim-Fast without even having a degree in nutrition. Outside of the millions of people who use his products every day to lose weight, who is going to trust him with their health since he doesn't even have a college degree?

 Sean John Combs – The man who is en route to becoming the first hip-hop billionaire in part because of his ownership in the Ciroc Vodka brand did not graduate from college because he was spending his time discovering and promoting Mary J. Blige, The Notorious B.I.G., Jodeci and other R&B stars. If this man ever wants to become truly successful, he will go back to Howard University and get that degree.

 Shawn Fanning – This is the music industry-killing devil who created Napster and went on to become a multi-millionaire. If he would have stayed in college, he would have learned to follow the rules.

 Simon Cowell – This famous TV producer, judger of people, American Idol, The X Factor, and Britain's Got Talent star dropped out of high school. He has been negative ever since. He obviously needs a college degree to calm him down because I've never met a college graduate who is mean.

 Steve Jobs – This hippie dropped out of college and frankly I don't even know who he is.

 Steve Madden – Steve dropped out of college and now spends his entire life making shoes. He may be worth millions, but I'm sure that you and I are not impressed.

 Steve Wozniak – Ok, so I did know that Steve Jobs co-founded Apple with this guy. Sure, both became billionaires, but they experienced what I call a "hollow success" because they did not take the time to earn a college degree.

 Theodore Waitt – This man became a billionaire by selling a PC to every human possible during the 1990s. I bet that he regrets not having a degree.

 Thomas Edison – Tommy Boy wasn't smart enough to graduate from high school, yet he was crazy enough to invent the modern light bulb, recorded audio and recorded video. I am never impressed with crazy people who don't graduate from high school.

 Tom Anderson – This dude co-founded MySpace after dropping out of high school. He made his millions, but who ever had a MySpace account anyway?

 Ty Warner – I think the only thing weirder than collecting Beanie Babies is to have invented them. To cover up this weird Beanie Babies fixation, this billionaire has gone on to purchase real estate. College would have taught him that it is not normal for an adult to be interested in stuffed animals.

 Vidal Sassoon – This dude founded Vidal Sassoon after dropping out of high school. Had he graduated from college, I'm sure his product would have been better.

W. Clement Stone – This guy started the billion-dollar insurance company called Combined Insurance. He then went on to start Success Magazine and write books to keep himself busy because he felt so bad that he didn't have a college degree.

 Wally "Famous" Amos – This man did not graduate from high school and spent almost his entire working career making people fat by selling them Famous Amos cookies. If he had graduated from college, he might have made a product that makes people thin and able to live forever while tasting good, you know, like Aspartame. No, wait. Aspartame is the sugar substitute created by college graduates that has been shown to cause cancer. Okay, you win this round Amos! But, I shall win in the end! You'll soon regret not having earned that degree.

 Walt Disney – This struggling entrepreneur who never really figured it out co-founded the Walt Disney Company with his brother Roy. He didn't even graduate from high school, which is probably why he spent his entire life drawing cartoons.

 Wolfgang Puck – Okay, so my wife and I buy his soup. Okay, so I have eaten at his restaurant a few times. But I can't respect a man who dropped out of high school at the age of 14. Yes, he's opened up 16 restaurants and 80 bistros. So what? Respecting people like this sets a bad example for kids because not everyone can go on to become a successful entrepreneur, but everyone can incur $100,000 of student loan debt before finding a soul-sucking job doing something they don't like in exchange for a paycheck that is not sufficient. For these people, the only things they have to look forward to are their two weeks of vacation and the chance they have to retire when they are so old that their body has begun to break down.

. . . .

SUPER MOVE #14 – Don't wait to bill your customers

Collect your payment at the time that your business provides the service or product. Don't become poor because you are "in an industry where everyone sends the customer a bill." Most businesses fail because most people in the world of business don't know what they are doing. At the absolute minimum, you must give the customers a bill for the services you are providing at the actual time that you provide the services or products.

Avoid Death by Invoice

SUPER MOVE #15 – Charge late paying customers a finance charge

Clearly explain to your customers that if they wish to not pay in full, they will be charged a finance fee or finance charge.

» Put this language into your standard contracts and hold your customers accountable to honoring your payment terms.

» You must make sure that your contracts include a monthly finance charge for all bills that are not paid on time.

» I recommend that you include a clause in your contract stating that the client is responsible for all reasonable fees and costs associated with the collections process.

» Always insist that your customers sign their contracts in their name and not in the name of their business so that they are personally liable for paying you.

SUPER MOVE #16 – Speed up your service and product delivery speed

Many companies I have helped were used to billing a customer for a service or product and then taking a nuclear half-life to deliver the product or service. This is not good. As a general rule, your business will get paid in full when you finish producing or delivering your products and services. Thus, you want to get your work done and delivered as soon as possible. Also, when you deliver products and services with a quick turn-around time, people assume that you care more and they are many times more likely to refer you more business.

SUPER MOVE #17 – Take every legitimate payment source known to man

I see so many small businesses that refuse to take American Express, Discover Card, or other payment options because of the fees that these companies charge. However, what does it cost you to not gain the business from customers who can only pay using these options? A lot.

Look at the true cost of accepting these forms of payment and then just add it into your normal everyday prices. Literally, just increase your prices by 3% across the board and go on with business as usual while taking the new forms of payment. To make your life easier, I have listed the payment systems that you should accept if possible and we have produced training videos to show you how to get set up with each one of these payment systems.

Cash – I would accept cash unless any of the following statements are true:

» You are selling high-dollar items and you don't want $106,000 in your register.

» You are selling items in a very high crime area and you are not fond of getting robbed. (You should also get the heck out of there as well.)

» You are a retail business that has a self-service model.

» You are involved in selling enriched uranium to the Iranian government.

To learn how to start accepting cash payments for your business, visit: www.ThriveTimeShow.com/TreasureTrove.

Checks – I would accept checks from your customers unless the following statements are true:

» You don't like messing with customers who have to write out checks and then dealing with the potential of bounced checks. I personally no longer accept checks from customers for most of my business ventures. If you do accept checks, there are now many websites out there that will allow you to verify that the check will go through even before you take it, websites such as: http://www.achworks.com/

To learn how to start taking check payments for your business, visit: www.ThriveTimeShow.com/TreasureTrove.

Credit Card – I would accept credit cards from your customers unless any of the following statements are true:

» You want to live in a van down by the river.

» You want to be homeless.

» You can't figure out how to raise your prices 3% across the board to cover the cost of taking credit cards as a form of payment.

Mobile Payments – I would accept mobile payments from your customers unless any of the following are true:

» You hate money.

» You have too much money.

» You believe in the Illuminati and you believe that the following mobile payment systems are funding the takeover of the world and the creation of "chem trails":

» www.samsung.com/Pay

» www.visa.com/MobilePayments

» www.paypal.com/here

» www.android.com/pay

» www.apple.com/apple-pay

» www.squareup.com

To learn how to start accepting mobile payments for your business, visit: www.ThriveTimeShow.com/TreasureTrove.

Money Order – I would accept money orders unless the following is true:

» You don't want to work with low-income consumers who are unable to qualify for a credit card.

If you do decide to accept money orders, then you must always verify their authenticity. Don't accept them without first verifying them.

Automatic Clearing House (ACH) - I would accept ACH payments unless any of the following statements is true:

» You believe money to be the root of all evil, based on a gross misinterpretation of 1 Timothy 6:10 which actually says, *"For the love of money is a root of all kinds of evil. Some people, eager for money, have wandered from the faith and pierced themselves with many griefs."* The love of money is evil; not the money itself.

» You enjoy playing the "Let's See If We Are Going to be Able to Pay the Bills Game" each month.

Consumer Financing and Payment Plans - I would work hard to set up third party payment plan options for your customers, if at all possible, unless:

» You cannot strike a deal with third party payment plan providers such as Wells Fargo, Synchrony, or CareCredit (for the Medical Services industry). I would strongly suggest that you not offer in-house consumer financing on products and services because as soon as you do, you shift your company's focus from your core niche to becoming a collections agency.

To learn how to set up consumer financing for your business, visit: www.ThriveTimeShow.com/TreasureTrove.

Web-Based Transactions and Online Shopping Carts - I would create an online shopping cart for the products and services you offer unless any of the following are true:

» You don't want to publish your prices online because you custom quote every project.

» You need your customers to buy your products and services in person because you offer an experience with your products and services that cannot be duplicated online.

» You are totally unwilling to learn how to set up an online shopping cart that has the potential to produce copious amounts of cash for your business.

SUPER MOVE #18 – Assume your bookkeeper or CFO is stealing money from you all of the time

I worked with three small business owners this year who discovered that the person handling their finances had stolen at least $20,000 from them. One person had over $80,000 stolen from her. Trust no one. Insist on having the weekly accounting meeting that I discussed previously.

SUPER MOVE #19 – Track your financial data so that you can better weather predictable seasonal up and down cycles in your business.

Most brides want to get married in May, June, September, or October and most companies want to have their politically incorrect Christmas parties during the

"In God we trust. All others bring data."

-W. Edwards Deming

(Famous management expert and best-selling author who many create as being the catalyst behind the post World War II economic miracle of industrialization that Japan experienced between 1950 and 1960)

"You've found market price when buyers complain, but still pay."

-Paul Graham
(Co-founder of the Y-Combinator business incubator famous for helping to launch Reddit, Airbnb, Dropbox, and Weebly)

month of Christmas (December). Thus, I had to plan for this in my entertainment business. Every year, I had to make sure that we were fully staffed with DJs during peak seasons and with enough quality salespeople during the off months to bring in enough deposits to keep the business going until we hit the busy months again. It was very feast or famine at first. However, after about three years of tracking the cash flow cycles, I began raising the deposit amounts during the months where we weren't doing many shows and raising the prices during the months when we were doing a ton of shows. This little move is referred to as "price elasticity." I first learned about this SUPER MOVE when reading, Nuts: Southwest Airlines' Crazy Recipe for Business and Personal Success by Kevin and Jackie Freiberg.

To stabilize your cash flow through the year, take the following five action steps:

1. Enter the income and expenses for the past 12 months into a spreadsheet.

2. List a minimum of three factors that are causing each month to be up during the peak months.

3. List a minimum of three factors that are causing each month to be down during the slow months.

4. Write down three ideas for how you could sell more to your existing customers during slow months.

5.   Consider creating a sales holiday or event to stimulate business in a slow month. You could come up with a NO INTEREST FOR FOUR YEARS special during a slow month. You could come up with a buy-one-get-one-free special. You could come up with a 4th of July Blow Out Special! You could attempt to create the World's Largest Snow Cone to attract customers who are staying inside and out of your store because it's so cold. You could rent an inflatable gorilla and have massive inflatable slides in front of your appliance store to celebrate your Customer Appreciation Weekend. I actually worked with a major appliance store to invent sales events and sales holidays and it works! People see the inflatables, the signs, and the balloons and they show up and buy stuff.

Fun Fact:

Thrive15.com investor and mentor Arthur Greeno actually attempted to build the world's largest snow cone and earned both national attention and tons of customers who ventured out into the terrible winter weather to take a glimpse at his magical snow cone and buy some chicken. Watch the story at: http://www.newson6.com/story/14008387/largest-snow-cone.

Ample Example:

Hobby Lobby is famous for placing most of their inventory on sale at 50% off at one point during each month. They basically set their prices much higher than they need to be and then they offer deep discounts each month on seemingly random items to convince you and me to come in to buy that item. Then while we are there, we end up buying a bunch of other items at full-price. I wouldn't call this a loss leader strategy because Hobby Lobby still makes good profits on items they are selling for 50% off.

Here are a few bonus suggestions:

» Write down three ideas you have to bring in more revenue by encouraging your customers to pre-book or pre-buy your services.

» Write down three ways you could trim labor costs during your slow months.

» Write down three ways you could move around the members of your team to different departments where you might need more help during certain seasons of the year.

» Write down any inventory items you could purchase in bulk ahead of a busy season to help increase your profitability during the busy months.

» Write down three ways you could increase your capacity to bring in more money during the peak seasons by being able to work with more customers.

» Consider selling a monthly or upfront service contract with the purchase of an item. For example, if you are a contractor and you install sinks, showers, wood floors and cabinets, consider selling a service contract for 5% of the price of the item that guarantees that you will come back and fix anything that breaks during the first 12 months after installation.

» Consider offering a next step service. For example, if you are a men's grooming business that offers men's haircuts, consider also selling style consulting, hair products, and men's clothing items such as socks, scarves, watches, etc.

» Consider offering a long-term contract to your customers in exchange for a discount. This can help you better forecast your company's financial future.

» EXTRA Bonus Idea: Consider eating ramen noodles for every meal. I've done it for a few months. Not good, but it's cheap and loaded with unhealthy sodium. Deer will start seeking you out as a human salt-lick.

SUPER MOVE #20 – Schedule a weekly time to watch your expenses like a hawk

I realize that very few hawks literally watch financial numbers, but you get what I am talking about. Typically, when a business owner starts their business they are

frugal out of necessity. However, over time as more and more money starts flowing in, many entrepreneurs start adding monthly expenses that are not justified by a proportionate increase in income. When you first start out in business, you hire a salesperson who also helps you run errands. Over time, you hire a salesperson who is a sloth, but because you are too busy to either train them or fire them, you hire another salesperson who also turns out to be dysfunctional. Soon your profits disappear and you find yourself frustrated and with a big staff of non-performers. Don't let this happen to you. You must schedule a weekly time to look at all of your expenses and ask yourself if each expense is helping you to make more money or not. If it's not, blow it up.

Ample Example:

I once worked with a fitness-related business that hired a super sales guy and trainer. This guy was great at training people and at selling. In fact, he did so well that the business grew from the owner and this sales superstar to a team of eight trainers. These other trainers were never fully trained and so they did not know how to bring in new business. Furthermore, they were bad trainers so they did not help keep business either. However, they did get paid. When I sat down to work with the owner, I quickly discovered that he was investing zero time in training his new team members or holding them accountable. He was focused on trying to generate new customers when in fact, his closing percentage had gone down from nearly 90% when it was just he and the other guy to a low of just 5%. Can you imagine how awful he felt when I pointed out the numbers to him? Here he had been spending thousands and thousands of dollars on marketing and his team wasn't even returning the calls of the inbound inquiries from potential customers or returning the customer service-related calls of his existing customers.

"Control your expenses better than your competition. This is where you can always find the competitive advantage."

-Sam Walton
(The self-made billionaire founder of Walmart and Sam's Club)

SUPER MOVE #21 – Seek out ways to buy more from fewer vendors in exchange for better pricing

If you are buying your pens and printer paper from Vendor X and your paper towels from Vendor Y, reach out to them and let them know that you are considering consolidating all of your expenses to one vendor in exchange for a deeper discount and better overall pricing. See if you can join a buying co-op group within your industry or if you can qualify for Chamber of Commerce or trade association-related discounts.

Ample Example:

As a sick example, I recently spoke to an association of funeral home professionals (as opposed to funeral home amateurs) and I discovered that both you and I could save money on the purchase of good quality name-brand embalming fluid if we became a member of their professional association. I dislike myself for using this example.

SUPER MOVE #22 – Let your vendors know that you want them to compete for your business without being a jerk about it

It's very important that you let your vendors know that you are looking for a good and fair deal with each vendor. Let them know that the pig vendors will get fat and the hog vendors that attempt to take advantage of you will get slaughtered when you switch to another, more fair vendor. It's occasionally important to reference the name of a vendor's direct competitors if you feel that you are not getting a good deal or are being taken advantage of.

SUPER MOVE #23 – Don't sign any long-term contracts that automatically renew

Make sure you do not sign any standard long-term contracts provided by vendors that state you will automatically renew your contract at the end of the term. Cross out that standard language and refuse to sign.

SUPER MOVE #24 – Incentivize cost-saving strategies by team members

Reward your staff for saving money. Any time a member of your staff saves you money on a recurring expense, I would recommend that you make it standard policy to give them a bonus of 10% of the savings, paid out one time. Southwest Airlines has created a culture where the members of the team are so focused on cutting costs that it has become almost legendary.

☺

Fun Fact:
When Southwest Airlines flight attendant Rhonda Holley was helping to clean up the plane by collecting all the empty cups from the cabin of the Southwest Boeing 737, she discovered that the Southwest logo was being printed on the trash bags. When she saw this, she had two quick epiphanies. 1 – Passengers knew what plane they were on whether they saw the logo on the trash bag or not. 2 – Trash bags are always immediately thrown away after use and no passengers see them again. She wrote into the Southwest leadership team headed up by Colleen Barrett to see how much money it was costing the company on an annual basis to print the logos on the trash bags. Colleen Barrett called her and famously said, "You've just saved us $300,000 a year. We're not going to be printing logos on the trash bags anymore."

Kevin & Jackie Frieberg, "How Stanley Steemer and Southwest Airlines Create Ownership," Freibergs.com. http://www.freibergs.com/resources/articles/leadership/stanley-steemer-and-southwest-airlines/

SUPER MOVE #25 – Use variable based and merit-based pay systems everywhere

You want your expenses to go up as your revenue goes up and down when your revenue goes down until you know your unit economics well enough to not lose your shirt by overpaying for everything. Whenever possible, don't pay people a flat salary. Pay your people based upon their weekly performance. When people get paid bonuses based upon their weekly performance, the small details matter and most people work hard to earn their bonuses. When you pay somebody a flat amount or an hourly amount, you will find them cutting corners to go home early, to extend their breaks, and to invent incredibly creative ways (also known as lying) to justify the insane pay sheets they are turning in.

• •

Definition Magician:
Unit Economics - the direct revenues and costs associated with a particular business model expressed on a per unit basis. For instance, in a consumer Internet company, the unit is a user.

• •

 SUPER MOVE #26 – Set a good example for your team by not buying crap that you don't need

In the world of business, everyone judges you based upon what you do and not based upon what you say. So when you, as a leader, sit down on your golden throne and sip the most expensive alcohol you can find from your golden chalice, it becomes very hard for people to take you or your cost-cutting initiatives

> "You can't build a reputation on what you are going to do."
>
> **-Henry Ford**
> (The famous entrepreneur who revolutionized the automobile industry with the creation of Ford Motor Company and the mass use of the assembly line concept of production)

seriously. By flying coach when possible and taking your staff out to eat on business trips at Outback and not a super-high-end steakhouse, you will set a powerful example for your team.

SUPER MOVE #27 – You must become obsessed with incrementally improving your margins as you grow your brand

Over time, you will find that customers will become increasingly loyal to your brand and when they do, you want to reap the harvest from the sweat equity you've put in over the years by incrementally raising your margins. I am going to drop three knowledge bombs on you that will blow your mind when you realize the power of a well-maintained brand backed by incremental pricing increases. Get ready.

. . . .

The Value – The $60 bottle of Antique Gold champagne that was discontinued by Cattier was repackaged under the name of Armand de Brignac and sells for over $300 per bottle.

The Story – It all started back in 2006 when the manager of the company that produces Cristal champagne was asked by a reporter from the Economist why rappers love his champagne so much. His response was, "We can't forbid people from buying it."

This comment infuriated Jay-Z and he began looking for a new champagne to rap about (and a company that he could own behind the scenes). Later that year, he featured a bottle of a new type of champagne that no one had ever heard about in one of his trend setting rap videos, "Show Me What You Got." Over time, this new brand of champagne called Armand de Brignac, nicknamed Ace of Spades because of the large and very prominent logo on each bottle, was introduced into the marketplace. The people at Cattier, the company that produces the champagne, said of the new brand, "(Armand de Brignac) making its North American debut this year, after enjoying success as a premium, high-end brand in France." Although the brand was later discovered to just be a rebranded version of the $60 per bottle Antique Gold that Cattier had discontinued in 2006, it is still flying off the shelves – at $300 a bottle.

Once this revered rapper who is worth approximately $550 million (according to Forbes) told the world they should be drinking a $350 bottle of champagne, the world began to buy the champagne and actually felt good about it. This, my friend, is proof positive of the value of incrementally raising the margins of something based upon the perceived value of the brand.

. . . .

The Value – The $300 Beats headphones are consistently rated below the $140 ATM-50s, but the headphones continue to sell because Dr. Dre and other celebrities have discovered that they can increase their margins to over 300% and consumers will still pay for the headphones because they are worn by celebrities.

The Story – Born in 1965, Andre Romelle Young is now better known as Dr. Dre. Growing up in the projects of Compton, California, Andre was constantly around gang violence and turned to music as his passion. In 1984, Dre became inspired by the DJ Grandmaster Flash song, "The Adventures of Grandmaster Flash on the Wheels of Steel" and began going to clubs to watch local DJs perform. He started out DJing under the name of Dr. J, after his favorite basketball player, but later changed his stage name to Dr. Dre.

In 1986, Dre met O'shea Jackson whom most people know as Ice Cube and began collaborating with him on songs for Easy E's record label, Ruthless Records. Soon they formed an iconic gangster rap group called N.W.A., which that lasted until 1991 when Dr. Dre decided to leave the group at the peak of its popularity. After he left, he founded Death Row records with his bodyguard at the time, Suge Knight. Death Row records produced hit after hit for Snoop Dogg, 2Pac, Dr. Dre himself, and countless other artists.

After leaving Death Row, Dre started his own label called Aftermath Entertainment. He signed Eminem to a recording contract in 1998 and 50 Cent to a contract in 2002. As a Grammy-winning recording artist who has stayed relevant for nearly three decades and as someone who is known for having a great ear for music, I believe that Dre is justified in pricing his headphones for $300 per pair if people are willing to buy his brand. In fact, so many people bought his $300 headphones that Apple ended up buying up Beats Audio for $3 billion dollars, keeping Dr. Dre on staff in a senior leadership position.

• •

The Value - The cost of the Nike and Jordan brand shoes will continue to be high because as Forbes reports, the price of the shoe has nothing to do with the cost of producing it and everything to do with the value of the brand.

"Nike holds as much as 60% of the U.S. market share for athletic footwear. The company's Jordan brand of basketball shoes alone contributes around 60% of the revenues to the entire U.S. basketball footwear category... Customers have regularly shown a willingness to fork out high amounts of cash to get their hands on shoes modeled around iconic names such as Michael Jordan, Kobe Bryant, and Lebron James."

(Trefis Team, "Factors Underlying Our ~$68 Valuation of Nike," Forbes, March 4, 2014. http://www.forbes.com/sites/greatspeculations/2014/03/04/factors-underlying-our-68-valuation-of-nike/#619685ab4e72)

The Story – When Michael Jordan was picked by the Chicago Bulls as the third overall pick in the first round of the 1984 NBA draft, he was very good and many general managers knew he was very good. However, the Houston Rockets felt that Hakeem Olajuwon was a better fit for their organization so they drafted him with the first overall pick and the Portland Trail Blazers thought that Sam Bowie was a better fit for their organization so they drafted him with the number two overall pick. Michael Jordan would prove to be perhaps the most competitive and hard-working athlete of all time as he demonstrated time and time again by doing things just like these:

» Named the Rookie of the Year

» Won 6 NBA Championships

» Won 4 NBA Most Valuable Player Awards

» Punched teammate Steve Kerr in the face during practice for not hustling enough.

» Shaquille O'Neil explained on the Dan Patrick Show that Jordan actually told a defender during a game what he was going to do to him and then he actually did it: "'I'm coming down. I'm going to dribble it between my legs twice. I'm going to pump fake and then I'm going to shoot a jumper. And then I'm going to look at you.' And that's exactly what he did."

» To combat his opponent Dikembe Mutumbo's trash talking during a game, Jordan actually looked over at him and said, "Hey, Mutumbo. This one's for you" before shooting and making a free throw with his eyes closed.

» He trashed all his doubters in his Hall of Fame induction speech, saying of Bulls GM Jerry Krause, "I don't know who invited him … I didn't."

Now despite having been retired for nearly 15 years, Jordan still earns over $100 million per year largely from endorsement income, like the income he derives from the Jump Man image that he co-owns with Nike. He and Nike have incrementally focused on raising margins as they have grown the brand's perceived value.

Kurt Badenhausen, "How Michael Jordan Still Makes $100 Million A Year," Forbes, March 11, 2015. http://www.forbes.com/sites/kurtbadenhausen/2015/03/11/how-new-billionaire-michael-jordan-earned-100-million-in-2014/#bfeb99036c5b

· ·

Fun Fact:

"Nike and Reebok produce most of their shoes in South Korea, Taiwan, China, and Indonesia. With their minimal production costs, basketball shoes are quite profitable. The wholesale cost of the $130 Air Jordan is $68.75, said John Ruppe, Nike's manager for basketball-shoe marketing. The cost of making them is about $30."

Glenn Rifkin, "All About/Basketball Shoes; High Tops: High Style, High Tech, High Cost," New York Times, January 5, 1992. http://www.nytimes.com/1992/01/05/business/all-about-basketball-shoes-high-tops-high-style-high-tech-high-cost.html?pagewanted=all

· ·

I don't care whether you are an artist, a bakery, a dentist, or a plumber. You must become obsessed with incrementally improving your margins as you grow your brand.

SUPER MOVE #28 – Focus on profitably creating value for your ideal and likely customers in a profitable way

When I built my DJ business, I actually used to feel guilty if I wasn't DJing weddings on Saturday nights. I used to feel bad when I didn't get a chance to personally do sales presentations because I felt like I was worthless. However, once I discovered that I was never going to achieve my financial freedom or my time freedom goals by spending my days and nights DJing and doing sales presentations, I became 100% committed to building duplicable and scalable systems that had the capacity to deliver value to my customers and profits to me and my team.

You must not lose focus of this concept, though it is easy to do so because people celebrate hard working small business owners as if they are the only true non-capitalist pigs in the world and they vilify large businesses as though the owners of these companies wake up each morning wanting to steal ice cream cones from little kids and punch unsuspecting sweet old ladies. It should be your goal to make enough money to achieve financial and time freedom. That is not a bad thing.

> "Great companies first build a culture of discipline... and create a business model that fits squarely in the intersection of three circles: what they can be best in the world at, a deep understanding of their economic engine, and the core values they hold with deep passion."
>
> **-Isadore Sharp**
> (The founder of Four Seasons resorts)

SUPER MOVE #29 – You must pay yourself well or nobody is going to want to buy your business or want your job

It is OK and even wise to reward yourself from the fruits of your business after

sacrificing for years to build a great product, service, team and company. As you begin to pay yourself well, eventually people within your company will want to earn as much as you are earning. If they truly show initiative, you can promote them and grow the business so that you can make even more money by adding even more value to even more customers.

When your business really begins to grow, you will attract the attention of outside investors who will want to

> "By loving yourself, you're going to be a happy person. A lot of people don't like themselves for whatever reason."
>
> *-John Paul DeJoria*
> **(The billionaire co-founder of Paul Mitchell and The Patron Spirits Company)**

either invest in your business, buy your business, or merge your business with their business. However, when the prospective buyer asks how much money the owner is currently paying himself and discovers that the owner is not personally making any money, the buyer might begin to worry that your company might not be a smart investment.

To learn more about determining how much you should pay yourself, visit: www.ThriveTimeShow.com/TreasureTrove

SUPER MOVE #30 – Don't Marginalize Your Margins

As a business owner, you must know about two different kinds of margins (in addition to the margins of this book in which I hope you are writing). The first type of margin that you want to focus on is your operating margin. This is calculated by basically taking every dollar of sales and figuring how much of each sale ends up as an operating profit (pretax) for your organization.

For example, if you brought in $2,000,000 of sales and ended up with a pretax profit of $500,000, then your total operating profit margin would be 25% and you would be happy and the government will tax the crap out of you. If you wanted to earn an extra $100,000 this year without creating any new revenue sources, you would need to find a way to cut your expenses by 5%.

$2,000,000 x .05 (5%) = $100,000

I hope you are tracking with me. If not, it's because I'm a poor teacher, not because you are a poor learner. To help you learn with greater ease, we have recorded a more in-depth video training about this subject available at: www.ThriveTimeShow.com/TreasureTrove.

The other type of margin that you need to fully grasp is known as the gross profit margin. This number represents how much money you have left after an individual sale, after you take out what it really costs to create, make, put together, deliver, bake, or otherwise produce the product or service you just sold.[350] Knowing this will make you really popular in bars and will help you grow your business faster, as much as it pains me to discuss and you to learn.

• •

Definition Magician:
Gross margin is the difference between revenue and cost of goods sold (or COGS), divided by revenue, expressed as a percentage. Generally, it is calculated as the selling price of an item, less the cost of goods sold (production or acquisition costs, essentially. (from Investopedia.com)

• •

You determine this by taking your total gross sales and subtracting the total cost of goods sold (for the actual product or service that you just sold) from this amount. To help hammer home this idea, let's go back to the example above about owning a business that produces $2,000,000 of gross sales per year. If you had a total cost of goods sold of $500,000, that would mean that your gross profit was $1,500,000. When you explain or describe the gross profit as a percentage, you get your profit margin of 75% and people think you are really smart and your wallet magically gets bigger.

$$\$2,000,000 - \$500,000 = \$1,500,000$$

$$\$1,500,000 \div \$2,000,000 = .75 \ (75\%)$$

Once you know your total gross profit margin, you are then able to make more intelligent budgeting decisions. Once you know what your total gross profit margin is, you then know how much money you're going to have left to spend on fixed overhead, sales, flat screen TVs for your customers to enjoy, and swag items such as small koala-themed stuffed animals that you can give to your customers to let them know that they are koalified for a loan (see www.GetKoalified.com). You laugh, but I actually worked with a mortgage provider to help him brand his mortgage lending business and we chose koalas to be our official mascot, but before doing so, we had to discuss how much each koala would cost. The owner then had to make his decision based upon his belief in the "stickability" of the idea in the heads of his potential ideal and likely buyers and his knowledge of his gross profit margin.

When you really know this number, you can really look into your pricing to discover which customers are the most profitable and which customers are almost not worth attracting or keeping.

SUPER MOVE #31 – Invest more in high-profit clients, services, products, and people and cut low-profit clients, services, products, and people

You will soon realize that you can always make more money, but you can't make more time. Because of this, after you know your numbers, you must objectively look at your clients, services, products, and people and ask yourself:

"Should you find yourself in a chronically leaking boat, energy devoted to changing vessels is likely to be more productive than energy devoted to patching leaks."

-Warren Buffet
(Self-made billionaire and philanthropists often referred to as the best investor in the world)

1 - What do you need to invest more time and money in?

2 - What is it that you need to invest less time and money in?

To help make this process easier, we have created an incredible interactive tool to guide you through the process at www.ThriveTimeShow.com/TreasureTrove.

SUPER MOVE #32 – Make brand-focused, shrewd decisions when it comes to pricing and purchasing

According to Webster and their team of definition-knowing people, the word "shrewd" means "having or showing an ability to understand things and to make good judgments: mentally sharp or clever" (Merriam-Webster Online Dictionary, s.v. "shrewd"). When I say you need to make shrewd decisions when it comes to pricing and purchasing, I mean that you really need to understand your goals, ideal and likely buyers, your brand, and your ideal profit margins and you need to act with this

"It doesn't matter which side of the fence you get off on sometimes. What matters most is getting off. You cannot make progress without making decisions."

-Jim Rohn
(Bestselling author and renowned motivational speaker)

knowledge in mind. For instance, don't get all nostalgic and emotional when setting your prices and over-the-top loyal when buying a $500,000 building. Do things that will benefit the brand. Get the facts and then act.

To help you make better business decisions by gathering the facts and then acting, we have put together a decision-making worksheet for you at: www.ThriveTimeShow. com/TreasureTrove.

Reevaluate Your Pricing Model

As a general rule, startup founders and small business owners who are struggling to gain initial business must sell their products at any price they possibly can. This is what you have to do to close some deals and pay the bills before you have to begin eating old shoes for dinner like the people on Christopher Columbus' ship who ran out of food. Generally over time, the business will raise prices to keep up with inflation (the devaluation of our fiat and paper currency due to government's inability to stick within a budget and ability to print money whenever the heck they want). However, in 9 out of 10 cases, I have discovered that most business owners have never truly thought about whether they should completely rework their pricing model to create much greater profits for themselves and their team.

To help you determine what price you should be charging, we have put together an incredible pricing worksheet for you that is available at: www.ThriveTimeShow.com/TreasureTrove.

To help you begin to really think about your pricing in a new and potentially game-changing way, I put together the following list of questions you can ask yourself:

» Why do you charge what you charge?

» What do your closest competitors charge for similar products and services?

» What would happen to your business if you radically raised your prices?

» How much does the problem that your products and services solve currently cost your ideal and likely customers?

» How could you use industry facts to immediately make your pricing seem more reasonable and more appealing?

» What could you do to increase the emotional value of your product and thus, the price you could charge?

» What is a key endorsement that you could secure to dramatically increase the perceived value of your product?

» How can you use testimonials to dramatically increase the price people are willing to pay for your products and services?

» How could you combine another service or another product with your existing services and products to offer a more valuable, higher priced solution?

My friend, I really want you to think long and hard about how you can increase your prices to make more profit from each customer in a way that still creates a win-win relationship between you and the customer. It's very easy to fall prey to a pricing war, trying to land customers with rock bottom, no-brainer pricing. However, over time as your company gains momentum and customers, you don't want to keep your prices artificially low just because that is what you've always done.

12 Tell-Tale Signs that Your Pricing Is Too Low

1. The demand for your product exceeds your ability to produce it (you can't keep up).

2. It takes your business more than three weeks per month to break even, yet you can't produce any more products or services because the demand for your services and products is already too high.

3. Your prices are much lower than everyone else's in your market and you have no specific reason for keeping your prices low.

4. By solving a specific problem, your product or service is saving your customer 11 times or more than what they are paying you.

5.   You are not making over a 30% gross profit margin on each transaction (if you are in oil and gas, commodities, and certain industries, you obviously can't operate at a 30% profit margin, but in most industries, I would recommend that you aim for a 30% profit margin, minimum).

6.   You keep finding yourself working with more and more non-ideal and non-likely buyers. (Hint: You want to work with fewer non-ideal and non-likely buyers and more ideal and likely buyers.)

7.   You haven't raised your prices this year.

8.   You are offering 10x more value than your competition.

9.   You have done the math and have determined that it is impossible for you to ever achieve both financial and time freedom at your current prices.

10.   The COGS (cost of goods sold) has gone up, but your prices have not.

11.   You charge by the hour and thus the more efficient you get, the less money you make.

12.   Your branding is significantly better than when you started; yet you have not raised your prices.

13.   Your public relations efforts have helped you secure some third-party media features and a few credibility-building media appearances, and you have not raised your prices.

Marinate on the Possibility of Changing How You Charge

I have successfully worked with many service companies to help them move from a one-time charge-based business model to an ongoing revenue stream model. Is this possible for your business? I've helped a men's haircut business that was struggling with inconsistent revenue and the financial and staffing problems this creates, a music school with the same problem, a winery with the same problem, a basketball facility with the same problem, a hockey venue with the same problem, a medical facility with the same problem, a spa with the same problem, a PR firm with the same problem, a graphic designer with the same problem, a website development company with the same problem, a search engine optimization company with the same problem, a fitness company with the same problem, a gift giving product company with the same problem, an attorney with the same problem. In each case, switching their pricing and business model from a one-time charge to a membership model helped to bring consistency to their income and more value to their customers. The best business models allow your business to develop life-long relationships with customers who truly appreciate the value that you add to their lives and the problems that you help them solve.

"IN A CROWDED MARKETPLACE, FITTING IN IS FAILING. IN A
BUSY MARKETPLACE, NOT STANDING OUT IS THE SAME AS
BEING INVISIBLE."
— SETH GODIN
BEST-SELLING AUTHOR OF "PURPLE COW"

Chapter 27

Determine the Ideal Staffing Size and Work on Developing an All A-Player Team

Sit down and invest the time to make a staffing ratio chart. If you don't know where to start, don't stress. We have an interactive tool available to help you 24/7. As an example, with our photography business, I know that one diligent and honest sales person who can sell $11,000 of photography services per week produces enough revenue to support eight part-time photographers and two full-time editors while producing approximately a 30% gross operating profit for the company. I know that every year the editors will come to me and say that they feel overworked during the wedding season and then they will be practically begging for work during the winter and non-wedding season months.

The goal here is to create the following systems within your company to help you always maintain the optimal levels of staffing without ever being over or understaffed.

1. Create a time in your calendar for weekly job postings.

2. Create a time in your calendar for weekly interviewing (I prefer the group interview because it saves time).

3. Place an agenda item in your weekly meeting with your managers to ask about any current or foreseen staffing problems.

4. Block out an ongoing training time in your weekly schedule to help train up honest and diligent people so that you can punt the skilled people who are not honest and not diligent. You can teach skill, but you cannot teach character.

Remember as you grow your team, an A-player will run circles around a B- or C-player. I have literally hired one person who was able to do the work of 5 B-players. You especially see this in sales.

I have worked with many contractors over the years and almost universally see an A-player who literally works four times faster than everyone else and who has less call backs (where the technician has to go back to the property to fix something that wasn't done right to begin with).

Don't let the B- and C-players suck your soul or your finances. The mental grind and the amount of emotionally focused coaching required goes down dramatically when you hire only A-players. Remember, you must always be interviewing because if you don't, you may miss that A-player out there who would allow you to fire that constantly yawning, slow-thinking, negativity-spreading, gossip-creating C-player you wanted to fire yesterday, but couldn't.

> "When you're in a start-up, the first ten people will determine whether the company succeeds or not. Each is 10 percent of the company. So why wouldn't you take as much time as necessary to find all the A-players? If three were not so great, why would you want a company where 30 percent of your people are not so great? A small company depends on great people much more than a big company does."

-Steve Jobs
(The co-founder of Apple and the former CEO of Pixar)

> "If you pick the right people and give them the opportunity to spread their wings and put compensation as a carrier behind it, you almost don't have to manage them."

-Jack Welch
(Arguably the most successful CEO of his time. He grew GE exponentially during his tenure with the company.)

"I noticed that the dynamic range between what an average person could accomplish and what the best person could accomplish was 50 or 100 to 1. Given that, you're well advised to go after the cream of the cream. A small team of A+ players can run circles around a giant team of B- and C-players."

-Steve Jobs
(The co-founder of Apple and the former CEO of Pixar)

"SOME PEOPLE DIE AT 25 AND AREN'T BURIED UNTIL 75."
- BENJAMIN FRANKLIN
FOUNDING FATHER OF THE USA

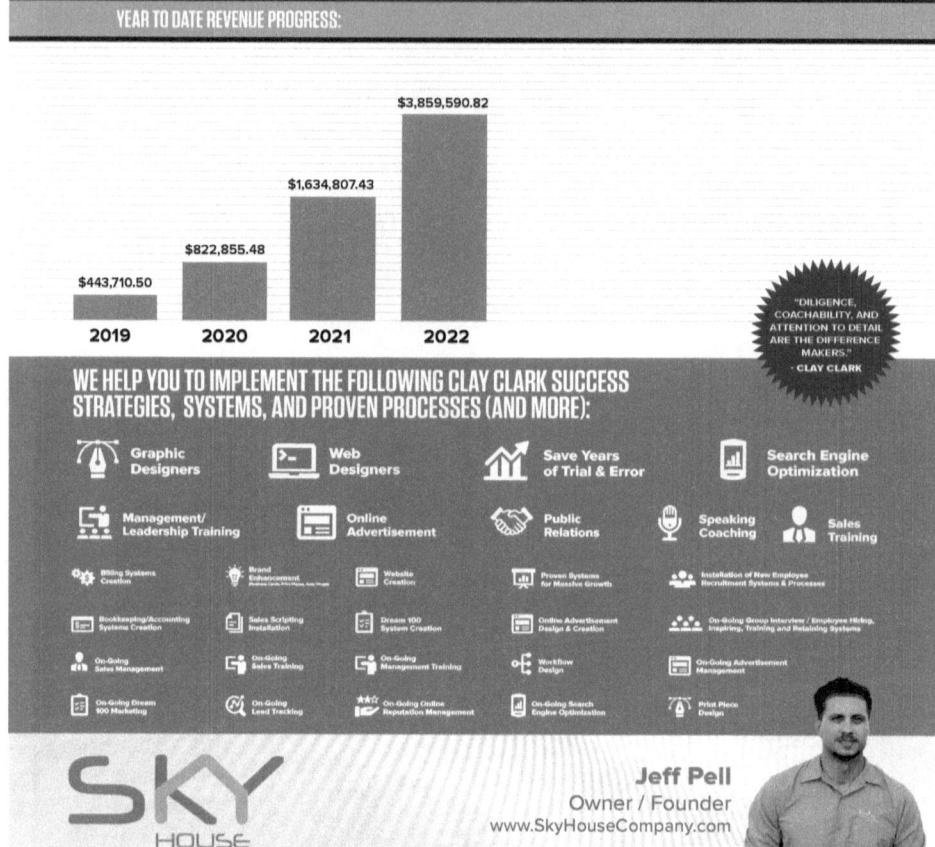

Chapter 28

Look at the Numbers Before You Leap into a Big Capital Investment

It's very important that you look at a major purchase from every possible angle, analyzing all the facts involved before you make any commitments. More times than not in the fast-paced world of business, business owners disregard this warning and begin taking small steps down the wrong path toward the infrastructure from hell as their company scales. As an example, many new business owners start out buying the products and services they need from people they know.

Let's say you purchased your computer parts from "a guy you know" who lives in Brooklyn, New York, who used to date your sister's friend Andrea. Louie "the computer guy" was a great solution when you only had one location of Ray's Pizza. Now, however you have multiple thriving locations of your Ray's Pizza and Louie clearly does not know how to help you set up your IT systems for your nationwide expansion. Your business has clearly grown at a rate that has outpaced Louie's rate of self-improvement and ongoing education.

At the same time Vinnie, a guy you know because he went to high school with your step-brother Joe, is no longer able to build you a website that looks modern and that is mobile compliant. You know this all to be true, but for some reason you are not willing to make a change of vendors because of your allegiance and unquestioned loyalty to Vinnie who went to high school with your step-brother Joe and Louie who

"The time to take counsel of your fears is before you make an important battle decision. That's the time to listen to every fear you can imagine! When you have collected all the facts and fears and made your decision, turn off all your fears and go ahead!"

-George Patton, Jr.
(He was a member of the U.S. Army who was in charge of the U.S. Seventh Army in many of the battles fought in the European and Mediterranean regions. He is best known for his leadership of the U.S. Third Army in both France and Germany after the Allied Invasion of Normandy in June of 1944.)

used to date your sister's friend Andrea. At this point, you must ask yourself the question, "if you hadn't already spent the money and invested the emotional energy into the providers, tools, and vendors that you are currently using, what would be the most logical decision to make moving forward before investing a large amount of additional capital into a solution?"

Only Invest in Items that Will Help You Grow Your Company

It's super important that you understand the HUGE difference between a strategic expense (business growth focused) and a nonstrategic expense (not business growth focused). You invest in a strategic expense to help you deliver the products and services that you produce more efficiently or to help you sell more to your ideal and likely buyers. Investing in hiring sales people, technological upgrades, better marketing materials, enhanced online marketing and search engine optimization could all be considered strategic expenses. Nonstrategic expenses do not help you to become more efficient in delivering your products and services and do not help you sell more to your ideal and likely buyers. The B- and C-players on your team (assuming you haven't coached them up or fired them by now) will almost exclusively be the ones making the case for more nonstrategic expenses. They want a bigger flat screen for the break room, they want to celebrate staff birthdays, they want to buy a cake for the person you are firing to celebrate their last day of work. These people will make you homeless if you listen to them.

As a general rule, you want to invest more than your competition in the area of strategic expenses, regardless of how much you are winning or losing in the marketplace. You also want to be intense about cutting out all nonstrategic expenses.

Financing Exponential Growth

When you start growing quickly, you may find yourself running out of cash because everything begins to cost a lot of money. The quicker your company grows as a result of you implementing scalable systems, the sooner you are going to need additional means of funding. It is very important that you not be caught off guard by this need for funding, which means you should work to secure these additional sources of funding well before you need them. Although some of my recommendations may freak out new entrepreneurs, I am listing the most reasonable and practical sources of funding that are available to you as an entrepreneur who has proven your business model.

The 14 Best Ways to Fund Your Business Growth

1. **Credit Cards** – Am I kidding? No. I have met many top entrepreneurs who very successfully funded their business using no-interest 18-month credit cards. Companies like Barclay, American Express and others understand that many times a business owner needs funding but you may not have a line of investors begging to invest in you. Thus, they have created no-interest 18-month credit cards with large limits. This may be a great solution if you know that you will be able to pay off the balance of the cards in the next 12 months.

2. **Family and Friends** – Am I kidding? No. Sam Walton (Walmart), Jeff Bezos (Amazon), and countless other entrepreneurs secured funding from people that they know. Sam Walton's father-in-law lent him the money to start his first business. The parents of Jeff Bezos pretty much emptied out their retirement fund and invested $300,000 in his business because nobody else wanted to invest yet. If you 100% believe in your business model and it is working, then you should absolutely consider borrowing money from friends and family. I recommend borrowing smaller amounts of money from more people such as $10,000 from 10 people instead of $100,000 from one person. Typically, having one major investor creates problems as they try to dominate each and every one of your business decisions because they have sunk so much of their personal money into your business (and wouldn't you).

3. **Create a Premium Package** – Typically the top percentage of your customers (economically speaking) don't care about the price you are charging at all. In fact, they value the most exclusive VIP experiences possible. I recently worked with a sports coach who introduced a premium package to his clients and was

able to land five Premium Package deals that pay $1,500 per month versus his typical price point of $150 per month. The clients he sold the packages to loved the exclusivity and they didn't really even care about the price.

4. **Offer Discounts for Payment in Advance** – Change your pricing model or your packages to create a situation where more of your customers will pay some or all of the balance up front before the service or products are delivered.

5. **Raise Prices by 5%** - Typically when you raise prices by 5%, your customers will not lose their minds and only about 5% of your customers will openly complain. Meanwhile, you can take that extra 5% and grow your business.

6. **Lease Instead of Buy** – You may want to consider leasing equipment instead of buying it up front and outright. When I was growing my entertainment company, I did this with the purchase of our phone system. The phone system would have cost $70,000 to buy outright (this was old school before Voice Over IP phones had been created yet).

7. **Connect with Your Local Banks** – Make your business bank-friendly by bringing consistency to your expenses, locking in long-term contracts with key customers, improving your margins, creating an accurate and up-to-date profit and loss statement, and creating an accurate and up-to-date balance sheet. Get your credit score up over 750 and gather at least five references from key customers. We'll talk more about this in a minute.

8. **Trade Out with Vendors and Suppliers** – Rack your brain and look for vendors that would be willing to trade out services or products instead of cash so that you can save more money and have more capital available to invest in STRATEGIC EXPENSES.

9. **Vendors** – Talk to your key vendors who make more when you make more and strategically and discreetly share with them your expansion plans. You wouldn't believe how many people are actually interested in funding the growth of a company that will then cause their business to grow as a result of their investment. Many of these people see you work every day and they understand the value you bring to the marketplace. These people are your fans.

10. **Credit Lines** – I will openly and honestly say that credit lines scare me TREMENDOUSLY because they are very, very fickle. I would compare operating your business using a credit line with having your house wired directly into a nuclear reactor because you like the energy efficiency. Sure, it's awesome having access to unlimited cheap energy, but if that baby has a leak, you are going to wish you lived in a log cabin and had to chop wood every day to heat your house.

Essentially, a bank can have a board meeting to discuss liquidity issues they are having (not having enough cash on hand) and your business can come up in the discussion. The bankers can openly discuss the best way to get the most cash into the bank as soon as possible to meet regulatory compliance and the suggestion to call your credit line due can be suggested and approved in minutes then BOOM! You will get a letter from your banker telling you that you must pay off your credit line in full right away or the bank has the right to repossess any of your assets that were put up as collateral to get the loan in the first place. This means that your business can be motoring along making a nice profit and then BOOM, it's over. You must come up with the entire amount of your credit line immediately or the bank will start taking your stuff. This is insane to me.

Many business owners say that credit lines have proven to be a great resource of the cash they need to fund their daily operations, but they are literally one decision and one call away from losing it all. If your business is too reliant upon short-term credit lines to fund operations, you need to focus on really increasing the quality of the relationship with your banker now. You need to consistently and accurately communicate with your banker and you had better have a great relationship with God. Because you are going to need divine intervention when that bank calls your credit line due all at once. Make sure that you never bounce a check and that you have a backup plan in place in case that bank decides to immediately reduce or close your credit line.

11. **3% Automatic Savings and Capital Reserve Funding** – With my photography company, we take 3% of all sales revenue and put it into a reserve bank account. We have set this up to happen automatically so that it is never an emotional decision to save or not save. This is not even something we discuss. We just do it. Because we made the decision one time to automatically save 3% of our gross revenue into a capital reserve fund, we have effectively decided to never have an emergency again. We are never in a cash crunch when bad things happen or when we need to fund our growth.

12. **Reduce the Time Involved in Your Sales Cycle** – Systemically reducing the amount of time involved in your average sales cycle will help you tremendously for almost countless reasons. The momentum in your office is unbelievable when deals close fast. The morale in your office increases dramatically when the members of your team see that deals are closing quickly. The energy and the emotional state of your average employee is peaked when deals are closing all day left and right…BOOM.

    For an in-depth training about how to dramatically decrease the length of your average sales cycle, visit: www.ThriveTimeShow.com/TreasureTrove.

13. **Receivables-Based Financing** – Raising money with receivables-based financing is expensive, but if it is your only route to financing, then you need to consider it. Essentially, a company like SwiftCapital.com will purchase your receivables at a discounted rate and will give you the cash you need today. They set up fixed payments from your business checking account that they deduct each week until all the receivables purchased have been paid back. The rate of interest that these companies charge can be very high so make sure that you know what you are getting yourself into before moving forward with companies like Kabbage.com, SwiftCapital.com, and CanCapital.com.

14. **Investors / Dancing with Potentially Key Partners or the Devil** – I have tried to not reference Satan, the Devil or the Anti-Christ in this book thus far, but now it is time. Whenever you take on an investor, you must realize that you are

taking on a partner who is going to want to give you advice, good or bad, for the long haul. Occasionally, I will speak with a young man who is upset that his father-in-law is constantly judging him and telling him what to do after he let his father-in-law buy him a house or pay for his vacation. My friend, taking on an investor definitely involves you taking on their influence, their feedback and their world-view, good or bad.

As a general rule, I have found that the local banks that you deposit your money with each and every week will be willing to invest in your business if you are operating at a 30% operating profit margin, if you have been a faithful and good customer with them, if you have a good credit score and if your loan package is Small Business Administration Loan compliant (SBA compliant). When banks lend money to a startup, it is very risky if you do not have enough collateral (stuff that the bank can take back if you don't pay the loan off). However, if the bank can secure for you an SBA Loan, the deal becomes less risky because the Federal Government is actually going to guarantee approximately 85% of the value of your loan.

For an in-depth training on how to secure a small business loan from your local bank, visit: www.ThriveTimeShow.com/TreasureTrove.

When attempting to secure a small business loan, you need to be super aggressive when it comes to preparing a bankable packet before you ask a bank to lend you money. You only have one shot to make a first impression and it is absolutely critical that you knock your initial presentation to the bank out of the park.

For an interactive and updatable worksheet to help you create an accurate and up-to-date Balance Sheet, visit: www.ThriveTimeShow.com/TreasureTrove.

For an interactive and updatable worksheet to help you create an accurate and up-to-date Profit and Loss Statement, visit: www.ThriveTimeShow.com/TreasureTrove.

Download a Small Business Loan Documents Checklist at: www.ThriveTimeShow.com/TreasureTrove.

Once you have your documents together, you must then commit to pitching to a minimum of 10 banks so that you will have multiple lending options to choose from. A wise business owner (and by now, you are one) will create an atmosphere where banks are competing with each other to lend you money. The better your loan packet, the more banks will want your deal. I do not know of a single small business owner who has not had to pitch his loan packet to at least several banks before getting the loan he needed.

When seeking a small business loan, you must keep these three key principles in mind:

1. **Banks make money by lending money.** They are not doing you a favor by lending you money. In fact, banks actually lose money (as crazy as it sounds) when they just take in deposits all day because they pay their customers interest on the money they deposit.

2. **Banks are just like any other business in that sometimes things are going well and sometimes they are not.** Sometimes a bank cannot lend you money because they are struggling to meet their liquidity requirements and not because you have a bad pitch or a bad loan package.

3. **He who has the most options always wins.** Make sure that you have at least three banks competing for your business and your loan at one time so that you can choose the loan package that is the best for you and your business.

Learn to Look at Your Business Like a Banker Would

Most entrepreneurs go into bank meetings and make absolute fools of themselves by going on and on about their passion, the market's need for their product and their passion for their passion. When they start getting asked the questions that bankers want the answers to, they generally get very quiet and this is not a good thing. Bankers generally don't care about the product or service that you are passionate

"Robert Hemphill was the credit manager of the Federal Reserve Bank in Atlanta. In the foreword to a book by Irving Fisher entitled 100% Money, Hemphill said this: If all the bank loans were paid, no one could have a bank deposit, and there would not be a dollar of coin or currency in circulation. This is a staggering thought. We are completely dependent on the commercial banks. Someone has to borrow every dollar we have in circulation, cash, or credit. If the banks create ample synthetic money we are prosperous; if not, we starve. We are absolutely without a permanent money system. When one gets a complete grasp of the picture, the tragic absurdity of our hopeless situation is almost incredible—but there it is."

- G. Edward Griffin
(An American author, lecturer, and filmmaker. He is the author of *The Creature from Jekyll Island*)

"I knew that if I failed I wouldn't regret it, but I knew the one thing I might regret is not trying."

-Jeff Bezos
(Founder of Amazon)

"Don't worry about failure, you only have to be right once."

-Drew Houston
(The co-founder and CEO of Dropbox)

about at all, or if they do care, they care very little. Banks simply focus on your margins, your key performance indicators, the gross operating profit, your gross profit margin, your break-even point, your leadership team, the scalability of your business model, and the consistency of your financial performance.

Improve Your Personal Credit and Financial Statement

You want to make sure that you have a traditional financial statement completely filled out and ready to go before meeting with your banker so that you can put on an absolute laser show when you are presenting to this person. Bankers are typically taught to turn off that "passion finding and super connector personality" when they are analyzing deals because emotions tend to cloud their judgment.

To download an interactive worksheet to guide you through the process of creating a personal financial statement, visit: www.ThriveTimeShow.com/TreasureTrove.

It's important that you are aware of your personal credit score before meeting with your lender for the same reason it's important to know if you have a big piece of lettuce stuck in your teeth before you get up to give a big speech. Not knowing this can make you look foolish. You have to know if you have missed any payments, if you are behind on any payments or if you are operating at the absolute maximum of your credit limit. Whether you know these things or not, trust me, your banker will know.

Be Open and Honest When Communicating with Your Banker without Exposing Your Sins that Have Nothing to Do with Your Loan

When dealing with your banker, it's important that you disclose any issues that you have had in the past that are well documented and easily findable by a banker. If you do not do this, then you are going to create an aura of distrust between you and the banker and this is often irreparable. However, you don't want to tell your banker that you once were arrested by the campus police at your local college when you were discovered streaking with the rest of the fraternity. If that is not on your record, don't voluntarily create problems for yourself. At the end of the day, be open and honest about your financial situation, but don't tell the banker about your marital problems and about that weird rash you have had on your left foot since you went camping 18 months ago.

When you bring money into your business, you are almost always forced to also place a value on your company.

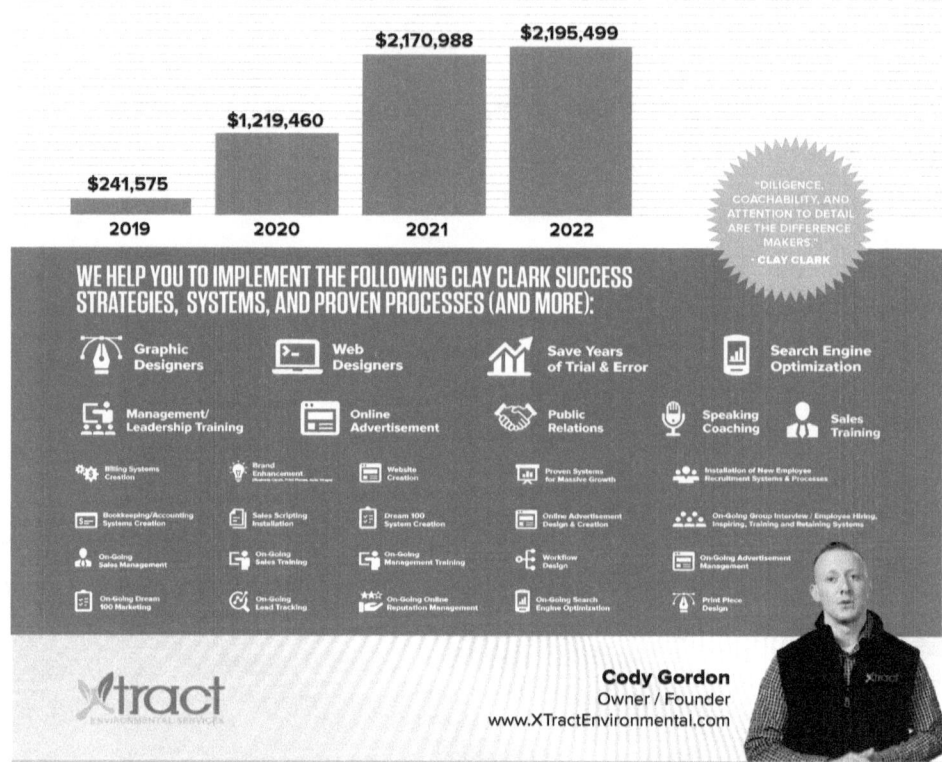

Chapter 29

Raising Capital: Investor Capital 101

If you sincerely desire to raise capital for your business via the route of bringing in outside investors, it is going to require approximately 40 hours of your time to get prepared to pitch and approximately 10 hours of your time to practice "The Art of the Pitch." More often than not, a seasoned investor (who didn't acquire his money from a trust fund or winning the lottery) will reject your pitch deck and not your actual business plan. They essentially do not give your business idea / pitch a chance because they believe that your pitch deck looks so bad (or is non-existent) that they can't fathom how you could possibly grow a successful business. If you don't know what a pitch deck is, don't feel bad. I didn't know what a pitch deck was either.

. . . .

Definition Magician:

A pitch deck is a quick presentation, most commonly produced using Keynote, Prezi, or PowerPoint to give a compelling presentation of your business plan to a group of potential investors. It's normal to use your pitch deck during both virtual / online meetings and face-to-face meetings with potential investors, partners, and the co-founders of your company.

. . . .

To bring in investor capital, you must put in the time needed to create a PowerPoint presentation that proactively and clearly answers all of the questions that a potential investor would ever have before they ask. The "Perfect Pitch Deck" deck outline is accurately described by Naval Ravikant, founder of AngelList.com, in his book titled Pitching Hacks. According to Naval, his favorite deck template comes from David Cowan at Bessemer Venture Partners. You can find other templates, but this is the best. Here's Naval's adaptation of David's template, taken directly from Pitching Hacks:

1. **Cover.** Include your logo, tagline, and complete contact information.

2. **Summary.** Summarize the key, compelling facts of the company. Make sure you cover all the topics that are in your elevator pitch — in fact, just steal the content from the elevator pitch.

3. **Team.** Highlight the past accomplishments of the team. If your team has been successful before, investors may believe it can be successful again. Include directors or advisors who bring something special to the company. Don't include positions you intend to fill — save that for the milestones slide. Put yourself last: it seems humble and lets you tell a story about how your career has led to the discovery of the...

4. **Problem.** Describe the customer, market, and problem you address, without getting into your product. Emphasize the pain level and the inability of competitors to satisfy the need.

5. **Solution.** Introduce your product and its benefits and describe how it addresses the problem you just described. Include a demo such as a screencast, a link to working software, or pictures. God help you if you have nothing to show.

6. **Technology.** Describe the technology behind your solution. Focus on how the technology enables the differentiated aspects of your solution. If appropriate, mention patent status.

7. **Marketing.** Who are the customers? How big is the market? You summarized this in your Problem slide and this is your opportunity to elaborate. How are you going to acquire customers? What customers have you already acquired?

8. **Sales.** What's your business model? If you have sales, discuss the sales you've made and your pipeline. What are the microeconomics and macroeconomics that turn your business into a $X million revenue business? Emphasize the microeconomics (each user is worth $1/year because...) instead of the macroeconomics (if we can get 1% of a $10B market...).

9. **Competition.** Describe why customers use your product instead of the competition's. Describe any competitive advantages that remain after the competition decides to copy you exactly. Never deny that you have competitors — it's okay to compete. Against anyone.

10. **Milestones.** Describe your current status and prospective milestones for the next 1-3 quarters of your product, team, marketing, and sales. Use a table with the quarters on the x-axis and the functions on the y-axis. Also include

quarterly and cumulative gross burn (your expenses, assuming zero revenue) for the next 1-3 quarters. Don't build a detailed financial model if you don't have past earnings, a significant financial history, or insight into the issue. What hypotheses did you test in the last round of financing and what were the results? What hypotheses will you test with this round?

11. **Conclusion.** This slide can be inspirational, a larger vision of what the company could accomplish if these current plans are realized, or a rehash of the Summary slide.

12. **Financing.** Dates, amounts, and sources of money raised. How much money are you raising in this round? Restate the hypotheses that you will test in this round.

To download a best-practice template of what a fully-completed pitch deck looks like, visit: www.ThriveTimeShow.com/TreasureTrove.

One more word about bringing on investors. My decision to bring on Doctor Robert Zoellner as the lead investor and CEO of Thrive15.com has been the best decision of my life, outside of my decision to marry my wife Vanessa (15 years ago). Z has been the best influence and mentor in my life and has been a father figure to me in many ways. He knows his stuff and he truly understands the needs of the average small business owner. He is the best. However, during the process of raising money to fund Thrive15.com, I was approached by many investors who would have been an absolute disaster to bring on. Their worldviews are not consistent with mine and their overall mindset would have been poisonous to the Thrive15.com culture.

When you bring on an investor, you want to make sure that the money you are infusing into your business is worth the equity and the influence that you are giving up. Make sure that you have adequately researched your investors so that you are not bringing on Satan as the new member of your team. Years ago when I was a young grasshopper business owner, I made the mistake of bringing on an investor with a high net worth and very low character score. I did not know that this was the case until he attempted to have sex with one of my employee's fiancé and shared nude photos of his wife with our sales team. When I first met him, he seemed nice and he had all of the positive and scripture-based Hobby Lobby décor one could buy adorning his home. However, there were subtle warning signs that I turned a blind eye to because I was so focused on achieving our goal and I wanted to believe that he was a good guy.

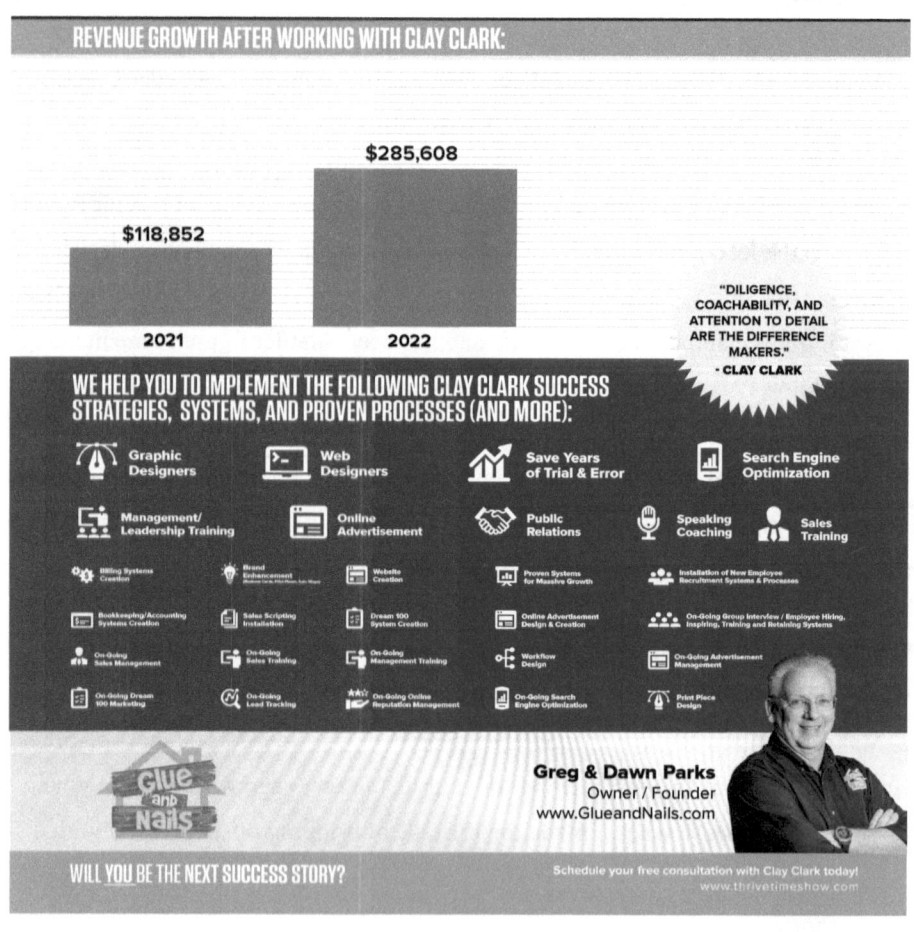

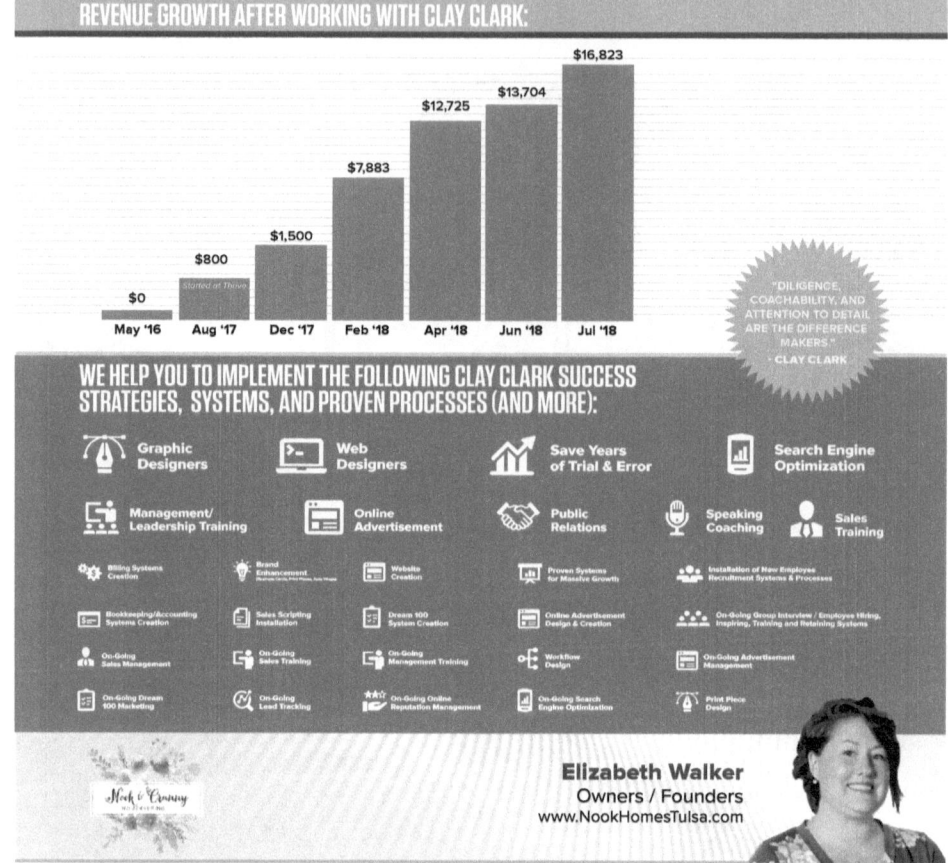

REVENUE GROWTH AFTER WORKING WITH CLAY CLARK:

"DILIGENCE, COACHABILITY, AND ATTENTION TO DETAIL ARE THE DIFFERENCE MAKERS."
- CLAY CLARK

WE HELP YOU TO IMPLEMENT THE FOLLOWING CLAY CLARK SUCCESS STRATEGIES, SYSTEMS, AND PROVEN PROCESSES (AND MORE):

Graphic Designers

Web Designers

Save Years of Trial & Error

Search Engine Optimization

Management/ Leadership Training

Online Advertisement

Public Relations

Speaking Coaching

Sales Training

Elizabeth Walker
Owners / Founders
www.NookHomesTulsa.com

Chapter 30

Protect Your Business from the Predictable Fraud and Theft

My belief in the inherent goodness of the human race is very low, not because I am a pessimist, but because I see patterns (essentially, I am not blind). Having been self-employed in some capacity since the age of 15, I have seen the truly horrible and the truly great aspects of the human race time and time again.

» The Highlights I Have Witnessed from the Human Race Since Being a Business Owner:

» I have literally seen multiple employees start walking to work two hours before start of business because they didn't want to be late for work and their car would not start.

» I have witnessed first-hand an employee (who was not wealthy) ask if he could transfer 100% of his check to another employee to help him pay his medical bills.

» I have witnessed first-hand an employee go without sleep for nearly 48 hours straight to fill in for another employee whose wife was having a baby.

» I have witnessed an employee read their entire one-year's required reading list within their first month of employment so that they would "set themselves up for success."

The Lowlights I Have Witnessed from the Human Race Since Being a Business Owner:

» I have witnessed an employee methodically use my business credit card to pay to fill up 25% of his boat gas tank each week.

» I was informed by a groom that one of my employees propositioned a bride-to-be for sex literally three hours before her wedding.

» I have watched video tape (with audio) of an employee explaining how they would attempt to fake an injury by falling in front of our business.

» I dealt with an employee who decided to check into a hotel – UNDER MY NAME - with unlicensed semi-automatic firearms that were discovered during the check-in process.

Install This Proven 20-Point System to Guard Yourself Against Employee Fraud and Theft

In my experience consulting with both small and large businesses, I have developed five proven ways to help guard your business from predictable theft and fraud. Unfortunately, small and medium-sized businesses get attacked by con artists and criminally minded employees all the time. If you own a business and you are not being proactive about protecting that business from predictable fraud and theft, you are going to lose your shirt; it is just a matter of time.

· ·

 Fun Fact:
75 percent of the 2,600 surveyed employees admitted to stealing pens and pencils, while 38 percent said they stole company stationery.

Matt Villano, "Sticky Fingers in the Supply Closet," New York Times, April 30, 2006. http://www.nytimes.com/2006/04/30/business/yourmoney/sticky-fingers-in-the-supply-closet.html

· ·

Fraud and Theft Guard #1: Fire people who are dishonest in the little things

Years ago when I was a young grasshopper entrepreneur, I didn't have a pattern of theft and fraud from which to draw my wisdom. However, now that I have personally consulted with companies from over one hundred industries, I can tell you that you must absolutely fire people who are dishonest in the little things. Employees who lie about their time card and who lie about what time they came into work will lie about everything and you need to fire them before they rob you blind. The criminal mind doesn't just show up to work one day. The employees who will rob you blind start off stealing your money by lying about their hours and by not fully completing their checklists. Then they take your money. When you fire an employee for ethical violations, I highly recommend that you make an example of them so that everybody within your organization knows that this kind of behavior will not be tolerated in any way shape or form.

"Public hangings are teaching moments. Every company has to do it. A teaching moment is worth a thousand CEO speeches. CEOs can talk and blab each day about culture, but the employees all know who the jerks are. They could name the jerks for you. It's just cultural. People just don't want to do it."

-Jack Welch
(Former CEO of GE who grew the company by 4000%)

Fraud and Theft Guard #2: It's important that you always insist that two different people are involved in the depositing and withdrawing of money within your business

Years ago I was blessed to be able to hire my father to work with me (which was a big goal of mine growing up). He was and is the most honest human I have ever been around. This man does not have the capacity to tell a lie, yet we all have the capacity to screw up and mess up our numbers. If I was in his position working as the company's bookkeeper, I would occasionally mess up the numbers as well. That is why you need to create systems where one person calculates the numbers and one person verifies the numbers any time you are depositing or withdrawing money within your business.

As an example, the person who opens your business mail should go to the effort of listing all the checks received on a spreadsheet file of some kind. Then this person should prepare these checks for depositing. After the spreadsheet has been created and the checks are prepared for depositing, the second person must double-check their math to make sure that they did not make an intentional or unintentional mistake. By implementing this system, you will almost completely remove the temptation for fraud that many people struggle with. You will also create a situation where two people would have to actually be involved to rob your business. This creates a powerful accountability system that will protect the financial health of your business.

Fraud and Theft Guard #3: Create a non-erasable financial history for your business

It's very important that you create a non-erasable financial history for your business so that committed criminal minds cannot take advantage of you. As a quick note, I want to dedicate the intensity of this portion of the book

> "For the 61 percent who admit to wasting 30 minutes to an hour, the lost productivity may not seem like a big deal. But for a small business owner, even 30 minutes each day adds up to 2.5 hours a week and 130 hours each year."

> *-Jayson Demers*
> ("How Much Time Do Your Employees Waste at Work Each Day?" Inc. Magazine)

to all the people who have screwed me over the years. Without exaggeration, I have been robbed of approximately $500,000 to this point in my career. I've dealt with the guy who falsified invoices to get paid higher commissions. I've dealt with the man who used my business card to fill up his boat with gas during my landscaping days. I've dealt with countless employees who have lied about and exaggerated their hours over the years. I've issued countless refunds and have even had to settle to prevent lawsuits with dozens of customers over the years because an employee of mine chose to be negligent and screw over the customer. My friend, this is unfortunately the way life is.

Fun Fact:

"According to a survey by psychotherapist and consultant Dr. Brad Blanton, 93% of respondents out of forty thousand Americans admitted to lying regularly and habitually in the workplace."

Keld Jensen, "Three Shocking Truths About Lying at Work," Forbes, June 24, 2013. http://www.forbes.com/sites/keldjensen/2013/06/24/three-shocking-truths-about-lying-at-work/#3885b03d1a3c

Fraud and Theft Guard #4 - You must become passionate about numbering your accounts payable invoices and keeping a separate log of who actually has each invoice series.

This is important because when someone attempts to take advantage of you by creating fraudulent invoices from a fictitious company that your company just happens to pay, you can nail them…and I have! (Yay me.)

Fraud and Theft Guard #5 – Keep your company checks in a locked and secure location

Recently I dealt with a low-quality human who actually attempted to write himself checks by stealing some of my corporate checks that he found on my desk when I got up and went to the restroom. I had discovered that this guy was lying about the hours that he was working on his search engine optimization tasks, so I was watching him like a hawk when it was discovered that he had attempted to write himself two paychecks during that week.

Fraud and Theft Guard #6 – Verify that your financial software is set up with individual log-ins for various team members who need access to that information

Whenever you set up your financial software for your business, you must go through the process of creating different log-ins for the various members of your team who need access to the critical financial information. Thankfully, I have yet to be robbed by somebody who was logging into QuickBooks to cover their tracks so that no one could detect what they were doing, but I have worked with a client who had this happened. Basically, to save money on the number of licenses he needed to purchase, this client created only one QuickBooks login and the man he hired to do the books for his business quickly discovered this. He began to set up new vendors within the system that he would pay on occasion. Later it was discovered that he was the "owner" of these eight to ten different companies that were getting paid a little here and a little there each month. As of the writing of this book, both QuickBooks and Peachtree have functionality set up to allow you to create individual logins for the various members of your team who need access to your accounting information.

Fun Fact:
"A global survey by Workforce Management company Kronos found that as many as 58% of employees call in sick on days they want to watch or attend a sporting event...This very simple kind of twisting the truth can cost organizations 8.7% of payroll each year, according to the study."

Lydia Dishman, "Here's the Truth About Lying at Work," Fast Company, July 14, 2014. http://www.fastcompany.com/3032863/the-future-of-work/heres-the-truth-about-lying-at-work

Fraud and Theft Guard #7 – Actively show that you are engaged and involved in the weekly accounting process

When the criminal mind notices that you don't notice certain things or that you are too trusting of certain people, it goes to work. Thus as a business owner, you need to show that you are engaged in the accounting process and that you weekly review the financial documents associated with your company. Yes, you must delegate to members of your team when you can, but know you cannot trust people. You can put your faith in God if that is how you choose to believe, but you cannot put your faith in people or you will be taken advantage of. To stay actively engaged in your business, I recommend that you take the following action steps on a weekly basis:

1. Schedule a weekly accounting meeting with your accounting team in which you question and highlight any purchases that seem unusual to you.

2. Listen to the members of your team, but listen to your inner voice and conscience if something seems out of the ordinary or weird. If your internal alarms are going off, then you are probably correct.

3. If something seems outside of the boundaries of your normal weekly numbers, strongly question it and demand answers with proofs.

4. Look for people who are extremely defensive when asked questions that enforce accountability, transparency, and verification that your numbers are correct. Most people who lie consistently will be offended at the thought of you holding them accountable or questioning their actions.

• •

 Fun Fact:
"In an updated regulatory filing released Wednesday, the social media company (Facebook) said that 8.7 percent of its 955 million monthly active users worldwide are actually duplicate or false accounts."

Heather Kelly, "83 million Facebook accounts are fakes and dupes," CNN.com, August 3, 2012. http://www.cnn.com/2012/08/02/tech/social-media/facebook-fake-accounts/

• •

Fraud and Theft Guard #8 – Set up guardrails to control your cash

You need to make sure that your business bank statements are mailed to your home. As a business owner, you should open and review your bank statement in great detail so that your bookkeeper knows you are watching him. Highlight any aspects of your bank statement that seem incorrect or off in any way.

Mystic Statistic:
"Workers' comp fraud accounts for about 1 percent to 2 percent of all workers' comp payments, according to J. Paul Leigh, a professor of the University of California, Davis."

Greg Hunter, "Workers' Comp Scams That Push the Limits," ABC NEWS, http://abcnews. go.com/GMA/story?id=127996

Fraud and Theft Guard #9 – Engage in the habit of doing monthly bank statement reconciliations

In a perfect world, you will do these monthly bank statement reconciliations with someone who is not the person responsible for making your ongoing bank deposits. The key here is to trust no one. Honest people make accidental mistakes; dishonest people make intentional mistakes.

Fun Fact:
The Pope John XII was deposed by the Roman Emperor Otto in 963 for stealing church offerings amongst other more scandalous activities. He was reported to have died from a stroke while in bed with a married woman.

Joseph S. Brusher, Popes through the Ages. (Princeton, N. J.: Van Nostrand, 1959).

Fraud and Theft Guard #10 – Set up a post office box for your accounts receivable to be mailed to

One often overlooked super move that can dramatically decrease the chance for your company to experience fraud and theft is to make sure that your accounts receivable (money owed to you) are mailed to a specific PO Box that is different from your office mail address.

Fun Fact:
"One out of three companies that go bankrupt each year do so as a result of employee theft. Almost 80 percent of workers admit that they have or would consider stealing from their employers."

Nicole Jacoby, "Battling Workplace Theft," CNN Money, August 19, 1999. http://money.cnn.com/1999/08/19/investing/q_employeetheft/

Fraud and Theft Guard #11 – Set up a sweep account

A sweep account is simply an account with loose financial controls into which you place money received from customer payments. At the end of each week you should transfer / sweep all of the money out of your sweep account and place it into a second account that is super secure and that offers much tighter financial controls, where you as the owner and your spouse are the only people authorized to access the funds. Do not blindly trust people with your banking information or you will be taken advantage of.

Fun Fact:
"Right now, we're hearing much celebrating from the media, the White House and Wall Street about how unemployment is "down" to 5.6%... Right now, as many as 30 million Americans are either out of work or severely underemployed."

Jim Clifton, "The Big Lie: 5.6% Unemployment," Gallup.com, February 3, 2015. http://www.gallup.com/opinion/chairman/181469/big-lie-unemployment.aspx

"Anything that can go wrong, will go wrong."

-Edward Murphy, Jr.
(The American aerospace engineer whose life was spent developing safety systems for the aerospace industry. He is the man for whom Murphy's Law is named.)

Fraud and Theft Guard #12 – Do not keep pre-signed blank checks around to be used as you see fit in the future

Keeping pre-signed blank checks around to be used as you see fit in the future will end in your certain financial demise. At some point, you will be taken advantage of as somebody other than you gains access to these checks and uses them without your permission. This will end badly 100% of the time. If you are doing this, stop.

Fraud and Theft Guard #13 - Only allow senior management to write-off losses

It's very important that you only allow yourself or members of your senior leadership team to write-off losses. When you write-off a loss from a client who has simply chosen not to pay you, this is very bad. Writing off bad debt from your clients is not a good thing. When you do this, you typically negate the profit you made or would have made on ten deals. Don't allow the writing off of bad debt to become a casual thing.

"Casual conversations and casual implementations will lead to perpetual frustration."

-Clay Clark

Fraud and Theft Guard #14 - Always use pre-numbered accounts receivable invoices and keep an accurate invoice log

Mystic Statistic:

"24% of respondents said they had detected an increase in stolen nonmonetary items, such as retail products and office supplies"

Sarah E. Needleman, "Businesses Say Theft by Their Workers Is Up," Wall Street Journal, December 11, 2008. http://www.wsj.com/articles/SB122896381748896999

Using pre-numbered invoices while maintaining an accurate invoice prepares you for when bad things happen, and they will. When a problem occurs, you will be able to find the source of the problem much easier when implementing these systems. Choosing not to follow these systems will turn the very bad day when fraud was discovered into the very bad month during which you spend every waking hour attempting to track your documents so you can figure out what happened.

Fraud and Theft Guard #15 - Require senior management to review the accounts payable each week

Not Fun Fact:

"Stateside... employee theft accounts for 43% of lost revenue."

Anne Fisher, "U.S. retail workers are No. 1...in employee theft," Fortune, January 26, 2015. http://fortune.com/2015/01/26/us-retail-worker-theft/

It's very important that your senior management sign off on the payment of accounts payable to prevent your business from paying for services and products that you did not buy and to prevent your business from paying fake invoices altogether. Over the years, I have witnessed scenarios in which a well-meaning bookkeeper paid invoices that were fake and not associated with an actual order of a product or service by the company. In fact, I know of one instance in which a bottom feeding businesses was prosecuted for routinely invoicing their former customers for small amounts. They would write "past due" on the invoices and simply send out these bogus invoices to thousands of customers at a time. Unsuspecting bookkeepers who were allowed to pay invoices of $200 or less without management's approval simply paid these like any other invoice. This fraudulent company was able to generate thousands and thousands of dollars of revenue by invoicing these oblivious business owners for small amounts each month. You must insist that your senior management signs off on the payment of all accounts payable each week to ensure that you're only paying what you actually owe.

Fraud and Theft Guard #16 - Restrict access to your corporate credit cards to a very small number of trusted people

· ·

 Not Fun Fact:
"Fraud and theft occurs in more than 35 percent of all small businesses."

Matthew Garrett, "Your Best Employee Stinks And May Be Stealing From You," Forbes, October 1, 2013. http://www.forbes.com/sites/matthewgarrett/2013/10/01/your-best-employee-sucks-and-may-be-stealing-from-you/#47eb16d650c0

· ·

Unless you want to end up buying your employees candy bars, Red Bulls, gasoline, alcohol and random adapters that they feel they need for their personal homes, I highly recommend being very strict about who gets to use your company credit card. I would require detailed receipts to support all credit card purchases that they turn in. Work off of the assumption that everyone is lying to you and create a system that requires them to prove their innocence each week by turning in detailed receipts. Require your employees to turn in a detailed monthly expense report that they sign and guarantee is both accurate and truthful. If you implement this system, honest employees will have no problem complying and dishonest employees will be rooted out and caught.

Fraud and Theft Guard #17 - Pass out paychecks at the actual worksite to verify that you don't have any bogus employees

Not Fun Fact:

"A new survey from CareerBuilder.com of more than 2,500 hiring managers found that 56% have caught job candidates lying on their resumes. The most common fib seems to be embellishing skills or capabilities."

Martha C. White, "You Won't Believe How Many People Lie on Their Resumes," CNNMoney, August 13, 2015. http://time.com/money/3995981/how-many-people-lie-resumes/

I have seen this scam attempted over and over in the construction industry. A new employee at a huge job site realizes that people get paid but the boss and management never see them. He gets the idea to create a fake person and begins to turn in fake hours that were "worked" by this fake person. The boss is out of touch with who is who on the job site, so this con artist got an extra paycheck whenever he needed it. To prevent this from happening to you, pass out the actual paychecks at the job site so that you can catch any bogus employees playing this game.

Fraud and Theft Guard #18 - Require that all overtime must be approved by management before being worked

Not Fun Fact

"The number of people who now admit to wasting time at work every day has reached a whopping 89%."

Cheryl Conner, "Wasting Time At Work: The Epidemic Continues," Forbes, July 31, 2015. http://www.forbes.com/sites/cherylsnappconner/2015/07/31/wasting-time-at-work-the-epidemic-continues/#274adcd63ac1

There are many slugs and dishonest people out there who love to work as slowly as possible so that management must pay them overtime in order to just get the job done. However, in well-run companies, management knows how many hours it should take to complete a job and requires their managers to actually sign off on the working of overtime hours before those hours are allowed to be worked.

Fraud and Theft Guard #19 - Verify that all software is registered to your company

Mystic Statistic:
"The U.S. Chamber of Commerce estimates that 75% of employees steal from the workplace and that most do so repeatedly."

"Employee Theft: Are You Blind to It?" – Rich Russakoff and Mary Goodman – CBSNews / MoneyWatch

Many times employees will attempt to license the software that you are buying for your business in their personal name so that they can use the cloud-based software from home. If they're allowed to do this, it will mean your business has to purchase an extra license of the software. You need to make sure that all software that is purchased is licensed to your business.

Fraud and Theft Guard #20 - Work off of the assumption that most people are evil and you are looking for the few good people

Mystic Statistic:
"The industry where interviewers have discovered the most phony claims on resumes: financial services (73%), followed by leisure and hospitality (71%). Information technology and health care, both at 63%, tied for third place."

Anne Fisher, "Resume lies are on the rise," Fortune, September 10, 2014. http://fortune.com/2014/09/10/resume-lies-are-on-the-rise/

I see it every week - Thrivers all around the world who have been totally shocked by an employee who has robbed them blind. Having been robbed by an employee multiple times, I really do empathize if this has happened to you. However at a certain point, we have to become smart about the people we hire and bring into our businesses. Give everyone a shot regardless of their race, age, gender, and worldviews, but you must be relentless about paying for professional background checks for each and every member of your team. Have your employees sign an employment agreement that states that you have the right to insist on random drug tests and credit checks whenever you see fit. When you ask people who routinely scam their employer to sign this type of form, they will resist, which is a great way to fire them before you hire them.

Mystic Statistic:
"Nearly one-third of all employees commit some degree of employee theft according to the Department of Justice."

Rich Russakoff and Mary Goodman, "Employee Theft: Are You Blind to It?" CBSNews / MoneyWatch, July 14, 2011. http://www.cbsnews.com/news/employee-theft-are-you-blind-to-it/

Set up Systems to Prevent the Temptation for Fraud the Ability for Massive Theft to Occur and Then You Can Get Back to Focusing on Your Business

I wrote this portion of the book to empower you so that you won't get robbed blind. I personally have been the victim of employee theft and fraud and when it happens, it totally pulls your focus away from growing your business. While you and your leadership team search for the source of the fraud, the trust that every other member of your team has earned can potentially be killed. By setting up these systems, you won't have to be super-paranoid every second of every day. This is preventive maintenance. However, if you choose not to set up these systems, you may as well start now to emotionally and mentally prepare yourself for the day you will be robbed blind because I promise you, it's coming.

Now that we have thoroughly tackled nearly every aspect involved with handling the financial aspects of growing your business in a scalable and duplicable way, let's focus on helping you build a team of employees that you can win with.

The Perfect Meeting Agenda

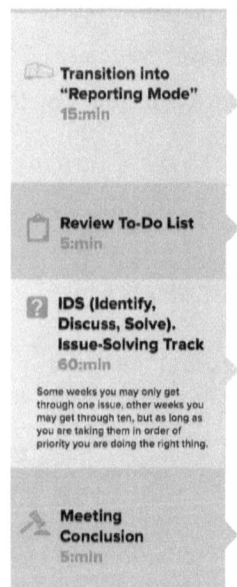

Transition into "Reporting Mode"
15:min

1. Review Scorecard - Make sure scorecard numbers are on track. *(5 minutes)*
2. Rock Review - Make sure priorities are on track. *(5 minutes)*
3. Customer or Employee Headlines - Share good and bad news in one sentence headlines to keep everyone informed about what is going on with all of your people.

If there are any scoreboard discrepancies, priority issues or headlines that need to be addressed, those items should be added to the "Issues List."

Review To-Do List
5:min

These are 7-day action items. Review last week's list to ensure that they are complete.
RULE OF THUMB: 90% of the to-do list should be getting done each week.

IDS (Identify, Discuss, Solve). Issue-Solving Track
60:min

Some weeks you may only get through one issue, other weeks you may get through ten, but as long as you are taking them in order of priority you are doing the right thing.

Load up your issues list and then prioritize those items based on what is the 1st, 2nd and 3rd most urgent isssue. If everything is of the importance, nothing gets done. Tackle each item on the list using Gino Wickman's system of indentifying, discussing and solving the issue.

1. Identify the real issue. Dive in and really find the true problem before the problem solving begins.
2. Begin discussing the issue with a spirit of candor. Attack the problem, not the people.
3. The entire focus must be on problem solving. Once you solve the problem, schedule the action steps on the "to-do list"

Meeting Conclusion
5:min

1. Recap the to-do list.
2. Discuss any messages that need to be shared out to the rest of the company.
3. Quickly rate your meeting on how you did today from 1-10 (10 being best.) 8 is the minimum standard. If you are not reaching an 8, discuss why and begin to self correct.

Note: To learn more about how to construct the agenda and outline for a perfect meeting read "Traction" by Gino Wickman.

"I would prefer not to focus on sales, I'd rather put my focus on developing a great product."

A STARVING WANTREPRENEUR
Someone who is definitely not you and who you definitely don't want to be

IT'S NOT ABOUT HOW MUCH YOU MAKE,
ITS ABOUT HOW MUCH YOU KEEP.
-CLAY CLARK

Chapter 31

BOOMING BUSINESS FOUNDATIONAL PRINCIPLE #4 – HUMAN RESOURCES TEAM

How to Hire, Inspire, Train, Empower, or Fire People

Once you have learned how to consistently sell something that your ideal and likely buyers are eager and happy to pay for, you are going to have to learn how to manage people. This section of the book deals exclusively with how to recruit, hire, equip, train, empower, evaluate, compensate, coach up, and fire people when needed. I'm also going to devote some time to discussing how to stay in compliance and meet all the requirements imposed on us by the state and federal governments when hiring employees.

Although I am going to keep this section of the book simple and pragmatic, I want to take a moment to dive into what I have discovered to be, for the majority of business owners, one of most difficult areas of scaling a business once they learn how to systematically sell a product or service – the management of people. I have witnessed many business owners (most business owners, actually) struggle to manage people because it involves doing everything that you were told not to do as a kid by your parents and your teachers.

Breaking Through the Mental Barriers to Properly Managing People

Growing up, you were probably told some of the things I'm going to list here. To become an effective manager, you must unlearn much of what you were previously taught.

1. **You were told to demonstrate unconditional love to your fellow man.**
   In the world of effective business management, you must fire people who will not work hard and who refuse to be actively engaged in the pursuit of wowing your ideal and likely buyers.

"If you aren't fired with enthusiasm, you will be fired with enthusiasm."

-Vince Lombardi
(An American football player, executive and coach who is most known for his role as the head coach of the Green Bay Packers during the 1960s, winning the first two Super Bowls in both 1966 and 1967)

2. You were told to bring enough cookies or candy for everyone in the class.
In the world of effective management, you must create a clear distinction between how you treat your all-stars and how you treat everybody else. An effective manager only gives cookies to his top performers. In fact, you may even want to take the cookies from the underperformers and give them to the diligent and honest team members.

3.   **You were told not to judge people.**
In the world of effective management, you have to hold people accountable for delivering on your brand's promises. Therefore, you must judge people by their performance.

4.   **Listen to what everyone has to say.**
In the world of effective management, you only want to listen to your ideal and likely buyers and to the constructive criticism provided by people who clearly know what they are talking about.

5.   **You shouldn't compare yourself to others.**
In the world of effective management, you have to look at members of your team and decide who is the best fit for the job based upon their daily performance. You must

"When looking for people to hire, you must look for people with integrity, intelligence, and great energy. However, if they don't have integrity they will screw you. If you can't find people with integrity you should focus on hiring dumb, lazy people."

- Clay Clark
(Billionaire founder of Berkshire Hathaway and considered by many to be one of the best managers of people and most successful investors of all time)

become very good and confident in comparing the work performance of the members of your team.

6. **You should trust people and believe that most people are inherently good.**
In the world of effective management, you simply cannot afford to run around trusting people. You must build systems to help you prevent fraud and you must keep an eye out for fraud at all times or you are going to have cash stolen out of your register, customers missing their orders and your taxes unpaid. In the world of business, only the paranoid people survive.

> "Complacency breeds failure. Only the paranoid survive."
>
> *-Andy Grove*
> (One of the founders of Intel and their former CEO)
>
> "You can't get much done in life if you only work on the days when you feel good."
>
> *-Jerry West*
> (National Basketball Hall of Fame player and a renowned sports executive)

7. **It's okay to yawn if you are tired.**
In the world of effective management, you must decide to bring energy to the workplace every day. If you yawn during a meeting with your boss or in front of a customer, you just disrespected them in a powerful and almost unforgiveable way.

8. **It's important to share how you feel.**
In the world of effective management, it does not matter how you feel. It only matters what you do.

I've discovered that most small to medium-sized businesses have assembled a weak team that consists of their brother-in-law, people they know from high school and people they should have fired four months ago. This is usually the result of an owner who is really scared about the concept of hiring people who may actually be more intelligent than him or because the owner is really weak when it comes to the process of hiring, inspiring, training, and requiring employees to be accountable. Because of this, the business owner is stuck in a perpetual reaction mode as he attempts to figure out how he is going to fill in for Employee A who called in sick and how to apologize to the customer for the negligence of Employee B. Over time, conditions deteriorate and employees who choose not to perform begin to be treated as though they are victims who need coaching, mentoring, and encouragement instead of being treated like the negligent, revenue sucking, energy stealing, company-demotivating, wrong hires that they are.

My friend, you want to hire the best people you possibly can so that you can focus your time on my three Ps of business:

1. Making great products

2. Working with people you like

3. Producing a life-changing profit

As you grow your company, focus on bringing on team members who are committed to helping you achieve the big, hairy, audacious goals of your company. Once you have built an incredible team, your business' potential will finally be unleashed. When you take the combined passion, talents, and life experiences of an honest, diligent, and skilled workforce and put it behind your proven product or service that has already begun to gain traction (sales), get ready for game-changing growth. When you take the combined laziness, lack of accuracy, negativity and lack of skill found in a negligent workforce, it doesn't matter how good your product or service is, your company will struggle. The mindset, the talents, and the experience of your team members always prove to be the big connection between your great systems and great results.

THE TEAM WITH THE BEST PLAYERS WINS!

Create an Environment Where Talented, Honest and Diligent People Want to Work

Over the years, I've had the opportunity to speak to many corporations at countless events. One of my favorite events I've ever been invited to speak at was a business leadership training for a professional contractor's association hosted at the home offices of Mike Counsil Plumbing (www.MCPlumbing.com) in San Jose, California. Every aspect of their business is run in a first-class way and because of this, it was an absolute pleasure to be around their staff and at their facilities. Mike Counsil and his team are focused on creating an environment that absolutely blows away the work environment and atmosphere at any other construction company's home office, and his company is thriving because of it. Every employee I spoke with loves working there. Their training systems are first class and consistent. The tracking of their daily key performance indicators are transparent and recorded on a big digital board for everyone to see and their décor is inspiring. Mike's vision for his company's future is sincere, future-focused, and all about growth. Mike Counsil Plumbing is an example of a business that is doing it right.

It's important to work towards hiring a team of A-players (or coaching your current team up to be A-players) while regularly firing the C-players. To bring clarity to the definition of A-, B-, and C-Players, I have written out the descriptions of each below.

A-Players:

1. They arrive to work early and stay until the job is done.

2. They embrace ongoing learning and don't push back when assigned something that is new and challenging because they like big challenges.

3. They hold themselves to a higher standard than management does so they can show that they really don't need a boss.

4. They are hungry for more work and more obstacles to overcome.

5. They are goal oriented and want to win.

6. They have a growth-mindset that is focused on constant improvement.

7. They consistently get their jobs done without broadcasting their emotional state to the room. With these people, you usually can't tell whether they are going through a personal tragedy or have won life's lottery because they will get their work done either way.

8.   They can't stand to work around B- and C-players who represent mediocrity and people who are slowing them down.

"I noticed that the dynamic range between what an average person could accomplish and what the best person could accomplish was 50 or 100 to 1. Given that, you're well advises to go after the cream of the cream. A small team of A+ players can run circles around a giant team of B and C Players."

-Steve Jobs
(Co-founder of Apple and the former CEO of Pixar)

B-Players:

1.   They arrive to work right on time and leave work right on time or two minutes early.

2.   They push back at the thought of ongoing learning and tend to ask if they are going to be paid for it because "it's not technically part of their job description."

3.   They hold themselves to the standard that management sets and actively demonstrates. They constantly compare themselves to their co-workers to justify their lack of effort and excellence.

4.   They don't want more work and they spend any free time they have planning their next vacation.

5.   They are not goal oriented and they hope the company wins just enough so that they don't have to look for another job.

6.   They have a fixed mindset that is based upon their belief that each person is born with a certain amount of skills and that is all there is to it.

> "I've learned over the years that, when you have really good people, you don't have to baby them. By expecting them to do great things, you can get them to do great things. The original Mac team taught me that A-plus players like to work together, and they don't like it if you tolerate B-grade work."

-Steve Jobs
(Co-founder of Apple and the former CEO of Pixar)

7. They consistently get their jobs done while bringing their up and down emotions to the workplace each day.

8. They love working with other B- and C-Players who justify their slow work pace and who they can go out to eat with and talk to about everything except for how to do their job better.

C-Players:

1. They arrive to work 5 to 10 minutes late and always have a traffic-related, personal or medical excuse.

2. They systematically make teaching them so hard that management gives up on them, but doesn't fire them. Since they are branded "unteachable," they get less put on their plates than anyone else.

3. They have no standards and want to do the least amount of work possible during each workday. When you walk into the room, they minimize their social media and their chat room programs and pretend to be working.

4. They find ways to leave work early every day and to take extended breaks. They fudge on the amount of time it takes for them to accomplish nearly every task and they need to be praised for just doing their job or they will have an emotional breakdown.

5. They view success as based largely upon luck and they are actually bitter toward people who are more successful than they are.

"Steve Jobs has a saying that A-players hire A-players; B-players hire C-players; and C-players hire D-players. It doesn't take long to get to Z-players. This trickle-down effect causes bozo explosions in companies."

-Guy Kawasaki

(Venture capitalist and part of the marketing team that was responsible for introducing the original Macintosh computer line to the world in 1984)

6. They have a fixed mindset that is based upon their belief that each person is born with a certain amount of skills and that is all there is to it.

7. They only work hard when they emotionally feel like it, and they usually don't.

8. They love working with other B- and C-Players who justify their slow work pace and they go out of their way to spread gossip and negative feelings around the office to bring the room down to their way of thinking.

A-PLAYER CULTURE CREATION 101!

8 Steps to Creating an A-Player Office Culture

Here are eight action steps you need to apply within your office to create an environment where talented, honest and diligent people will want to work.

1. **You must write out your company's values.** Taking the time to write out your company's values causes you to pause and think about what you really believe and why you really believe it. Your values must be strong enough that certain candidates will shy away from working with you, while other candidates will become excited about working with you because of your values. Don't go through the motions like most businesses just writing out some generic, politically correct, insincere values that don't matter to you or your team.

2. **Invest the time needed to describe the character traits of your perfect team member.** It's important that you invest the time to document the values, beliefs, and mindsets of your utopia team member so you can tailor your job posts and your environment to appeal to them.

3. **Be intentional about your décor.** Your décor must say something about you, your values, where your company has come from and where it is going. When customers and potential new hires walk into your office for the first time, they should be wowed, inspired or somehow emotionally touched by your décor. If your décor is just safe, generic, and professional, you are not going to create a work environment that people can't wait to get back to each morning.

4. **Hire only A-Players (and B-Players, if you have to).** When you are growing your business, I understand that pragmatically we all need people with a pulse on our team to get certain jobs done. However, I would encourage you make it

"There wasn't anything disciplinary I had to do. I had to do some disciplinary things with Dennis Rodman, but we signed off on them. 'Dennis, I'm gonna fine you for being late,' because he's late every day. And he said, 'I went to the team and I said Dennis is gonna be late, I'm gonna fine him, but we can't act out of sorts with this and become childish because we have to make allowances for his behavior.' He said that Bulls team was mature enough to allow Rodman that space to be out of bounds. But he'll pay for it. He'll be fined. But we're not going to get caught up in Dennis Rodman's eccentricities, his tardiness, and everything else. We're not letting that drag us down, or make that an opening for then everyone else to get out of line."

-Phil Jackson on The Lowe Post Podcast with Howard Beck
(11-Time NBA Championship-winning coach and former NBA player)

your goal to have an A-Player-only work environment. It's okay to have some B-Players whom you are actively coaching to become A-Players, but you really do not ever want to have a bunch of C-Players on your team.

5. **Discover the goals of each team member and find a way to make those goals work for your business.** As a manager of people and as the leader of a company, you must learn to see the entirety of each person and manage people on an individual basis. Yes, you need to hold people accountable to the policies that are well documented within your employee handbook, but you also need to know what is going on when enforcing these rules and policies. It's important that you or your management team invest the time to meet with each team member to discover his or her goals, wants, and needs.

If you are coaching a team and want to win consistently, you must understand the individual personalities and the strengths of each player and how these contribute to the overall team dynamic. Take a moment and think about one of the most consistently winning sports franchises in recent history - the NBA's 6-time championship winning Chicago Bulls. When Phil Jackson was coaching the Bulls to their six NBA championships, he was managing a different roster every year. At one point, he was coaching the NBA's rebounding leader and the man that many thought to be the most un-coachable player in the NBA, Dennis Rodman. He also coached the NBA's best and most competitive player, Michael Jordan, and one of the NBA's greatest players of all time, Scottie Pippen. The beauty of what Jackson did was that he was able to win year after year, regardless of which personalities and personnel were on his team.

> "The quality of a leader is reflected in the standards they set for themselves."
>
>
> **-Ray Kroc**
> (The man who franchised McDonald's and who bought the San Diego Padres in 1974)

6. **You must show that you genuinely believe in your team while holding them accountable for the achievement of high standards.** The A-Players of the world want to be pushed and they want to be respected. A-Players love it when you share information with them about the state and the direction of the company. A-Players also actually love to produce great work and this desire is contagious. When one A-Player sees another A-Player delivering great work, he or she wants to produce great work as well.

7. **Fire intentional underperformers as soon as possible.** When you spot someone at your office who is intentionally doing a poor job, you must intervene immediately. Let the employee know that you are aware that they are choosing to underperform and they must correct their behavior immediately. Write them up and ask them what is going on and why they are choosing to behave this way. Then let them know that you believe in them, but if they choose to continue underperforming, they will be fired. It's very important that you do not put up with poor performers. When you keep poor performers around, you are going to have to invest a ton of your time into the training, coaching, and mentoring of them to the point that you will not have the time left in your schedule to invest in your top people. Keeping bottom feeders and poor performers around has a way of demotivating the A-Players on your team when they begin to notice that you seem too accepting of mediocrity.

8. **Install a merit-based pay system to reward great performance and to penalize poor performance.** Pay should be directly tied to performance. In addition to rewarding people in their paycheck, try to catch people doing a good job so that you can reward your high achievers in front of the group. It's very important for the emotional state of your business that you reward big wins within your office immediately, publicly, and with sincere enthusiasm. This creates momentum when people see this cycle of high performance equaling both rewards and praise. Praise achievers as soon as possible by commending them in a meeting, buying them lunch, announcing their success to the entire team via a group voice mail, announcing it in a company memo and newsletter, giving them the "Employee of the Month Parking Spot", or some other perk.

The Thrive15 Method   1. DEFINE 2. ACT 3. MEASURE 4. REFINE

"People think focus means saying yes to the thing you've got to focus on. But that's not what it means at all. It means saying no to the hundred other good ideas that there are. You have to pick carefully. I'm actually as proud of the things we haven't done as the things I have done. Innovation is saying no to 1,000 things."
- **Steve Jobs, Founder of Apple and former CEO of Pixar**

"The Diligent Doer"

A. Knows their "why".

B. Knows their daily Key Performance Indicators.

C. Uses one weekly meeting to work on their business; to discuss their problems and produce systematic solutions.

D. Assigns detailed and granular action times (who, what, when, why) items

E. Follows up. Builds accountability.

F. Insists on organization and proper nomenclature.

Meets the same time weekly

1. Asks why?
2. Tracks KPI's
3. Sets Goals

"Most people are sitting on their own diamond mines. The surest ways to lose your diamond mine are to get bored, become overambitious, or start thinking that the grass is greener on the other side. Find your core focus, stick to it, and devote your time and resources to excelling at it." - **Gino Wickman, *Traction: Get a Grip on Your Business***

"The Happy Hoper"

A. Not committed to their "why".

B. Focuses on creating many new ideas, not the execution of previous ideas.

C. Uses endless emails, texts, meetings, and calls to discuss their individual burning fires.

D. Assigns vague, general concepts and ideas without details.

E. Allows people to make them feel bad about holding others accountable.

F. Insists on disorganization and the absence of nomenclature.

Misunderstanding — No Communication — No Traction — Frustration — Emergencies — No Deadlines — Endless Email Threads

"Most entrepreneurs are merely technicians with an entrepreneurial seizure. Most entrepreneurs fail because you are working IN your business rather than ON your business." - **Michael Gerber, Bestselling author of *E-Myth***

During this book, I will teach you the 13-point success system that Dr. Z and I have made and personally implemented in our own lives and businesses, but the system will not work if you do not have a real product or service that the world really wants. To create time and financial freedom intentionally make trade offs. What will you be willing to give up?

- **TV**
- **Social Media**

- **Negative Relationships**
- **Sleep**

- **Distractions**
- **Social Events**

Phase 4

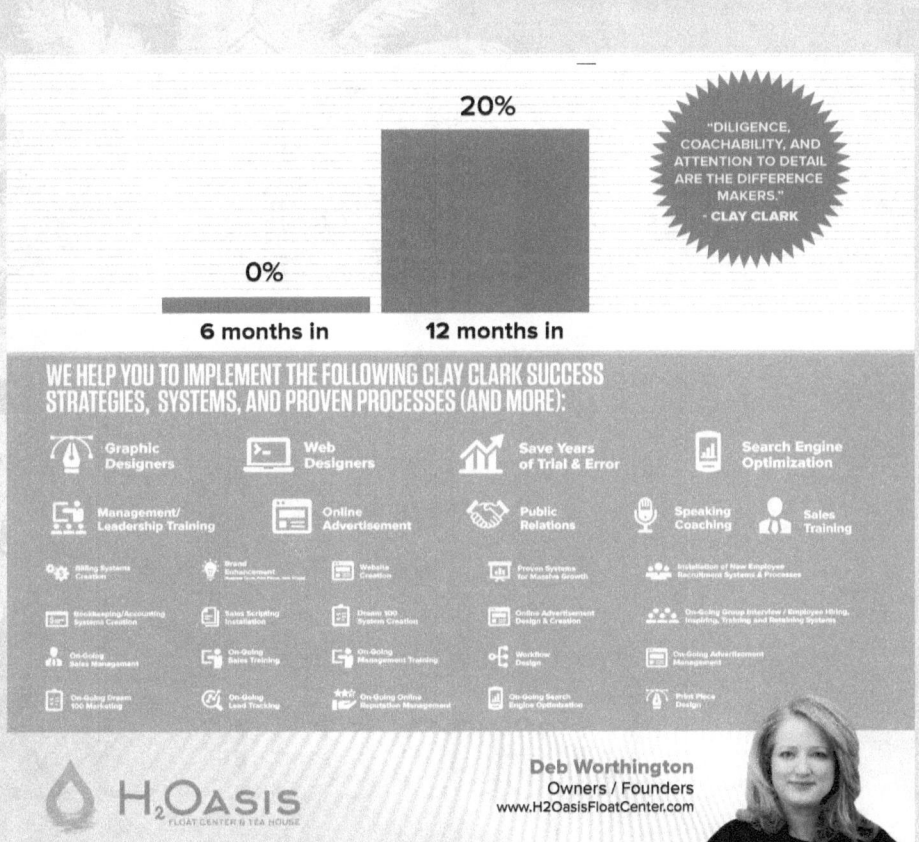

Chapter 32

Optimize Your Personal Happiness and Personal Life Satisfaction

"The people who make it to the top — whether they're musicians, or great chefs, or corporate honchos — are addicted to their calling ... [they] are the ones who'd be doing whatever it is they love, even if they weren't being paid."

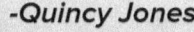

-Quincy Jones
(American record producer, conductor, arranger, composer, musician, television producer, film producer, instrumentalist, magazine founder, entertainment company executive, and humanitarian responsible for 79 Grammy Award nominations, 28 Grammys, including a Grammy Legend Award in 1991, and producer of Off the Wall, Thriller, and Bad albums for Michael Jackson)

"You've got to find what you love. And that is as true for your work as it is for your lovers. Your work is going to fill a large part of your life, and the only way to be truly satisfied is to do what you believe is great work. And the only way to do great work is to love what you do. If you haven't found it yet, keep looking. Don't settle. As with all matters of the heart, you'll know when you find it. And, like any great relationship, it just gets better and better as the years roll on. So keep looking until you find it. Don't settle."

-Steve Jobs
(Co-founder of Apple, and Founder and former CEO of Pixar and NeXT)

It is vitally important that you love what you're doing. We've seen many business owners who do not follow the principles that have been outlined throughout this book, and eventually they become a hostage of their own organization. Do business the way YOU want to do business, not the way that your customers or employees want to do it. You are going to spend an extraordinary amount of time with your business, so take care to develop a good relationship with it. Without developing goals for your seven F's (Faith, Family, Finances, Friendships, Fun, Fitness, and Focus), the rigors and challenges of operating and growing the business will be your only daily focus.

You are given one life to do great things, and that is not isolated to doing only great things in business. You are empowered to great things in each of your seven F's. Develop an incredible faith. Be the most healthy person possible so you can live long enough to reap the rewards of your labor. Spend time with family. Build relationships with genuine people. Create wealth

> "Life is like riding a bicycle. To keep your balance, you must keep moving."
>
> *-Albert Einstein*

in abundance. Growth in these areas not only moves you forward toward your goals, but it also enhances your balance and satisfaction. We've seen many business owners neglect one or more of these areas for too long and become unbalanced, discouraged, and dissatisfied with their business. There are certainly seasons where the focus will shift between each of the five F's, but the important thing is to not lose sight of any of them entirely. The easiest way to do this is to remind yourself every day of each of your goals. Through achievement and progress, you will find balance and satisfaction.

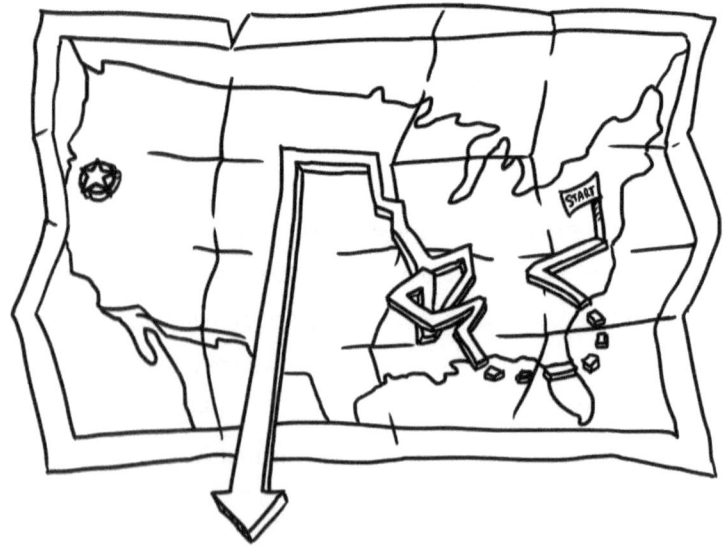

PLOT YOUR COURSE OR YOU WILL NEVER GET THERE

"YOU MUST CREATE A BUSINESS MODEL THAT
PRODUCES REPEATABLE, PREDICTABLE, &
PROFITABLE SUCCESS."

- CLAY CLARK

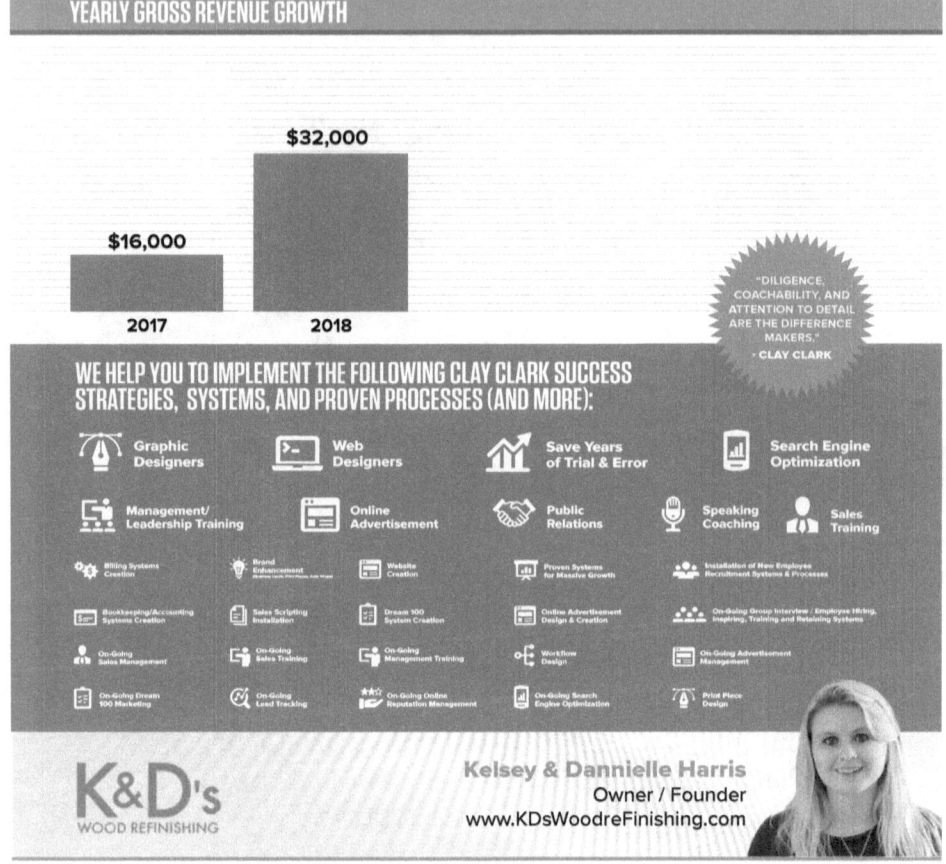

Chapter 33

Time Management Mastery Super Moves

Now that you are equipped with a fire hose of knowledge, action items, and steps to build a more scalable business, you may be wondering, "How in the world am I going to find time to implement all this?" IT IS GOING TO TAKE TIME. Most business owners are so busy working IN their businesses that they rarely have time to work ON their businesses. On those rare occasions when they finish their work at a respectable hour when the sun is still out, they are usually too exhausted to deep dive into creating documents, systems, and processes, which all require close attention to detail. By scheduling time to work ON your business, you will slowly begin to transition your business to one that can operate without your direct involvement. However, just like any other appointment, if you don't put it on your calendar, it will not get addressed.

Business owners who are already working 70, 80, or 90 hours per week in their business can't stomach the thought of tacking on an additional three hours per day to work ON their business. Well, take heart! I have provided you five Super Moves for effective time management that will free up the needed time to work ON your business.

Time Management Mastery Super Move #1 – Don't ever hesitate to blow up items on your to-do list

I'm going to teach you the specific moves that you can use to blow up certain items on your to-do list, but it's important that I take a moment to verify that you are truly tracking with what I am saying here. You must become very comfortable with simply saying "no" to things other people try to put on your to-do list. When someone says, "Call me and remind me to do this or that," you need to respond in a nice tone of voice, "I believe

"This isn't about managing your time. It's about keeping your life organized and under control. Design your days and be intentional about what you spend your time doing."

 -Clay Clark

in your ability to remind yourself and if you can't, I'm not going to be responsible for reminding you to do things."

1. **Delete that funk.** Many times activities get e-mailed to you or put on your calendar and you just need to delete that stuff. Every day, I get an e-mail from a person who didn't invest the time needed to ensure that their message is grammatically correct, telling me that I need to call them back about X, Y, and Z because of A, B, and C. If the person is not my wife, one of my business partners, or a customer, I simply delete that funk.

2. **Don't do anything.** Sometimes people want to give me updates about updates, and updates about the updates, and everything that is being communicated has zero impact on my life or the status of our business. This basically describes the agenda of a typical networking event. Some dude gets up and makes some announcement about some esoteric legislative mindset, and then some other dude gets up and talks in generalities about the state of the economy, and then some sincere lady gets up and talks about her vision for a cleaner community. As for me and my wallet, we are not going to sit through those kinds of gatherings just so I can pass out my business card to the 76 multi-level marketing professionals, three realtors, and two insurance agents who are guaranteed to be in attendance.

3. **Delegate it.** There are many things that you should delegate. In my office, I am always asked to get involved in stupid stuff that doesn't matter. The decision of whether to order our paper towels online or directly from Office Depot is one such instance. True, if we order them online, they will take longer to arrive, but if we buy them direct from Office Depot, our paper towel budget will be about $4.00 per week more. Seriously? This is an example of something I should delegate to somebody who is empowered to make the decision while protected by Guardrails. This person knows what towels should cost and knows that it is not acceptable to ever run out. If the person in charge of the towels shows that they do not have the mental capacity to make this decision, then I need to find a new paper towel ordering person. Don't embroil yourself in stuff that does not make highest and best use of your time.

4. **Create a system enhancement that makes the repetitive questions disappear forever.** If you get asked the same questions from customers every day, it is probably because the sign indicating where your customer restroom is located is not large enough. Lee Cockerell, former executive vice president of Disney World Resort, once told me about how much time Disney had invested to ensure that the signage at their properties are clear and obvious. The people at Disney World see over one million guests per week, so they knew they had to create a systems enhancement that made the repetitive questions disappear forever or everyone would spend their entire vacation asking where the bathrooms and the gifts shops were.

Time Management Mastery Super Move #2 – Stop listening to the feedback of people who are not your ideal and likely buyers and who are not truly experts

Most people do not like their lives and do not have successful businesses, thus you should not listen to most people about most things related to your business. Simply cut off people who are negative or become an excellent selective listener.

> "Everyday is a gift from God. What you do with it is a gift to God."
> -*Clay Clark*

. . . .

 Mystic Statistics:
A Gallup survey shows that 71% of workers are "not engaged" or "actively disengaged" from their work.

Carmine Gallo, "70% of Your Employees Hate Their Jobs" Forbes – November 11, 2011. http://www.forbes.com/sites/carminegallo/2011/11/11/your-emotionally-disconnected-employees/#5a0823dbe89b

According to Bloomberg, 8 out of 10 entrepreneurs who start businesses fail within the first 18 months.

Eric T. Wagner, "Five Reasons 8 Out of 10 Businesses Fail" Forbes, September 12, 2013. http://www.forbes.com/sites/ericwagner/2013/09/12/five-reasons-8-out-of-10-businesses-fail/#475ea4935e3c

. . . .

Time Management Mastery Super Move #3 – Ordain your destiny daily

Each day when you first wake up, look at your to-do list (not your text messages, your social media updates, or your e-mail) and write down the items that you definitely will get accomplished that day. Then schedule a specific time to get those tasks accomplished. When you begin your day by ordaining your destiny, deciding what items you are going to get done, and blocking out the time needed to get those items done, you will find yourself becoming DRAMATICALLY MORE EFFICIENT, FOCUSED, AND EFFECTIVE.

> "The reasonable man adapts himself to the world; the unreasonable one persists in trying to adapt the world to himself. Therefore, all progress depends on the unreasonable man."
>
> *-George Bernard Shaw*
> (Famous and successful Irish playwright who was able to block out the time needed to write 60 plays)

Time Management Mastery Super Move #4 - You must block out time every week for your highest and best use activities only

If you can't keep from being distracted in your office, you need to work from your truck, a hotel, the middle the forest, or anywhere other than my Man Cave (which is where I will be). Do whatever you have to do to block out the time for your highest and best use activities. Turn your phone off, turn your e-mail off, and get it done. When I first met David Robinson (the NBA Hall of Famer), I was shocked to discover that he had multiple cell phones, until he told me that one is for his wife and kids and the other one is for everybody else (myself included). This was smart because as a two-time Olympic gold medal winner, NBA Champion, and former MVP who has since gone on to become a big-time investor in a $300 million investment fund, his phone never stops ringing. He had to find a way to create clear boundaries for himself and by having two cell phones, he was able to do that.

"A person's success in life can usually be measured by the number of uncomfortable conversations he or she is willing to have."

-*Tim Ferriss*

(Bestselling author of *The 4-Hour Work Week*, **venture capitalist and podcaster)**

Time Management Mastery Super Move #5 - Create an "I'm going to stop doing this" list

I run into so many people who keep doing things because they've always done them, until they reach the point of exhaustion. You must start delegating or deleting things from your list if you ever hope to move on to doing bigger and better things.

 Ample Example:

Years ago I worked with a gourmet dessert company whose owner was fascinated with the concept of making gourmet cupcakes that were super time consuming to make and not at all profitable. In all seriousness, it was well documented so she knew that she could only make at best 50 cents per cupcake on each gourmet cupcake she sold, but she was loyal to this dysfunction. She would routinely turn down purchases from customers who were willing to pay big dollars for her gourmet cakes, because she could not stop making those unprofitable, resource-draining, and time-consuming cupcakes. She would say "her customers loved them" and she "didn't want to upset her customers" and "the customer is always right." She literally could not afford to fix her delivery van when it exploded because she continued to cling to this belief in her cupcakes.

I wish this story ended well, but it did not. Even after my wife and I decided to buy her a van to help her, she still would not stop operating out of dysfunction. We realized that we were working with someone who was loyal to dysfunction and so we just let her kill herself slowly by making those God-forsaken unprofitable cupcakes.

Just because you have always done something does not mean that you have to keep doing it. If you are having routine computer issues, accounting issues, human resource issues, or other issues, you must be committed to making changes, regardless of whether or not they are uncomfortable or not.

Unlocking the Power of Disciplined Time Management

Whenever I speak to people about the importance of disciplined time management, they tend to make the same face as if you were about to disclose all the sins they have ever committed. Don't freak out about disciplined time management. In fact, I encourage you to greatly simplify this idea in your mind because it is not as overwhelming as advertised. At the end of the day, disciplined time management comes down to controlling just six simple variables:

1. **Make sure that you are working at the right time of day.** For me, I simply cannot get things done while my teammates, their emotional baggage, their questions, their joy, their pain, and their issues of the day swirl all around me. I must plan my day from 3:00 AM to 9:00 AM. This is what I call my "meta time." It is the time each day when I can truly think above and beyond my current circumstances and can get massive quantities of work done and done.

> "Lack of direction, not lack of time, is the problem. We all have twenty four-hour days."
>
> **-Zig Ziglar**
> (Bestselling author and renowned motivational speaker)

- -

 Definition Magician:
The word "Meta" comes from the Greek word meaning "after" "beyond" or "higher."

- -

2. **Make sure that you are working in the right environment.** I am writing this book from within the beautiful confines of my speakeasy-themed Man Cave. This room is almost sacred to me as it is a place where I can shut off the outside world, crank up the bagpipe music that I often listen to, and just get it done. Back in the day before I could afford to build a speakeasy-themed Man Cave, I had to work out of my apartment with my phone off and with headphones on to escape from the interruptions of the world.

> "Concentrate all your thoughts upon the work at hand. The sun's rays do not burn until brought to a focus."
>
> *-Alexander Graham Bell*
> (Inventor of the world's first modern telephone)

3. **Make sure that you turn off all distractions.** As I write, I am celebrating my 38th consecutive hour of having my phone turned off. I don't check e-mails, I don't answer the door, I just crank up my bagpipe music and I get stuff done. I am not interested in social media updates or who may be calling, I am just 100% focused on writing the best business book in the history of the planet so that you can change your life and so that I can fulfill my mission to mentor millions before I look like the late, great Andy Rooney.

. . . .

 Fun Fact:
Andrew "Andy" Rooney was an American radio and television writer who was best known for his weekly broadcast "A Few Minutes with Andy Rooney," part of the CBS News program, 60 Minutes from 1978 to 2011. At the time of his death, his eyebrows each looked like a fully-grown adult cat.

. . . .

"You become the average of the five people you spend the most time with."

 -Clay Clark

4. **Make sure that you insert accountability into your life.** It's important that you have a business coach or business partner who holds you accountable. If you can achieve success without a business coach or partner in your life, then you are a better businessperson than Bill Gates (the co-founder of Microsoft). Everybody needs someone to keep them on track and hold them accountable for hitting deadlines, getting stuff done, and not letting emotions get in the way of the perpetual motion needed to achieve big time business success.

"We need to re-create boundaries. When you carry a digital gadget that creates a virtual link to the office, you need to create a virtual boundary that didn't exist before."

 -Daniel Goleman (Psychologist and bestselling author of *Emotional Intelligence*)

5. **Set boundaries with your time.** I have thousands of people who reach out to me each month, many of whom are very happy, though some are upset. I work with great customers in our core businesses who write super positive things about me and our brands on social media, then there are other people who hate me for standing up for my core beliefs, firing their wife, firing their son, driving a Hummer, etc. With all of this, it would be easy for me to get overwhelmed. It's up to me to set up boundaries in my life for when I will check social media, check e-mail, answer my phone, etc. It's up to me to decide when I will be involved in a business meeting and when I will not be. I have to set my own boundaries.

"But you are the average of the five people you associate with most, so do not underestimate the effects of your pessimistic, unambitious, or disorganized friends. If someone isn't making you stronger, they're making you weaker."

-Tim Ferriss
(Best-selling author of *The 4-Hour Work Week***, venture capitalist and podcaster)**

"By the time we got to 100 people, we hired all the people with the right skill sets and experiences, but not all of them were culture fits. And when we got to 100 people, I remember, I dreaded getting out of bed in the morning to go to the office."

- Tony Hsieh
(CEO of Zappos, explaining that at his first successful business, LinkExchange, he began to hate the company and ultimately sold it because he couldn't stand the people he had to work with every day)

6. **Set boundaries with the people with whom you choose to engage.** People do not deserve your time simply because they request it. In fact, if you did have to say yes to every person who ever asked for a minute of your time, you would not ever become successful. Once you start to achieve any success at all, more and more people will begin reaching out to you and requesting moments of your time. I have had to become increasingly good at saying no to time-sucking, negative, reactive and pessimistic people or people I just do not like.

To analyze objectively how good you are at managing your time effectively, take the Time Management Effectiveness Assessment at: www.ThriveTimeShow.com/TreasureTrove.

Learning How to Manage Your Distractions (Social Media, E-Mails, Text Messages, Missed Calls, etc.)

"Your e-mail, text message, and social media is your to-do list that you are allowing to be made by other people. Don't let it control your life. Set boundaries or spend your day responding to random-ass updates of your cousin who was offended that you didn't respond to the picture they tagged you in."

-Clay Clark
(Founder of Thrive15.com and former U.S. Small Business Administration Entrepreneur of the Year)

Having been self-employed for so long, I no longer struggle with saying no to things; however, I used to. Therefore, I am going to attempt to be empathetic while being very pragmatic as I lay out the rules you need to implement in your life to better manage your e-mail, your social media, your text messages and the constant distractions that people with less intentional life plans are using to try to slow you down.

"Social media wasn't invented to make you better — it was invented to make the companies money. You are an employee of the company and you are the product that they sell. They have put you in a little hamster wheel and they throw little treats in now and then — but you've got to decide, what's the impact you're trying to make?"

-Seth Godin
(Bestselling author, entrepreneur and marketing expert)

1. Inform your team that you expect customer service and sales emails to be handled in real time and inboxes to always be at zero at the end of the workday.

2. Educate and inform your clients and your staff that henceforth, you are only going to be checking your email once each morning.

· ·

 Fun Fact:
"You don't really need science to know this, but technology makes it much easier to get distracted, whether that's stepping away from an important project to check your smartphone, or flipping between multiple browser tabs without really focusing on any one. It has been proven that toggling between multiple tasks at once doesn't actually work — in fact, you just wind up performing all your duties even worse... No, 'Internet addiction' isn't just some BS term parents throw around to terrify youngsters who spend too much time playing Candy Crush. Spending too much time on the Internet can actually cause changes in the brain that mimic those caused by drug and alcohol dependence, according to a 2012 study."

Rebecca Hiscott, "8 Ways Technology Makes Your Stupid," Huffington Post, July 25, 2014.
http://www.huffingtonpost.com/2014/07/25/technology-intelligence_n_5617181.html

· ·

3. Quit responding to social media unless it pays you to do so. My wife and I live on land with a forest right behind our house, but I don't feel a psychological urge to run into the woods and pick up a branch every time one falls from the hundreds of trees. However, I used to feel the need to respond to every social media update that I was somehow involved in. What a fruitless waste of time.

4. Disconnect your social media from your cell phone updates. Every time someone writes about you, tags you, messages you or reaches out to you, you do not need to know. Constantly interrupting your train of thought with the random updates from potentially hundreds of thousands of people out there who have the ability to reach you at any time can

"Be present. Be meditative. Form real friendships."

 -Naval Ravikant
(Founder of AngelList. com and venture capitalist)

"Being present is a present. Intentionally choose to be both mentally and physically present and engaged in what you are doing at all times."

 -Clay Clark

cause you real psychological damage. Seriously. Harvard and other leading schools have done research on what happens when a person has to make too many decisions during a workday and their findings are not positive.

· ·

 Fun Fact:
A report by Common Sense Media shows that teens spend a mind-boggling nine hours a day using media.

· ·

5. Start the subject line of an email with the name of company or the main person involved in the email. Do not send blank or vague subject lines.

6. To reduce the number of e-mails that you receive every day, you must reduce the number of e-mails that you send every day.

7. Do not respond to your email in real-time. Respond to all your email once per day and then get the heck out of there. If you are in a position of leadership, you will lose your mind trying to stay on top of it in real-time.

> "Focus and simplicity. Simple can be harder than complex: You have to work hard to get your thinking clean to make it simple. But it's worth it in the end because once you get there, you can move mountains."

8. Don't engage in nuanced conversations via email. Reserve those types of conversations for in-person or over-the-phone.

 -Steve Jobs
(Co-founder of Apple and the former CEO of Pixar)

9. Don't send long emails.

10. When possible, respond to long emails filled with many questions with the answer, "I'll call you about these items ASAP." Then make sure to cover all the items in the email during your phone conversation.

11. Write your emails using numbered bullet points when discussing multiple issues. Do not weave many questions and subjects into the body of an email paragraph.

12. If you believe that the topic of your email may be very sensitive to the reader or that it may actually offend or upset the reader, do not send it.

13. Do not ever write something in an email that you would not be willing to say directly to the person.

14. Get your inbox reduced to zero each day. Don't leave hundreds of half-responded to or not responded to emails in your inbox.

15. Commonly use the carbon copy (CC) feature on your email, but never use the blind copy (BC) feature on your email, if possible.

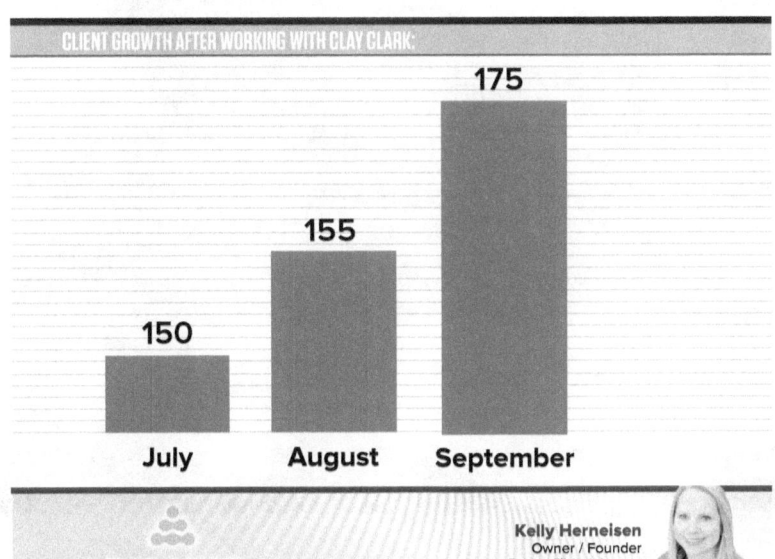

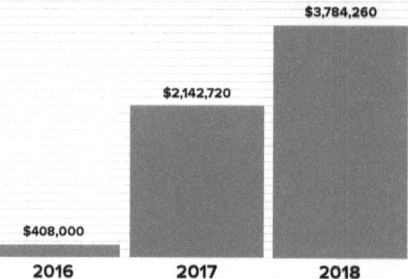

"MOST ENTREPRENEURS ARE MERELY TECHNICIANS WITH AN
ENTREPRENEURIAL SEIZURE. MOST ENTREPRENEURS FAIL BECAUSE THEY ARE
WORKING IN THEIR BUSINESS RATHER THAN ON THEIR BUSINESS."
- MICHAEL GERBER
AUTHOR OF "THE E-MYTH REVISITED"

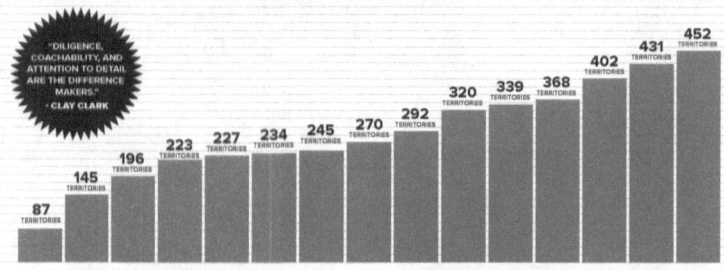

YEAR AFTER YEAR CONSISTENT GROWTH

"DILIGENCE, COACHABILITY, AND ATTENTION TO DETAIL ARE THE DIFFERENCE MAKERS."
- CLAY CLARK

2006	2007	2008	2009	2010	2011	2012	2013	2014	2015	2016	2017	2019	2020	2021
87	145	196	223	227	234	245	270	292	320	339	368	402	431	452

WE HELP YOU TO IMPLEMENT THE FOLLOWING CLAY CLARK SUCCESS STRATEGIES, SYSTEMS, AND PROVEN PROCESSES (AND MORE):

- Graphic Designers
- Web Designers
- Save Years of Trial & Error
- Search Engine Optimization
- Management/ Leadership Training
- Online Advertisement
- Public Relations
- Speaking Coaching
- Sales Training

Billing Systems Creation · Brand Enhancement · Website Creation · Proven Systems for Massive Growth · Installation of New Employee Recruitment Systems & Processes · Bookkeeping/Accounting Systems Creation · Sales Scripting Installation · Dream 100 System Creation · Online Advertisement Design & Creation · On-Going Group Interview / Employee Hiring, Inspiring, Training and Retaining Systems · On-Going Sales Management · On-Going Sales Training · On-Going Management Training · Workflow Design · On-Going Advertisement Management · On-Going Dream 100 Marketing · On-Going Lead Tracking · On-Going Online Reputation Management · On-Going Search Engine Optimization · Print Place Design

Jonathan Barnett
Owner / Founder
www.OxiFresh.com

Chapter 34

Can You Afford Not to Have a Personal Assistant?

I am now celebrating my 20th year of self-employment, and I can tell you from firsthand experience, I have almost always utilized a personal assistant to help me get more things done and to leverage my time. As an example, writing this book has required almost 95 hours of my time thus far, and we have not yet begun editing it. However, I have been able to write this book and stay on top of my responsibilities as a father, businessman, and speaker because I have prioritized making sure that

> "Unless you value yourself, you will not value your time, and you will not do anything with it."
> *-Clay Clark*

I surround myself with quality people to whom I can delegate effectively. Call them whatever you want; I call them personal assistants.

My first experience with successfully leveraging my time was when I was in high school and attempting to scale the business model of promoting dance parties where I would charge people $5 to attend. I paid a guy named Leif (I grew up in Minnesota) to help organize the equipment, manage the crowds and help promote the event because there simply were not enough hours in the day for me to get everything done that needed to be done for the big event. I wasn't rich at the time I hired Leif, but I did realize the value of paying him a percentage of what I was making so that I could make more money and deliver more value to my ideal and likely buyers.

 Deep Thought:
Remember, just because you choose to delegate something to someone else does not mean that you are not responsible for whether those things get done. By definition, delegation means to give a task to somebody else with responsibility to act on your behalf. However, at the end of the day, you are still responsible for achieving results and getting stuff done. It's ok to be a delegator, but do not become an abdicator and a blamer. To abdicate means to fail to fulfill a duty or responsibility. Don't be the person who abdicates and then blames. Be a delegator. There is a difference.

Today, I almost always work with an assistant of some kind whom I am paying to help free up my time so that I can focus on their highest and best use. To help you free up the time needed to get more stuff done, I have put together a list of the tasks that I would highly recommend that you hire a personal assistant to help you with:

1. Prepping the office for big presentations and meetings _____

2. Greeting guest and clients at the door _____

3. Picking up clients at the airport _____

4. Organizing your travel _____

5. Taking notes during meetings _____

6. Scheduling appointments _____

7. Driving almost anywhere _____

8. Mailing items _____

9. Buying office supplies _____

10. Cleaning up the office _____

11. Organizing the office _____

12. Getting items notarized _____

13. Buying items online (assuming that you have a budget in place) _____

14. Printing documents _____

15. Managing the logistics and issues related to fixing your computers, scanners, printers, etc. _____

16. Collecting payments from clients _____

17. Researching quick and specific items _____

There are some things I would not delegate to a personal assistant:

1. Responding to emails _____

2. Paying bills _____

3. Attending meetings on your behalf _____

4. Firing someone on your behalf _____

5. Handling employee disputes on your behalf _____

6. Strategic decision-making _____

Delegating Effectively to a Personal Assistant

The art of delegating effectively to a personal assistant is just that - an art that must be mastered in the same way that just giving someone paint does not make them an artist. To delegate effectively to a personal assistant, you must work hard to do your part in the following six areas:

1. You must clearly and concisely identify in writing the task that you want done.

2. You must document in writing the way you want the task to be done.

3. You must specify in writing when the item must be completed.

4. You must ask your assistant if they have any questions before the delegation has truly begun.

> "My job is to not be easy on people. My job is to make them better."
>
> -*Steve Jobs*
> (Co-founder of Apple and the former CEO of Pixar)

5. You must keep the lines of communication open and be ready to answer your assistant if and when they have any questions.

6. You must commit to following up with your assistant based on the assumption that they did not get the task completed correctly.

Every one of the Foundational Business Principles that we have taught you during this book has its own very common and predictable challenges associated with it, however we are here to help you. You don't have to kill yourself in the process of turning your business into a scalable and duplicable business that is capable of producing both the time and financial freedom that you desire.

If you have any challenges along the way, remember that our entire team is only one phone call away and we believe that you can do this!

Additional Resources:

If you have any business-related questions, find your answers by utilizing the following resources:

»   Visit www.ThriveTimeShow.com

Three Different Packages to Serve You:

As I've achieved tremendous success, I did not forget about the powdered milk I drank as a kid from time to time, or the Food Stamps we had to occasionally use to buy the food that we needed. Thus, I have worked thousands of hours and have invested millions of dollars into creating three different packages to help anybody on any budget who is willing to apply the effort needed to learn and apply the principles, processes, systems, best-practices, and strategies that we teach.

"No one lives long enough to learn everything they need to learn starting from scratch. To be successful, we absolutely, positively have to find people who have already paid the price to learn the things that we need to learn to achieve our goals."

-*Brian Tracy*
(Bestselling self-help author)

REVENUE GROWTH AFTER WORKING WITH CLAY CLARK:

$32,450 (2018)

$6,800 (2017)

2017   2018

"DILIGENCE, COACHABILITY, AND ATTENTION TO DETAIL ARE THE DIFFERENCE MAKERS."
- CLAY CLARK

WE HELP YOU TO IMPLEMENT THE FOLLOWING CLAY CLARK SUCCESS STRATEGIES, SYSTEMS, AND PROVEN PROCESSES (AND MORE):

- Graphic Designers
- Web Designers
- Save Years of Trial & Error
- Search Engine Optimization
- Management/ Leadership Training
- Online Advertisement
- Public Relations
- Speaking Coaching
- Sales Training
- Billing Systems Creation
- Brand Enhancement
- Website Creation
- Proven Systems for Massive Growth
- Installation of New Employee Recruitment Systems & Processes
- Bookkeeping/Accounting Systems Creation
- Sales Scripting Installation
- Dream 100 System Creation
- Online Advertisement Design & Creation
- On-Going Group Interview / Employee Hiring, Inspiring, Training and Retaining Systems
- On-Going Sales Management
- On-Going Sales Training
- On-Going Management Training
- Workflow Design
- On Going Advertisement Management
- On-Going Dream 100 Marketing
- On-Going Lead Tracking
- On-Going Online Reputation Management
- On-Going Search Engine Optimization
- Print Piece Design

JEAN BRIESE

Jean Briese
Owners / Founders
www.JeanBriese.com

"Though several people encouraged me to work with Clay, it was without question the pivotal moment in my business. I went from lacking some confidence to becoming empowered through knowledge with how to grow a business and my business grew dramatically."

-*Kat Graham*
(CEO BarbeeCookies.com)

» **Coaching Client Thriver** – If you desire to be personally mentored and coached through the process of turning your existing business into a duplicable and scalable business that can produce both the income and financial freedom that you desire, you can apply at: www.ThriveTimeShow.com/Coaching. Because we can only handle a limited number of coaching clients at time, we schedule an initial complimentary coaching session with you to determine if your business is a good fit for both parties before committing to take on both you and your business as a client.

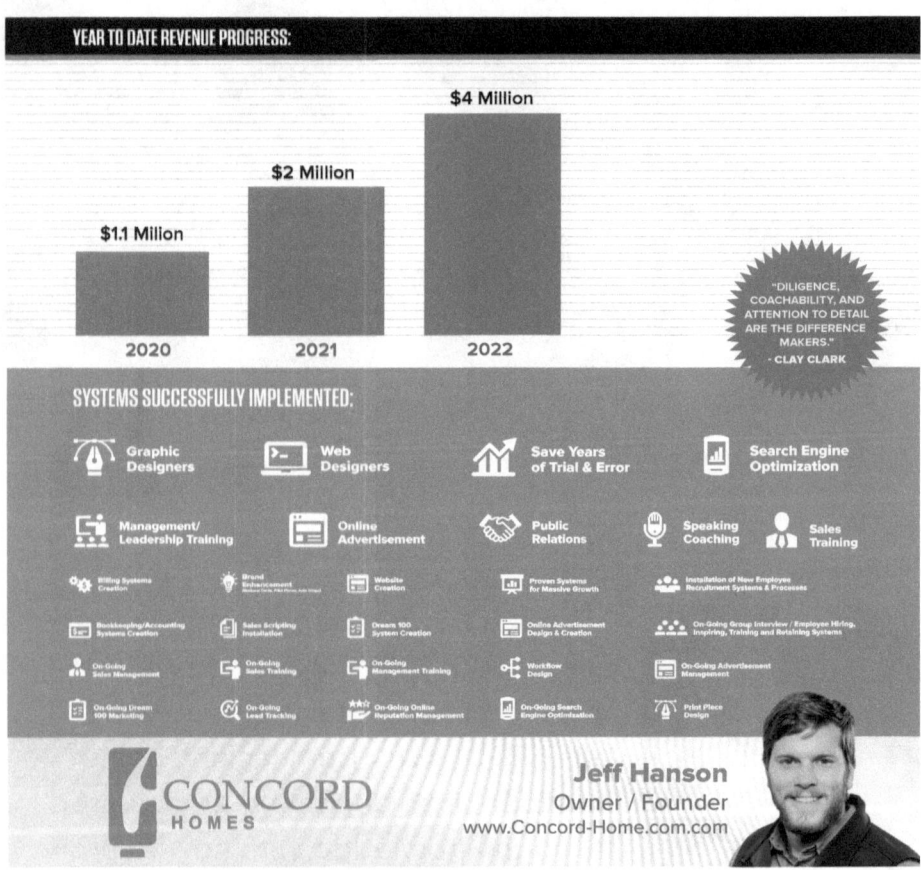

"Thanks for answering my questions. I have applied your advice and we are hitting goal numbers daily- and I am obsessive about it (they think I'm nuts- and I think that's a good thing). Previously we were scheduling 340 new patients a month and we are on track to do 460 this month! Yeaaaaaaaaahhhhh!!! Also- they do think I have a big stick. I'm the person who fires people for not performing lol."

-Jennifer Allen
(BodyCentral PT)

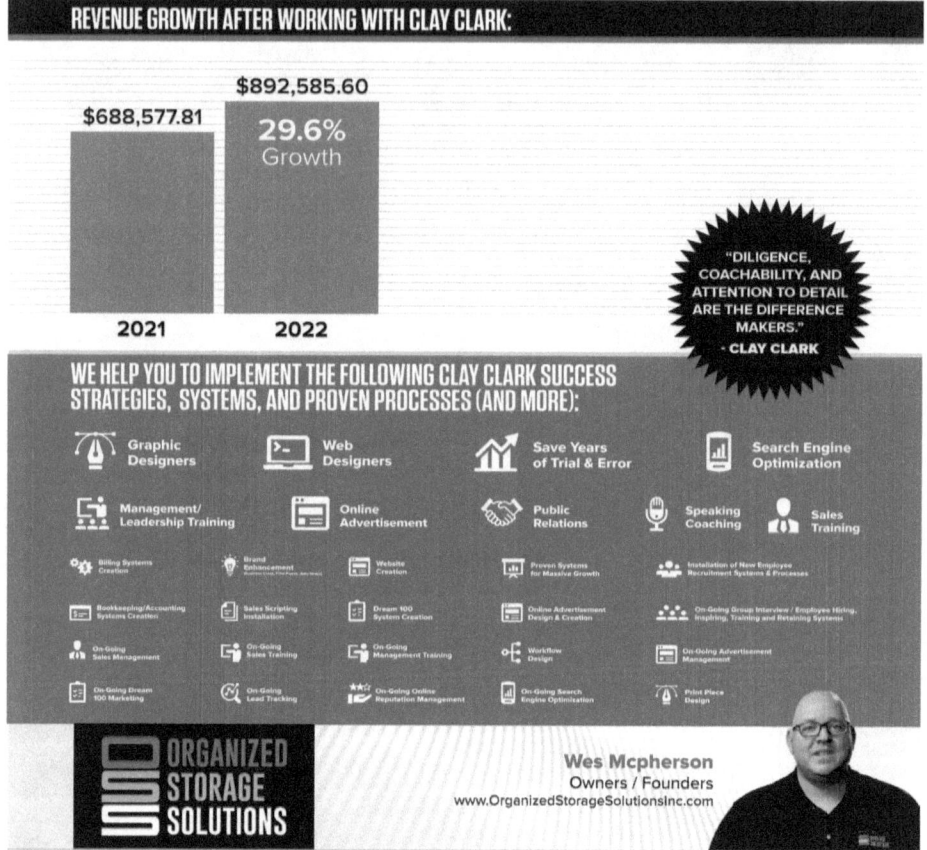

REVENUE GROWTH AFTER WORKING WITH CLAY CLARK:

$688,577.81 — 2021

$892,585.60 — 29.6% Growth — 2022

"DILIGENCE, COACHABILITY, AND ATTENTION TO DETAIL ARE THE DIFFERENCE MAKERS."
- CLAY CLARK

WE HELP YOU TO IMPLEMENT THE FOLLOWING CLAY CLARK SUCCESS STRATEGIES, SYSTEMS, AND PROVEN PROCESSES (AND MORE):

- Graphic Designers
- Web Designers
- Save Years of Trial & Error
- Search Engine Optimization
- Management/Leadership Training
- Online Advertisement
- Public Relations
- Speaking Coaching
- Sales Training

ORGANIZED STORAGE SOLUTIONS

Wes Mcpherson
Owners / Founders
www.OrganizedStorageSolutionsInc.com

Chapter 35

You Have the Time You Need to Produce a Duplicable Business that Can Create Both Time and Financial Freedom for You

I have had countless business people come up to me and say, "I would love to grow my business, but I just can't find the time." And they are 100% wrong, 100% of the time. I would guess that you are already putting in the hours needed to take your business to the next level. However, you can incrementally increase the value of each hour of your working day by upgrading the way you use your time through creating the systems and processes you need to grow.

Growing your business in a duplicable way is not an event; it will not happen with the touch of a button or with the brief placing of a call. We can help you completely change your life if you will allow us to guide you through the process of executing the best-practice systems that you have learned throughout this book.

What Are the First Things You Should Be Doing?

To help you get some big and quick wins and to establish a renewed sense of momentum within your company, I have put together a list of the SEVEN BIGGEST action items you need to implement within the next week. Each one of these action items will take less than 25 minutes to implement, but you must commit to doing them for them to work.

ACTION ITEM #1 – Define and clarify your personal F7 Goals (Faith, Family, Friendships, Fitness and Financial)

It's almost impossible to drift your way to success. You won't push back against outside pressures, your peers, and the culture around you if you don't know where you want to go. Invest the time to type in and print out your F7 Goals today at: www.ThriveTimeShow.com/TreasureTrove.

When you print out those goals, place them somewhere so that you can see them in the morning when you wake up, during the day when you are working and at night when you go bed. You can get to where you want to go, if you will only invest the time to define where it is that you want to go.

> "Drifting, without aim or purpose, is the first cause of failure."
>
> *-Napoleon Hill*
> (Bestselling self-help author and the former apprentice of the world's wealthiest man, Andrew Carnegie)

ACTION ITEM #2 – Define your ideal and likely buyers

You must invest the time needed to create a document that clearly identifies who your ideal and likely buyers are and who they are not. This will save you thousands of dollars down the road in fruitless marketing efforts and it will impact nearly every business decision that you make.

ACTION ITEM #3 – Determine the costs associated with achieving your ideal lifestyle

It is great to have massive goals, but you must really get out the calculator, a pen, and paper to figure out how much your goals are really going to cost you monetarily during each year. If you want to have kids, hospitals are not free. If you want to get in shape, gyms are not free. If you want to get engaged but have yet to convince your fiancé that your engagement shouldn't involve the purchase of diamond ring simply because De Beers executed a brilliant marketing strategy that has now convinced that world's market that a man who is proposing to a woman must invest his hard-earned money into buying her a diamond ring if he truly cares about her and the relationship, getting engaged is not free.

NOTE: To help you stay organized and to track the estimated cost of living for your ideal lifestyle, visit: www.ThriveTimeShow.com/TreasureTrove.

Fun Fact:
Today, the De Beers Group of Companies seems to be the most magical company in the diamond industry. They play a leading role in the diamond exploration, diamond mining, diamond trading, diamond retail sales and the industrial diamond market. However, 1938 is when the magic really began. De Beers hired the N.W. Ayer advertising agency to help make diamonds appeal to a broader audience. Ayer felt that the company needed to link the purchase of a diamond to something emotional to keep the sale of diamonds from going up and down during predictable economic cycles. He recommended that the company begin advertising diamonds as something that men should buy and give to women when proposing and getting married. According to the New York Times, Ayer told everyone on his team that he wanted to "create a situation where almost every person pledging marriage feels compelled to acquire a diamond engagement ring." Before World War II, less than 10% of engagement rings contained diamonds. However, once Ayer began marketing the phrase "A Diamond Is Forever" on all of De Beers' advertisements beginning in 1948, it became almost a given that men will buy their brides to be a diamond ring. And who came up with the idea that a man should save up two months of salary to buy a diamond ring before proposing? You guessed it; it was Ayer.

ACTION ITEM #4 – Determine Your Highest and Best Use to Scale Your Company

My friend, you and I are where we are because of how we spend our time. If you want to upgrade your life, you will need to upgrade how you manage your time. **NOTE:** To help you assess where you are clearly using your time both effectively and ineffectively, we STRONGLY encourage you to take the Time Management Assessment today at: www.ThriveTimeShow.com/TreasureTrove.

> "You will either pay now or later for how you spend your time."
> -Clay Clark

ACTION ITEM #5 – Join Thrive15.com and commit to investing 15 minutes a day to learn how to grow a successful business and how to build a successful life

In his exhaustive study of the habits of the rich, Tom Corley (bestselling author of Rich Habits – The Daily Success Habits of Wealthy Individuals [Langdon Street Press, 2010] and the founder of www. RichHabitsInstitute.com) discovered some incredible habits that the rich seem to almost universally have, many of which involve the ongoing pursuit of self-improvement and business mastery.

» 88% of wealthy read 30 minutes or more each day for education or career reasons vs. 2% of poor.

» 67% of wealthy watch one hour or less of TV every day vs. 23% of poor.

» 44% of wealthy wake up three hours before work starts vs. 3% of poor.

» 84% of wealthy believe good habits create opportunity luck vs. 4% of poor.

» 86% of wealthy believe in lifelong educational self-improvement vs. 5% of poor.

Stanford Professor Carol S. Dweck wrote a bestselling book focused on what makes people successful called, Mindset: The New Psychology of Success (Ballantine Books, 2007). In her book, she says, "Mindset change is not about picking up a few pointers here and there. It's about seeing things in a new way. When people change to a growth mindset, they change from a judge-and-be-judged framework to a learn-and-help-learn framework. Their commitment is to growth, and growth takes plenty of time, effort, and mutual support."

My friend, I don't want to say that you will be a pathetic loser if you do not commit to blocking out 15 minutes per day for ongoing education and business training on a consistent basis, but it's a fact. You will lose if you don't invest the time needed to study proven systems, strategies, and processes.

"CREATE A DEFINITE PLAN FOR CARRYING OUT YOUR
DESIRE AND BEGIN AT ONCE, WHETHER YOU ARE
READY OR NOT, TO PUT THIS PLAN INTO ACTION."
- NAPOLEON HILL
AUTHOR OF "THINK AND GROW RICH"

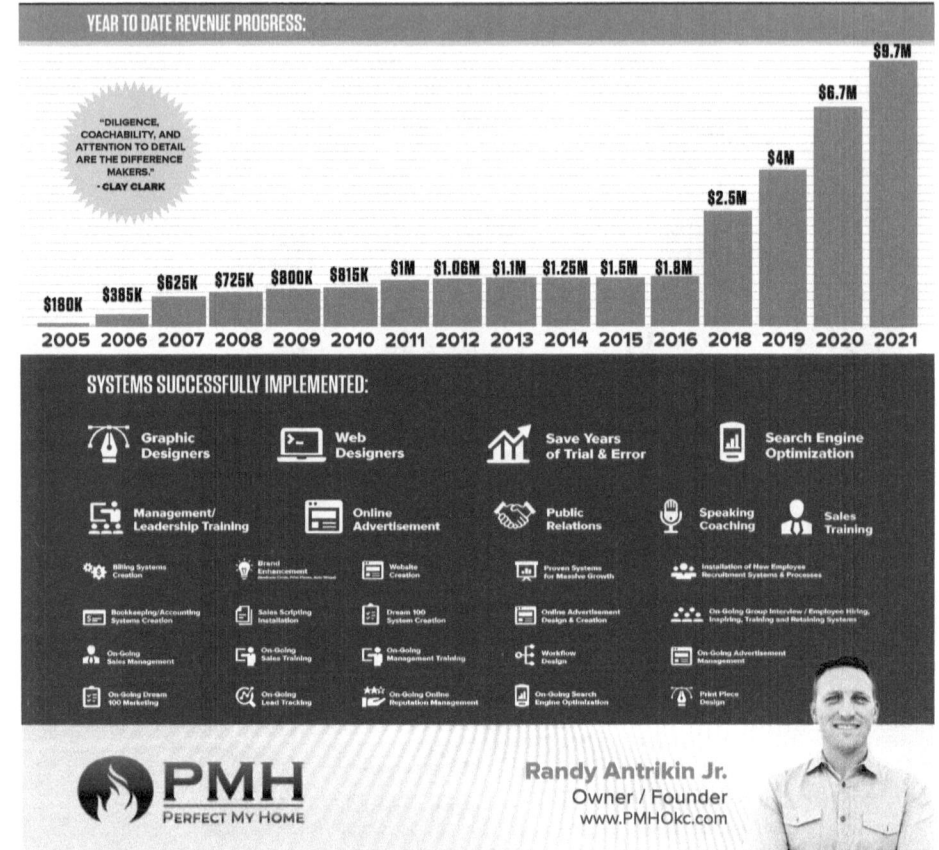

Chapter 36

Success Is Worth It

Growing up, I never thought I would become the U.S. Small Business Administration Entrepreneur of the Year or that I would become the successful founder of multiple businesses. I still remember the first time I was asked to entertain for a high-class venue (remember, I was a DJ in my early career). I still remember the first time I deposited $2,000 of profits into the bank after a fun weekend of entertaining. I can still remember what it felt like the first time I was able to turn back on the air-conditioning unit in our one-bedroom apartment because we had the money to afford the electric bill. I can still remember how it felt the first time www.DJConnection.com hit $1,000,000 in annual sales. I still remember how it felt when Elephant in the Room hit $1,000,000 in annual sales. I still remember what it felt like the first time I got asked to speak to a group of people. My friend, whatever your goals are, achieving success is worth it.

However, I don't want to put my goals on you. Maybe being debt-free and living in a van down by the river is your vision of success and that's OK. My mission to mentor millions is centered around helping those millions live the life of their dreams during this brief period of time we all get to experience on Planet Earth.

"When I was 5 years old, my mother always told me that happiness was the key to life. When I went to school, they asked me what I wanted to be when I grew up. I wrote down 'happy'. They told me I didn't understand the assignment, and I told them they didn't understand life."

- John Lennon
(An English singer and songwriter who became internationally famous as a member and co-founder of the Beatles)

REVENUE GROWTH AFTER WORKING WITH CLAY CLARK :

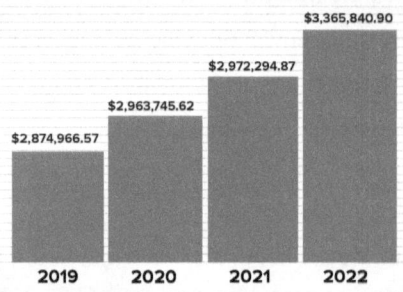

2019	2020	2021	2022
$2,874,966.57	$2,963,745.62	$2,972,294.87	$3,365,840.90

"DILIGENCE, COACHABILITY, AND ATTENTION TO DETAIL ARE THE DIFFERENCE MAKERS."
- CLAY CLARK

WE HELP YOU TO IMPLEMENT THE FOLLOWING CLAY CLARK SUCCESS STRATEGIES, SYSTEMS, AND PROVEN PROCESSES (AND MORE):

 Graphic Designers

 Web Designers

 Save Years of Trial & Error

 Search Engine Optimization

 Management/ Leadership Training

 Online Advertisement

 Public Relations

  Speaking Coaching

Sales Training

 Billing Systems Creation

 Brand Enhancement

 Website Creation

 Proven Systems for Massive Growth

 Installation of New Employee Recruitment Systems & Processes

 Bookkeeping/Accounting Systems Creation

 Sales Scripting Installation

 Dream 100 System Creation

 Online Advertisement Design & Creation

 On-Going Group Interview / Employee Hiring, Inspiring, Training and Retaining Systems

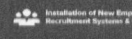 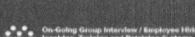

 On-Going Sales Management

 On-Going Sales Training

 On-Going Management Training

 Workflow Design

 On-Going Advertisement Management

 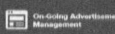

 On-Going Dream 100 Marketing

 On-Going Lead Tracking

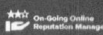 On-Going Online Reputation Management

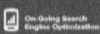 On-Going Search Engine Optimization

 Print Place Design

Bonus!

```
<header class="chapter-title">
```

```
<p>
```
CHAPTER 2
```
</p>
```
```
<h1>
```

ULTIMATE SEARCH ENGINE DOMINATION CHECKLIST

```
</h1>
```

```
</header>
```
```
<style>
    #page-background{
        background-color: rgba (0,0,0, 25);
    }
        header p{
            text-transform: uppercase;
            color: black;
            font-family: 'Proxima Nova ';
            font-weight: 600;
        }
        header  h1{
            text-transform: uppercase;
            color: white;
            font-family: 'Proxima Nova';
            font-weight: 900;
        }
</style>
```

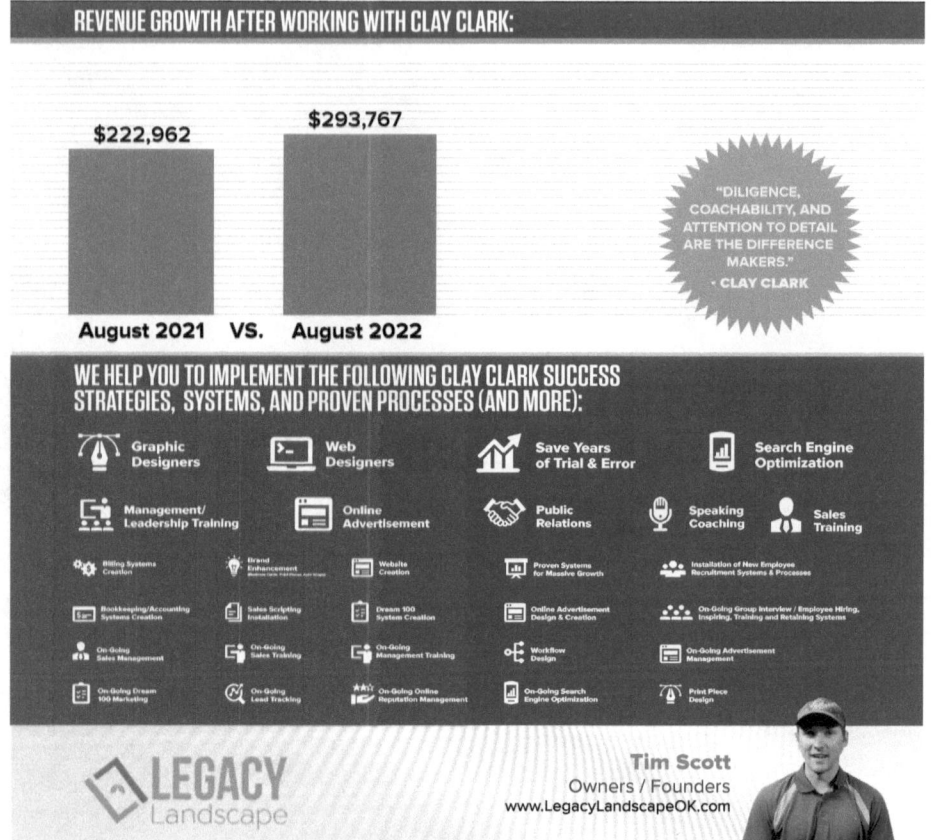

Chapter 37

In order for you to achieve total SEARCH ENGINE DOMINATION and DRAMATICALLY increase your level of COMPENSATION you must simply check off and complete all of the checklist items on this website evaluation. We humbly refer to this checklist as "The Ultimate Search Engine Domination Checklist."

The Ultimate Search Engine
DOMINATION
CHECKLIST
(AND WEBSITE EVALUATION):

_____ **Host your website with a reliable hosting service.** If your website is hosted with an unreliable hosting service you will rank lower in the search engines. We recommend using GoDaddy.com. Don't host your website with some local, janky hosting provider who lives with his mom in the basement.

_____ **Host your website with the fastest package that you can afford.** Google REALLY CARES about how long it takes for your website to load. Why? Because people get impatient and will quickly move on to another website if your website takes too long to load. On January 17th of 2018, Google formally announced the "Speed Update." Google's plan called for them to slowly roll out the new search engine ranking criteria to give web-developers plenty of time to make their websites load much, much faster. To test the speed of your website visit: https://developers.google.com/speed/pagespeed/insights/ To read more about Google's new speed requirements visit: https://www.forbes.com/sites/jaysondemers/2018/01/29/will-googles-new-page-speed-criteria-affect-your-site/#396634ed6a8f

_____ **Build your website on the WordPress platform.** "WordPress offers the best out-of-the-box search engine optimization imaginable." - Tim Ferriss (Best-selling author of The 4-Hour Work Week, The 4-Hour Body, The 4-Hour Chef, Tools of Titans, and Tribe of Mentors. He is also an early stage investor in Facebook, Twitter, Evernote, Uber, etc.)

Don't use any other website building platform than WordPress. If you hire coders to custom build your website on PHP or .NET you will end up hating your life as a result of having a website that nobody can update other than the entitled, nefarious employees who now have the ability to hold you hostage. Trust us here. We have personally coached hundreds of clients and every time our coaching clients have a custom built website the business owner at some point has been held hostage by the employee who is the only person who knows how to update the custom built, non-search engine friendly, and ridiculously complicated website. Building your website on WordPress puts the power back in your hands as a business owner because you can update the website yourself if you have to.

PRO TIP: USE WORDPRESS.ORG NOT WORDPRESS.COM
Wordpress.org is the open source platform used to power the best SEO compliant websites in the world. Wordpress.com is their platform that does not allow for plugins or optimal website optimization.

*Avoid wordpress.com

_____ **Build a mobile-friendly website.** What is a mobile friendly website? Check your website's mobile compliance at: https://search. google.com/test/mobile-friendly. If this link changes in the future just search for "Google mobile compliance test" in the Google search engine and you'll find it.

Install HTTPS encryption onto your website. HTTPS encryption stands for Hypertext Transfer Protocol Secure. What does that mean? HTTPS encryption makes your website more difficult for bad people to hack, thus making it tougher for very bad people to crash your website and to use your website as a way to steal the personal information of your valuable clients and patrons. Google ranks websites higher who have invested the additional money needed to add HTTPS encryption to their website. How many times would you use Google if every time their search results sent you to websites that had been hacked into by cyber criminals and internet hackers?

 Install the Yoast.com search engine optimization plugin into your website. What is Yoast? Yoast SEO is the best WordPress plugin on the planet when it comes to search engine optimization. Yoast was built and designed in a way to make search engine optimization approachable for everyone, and thus we love Yoast. Yoast makes it possible for people who are not complete nerds to proactively manage the search engine optimization of their website.

· ·

 What is a plugin?
A plugin is a piece of code or software that provides a variety of functions that you can add to your WordPress website. Plugins allow you to increase the functional capacity of your website without having to hire a bunch of nefarious, entitled custom coders who are typically hard to manage because you do not have any idea what they are working on or what they are talking about 90% of the time.

· ·

_____**Uniquely optimize every meta title tag on every page of your website.** The title tag is simply a hypertext markup language (HTML) element on a website that specifies to search engines what a particular web page is all about. "according to SEOMoz, the best practice for the title tag length is to keep titles under 70 characters." An example would be, "Full Package Media | Dallas Real Estate Photography | 972-885-8823"

> Full Package Media | Dallas Real Estate Photography | 972-885-8823
> https://fullpackagemedia.com/ ▾
> Looking for the best in the business when it comes to **Dallas** Real Estate Photography? You need to

 _____**Uniquely optimize every meta description on every page of your website.** The meta description is simply part of the hypertext markup language (HTML) code that provides a brief summary about a web page. Search engines like Google usually show the meta description in search engine results. Don't make your meta descriptions more than 160 characters in length. An ample example would be, "Looking for the best in the business when it comes to Dallas Real Estate Photography? You need to call Full Package Media today at 972-885-8823."

> Looking for the best in the business when it comes to **Dallas** Real Estate Photography? You need to call **Full Package** Media today at 972-885-8823.
> Careers · About Us · Contact Us · Client Login

_____**Uniquely optimize the keywords on every page of your website.** Meta keywords are a very specific kind of meta tag that will show up in the hypertext markup language (HTML) code on web pages and these will tell the search engines what the web page is really all about. An example of specific keyword optimization would be "Berj Najarian." You may be thinking, who is Berj Najarian?

Berj Najarian serves as the New England Patriots Director of Football and the "Chief of Staff" for the legendary Coach Bill Belichick who has won a total of 8 Super Bowl titles since beginning his coaching career in the National Football League. If someone is searching for "Berj Najarian" there is a high probability that they already know who "Berj Najarian" is and if you want to rank high in the search engines when people are searching for "Berj Najarian" you definitely want to make sure that you have declared your meta keyword phrase as "Berj Najarian."

Quick Note: If at any point while reading this you are beginning to feel overwhelmed just submit your website for an audit and deep dive evaluation and we'll do the heavy lifting for you. You can submit your website to be audited at: www.ThriveTimeShow.com/Website

 _____ **Create 1,000 words of original and relevant text (content) per page on your website.** Are we saying that somebody actually has to write, 1,000 original words of original and relevant text for every page of your website? Yes. Isn't there a hack? NO. Can't there be a better way? No. Can't you just go out and hire a company out of India to use "spinners" to slightly change existing text for you? NO. Can't you just copy content from another website? NO.

You can spend every minute of every day trying to find some blogger or some website experts out there that will tell you that someone on your team doesn't need to invest the time needed to create 1,000 words of both original and relevant content and you will eventually find them and they will be 100% wrong. However, they will gladly take your money. YOU OR A MEMBER OF YOUR TEAM MUST WRITE 1,000 WORDS OF BOTH ORIGINAL AND RELEVANT CONTENT FOR EVERY PAGE OF YOUR WEBSITE.

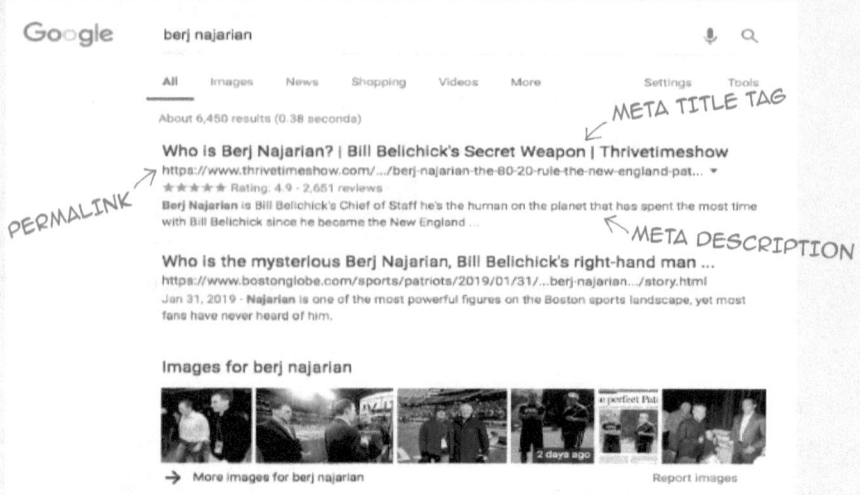

 _____ Create a Google search engine compliant .XML sitemap on your website. What is an .XML sitemap? XML stands for Extensible Markup Language. A quality XML sitemap serves as a map of your website which allows the Google search engine to find all of the important pages located within your website. As a website owner, unless you hate money, you REALLY WANT GOOGLE to be able to crawl (find, rank, and sort) all of the important pages on your website. Yoast.com has tools that will actually generate Google compliant .XML sitemaps for you. Don't worry, you can do this!

 Fun Fact:
I had to take Algebra 3 times en route to getting into Oral Roberts university and I was eventually kicked out of college for writing a parody about the school's president "ORU Slim Shady" which you can currently find on YouTube. If I can learn and master search engine optimization you can too!

_____Create a Google search engine compliant HTML sitemap. What's an HTML site map? A hypertext markup language sitemap allows the people who visit your website to easily navigate your website. This sitemap should be located at the bottom of your website and should be labeled as a "Sitemap."

Hiding your sitemap for any reason is a bad idea because Google assumes that if you are hiding your sitemap you are probably trying to hide something. Don't change the background of your website to be the same color as your sitemap's font or do anything tricky here. You want to make sure that your website's sitemap can easily be found at the bottom of your website. See the example below:

_____Create a clickable phone number. If you ever want to sell something to humans on the planet Earth you must make your contact information easy to find. Thus you want to make your phone number easily available to find at either the top right or at the bottom of your website. When coaching your web-developer, force them to make your phone number a "click-to-call" phone number so that users on your website who are using a mobile phone (almost everyone) can simply click the number to call you.

In our shameless attempt to make this the BEST, MOST HUMBLE, and
ACTIONABLE SEARCH ENGINE OPTIMIZATION book of all time we have
provided the following real examples from REAL clients just like you who we have
really helped to REALLY increase their REAL sales year after year:

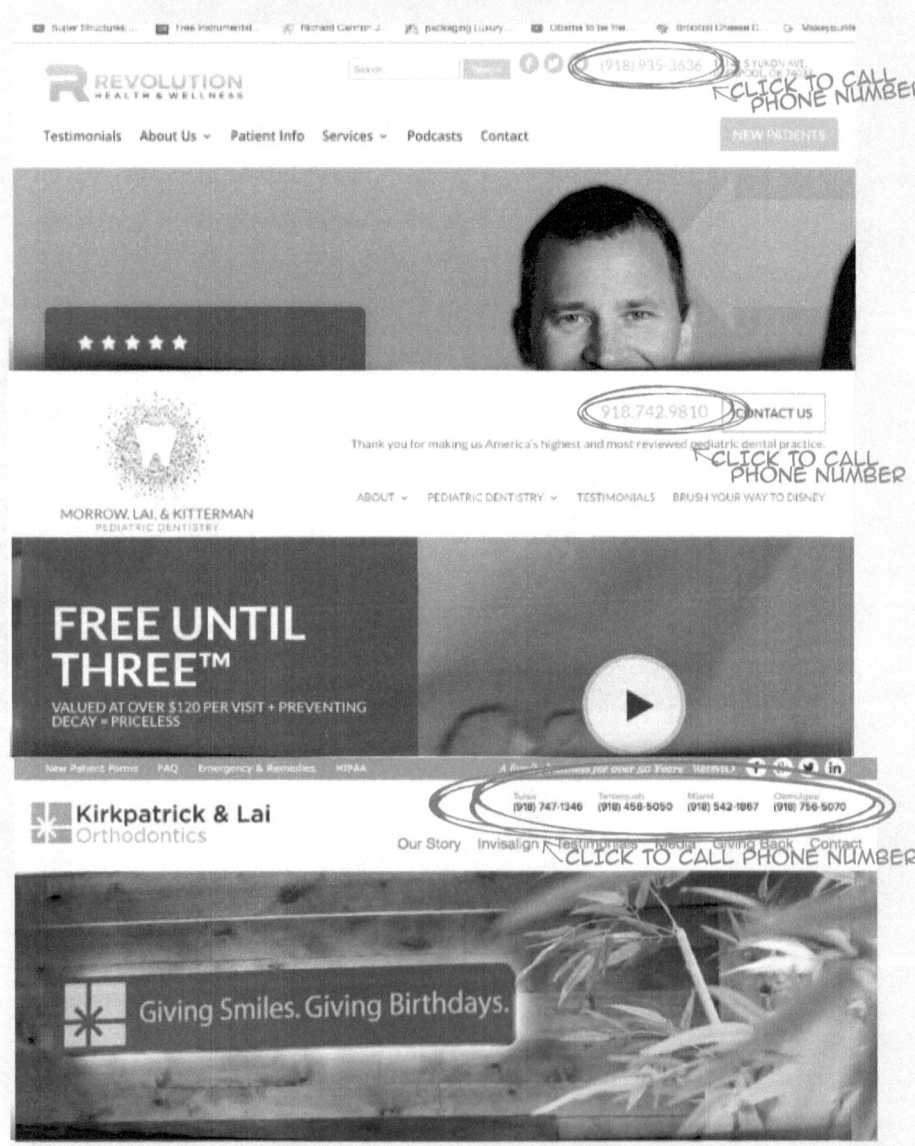

_____**Have a Social Proof. If you don't hate money and you are not a committed socialist, you will want to include some social proof near the top of your website.** What is social proof? "Social proof" is a phrase and a term that was original created by the best-selling author Robert Cialdini in his book, Influence. The best social proof examples are:

> a. Real testimonials from real current and former clients are super powerful.

> b. Media features and appearances on credible media sources like Bloomberg, Fox Business, Entrepreneur.com, Fast Company, etc.

> c. Proudly showing that you have earned the highest and most reviews in your local business niche.

> d. Celebrity endorsements from celebrities that have earned the trust of your ideal and likely buyers.

> e. Listed below is an example that will showcase to you what it looks like to use social proof effectively.

_____**Make the logo return to home.** Allow the logo on your website to serve as your "homepage" button. As of 2019, most people assume that if they click your logo they are going to be taken back to the homepage of your website.

 _____**Create original content.** You must create more original and relevant content than anyone else in the world about your specific search engine focus. If you want to come up top in the world for the phrase "organic supplements" you must then create the most original and relevant content on the planet about "organic supplements." If you want to come up top in your city for the phrase "knee pain Tulsa" then you must what? You must create the most original and relevant content on the planet about "knee pain Tulsa."

If you want to come up top in the search engine results for the phrase "America's #1 business coach" then you must create the most original and relevant content on the planet about "America's #1 business coach." Listed below are a few examples of receiving high search rankings due to having the most original, relevant content on the planet about that particular subject.

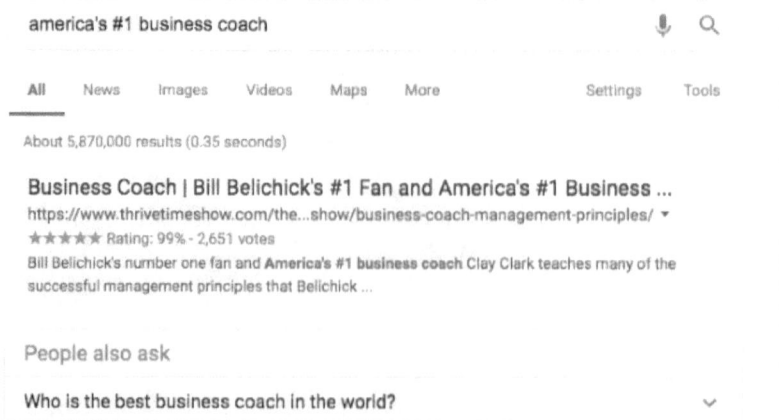

1.3 mi · 3019 E 101st St · (918) 299-4415 ext. 5384   WEBSITE   DIRECTIONS

The Little Gym of SE Tulsa
4.7 ★★★★★ (14) · Gymnastics center
3.3 mi · 6556 E 91st St · (918) 492-2626   WEBSITE   DIRECTIONS
Open · Closes 7:30PM
🌐 Their website mentions **gymnastics classes**

Twist & Shout Tumbling & Cheer
3.5 ★★★★ (8) · Gym
6.2 mi · 4820 S 83rd E Ave · (918) 622-5867   WEBSITE   DIRECTIONS
Closed · Opens 5PM
🌐 Their website mentions **tumbling classes**

≡ More places

Tumbling Tulsa | Tulsa Tumbling Lessons | 918-764-8804
https://justicetumblingco.com/ ▾
If you are looking for the best and highest reviewed **tumbling Tulsa** place, you need to call us at Justice
Tumbling today and see what makes us better.
Services · About · Schedule · Testimonials

Tulsa Cheerleading | Tumbling Tulsa | Tulsa Tumbling | 918-986-5785
https://tumblesmart.com/ ▾
Tulsa's Most Reviewed **Tumbling** Program. **Tumble** Smart Athletics. Free Evaluation **Lesson**Meet the
Owner. **Tumbling Tulsa** Gymnast Stars. Experience the

Google   tulsa knee pain   🎤   🔍

META TITLE TAG

Tulsa Knee Pain - Revolution Health Tulsa
https://www.revolutionhealth.org/.../tulsa-knee-pain-revolution-health-is-bring-in-a-re... ▾
Find the best treatment for your **Tulsa knee pain** right here in Tulsa. Find out more about Revolution
Health by calling at 918-935-3636.

PERMALINK   META DESCRIPTION

Tulsa knee Pain | Revolution Health Oklahoma
https://www.revolutionhealth.org/.../tulsa-knee-pain-find-the-top-and-quickest-result-f... ▾
The best prolotherapy is right here at Revolution Health for **Tulsa knee pain**.

Best Prolotherapy Treatments Tulsa | Tulsa Knee Pain
https://www.revolutionhealth.org/.../tulsa-knee-pain-find-the-best-possible-tulsa-knee-... ▾
Best QTH... Best Prolotherapy Treatments for your **tulsa knee Pain**

Non-invasive remedies relieve knee pain without surgery - Tulsa World
https://www.tulsaworld.com/...knee-pain.../article_6bdf681d-d017-554c-9ecc-fae529... ▾
Mar 13, 2019 · Dear Doctor K: I have osteoarthritis of the knee. Are there ways to relieve my **knee pain**
without drugs or surgery?

_____Create a "Testimonials," "Case Studies," or a "Success Stories" portion of your website if you want to sell something to humans who were not born yesterday.** Most shoppers today have become savvy and are aware of the fact that great companies generate great reviews (and occasionally bad ones) and that bad companies chronically generate bad reviews (and occasionally some good ones). Thus, most people will want to actually see testimonials, case studies or success stories from real clients that have actually worked with your company in the past.

In fact, not having testimonials, case studies, and success stories on your website freaks most people out to the point that they won't even call you or fill out your contact form.

How do we know this? Well, for starters, we are humans who happen to be also consumers and Forbes tells us that, "Almost 90% of consumers said they read reviews for local businesses. In other words, if you are not investing efforts into online reputation management, then you are missing out on having control of the first impression your business has." - Online Reviews and Their Impact On the Bottom Line by Matt Bowman - https://www.forbes.com/sites/forbesagencycouncil/2019/01/15/online-reviews-and-their-impact-on-the-bottom-line/#35d3b4955bde

"Perfectionism is often an excuse for procrastination."

- PAUL GRAHAM

(The entrepreneur investor, incubator, and coach behind AirBNB, Dropbox, and Reddit)

⊙ _____Include a compelling 60-second video / commercial (on the top portion above the fold) on your website to improve your conversion rate.** To provide you with an ample example of clients that we have personally worked with who have used a "website header video" in route to dramatically increasing their sales check out:

VIDEO PLAY BUTTON

_____Create a "top of the website" call to action that your ideal and likely buyers will relate to and connect with. You want to make it SUPER EASY for your ideal and likely buyers to call you, to schedule an appointment with you, or for them to do business with you in the most convenient way possible. As an AMPLE EXAMPLE check out EITRLounge.com and OXIFresh.com:

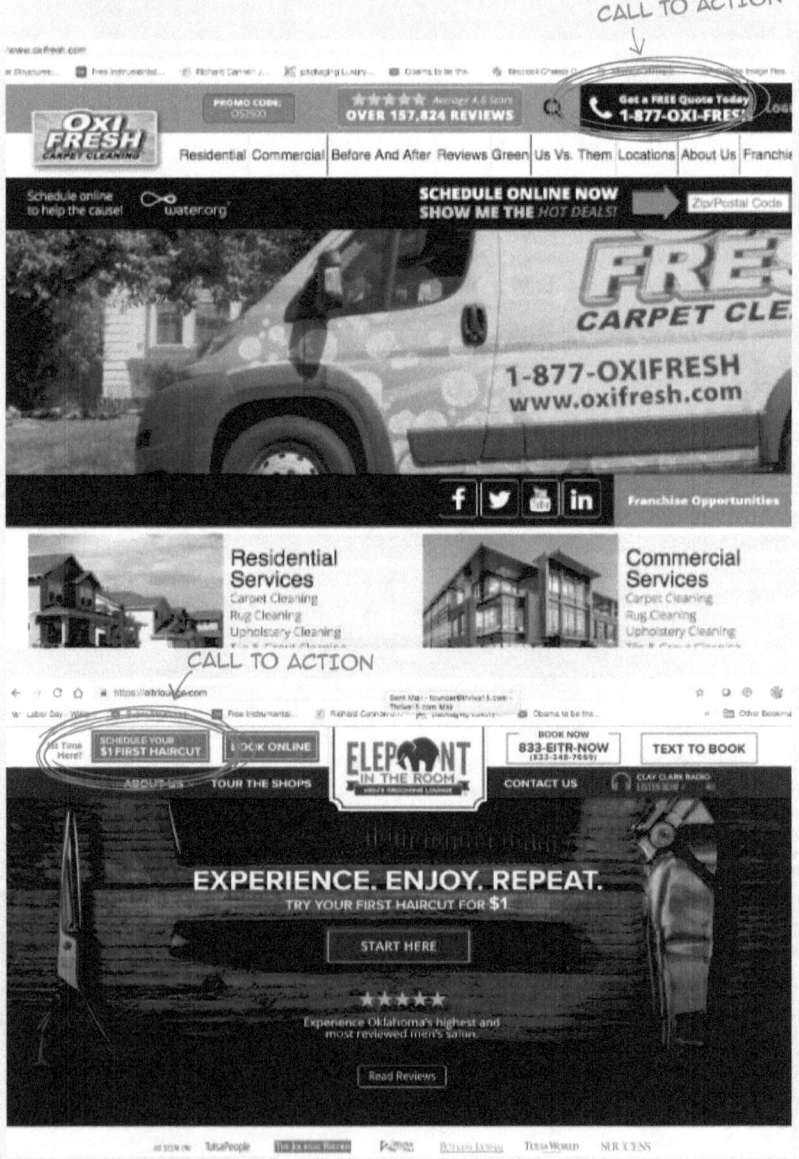

_____ Create a "No-Brainer" sales offer deal that is so GOOD, so HOT, and so IRRESISTIBLE that your ideal and likely buyers simply cannot resist the urge to at least try out your services and products out. As an example, we would encourage you to check out the following websites.

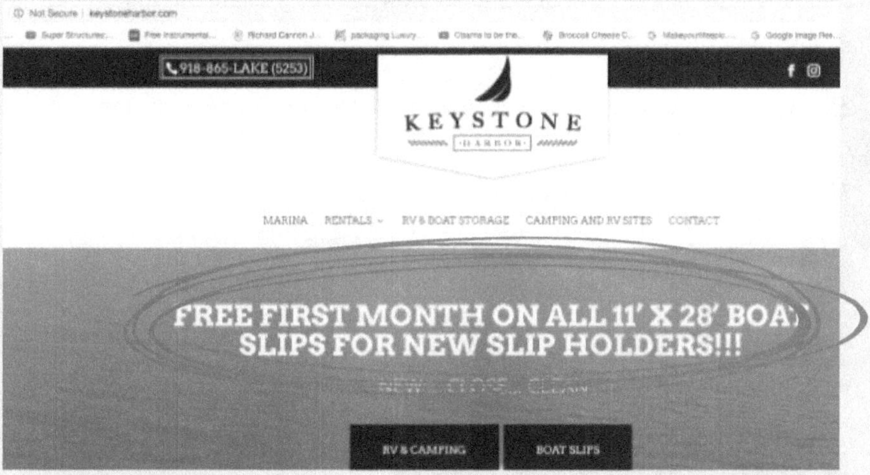

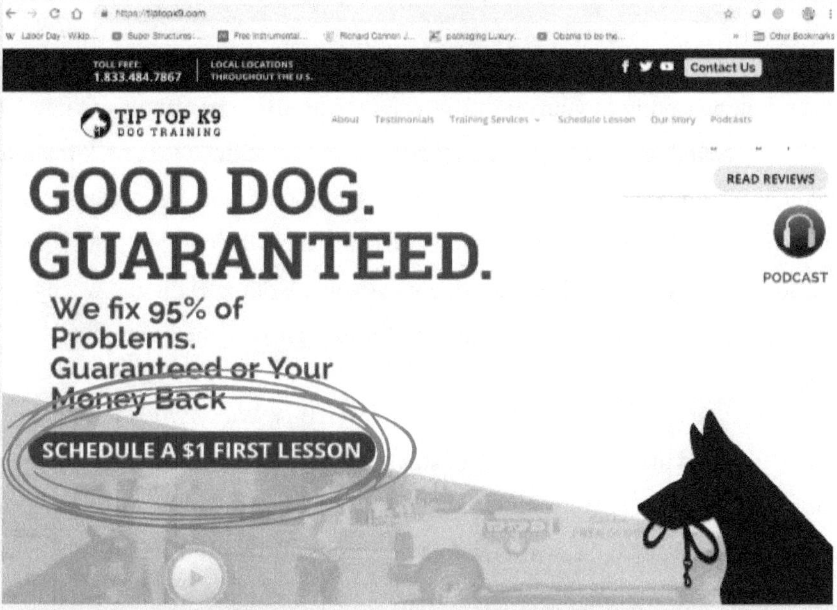

Introduction: The SEO Manifesto

If you are a human on the planet earth, there is a good chance that you have used the Internet to search for products and services you need or want. In fact, nearly every human I have met uses their smart phone to search for the products and services they need and want. Former Vice President Al Gore (the man who once claimed to have invented the Internet) has won. People are now officially using the Internet to shop. Thus, I would like to ask you three questions:

» *How much would it be worth to you for your business to be at the top of search results displayed by Google?*

» *How much is it costing you to not be at the top of Google search engine results?*

» *What terms are your ideal and likely buyers typing into the Google search bar on a daily basis to find the products and services that most closely relate to what your company offers?*

If you don't know the answers to these three questions, don't freak out, but also, don't move on without e-mailing us at info@ThriveTimeShow.com so that we can coach you through finding the answers to these questions.

Now, you might be a motivated and loyal Microsoft employee or a Yahoo employee and you might be saying to yourself, "But what if I use Bing or Yahoo and not Google as my search engine?" Don't stress, the game-changing systems I'm about to teach you will help you climb to the top of search engine results, regardless of which search engine your ideal and likely buyers are using. To get a baseline audit of your website so that you can quickly determine what you are doing right and wrong, just request a free website audit by e-mailing us at info@ThriveTimeShow.com.

I promise that you have the mental capacity to learn this. We've worked with and personally coached thousands of busy business owners like you and in every case, we have been able to teach anyone who is sincerely motivated to learn how to dominate search engine results. We know that search engine optimization is currently one of the most affordable, proven, and powerful marketing strategies available and we believe it to be a huge issue if you do not know how search engine optimization (commonly referred to as SEO) truly works. Search engine optimization should not be viewed as mysterious or overwhelming. It should be seen as just another core daily task that is executed by your business every day, just like turning the lights on and opening the door. Up to now, you probably have not learned the dark arts of search engine optimization because…

1. You have denied that your ideal and likely buyers actually use the Internet to find both the products and services they are looking for.

2. You have read too many search engine optimization blogs and have been falsely led to believe that the Internet is too complicated and that Google is always changing, so even attempting to optimize your website is a waste of time.

3. You have yet to discover a system for search engine optimization that is both clear and understandable.

To create the system that we are going to teach you today, please know that we first experimented on ourselves (members of our team are owners and partners in dozens of businesses). We then successfully taught this system and coached hundreds of clients through this process. Our team painstakingly invested thousands of hours into the creation of these effective search engine techniques, and have read countless best-practice search engine optimization books on the subject to create what is THE BEST SEARCH ENGINE OPTIMIZATION SYSTEM ON THE PLANET. If you would like to read more on the subject of search engine optimization, we highly recommend that you read the following books:

» **Get Rich Click** – by Mark Ostrofsky – This book is endorsed by Steve Wozniak who co-founded that little company called Apple.

» **Search Optimization All-in-One** – by Bruce Clay – This book is very detailed and has the potential to blow your mind…so be careful.

» **Honest Seduction: Using Post-Click Marketing to Turn Landing Pages into Game-Changers** – by Scott Brinker, Anna Talerico and Justin Talerico

After you finish reading the 1,500 pages of these books about how to harness the power Internet marketing, you will be a certified nerd and we will give you a high-five when you see us in person at a Thrive15.com workshop. Once you know what the heck you are doing, you must then commit to being a diligent doer and not a happy hoper. You must commit to taking the action steps that are required to win because knowledge is only potential power.

Getting to the top of search engine results is not an overnight process that will immediately begin sending your business

> "Knowledge is not power; it is only potential power that becomes real through use."
>
> **— Napoleon Hill**
> (Bestselling author for whom the founder of Thrive15.com, Clay Clark, named his son...Aubrey Napoleon-Hill Clark)

life-changing amounts of inbound leads from your website. However, I promise that if you follow these checklists that we are providing and our proven search engine optimization rules, you will rise to page one in Google search results. Let's do this.

The Google Domination Equation

Proper Google Website Architecture (must follow Google's canonical rules) + Proper Google Mobile Compliance + Reviews + Most Relevant Original Content + Most High Quality Backlinks = Top of Google Search Engine Results

Architecture + Mobile + Reviews
Content + Backlinks
= Google Domination

My friend, the bottom line is that the sites that have the most overall Google compliant architecture, the most mobile compliant architecture, the most original relevant content and the most backlinks, win. Once you wrap your mind around this idea, you can win. However, before you can win, you must first know what search terms (also referred to as "keyword phrases") are actually winnable. As an example, let's say you want to come up to the top of the Google search results for the word search term, "San Diego bakery." To show you if this search term is actually winnable, I'll walk you through the process.

» **Step 1** - Type "San Diego bakery" into the Google search bar and hit enter. http://www.twiggs.org/ came up top in the search results.

» **Step 2** – Go to SEMRush.com and run a report on their overall Google compliance score. Their overall score right now is a 78% out of a possible 100%, which is like getting a letter grade of a C.

» **Step 3** – Go to https://www.google.com/webmasters/tools/mobile-friendly/ and run a report on their overall Google mobile compliance score. Unfortunately, Google is showing their website is not mobile friendly.

» **Step 4** – Go to http://freetools.webmasterworld.com/ and click on "Indexed Pages" to determine how many pages of content the Twiggs.org people have. Currently they have 176 pages of content on their website (each page must have 1,000 words or more).

» **Step 5** – Go to SEMRush.com again to check how many backlinks the good people at www.Twiggs.org have. Currently they have 4,100 backlinks.

Equipped with this information, you now know that if you wanted to beat Twiggs.org for the term "San Diego bakery," you would need to have the following:

» Google architecture compliance score of 79% or more.

» A Google mobile compliance score that is found to be "mobile friendly."

» 352 pages of original content on your website (because you always want to have two times more content that your closest competition).

» 8,000 backlinks from various websites around the Internet.

» Thus, your total costs needed to win would be approximately:

» $3,000 to fix your website to get it both architecturally and mobile compliant.

» $3,520 to pay for the writing of 352 pages of original content for you.

» $16,000 to create 8,000 backlinks from various high quality websites around the Internet.

In total, you would need to invest approximately $22,520 to win.

Quick Thoughts from Clay:

Marinate on the math for a moment. For me, this number would be very encouraging both now and when I was starting my first business out of my college dorm room. I grew up without money. When I was in college, I worked at a call center, Applebee's,

Target and as an intern at Tax and Accounting Software Company. I worked nearly 80 hours per week during the summer as a home health aide at night and a very low-skilled construction worker during the day. Without reservation, I spent nearly $2,000 per month on Yellow Page advertisements and nearly $1,000 per month on bridal fairs – this while I was still in college. To afford this marketing, both my wife and I decided to live without air conditioning and to operate with one mobile phone and one car. We made sacrifices, but they paid off. If I owned a bakery in San Diego and I just discovered that for a total outlay of $22,520 I could beat my competition, I would be pumped and asking when we could get started!

Once you have determined your winnable keywords, it is time to begin the process of executing the proven winning strategy, which includes the following steps which we will teach you in a minute:

» **Step 1** – Create a website with the proper Google compliant website architecture
» **Step 2** – Create a website that is Google mobile compliant
» **Step 3** – Set up Google Places
» **Step 4** - Gather Reviews

» **Step 5** - Create the most relevant and keyword-rich original content possible

» **Step 6** - Create the most relevant and keyword-rich original content possible

» **Step 7** - Generate the most high-quality backlinks

The SEO Manifesto:

Search engine optimization is about getting in front of your ideal and likely buyers who are already searching for the solutions your company provides. If you are not on page one of Google's search engine results, you are invisible to customers...which is only cool if you are trying to hide from additional revenue, customers, and money.

Who Is Truly in Charge of Google Search Engine Results?

Google earns their money by creating the best search engine results possible for people who search the Internet. If no one is using their search engine because the results that they are displaying are not logical and relevant, soon Google will not be able to make any money from selling advertising. Thus, they are obsessed with making their search engine results the best in the world. As it relates to search engines, Google is the boss, the referee, the judge, and always the final word on who is deemed the "most relevant" website. If you follow their rules, you win. If you choose to not follow their rules for artistic, personal or psychological reasons, you will lose.

When in doubt, refer to Wikipedia. Google loves Wikipedia in the way that Thrive15. com's founder will always love Tom Brady and the Patriots. Google loves Wikipedia because Wikipedia has chosen to follow all of the rules of search engine optimization on a mass scale.

Why Is Google Always Changing?

Google is focused on providing the most relevant search engine results possible so they can convince most people to use their search engine when they are looking for the products and services they both want and need. The more people who are using Google, the more money they can charge advertisers. As technology has evolved, Google has had to evolve as well. As Google evolves, your business must also evolve if you want your customers to continue to be able to find you when searching the Internet.

The Magic Begins on Mobile

We must design our websites to look great on mobile devices because this is what the majority of Internet users (90%) are using to view our websites. We must also design our websites to look and work great on mobile devices because Google now requires websites to meet its mobile compliance standards if they are going to rank highly in search engine results. To see how highly or lowly Google is ranking your website, just shoot us an e-mail at info@ThriveTimeShow.com and we will run a free report for you.

To make sure you fully understand the necessary components of our search engine optimization system, we will first cover how it works. Then we will teach you how to do it. In order to dominate in Google search engine results, you must take the following action steps.

Step 1 – Create a website with the proper Google compliant website architecture

Your website must follow Google's canonical rules. Your website must follow the Google compliance checklist, which is available at www.ThriveTimeShow.com/ TreasureTrove. If you are a normal human, you are probably totally unaware of how your site ranks in terms of its overall architecture and canonical compliance. Don't let this overwhelm you.

- -

Definition Magician:
Canonical Rules - When referring to programming, canonical means conforming to well-established patterns or rules. The term is typically used to describe whether or not a programming interface follows the already established standards. You don't want to build a bizarre website that Google does not understand and thus, won't place high in search engine results.

- -

Step 2 – Create a website that is Google mobile compliant

Your website must meet Google's mobile search compliance rules or you will lose. I realize that you might not like all these rules, but because our good friends at Google are in charge, you'll have to take up any arguments with Larry Page or Sergey Brin (the founders of Google). If you want to check the current mobile compliance of your existing website, visit: https://www.google.com/webmasters/tools/mobile-friendly/.

If the good people at Google ever decide to change this link, please e-mail us at Thrive15.com and we shall help you find the new link. That's what we do.

Step 3 – Set up Google Places

Have you ever used your phone to search for a restaurant when out of town? Have you noticed that the local business listings that pop up at the top of Google search results for certain terms include user reviews and a number of stars appearing near the listing itself? Usually you can see the business' phone number and address there as well. Well that, my friend, is Google Places. OPTIMIZING YOUR GOOGLE PLACES ACCOUNT HAS THE POTENTIAL TO LITERALLY DOUBLE YOUR INCOME. We have worked with countless business owners from nearly every field and industry imaginable (apothecary pharmacies, chiropractors, dentists, fitness companies, lawyers, manufacturers, professional sports teams, and many more) who have been able to literally double the number of inbound calls and leads they were receiving simply by doing this! YOU MUST MAKE THIS HAPPEN. In order to get your company to show up in search engine results and to begin gathering those reviews so that you can show up prominently on Google maps, you will need to fully set up your Google Places account. Type in "Google My Business" in the Google search field, follow the link and then completely fill out every area of the form in order to have the most robust Google profile. During this step, you will have to provide a real physical address to verify that you are a real business. If you get stuck while attempting to do this, you will not be the first human on the planet who has ever done so. Just e-mail us at info@ThriveTimeShow.com; we will literally pick up the phone, call you and walk you through this process.

While optimizing your Google Places account, make sure you include the following:

1. Confirm that your address is both correct and consistent. If you are operating a home-based business, I recommend that you set up a UPS mailbox and consistently use that address. I realize that this seems blatantly obvious, however it is CRITICAL that your address remain consistent because of the way Google has set up the local search feature. You need to write your address the exact same way every time, because Google cares about this stuff when ranking websites; therefore, you and I need to care about this stuff. As an example, use either "Ave." or "Avenue" (pick one and stick with it, write it out or abbreviate) every time you set up an online address listing for your company on the Internet on websites like YellowPages.com, YEXT, Groupon, Moz, Axciom, InfoGroup, Factual, InsiderPages, Neustar, and the like. Failure to be accurate and consistent will negatively impact your overall ranking in Google. When I teach at workshops and other speaking events, some raise their hands right here and say, "But why does Google make you do that?" I typically respond with, "I don't make Google's rules. My game is to learn them and use them to generate copious amounts of money."

2. Verify that your hours of business are accurate. Many people now use Google to search for everything and they blindly trust Google to be right about everything. Think about how much money you could be losing if your Google listing says that you are closed during hours when, in fact, you are open. Unfortunately, most businesses discover that their hours are listed incorrectly when they go through this checklist.

3. Verify that your business is listed in the correct category. For most business owners like you, choosing the category that you are in is not confusing. As an example, if you serve food and you are a restaurant, you would obviously choose to be listed in the "restaurant" category. However, for industries such as public relations, marketing and advertising, you may need to put some thought into the matter to determine which category will generate the most calls to your business. You don't want to be oddly missing from Google search results in a business category that you should be dominating. Unfortunately, when diligent people like you take the time to audit their Google My Business listing, they often find that their business categories are incorrectly set up. Recently, we

worked with a mortgage broker whose business was incorrectly listed under the restaurant category. You can imagine that this had a devastating impact on the number of inbound calls he was receiving.

4. Add at least three to five paragraphs of really good content about your business. In this description, make sure to include the name of the local city you are in and how your company can uniquely solve the problems of your ideal and likely buyers.

5. Add as many high quality photos of your business, your checkout area, your offices and your products and services as Google will allow. Photos really do make a huge impact. In fact, the majority of Internet users today tend to gravitate towards websites that are filled with beautiful images and video. At the time of this writing, we are managing the online marketing campaigns for hundreds of business owners just like you. These business owners are always blown away when we show them their weekly website traffic analysis and they see for themselves how their website's visitors explore their website. Well over 80% of the people who visit a website do so using their mobile phone, and they tend to scroll up and down the website rapidly, stopping mainly on compelling photos, videos and a phone number to call. Most business owners fail on this step because they upload poor quality photos to their Google My Business listing. Doing this gives the impression that you are either a hillbilly or the owner of a poorly run business. People shouldn't judge us, but they do.

6. Consider adding a 360-degree view or a virtual tour of your business. If you've ever used Google maps, you are undoubtedly familiar with the feature known as "street view." When you click this view, you can walk around the street and actually get a 360° view of a neighborhood, street, or area. Although this is as disturbing as it is great, many consumers prefer to take a 360° virtual tour of your business before deciding whether or not to engage with your business. Again, if you are going to add this feature, you want to do it right.

7. Write a solid, engaging, and complete introduction to your business. This is the section where you describe your actual business. During this section of your listing, you should include links and the three carefully selected keywords you are focused on optimizing. For instance, if you are a Tulsa-based orthodontist,

you would want to focus on including the keyword phrases "Tulsa Orthodontist, Orthodontists Tulsa, Orthodontists in Tulsa."

8. Include the types of payment that you accept. You must be thorough when filling out your Google My Business account, even if it seems to be a waste of time. Believe me, it is not. If two businesses are equally matched, the Google My Business listing that is the most complete and most optimized will win.

Step 4 – Gather Reviews

Google has decided to put the most optimized registered local business with the most "authentic" positive reviews at or near the top of Google search engine results. This means that not only must you properly optimize your local Google business listing, but you and I must also start being very proactive about getting some reviews. You cannot afford to sit back and wait for Google reviews to come to you. Go get those reviews. Unlike our good friends at Yelp, who actually penalize business owners for asking for reviews (don't get me started), our buddies at Google allow you and me to ask our customers for reviews. This is great because once you have the most complete Google My Business account and the most reviews in your area, you will climb to the top of Google search results quickly, even if the reviews you have are not good.

Most business owners fail here by passively waiting for their customers to provide them with reviews and acting as though the negative reviews that have been written don't impact the buying decisions of potential customers. In this world of anonymous reviews, the trolls can quickly gain control, so you must proactively e-mail, call, and ask your happy customers to write a review for you. Most sane people will not typically go out of their way to request reviews.

If you are not proactive about asking for reviews from your happy customers, you will wake up one morning and discover that you have four negative reviews and no positive reviews. After working with thousands of businesses all over the planet, we have developed a pre-written e-mail that has proven to be very effective at helping good business owners like you generate positive reviews. However, I want to add this quick note. In nearly every market on the planet, we find that local business owners have to deal with disgruntled ex-employees, ex-spouses, competitors, and irate customers who are wrong. My friend, you must embrace the truth that this group of humans will be the only people writing reviews about your business if you are not intentional about gathering positive Google reviews.

You must respond to the reviews you have, particularly the negative reviews. I realize that you are not an idiot and that you weren't born yesterday, but I want to make sure that you fully understand this concept. If handled correctly, a negative review can actually provide you with an opportunity to improve the quality of your business and earn the loyalty of both current and potential customers who are watching to see how you will respond. If you come across as an irate business owner and personally attack everyone who gives you anything less than a five-star review, this is not good. Most business owners screw up this step by responding poorly to negative reviews. Respond sincerely and kindly and you will come out ahead.

To bring some clarity to what we just talked about, I have included a screenshot of a typical Google search listing on the following page.

Invest the time to call, text, and email every customer and human you know who has anything favorable to say about your business and ask them to write a review. Choosing not to do this is committing Google suicide, which, unfortunately, I have watched many business owners do over the years. Google has stated repeatedly that you are not allowed to pay people to write favorable reviews, so don't offer money for reviews. For the sake of repetition, just call, text, and email every customer and

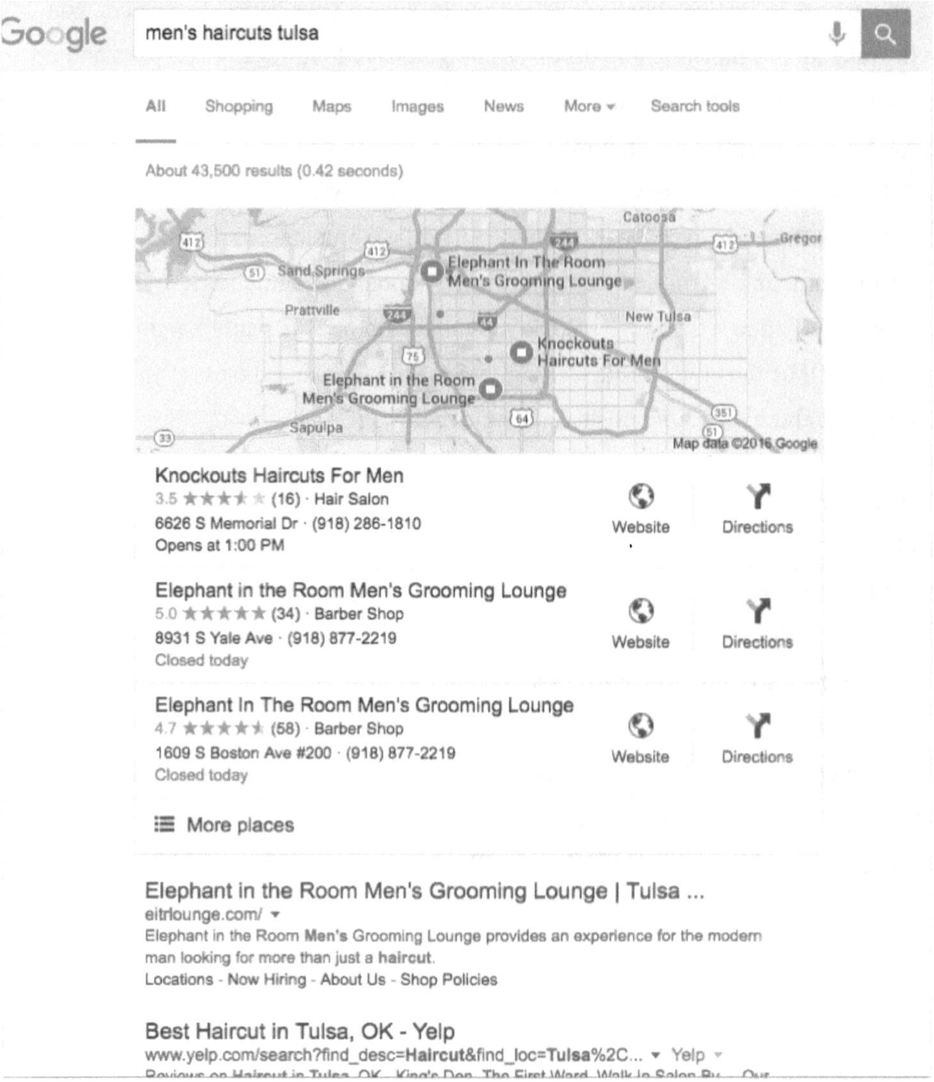

Google   men's haircuts tulsa

All   Shopping   Maps   Images   News   More ▾   Search tools

About 43,500 results (0.42 seconds)

Knockouts Haircuts For Men
3.5 ★★★★ (16) · Hair Salon   🌐   ⤴
6626 S Memorial Dr · (918) 286-1810   Website   Directions
Opens at 1:00 PM

Elephant in the Room Men's Grooming Lounge
5.0 ★★★★★ (34) · Barber Shop   🌐   ⤴
8931 S Yale Ave · (918) 877-2219   Website   Directions
Closed today

Elephant In The Room Men's Grooming Lounge
4.7 ★★★★ (58) · Barber Shop   🌐   ⤴
1609 S Boston Ave #200 · (918) 877-2219   Website   Directions
Closed today

☰ More places

Elephant in the Room Men's Grooming Lounge | Tulsa ...
eitrlounge.com/ ▾
Elephant in the Room Men's Grooming Lounge provides an experience for the modern
man looking for more than just a haircut.
Locations - Now Hiring - About Us - Shop Policies

Best Haircut in Tulsa, OK - Yelp
www.yelp.com/search?find_desc=Haircut&find_loc=Tulsa%2C... ▾ Yelp ▾
Reviews on Haircut in Tulsa, OK - King's Den, The First Ward, Walk In Salon By... Our...

Google search listing.

human you know who has anything positive to say about your business and ask them for a review. We will gladly share our proven, effective template email, text, and call script if you request them by e-mailing info@ ThriveTimeShow.com

Deep Thoughts from the Devil's Advocate:

Q: What if I don't want to ask people to write reviews and I just want them to come about organically?

A: You will be poor.

Step 5 – Create the most relevant and keyword-rich original content possible

Perhaps you've been online searching the phrase "free range chickens" or the word "dog" or the name "Ryan Tedder" and you noticed Wikipedia's page at or near the top of nearly every Internet search you perform. Perhaps you think it's odd that I would use the phrase "free range chickens" as an example...but we move on.... Have you ever asked yourself why our good friends at Wikipedia are nearly always near the top of Google search results? My friend, it's because Wikipedia follows nearly every one of Google's search engine compliance rules and they have more HTML text content than anyone else about that given subject.

Definition Magician:

(HTML) Hypertext Markup Language - A standardized system for tagging text files to achieve font, color, graphic, and hyperlink effects on World Wide Web pages. This markup is what tells the Internet browser how to show website images and words to the user.

So how do you generate more content than nearly anyone else about a given subject? You must write your content following these six steps if you ever plan to get to the top of Google search results during your living years (after we are dead, I'm not sure that you or I care if we are at the top in Google search results anymore).

Step A – Buy the Nuance Dragon Headset, which allows you to turn your talk into text. Basically, this device transcribes the words you speak into pages of text. Remember, you must have more original and keyword rich text on your website than your competition. This headset makes generating that content a little bit easier since you can just talk and the headset and your computer do the rest of the work. Buy this device on Amazon or at http://www.nuance.com.

Step B – Commit to writing more content than any of your competitors about the search term results that you are focused on winning. When you are writing this content, make sure that you reference the keyword that you are focused on winning such as "Tulsa orthodontists" at least six times per 1,000 words. Here is where the headset mentioned in Step 1 comes into play. Typically, 10 minutes of speaking will produce approximately 1,000 words of original relevant content. Google wants every page of your website to contain at least 1,000 words of content. Why, you ask? We are not to question why. Google is the boss and that is what they want, so that is what we shall do. In order to actually generate this content, you must set aside a specific time in your schedule to get this done. In my own core businesses, I pay a team of people to write this type of content for my companies every day. Yes, I said every day. You must have more original, relevant, and keyword-rich content than your competition if you want to win. To figure out how many pages of original content your competition has, go to http://freetools.webmasterworld.com.

Step C – Block out a specific time and place every day to write your content. You have to be intentional about this. Don't get nefarious here. Don't look for shortcuts or start copying text from other websites to save time. Google is a multi-billion-dollar company that invests countless dollars annually into catching businesses that are simply copying text from another website. Years ago, a homebuilder reached out to us to help him grow his business and increase the overall effectiveness of

his marketing. He asked us to look into why his website was perpetually found at the bottom of Google search results or even not found. After simply using the free tool that is available at http://www.copyscape.com/duplicate-content/, we found our answer. Much to his dismay, we showed him that his website was an exact replica of another website for a business located in the northeast United States. The web development company he hired to build his website simply copied the text from another homebuilder's website. They apparently assumed he would never check whether his copy was original or not, and they were right. You and I need to be much wiser about how content is created for our websites. Any time that we allow anyone to write content for our websites, we must ensure that it is original. We do this by using the free tool at http://www.copyscape.com/duplicate-content/.

If you ever get the urge to try to save both time and money by reducing the amount of content that you place on each page of your website, please understand that this is not a good idea. Google has a habit of not highly ranking, featuring, or indexing (showing in search results) website pages that do not have at least 1,000 words of content per page.

> "If you cannot do great things, do small things in a great way."
>
>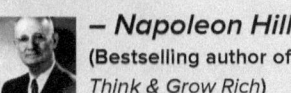
> *— Napoleon Hill*
> (Bestselling author of *Think & Grow Rich*)

If you or I are writing our own search engine optimization content, we have to move quickly to create massive amounts of content if we are going to beat our competition. Because of the volume of work involved, you may opt to hire some people to generate content for your business. Determine a pay scale for those people you will employ to write content that will win your chosen search term. As of 2016, I believe that a pay scale that allows your writers to earn around $20-$30 per hour (writing at a rapid pace) is fair. If you disagree, that is fine, but it is important that you use a merit-based pay program for your search engine optimization team.

Pay your writers what the quality of their content says they are worth. I am not exaggerating when I say that I have literally worked with hundreds and hundreds of business owners who have attempted to pay their search engine optimization content writers either a salary or an hourly wage and in all cases, the quality of the content they generated ranged between horrible and bad.

When evaluating the pay scale you will offer, remember that the geniuses who run both our federal government (Thrivers outside of the United States have problems with their governments too) and state governments don't know how to operate from a balanced budget. Because they generate debt on a weekly and monthly basis, they simply print money when they run out. This printing of money (known as fiat currency) decreases the value of our money each year. This is why the cost of living goes up every year. Keep this in mind and raise the amount you pay your people every two to three years to keep up with inflation.

"In the absence of the gold standard, there is no way to protect savings from confiscation through inflation. There is no safe store of value."

- Alan Greenspan
(American economist and former chairman of the Federal Reserve)

"Inflation is as violent as a mugger, as frightening as an armed robber, and as deadly as a hit man."

- Ronald Reagan
(40th president of the United States)

 Fun Fact:
Using the inflation calculator that is available at http://data.bls.gov/, you will quickly discover that a house that costs $238,062.22 in 2016 could have been purchased in 1971 for just $40,000. Thus, Clay Clark and the Thrive15.com team have often thought about investing millions of dollars into the creation of a time machine. Taking money into the past would be great. However, taking money into the future is just scary.

Definition Magician

"Fiat currency" is legal tender whose value is backed by the government that issued it. The U.S. dollar is fiat money, as are the euro and many other major world currencies. This approach differs from money whose value is underpinned by some physical good such as gold or silver called a commodity.

Fun Fact:

In October 1976, the government officially changed the definition of the dollar; references to gold were removed from statutes. From that point on, the international monetary system was made up solely of fiat money. Thus, the government can now spend money on whatever they want without a budget and whenever they run out of money, they can just print more. Good job, government.

Step 6 – Generate the most high-quality backlinks

Link building is the action of acquiring hyperlinks from other websites that link to your own website. Although you cannot control what people do on their websites, you can strongly encourage people to share about your website and add a link from their site to yours. A hyperlink from another website to yours is most often referred to as a "backlink." Google and other search engines will count the number of high quality backlinks that you have pointed toward your website as they crawl around the web in their never-ending quest to determine which site should be awarded the top position in their search engine results.

For those backlinks to be most effective, they must include the proper anchor text. Anchor text basically describes to the search engines the overall subject of the website page that is being linked to. Well-written anchor text will always include the main keywords you are focused on winning. You cannot control the words or actions of the other websites that are linking back to you, but in many cases, the individuals running those sites will ask you for a suggestion of what text you would like to be displayed in the backlink. Let me give you an example:

Score Basketball is proud to provide the best Tulsa basketball lessons in the region. For over 30 years, Coach Calvert and his team have provided northeast Oklahoma's most well-known and results-focused Tulsa basketball camps and personal Tulsa basketball coaching experience.

In this example, "Tulsa basketball lessons" serves as the anchor text. Those are the keywords this business owner is focused on winning. When Google sees that you and I have received a high quality backlink from a website that is using text like this, it celebrates this activity by moving us higher and higher up those Google search results.

Although you could spend a nuclear half-life in the Internet researching the various theories of search engine optimizers, bloggers and academics, I am going to make your life easier by listing for you here the EIGHT SUPER MOVES that work.

1. Creating Link Magnets

2. Create Link Bait

3. Gather Online Citations for Your Business

4. Guest Blogging and Podcasting

5. Guest Article Writing

6. Testimonial Links

7. Blog Writing (on your own website)

8. Asking Your Business Network to Link to You

1. Link Magnets

When I mention link magnets, I am referring to the various elements of your website that have been created in such a way that humans with a functional brain will

naturally want to link to them. In the same way that certain magnets attract certain metals, these quick moves that I am going to teach you will attract backlinks to your website as people find it to be both valuable and engaging. This process takes time to fully establish itself, but I have seen it work for many businesses, including my own. As an example, the resources that we make available at www.ThriveTimeShow.com/ TreasureTrove are useful and are often linked to by business owners who benefited from using them.

2. Link Bait

When we refer to link bait, we are referencing a steroid-enhanced version of a link magnet. Basically, link bait is something on your website that is intentionally designed to appeal to emotions or be engaging or provocative to get another human to provide a backlink to your site. A tremendous example of link bait is The Dollar Shave homepage (https://www.dollarshaveclub.com/). The video that is located on this home page has been viewed millions of times and is often linked to by other people who sincerely enjoy the commercial and just want to share it with others. Years ago, the world began to hear about Blendtec blenders because of their hilarious videos found on Blendtec's Youtube channel. Go check them out and you will quickly see why millions of people willingly provided a link to both the Blendtec videos and their website. They are hilarious and they showcase the product's actual blending power.

3. Gather Online Citations for Your Business

A citation is when another website references your business name, phone number, and address as listed on your website. The most common citations come from places you are probably familiar with: BingPlaces.com, Google.com/business, InsiderPages. com, SuperPages.com, Yelp.com, FourSquare.com, MerchantCircle.com, 411.com, Mapquest.com, and other sites like that. You see, our good friends at Google use citations to help them decide whether or not your business should be considered a relevant entity in their Knowledge Graph. The Google Knowledge Graph is an incredibly large base of knowledge that is used by Google in its never-ending pursuit to improve its already massive search engine results. Google's "disturbingly large" semantic search data is being continuously gathered from a variety of sources. As you talk or type into your phone the various items that you are using Google to look for, Google is learning more and more about you so that it can accurately (some say "disturbingly accurately") begin to understand your intent and predict what the most relevant search results should be just for you. The semantic search project is yet another massive project Google has taken on to dramatically enhance the consistency and accuracy of the search results generated for its users. The best tools to speed along the creation of hundreds of high quality citations for your website are Yext.com and Moz.com/Local. These are both paid services that we use when working with our clients and in our own business ventures.

4. Guest Blogging and Podcasting

If you are an expert in your field and are willing to commit the time needed to produce accurate, insightful and helpful content that can be either listened to or read by your ideal and likely buyers, then you should reach out to the various bloggers and podcasters within your niche to see if you can be a guest contributor for their blog or podcast. When you produce a quality piece of content, most bloggers and podcasters will provide a link back to your website from their website, thus generating a high quality and relevant backlink from a trusted source within your industry. For additional trainings on the specifics of how to systematically reach out to the top podcasters and bloggers within your niche, visit www.ThriveTimeShow.com/TreasureTrove.

5. Guest Article Writing

If you love to write or at least have the ability to generate expert and compelling content that your ideal and likely buyers are willing and maybe even want to read, you should reach out to various online publications to become a guest writer / contributor. Forbes.com, FastCompany.com and Entrepreneur.com are all top-rated sites that feature content on a consistent basis produced by guest writers.

6. Testimonial Links

If you have provided an extremely high level of satisfaction to your ideal and likely buyers, you need to begin gathering testimonial links from your clients. Basically, a testimonial link is a backlink to your website that is found within a paragraph that contains a large amount of sincere, relevant information touting your website as a source of wisdom and knowledge. Your customers' websites may contain a page dedicated to explaining how they are proud to partner with great vendors like you. Consider this example:

In Tulsa you can find a large variety of restaurants and bakeries that serve gourmet cookies. However, for the best cookies in Tulsa, you need to experience Barbee's Tulsa cookies. Barbee's has delicious cookies of all shapes and sizes and you can even now buy her cookies online. When we need to send our clients a special gift, without reservation we use BarbeeCookies.com and you should too.

7. Blog Writing (on your own website)

If you invest both the time and effort to create quality blogs and articles on your website that actually provide useful or entertaining information, many people will naturally want to link back to your website. When you write an article that is non-sales oriented, educational, informative, or entertaining, people will begin to link to you quite often. To make your life 2% better, I have provided a few examples of what I am talking about.

» Articles about topical and hot news issues: Writings about Justin Bieber's most recent attempt to get in trouble, Donald Trump saying something polarizing, or Great Britain's decision to leave the European Union as part of the Brexit movement are all examples of this kind of article. Perez Hilton has made a great living writing these kinds of articles: http://perezhilton.com/category/justin-bieber/ - .V4uLs5MrLMI

» Humorous or engaging content: If you are Jedi Master when it comes to writing funny stories about topics that humans enjoy, then this may just be your super move for generating high quality backlinks. If you recorded a daily video blog or a weekly podcast or wrote a daily blog about your unique perspective on life, your fans will begin to want to share your content with their friends. As they begin to share, more and more high quality backlinks will pour in. As an example, the good people at WestJet Airlines invested the time, money and energy into creating a video that has been shared by some 45 million to date. You can check out the video at https://www.youtube.com/watch?v=zIEIvi2MuEk.

» How-to guides: When you take the time needed to thoroughly explain how to do something in both an easy and concise way using visuals, videos, text, or infographics, people will naturally begin to share backlinks to your website. The Pioneer Woman (Ree Drummond) is a powerful example of somebody who is now making millions of dollars and generating thousands of backlinks thanks to her powerful How-to Guides. Visit her website at http://thepioneerwoman.com/cooking/.

» Top Ten lists: David Letterman feasted on the power of Top Ten lists during his career as a late night talk show host and you can too. When you write a helpful top ten list related to your industry, people will share it time and time again. Some examples of this are the Top Ten Ways to Be a Better Dad, the Top 10 Ways to Save More Money, and the Top Ten Ways to Properly Feed and Raise Organic Free Range Chickens. People will provide the backlinks you need if they find your content to be helpful. As an example, the powerful entrepreneurial podcast, Entrepreneurs On Fire, published a blog post titled, "Top 15 Business Books Recommended by Today's Top Entrepreneurs." That list has been shared 589 times, as of the writing of this book. See this blog post by going to http://www.eofire.com/top-15-business-books-recommended-todays-top-entrepreneurs/.

» Resources: If you and your team (which might consist of you and yourself) are willing to invest the time to document new research, surveys, case studies, compelling charts, infographics, or interesting graphs, this will also create backlinks to your website over time. We've employed this tactic ourselves as over the years, we have added dozens and dozens of practical resources, templates, and downloadables for entrepreneurs and business owners like you. These have generated plenty of backlinks for our site. Check out what we've done by visiting www.ThriveTimeShow.com/TreasureTrove.

8. Asking Your Business Network to Link to You

Many business relationships are very symbiotic, meaning that both parties need each other to be successful. To give you an idea of how this can work, years ago we helped a general family doctor generate nearly 100 high quality backlinks by convincing suppliers, the insurance reps, the pharmaceutical sales reps, and other people with whom he did business to provide a link on their website to his using the proper anchor text. Why did they do this? They did this because the good doctor agreed to feature them in his on-going podcast and because as his practice grew, many of these vendors benefited as a direct result of his success. The more patients he sees the more supplies he orders, the more prescriptions he writes, and the list goes on and on.

Bonus Step – Get it done.

I think Walt did a great job explaining this bonus step succinctly. Now that you and I know what to do, it really is up to us to just get it done. You must schedule both the time and the location you need to get your daily search engine optimization done and done. If you are struggling with your time management skills, we highly recommend that you check out the time management training segment on Thrive15.com, developed by the former Executive Vice President of Walt Disney Resorts, Lee Cockerell, who once managed over 40,000 team members.

> "One great way to get started is to quit talking and start doing."
> **- Clay Clark**

Now that we have covered the concepts involved in optimizing a website, it is now time to get into the nuts and bolts, the nitty gritty step-by-step checklist involved in properly executing an on-going search engine optimization strategy. If you were looking for light reading or even fun reading, this chapter is not it, but I'll do my best.

> "With self-discipline, almost anything can be achieved in every aspect of life. Those without self discipline will end up as a poor sloth by default."
> **– Clay Clark**

The Nuts and Bolts of Search Engine Optimization:

1. Understanding the Equation (You must know this, so we repeat it often)

2. The mechanics of optimizing website content

3. Uploading Articles / Text Content Checklist

4.   Fixing SEMRush Report Errors

The Google Domination Equation

Proper Google Website Architecture (must follow Google's canonical rules) + Proper Google Mobile Compliance + Reviews + Most Relevant Original Content + Most High Quality Backlinks = Top of Google Search Engine Results.

**Note: The managers and business owners who actually care about what they are doing and who are diligent about what they are doing, will win.

**Note: When building and optimizing a website, you must use a WordPress based website and the Yoast SEO plugin. If you decide to build a custom website instead of using a WordPress-based website with the Yoast SEO plugin, you are going to struggle endlessly with countless issues. The action items below have been written assuming that you are using a WordPress based website and the Yoast SEO plugin.

Every time you choose to add content to your website, you must optimize each and every page of your website. Listed below is a checklist of all of the steps that you must do correctly on each and every website page.

Optimizing Website Content

1.   _____H1 Tag Prioritize (H1 stands for header 1)

   a.   You must include the keyword within the first sentence of the content.

   b.   This text must be in complete sentence form.

   c.   DO NOT EVER DUPLICATE H1 text on other pages of your website. Google hates this and thus, I HATE IT TOO.

   d.   Example of well written H1 Tag – *Are you looking for the best haircuts in Tulsa?*

   Step 1:   Select the Page or Article that you wish to edit

   Step 2:   Select text that you want to make H1 text and enlarge it using "Heading 1" in the paragraph field

   Step 3:   Make sure that the H1 text is a complete sentence. (ie. Find Tulsa Men's Haircuts at the Elephant in the Room.)

Step 4: Check again to be sure H1 text is a complete sentence with a subject, verb and a period.

Step 5: Be sure the H1 text is at the top of the page.

2. _____ Article Description (This isn't the meta description)

a. Make sure to include a title for all content that you are writing, just like you would if you were writing a college paper.

b. Below the actual title of the content on each page, you must write the description.

c. DO NOT EVER DUPLICATE the description text or any text.

d. The phone number should appear on the top of every web page where content is being written.

> » Example - *This article is about how to find a quality men's haircut in Tulsa.*

> » Example - *This business coaching blog is about how to create a pro-forma that is usable.*

3. _____ Keywords (This isn't the meta keywords)

a. Use the keyword that you are focusing on six times per 1000 words.

b. The keyword you are focusing on must actually be woven into the article or blog content.

> » Example / Sample Paragraph: *At Elephant in the Room Men's Grooming Lounge, we are focused on providing the very best Owasso haircut. In fact, since first opening our doors at 1609 South Boston in the heart of downtown Tulsa, we have been able to grow our business exponentially as a result of focusing relentlessly on providing a premium grooming experience every time. Now as we expand out just to the north of Tulsa, we are excited about bringing the very best Owasso haircut to this rapidly growing city.*

4. _____ Content / Text

a. A minimum of 1,000 words of original high quality content must be created per page of the website you are focused on optimizing.

b. Producing 1,000 words of content is equal to spending approximately 10 minutes talking on a talk-to-text Dragon headset.

c. I would highly discourage you from attempting to write the content needed for your website's optimization by typing. I would strongly encourage you to use a talk-to-text transcription technology like Dragon so that you can save your time, money and sanity.

d. When creating content, make sure to answer the following questions as you talk into the Dragon headset.

   » Who is this content being written for?

   » Who is ideally searching for this content?

   » What is this content about?

   » Why does this content matter?

   » What do you want your reader to do as a result of this content?

   » Why are you passionate about this content?

   » How is your company different from everybody else in the market?

e. As you create content, you want to make sure that it will be scored highly by Google. In order to score highly, you must include synonyms related to the topic that you are focused on optimizing and you must receive a high readability score.

f. Content that receives a high READABILITY SCORE from Google will rank higher. Readability scores will be higher if you actually make sense and are saying something of meaning. Include synonyms and other industry related terms in your content. I highly encourage you to do a Wikipedia search for the keywords that you are focused on optimizing, then write down six words and terms related to the keyword. Focus on weaving these terms into each article that you write.

   » Example - *http://eitrlounge.com/articles/tulsa-barbershops-elephant-in-the-room-mens-grooming-lounge-best-south-tulsa-barbershop/.*

g. Use proper punctuation. Avoid long run-on sentences. Spell things correctly. Check your work after the article is written.

h. Company names, awards and personal names must be capitalized (Command 'Caps On')

i. The content of the article must be relevant to the company and always truthful.

j. All articles must be written in "Text Edit" and saved as an .RTF (no Word documents allowed). If you choose to save every file as a Word Document

(.docx), you will pay for it later as you are forced to reformat all the content that you add to the website. When you save a file as a Word document, it makes the process of uploading the content 30% harder.

k. You must verify whether content has been copied from another website by using http://www.copyscape.com/duplicate-content/.

5. _____ Upload to Dropbox.com (You must keep it organized)

a. You cannot allow your files to become disorganized by default. You must hold your team accountable for keeping your files organized.

b. Upload content to SEO Master Folder / Company Folder

c. Upload content to the correct Writer Folder using the initials of the writer first, the keyword that you / they are focused on second, and the article number third.

d. Create Keyword Folder for articles

» Example: *CMH – Haircuts in Tulsa*

» Example: *CMH – Haircuts in Tulsa – 1, CMH – Haircuts in Tulsa – 2, etc...*

6. _____ Fill Out Article Sheet (Insist that all content that is produced is turned in to your company's SEO Manager)

a. A third party must verify the quality of all content.

b. Run a test on all content via CopyScape.com to verify that content has not been plagiarized.

7. _____ Create More Relevant Content than Anyone in Your Niche

Step 1: Determine how much content your competition has had indexed by Google using this incredible tool: http://freetools.webmasterworld. com/. Click on "Indexed Pages."

Step 2: YOU CANNOT EVER DUPLICATE CONTENT. Doing this is like inviting Satan into your website. Google will flag your website for duplicate content and your website will drop like a rock from search engine results. Check for duplicate content using: http://www.copyscape.com/duplicate-content/

Step 3: Don't stop writing until you have written more high-quality and original text than your competition. Search around your office for original content that you have written in the past and get that uploaded to your website. Many companies have a gold mine of thousands of pages of transcripts or original content sitting on a computer somewhere. Use it.

8. _____ Featured Image (Add a new image for each article)

a. Every image that you add to your website must be optimized.

b. You must own the rights to every image that you add to your website.

c. At Thrive15.com, we subscribe to GettyImages.com and IStockPhoto.com so that we can use the massive library of high quality images both of these companies have carefully organized, paid for and archived.

Step 1: Select a place to put the image.

Step 2: Click on Add Media.

Step 3: Click on Upload Image (must be an image that you have the rights to).

Step 4: Name the image.

» When you save the image, use dashes. Example: owasso-mens-haircuts.

» When you title the image, use the same words, but remove the dashes.

Step 5: Set the image to medium size.

Step 6: Set the image to the left side of the page.

Step 7: Use the formatting buttons to wrap the text around the image.

Step 8: Title the image following this format:

» Example: Owasso Men's Haircut | Shaving Tools

» Example: Business Coaching | Woman in a Coffee Shop

Step 9: Name the Alt text: same as the title image.

» No description of image is needed.

Uploading Articles / Text Content Checklist

Once you are ready to upload the content that you and your team have written for your website, it is very important that you follow this checklist. Keep a log of uploaded content that includes the following details:

» Article Uploaded #: _____

» Initials of Uploader:_____

» Date of Article Upload: _____

» Keyword: _____

1. _____ Add Content to Website: No duplicate content is allowed.

    a. Go to Dropbox > SEO Master Folder > Articles

    b. Find the Client (Your Company's) Folder > Choose Writer Folder > Choose Keyword Folder

2. _____ Login to Client Website > Choose Posts / Articles

3. _____ Copy and Paste TWO 500 Word Articles into the Body (or one 1,000 word article)

4. _____ Scroll Down to the Yoast SEO Plugin

5. _____ Meta Title (Referred to as the "Snippet Editor" in SEO Yoast)

    a. Must not include more than nine words (less than 56 characters)

    b. Must include a "vertical bar" = | (located above the return / enter key)

    c. Must include the keyword and article title

        » Example – *Men's Haircuts in Tulsa | (Article Title)*

        » Example - *Men's Haircuts in Tulsa | Find a Superior Cut*

6. _____ Meta Description

    a. Write content that you want to show up on the actual Google search results.

    b. Keep this to two sentences, maximum. Include the keyword in the first sentence.

    c. Include the phone number / call to action in the second sentence.

    d. This content must fit into the SEO Yoast character rule limit.

» Example: *Are you looking for a premium south Tulsa Men's haircut? Call the award-winning Elephant in the Room team at 918-877-2219.*

» Example: *In this article award-winning business coach teaches management with the former EVP of Disney World, Lee Cockerell. Sign up for a free trial today.*

7. _____ Add the One "Focus Keyword"

    a. SEO Yoast will ask you to determine one "Focus Keyword" that you are focused on.

    b. Choose the "Focus Keyword" for SEO Yoast based upon what keyword phrase the content you are uploading was focused on.

    c. Provide six tag phrases (keyword phrases) that pertain to the keyword you are focusing on that can be found within the content that you are uploading.

    d. The keywords that you list must be included in the actual article.

        » Example - *Business Coaching*

        » Example – *How to grow a business, business coach, coaching businesses, how to find a business coach, business coach, accounting*

8. _____ Add Optimized Permalink (Also known as a "Slug" in SEO Yoast)

    a. The focused keyword that you are currently uploading content for must be included in the permalink.

    b. Do not attempt to automate this process. When you create an automated process, you will start to create duplicate content and Google will penalize you.

    c. Every permalink must be different.

        » Example - *http://www.eitrlounge.com/find-tulsa-mens-haircuts*

9. _____Compose Anchor Text Found Within Content

    a. You must include your keyword six times within every 1,000 words of your article and you must provide a link from this phrase out to content that relates to it (within your own website, if possible).

    b. Wikipedia uses anchor text everywhere. For an example of how they do it, to to https://en.wikipedia.org/wiki/Dog. Wikipedia has a hyperlink (a link to another webpage) embedded for the word Canidae, domesticated canid, selectively bred, Eurasia, and other words and phrases. When you click each of the phrases, you are taken to another section of Wikipedia's massive library of content. This is what you want on your website. Granted, you may not be as massive as Wikipedia, but you at least want to provide a few links out to related content found within your website. As an example, if you had content that mentioned the city of Orlando, you would either want to provide a link to a portion of your website that discusses the city of Orlando or you would want to provide a link out to the City of Orlando's website (http://www.cityoforlando.net/).

c.   Hyperlink out from words related to your OPTIMIZATION FOCUS to sites of high quality and integrity (high page rank).

» Example - *At the Elephant in the Room we guarantee that you will love your Tulsa men's haircut (link this text to our website).*

10.   _____ Embed a Video

a.   Pages featuring YouTube videos are ranked higher in Google search engine results.

b.   Remember, Google owns YouTube. If you were Google, wouldn't you rank websites higher that include content found within YouTube than websites that include content found within Vimeo?

c.   Adding videos to your web pages also increases the time that each visitor spends on each webpage, which increases your score. Google sincerely cares about the user experience and they want to reward websites that are able to keep people engaged and on a website longer.

d.   The video should be embedded right below the text written for it.

Step 1:   Go to YouTube to find a video

Step 2:   On Youtube.com, find a video THAT WAS CREATED BY YOUR COMPANY or by the client that you are optimizing for. You MUST select a video from the client's YouTube channel.

Step 3:   On YouTube.com, click the Share button

Step 4:   On YouTube.com, click the Embed button

Step 5:   On YouTube.com, copy code into Article / Update

Step 6:   On the WordPress-based website, switch from Visual to Text

Step 7:   On YouTube.com, select video size: 640 x 360

Step 8:   On YouTube.com, uncheck the box that says "Show suggested videos"

Step 9: On YouTube.com, copy the iframe embed code

Step 10: On the WordPress-based website, go back to your article

Step 11: Paste the iFrame embed code into the article right below the text written for it. (ie: This content is written for *client name*)

Step 12: On the WordPress-based website, switch back to the Visual tab to verify the video is actually there

Step 13: On the WordPress-based website, click Update

Step 14: On the WordPress-based website, open "View Article" in a new window to preview your work

Step 15: On the WordPress-based website, press Play to verify the embedded video works

Step 16: On the WordPress-based website, verify that no related videos pop up at the end of the embedded video

11. _____ Name All Images Correctly

 a. Make sure to name all images based upon your search engine strategy.

  » Example - On EITRLounge.com, the images appearing on that page should be labeled "*tulsa-mens-haircut-example-1,*" and "*tulsa-mens-haircut-example-2.*"

Step 1: Select a place to put the image.

Step 2: Click on Add Media.

Step 3: Upload the image (must be an original image for each article).

Step 4: Name the title of the image (when you save the image, use dashes, no spaces - example: *owasso-mens-haircuts*).

Step 5: When you title the image, use the same words, but remove the dashes.

Step 6: Set the image to medium size.

Step 7: Set the image to the left side of the page.

Step 8: Use the formatting buttons to wrap the text around the image.

Step 9: Title the image following this format: Owasso Men's Haircut | Shaving Tools Business Coaching | Woman in a Coffee Shop

Step 10: Name the Alt text: same as the title image.

  » No description of image is needed.

Fixing SEMRush Report related errors

Fixing SEMRush Report related errors

Step 1:   Go to semrush.com

Step 2:   Click log-in and use the appropriate user name and password

Step 3:   Click the + button (located next to Projects)

Step 4:   Choose a name and domain for the project

Step 5:   Click on Site Audit

Step 6:   Crawl all pages and click Start Edit

Step 7:   Click on Site Audit

Step 8:   Click on View All Issues

Step 9:   Once you click View All Issues, a mountain of errors will appear. This checklist tells you how to fix these errors.

1. Alt Tags – Coder must fix.

   Step 1:   Use the Divi template found within WordPress. Building a custom website is nearly always a disaster if you do not have full-time coders working for you.

   Step 2:   Use the Divi template.

   Step 3:   Use the Divi template.

2. Broken Images – A Coder / Web-Development Professional must fix.

3. Doc Type Not Declared – A Coder / Web-Development Professional must fix.

4. Duplicate Description (See the Meta description steps found in section 37.8, point 6.)

5. Duplicate Titles (Someone copied and pasted.)

6. External Links That Are Broken

   Step 1:   Click the "external links are broken" link to show all broken URLs

   Step 2:   Find 404 Errors to fix. (Ignore all other errors.)

7. HTTPS Encryption – Coder must fix. Google ranks websites higher that have invested the time and energy needed to install a Secure Socket Layer (SSL) as a sublayer under regular HTTP application layering. Whenever you use HTTPS on your website, you are choosing to make your website more secure and Google loves this.

8. Internal Links that Are Broken – A Coder / Web-Development Professional must fix.

9. Low Text to HTML Ratio – A Coder / Web-Development Professional must fix.

10. Missing H1 Heading – To create a proper H1 heading, review the trainings found in the previous two sections of this book.

11. Missing Robots.txt

    Step 1:   Click Plugins in the left sidebar

    Step 2:   Click the Add New button at the top

    Step 3:   In the Search Plugins bar, search for: Yoast SEO

    Step 4:   Click Install Now button

    Step 5:   Click the blue Activate link

    Step 6:   Go to SEO Tools Tab

    Step 7:   Click on File Editor

    Step 8:   Click Robot.txt button (this button tells Google which pages it can crawl)

12. More than H1 Heading – A Coder / Web-Development Professional must fix.

13. No Follow Attributes – A Coder / Web-Development Professional must fix.

14. Page that Returns 4XX Status Code

    Step 1:   Locate the broken link

    Step 2:   Delete the link OR link it to something that does exist

15. Pages that Cannot Be Crawled - Coder must fix.

16. HTML Sitemap (HTML = Humans to See… It MUST be visible! MUST be referred to as "sitemap" at the bottom of the page.)

    Step 1:   Go to Pages

    Step 2:   Click Add New button at the top

    Step 3:   Title it: Sitemap

    Step 4:   In the right hand column under Page Attributes, select Sitemap from template drop down.

    Step 5:   Click Publish.

17. .XML Sitemap

    Step 1:   Install SEO Yoast

18. HTTPS encryption--Coder must fix.

19. Submit Website to Google Webmaster Tools

    Step 1:   Must set up a Gmail account

    Step 2:   Submit site to Yahoo

    Step 3:   Search for Google Search Console

    Step 4:   Login to gmail https://www.google.com/webmasters/tools/home?hl=en

    Step 5:   Add a Property

    Step 6:   Paste the URL of the correct website (ie: https:/eitrlakewood.com)

    Step 7:   Click on Alternate Methods

    Step 8:   Click on HTML Tag

    Step 9:   Copy the metatag below

    Step 10:   Login to WordPress website

    Step 11:   Go to Appearance in the left bar

    Step 12:   Click on Editor

    Step 13:   Click Enable Editing

    Step 14:   Go to Theme Header on the right

    Step 15:   Look for the head within the theme header

Step 16:   Paste the metatag underneath the first head

Step 17:   Click Update File

Step 18:   Click on Verify within the Google Search Console

Step 19:   Click Continue

Step 20:   Verify that you are submitting your website for Google to crawl it within the right country preference

Step 21:   Click Search Traffic

Step 22:   Click on International Targeting

Step 23:   Click on Country and checkmark targeted users in the appropriate country

Step 24:   Click Save

Step 25:   Click on Crawl and Sitemaps

Step 26:   Click Add/Test Sitemap

Step 27:   Enter: sitemap_index.xml

Step 28:   Click Test

Step 29:   Verify there are no errors

Step 30:   Click Close

Step 31:   Click Add/Test Sitemap again

Step 32:   Enter: sitemap_index.xml

Step 33:   Click Submit

Step 34:   Click Refresh - Allow 24 hours for Google to index the site

Step 35:   Click Fetch as Google

Step 36:   Click Fetch and Render

Step 37:   Enter: sitemap_index.xml in the box

Step 38:   Click Fetch and Render again

Step 39:   After they're done pending, click Submit to Index for each

Step 40:   Select Crawl this URL and its Direct Links

Step 41:   Click Go

20. Too Low of a Word Count (must have at least 1000 words on the page)

Step 1: Copy the permalink of the page with not enough content

Step 2: Record the keywords for this page

21. Too Many On-Page Links

    Step 1 and Done: If the page is a blog or article, remove any links beyond

    Note: Do not remove a heavy amount of links from a "Press Page" that features all of your media wins or from your overall "Sitemap"

22. Too Much Text in the Meta Description--See above

23. Too Much Text in the Meta Title Tag--See above

24. URL Too Long (Slugs and Permalinks)

    Step 1 and Done: Follow SEO Yoast guidelines

During the year 2019, our clients grew at a rate of 104%. Why? Because I am focused on results and how you are going to feel when you achieve your goals and not how you feel as you are pushing through the pain needed to execute the plan and to experience real gains.

https://www.thrivetimeshow.com/testimonials

FACT: 96% OF BUSINESSES FAIL.
https://www.inc.com/bill-carmody/why-96-of-businesses-fail-within-10-years.html

FACT: OUR CLIENTS GROW ON AVERAGE 104% PER YEAR AND ABOVE.
(It is harder to grow at a large percentage as the size of a company increases)

The Shaw Homes Case Study: From $24 Million to $81 in Annual Revenue:

Aaron Antis - As 2015 drew to a close I was not sure where to go as a company to move us past the $24 million in revenue to the place where my drive and ambition wanted us to go. I had sold over $700 million in real estate personally but I couldn't figure out how to get the rest of my team to have the same drive and ambition to go higher than where they were. As we came into 2016, Steve Currington, a mortgage rep I knew in Tulsa introduced me to Clay Clark and we apprehensively signed up for a coaching service we could cancel anytime. I thought, I'll give this guy a few months to see if he actually can live up to the hype. I felt that I knew everything there was to know about sales and marketing and management but maybe he could teach me a couple new things.

Little did I know that we would go from $24 million in 2015 to $49 million in 2016, more than doubling our previous years production. Our proven systems worked in spades to spur incredible growth in leads and conversion rates through scalable systems and processes. 2017 brought growing pains from the massive growth of 2016 and Clay masterfully and patiently helped me navigate through the discovery that I had to grow and change in order for the company to continue growing. Clay's message to me remained consistent as he waited to see if I would continue to heed his advice.

Every year we have worked with Clay we have broken records and 2019 we did $80 million in sales. So far in 2020 we are a pace for $122 million in sales and breaking monthly sales records each month. Clay has been an inspiration to me as a leader, a lightning rod to our sales efforts and guide post for how to manage a growing company.

Lastly I have referred many business owner friends of mine to Clay that are all thriving and growing as well. With Clay being a former DJ I believe his microphone and platform to speak life into other people's businesses needs to continue to increase. He helps people, and I would love to see him help more people. If you have any suggestions please call me and I would be glad to talk.

Aaron Antis
www.ShawHomes.com
918.645.4441
Aantis@shawhomes.com
Industry - Home Builder

A Better Sewer
Jeff Watson
www.ABetterPlumberCo.com
2018 - 2019 Up 79%
Industry - Plumber

Accolade Exteriors
Stuart Weikel
www.AccoladeExteriors.com
2018 - 2019 Up 82%
Industry - Window Replacement

Amy Baltimore, CPA
Amy Baltimore
www.AmyBaltimoreCPA.com
2018 - 2019 Up 34%
Industry - Accountant

Angel's Touch
Christina Nemes
www.CapeCodAutoBodyandDetailing.com
2018 - $988,241.28
2019 - $1,646,327.37
Growth - 67%
Industry - Auto Body and Restoration Shop

Back to Basics Builders
Joe Burbey
www.HomeRemodelingMilwaukee.com
2018 - 2019 Up 35%

Client
Success Stories

Barbee Cookies
Kat Graham
www.BarbeeCookies.com
2014 - 2015 Up 140%
Industry - Bakery

Best Buy Window Treatment
Ergun Aral
www.BestBuyWindowTreatments.com
2018 - 2019 Up 76%
Industry - Window Treatments

Bigfoot Restoration
Marc Lucero & Stephen Small
www.BigFootRestoration.com
2018 - 2019 Up 112%
Industry - Disaster
Restoration and Repair

Bogard and Sons Construction
Andy Bogard
www.BogardandSons.com
2018 - 2019 Up 32%
Industry - Home Building
and Remodeling

Breakout Creative
Chris De Jesus
www.BreakOutCreativeCompany.com
Up 59% Total
Industry - Advertising

Brian T. Armstrong
Construction Incorporated
Brian T. Armstrong

www.BrianTArmstrongConstructionInc.com
2017 - 2018 Up 29%
2018 - 2019 Up 89%
Industry - Home Builder

C&R Contracting
Ryan Kilday
www.ColoradoContracting.com
2018 - 2019 Up 240%
Industry - Contracting and Remodeling

Catalyst Communication
Adam Duran
www.
CatalystCommunicationsGroupInc.com
2018 - 2019 Up 44%
Industry - Commercial Security Systems

Chaney Construction
Jim and Amy Chaney
www.ChaneyConstructionTX.com
2018 - 2019 Up 19%
Industry - Home Builder

Citywide Mechanical
Terrance Thomas
www.CityWide-Mechanical.com
2018 - 2019 Up 118%
Industry - Heating and Air

CK Electric
Chad Kudlacek
www.CKElectricOmaha.com
2018 - 2019 Up 25%
Industry - Electrician

Colaw Fitness
Charles and Amber Colaw
www.ColawFitness.com
2018 - 2019 Up 15%
Industry - Fitness Gym

Compass Roofing
Robert Alsbrooks & Sonny Ordonez
www.CompassRoofing.com
2018 - 2019 Up 103%
Industry - Commercial and
Residential Roofing

Complete Carpet
Nathan & Toni Sevrinus
www.CompleteCarpetTulsa.com
2017 - 2019 Up 298%
Industry - Carpet Cleaning

Comfort Pro
Steve Bagwell
www.ComfortPro-Inc.com
2018 - 2019 Up 28%
Industry - Heating and Air

CT Tech
Christopher Tracy
https://cttec.net/
2018 - 2019 Up 77%
Industry - IT Support

Curtis Music
Ron Curtis
www.CurtisMusicAcademy.com
2018 - 2019 Up 58%
Industry - Music Teacher

Custom Automation
Technologies Incorporated
Dan Hoehnen
www.CustomAutomationTech.com
2018 - 2019 Up 16%
Industry - Custom Automation

D&D Custom Homes
Dave Tucker
www.MidSouthHomeBuilder.com
2018 - 2019 Up 45%
Industry - Custom Home Builder

Da Vinci
Josh Fellman and Jerome Garrett
www.500KMSP.com
2018 - 2019 Up 1,097%
Managed Service Provider Consulting

Danco
Denise Richter
www.DancoPump.com
2018 - 2019 Up 17%
Industry - manufacturing
and distribution

Delricht Research
Tyler and Rachel Hastings
www.DelrichtResearch.com
2018 - 2019 Up 300%
Industry - Clinical Research

Dr. Breck Kasbaum Chiropractor
Dr. Breck Kasbaum
www.DrBreck.com
2018 - 2019 Up 50%
Industry - Chiropractic

Duct Armor
Tim Borgne
https://www.ductarmor.com/
2015 - 2016 Up 20%
Industry - Air Duct Repair

Dynamic Electrical So
Edward Durant
www.DynaElec.com
2018 - 2019 Up 16%
Industry - Electrician

ECS Electric
James Crews
www.ECSElectricllc.com
2018 - 2019 Up 26%
Industry - Electrician

Edmond Dental
Dr. Joseph Tucker
www.EdmondDentalatDeerCreek.com
2018 - 2019 Up 205%
Industry - Dentist

Electrical Investments
James Henry
www.ElectricalInvestments.com
2018 - 2019 Up 21%
Industry - Electrician

EnviZion Insurance
Austin Grieci
www.EZInsurancePlan.com
2018 - 2019 Up 800%
Industry - Auto Insurance

Full Package Media
Thomas James Crosson
www.FullPackageMedia.com
2018 - 2019 Up 15%
Commercial Real Estate Photography

Gable's Excavating Incorporated
Levi Gable
www.GEI-USA.com
2018 - 2019 Up 66%
Industry - Utility Contractor

The Garage
Roy Coggeshall
www.TheGarageBA.com
2018 - 2019 Up 19%
2017 - Present Up 70%
Industry - Auto Repair

The Grill Gun
Bob Healey
www.GrillBlazer.com
From Idea to Manufactured Product
8,725 Funders
Raised $920,009.00 Crowd
Funding the Invention
Industry - Retail Products

H2Oasis Float Center
Debra Worthington
www.H2OasisFloatCenter.com
Up 17% Total
Industry - Float Therapy

Handy Bros Services
David Visser
www.HandyBros-Services.com
2018 - 2019 Up 136%
Industry - Handyman

HealthRide
Ryan Graff
www.HealthRideTulsa.org
2018 - 2019 Up 10%
Industry - Non-Emergency
Medical Transportation

Healthworks Chiropractic
Jay Schroeder
www.HealthworksChiropractic.net
2018 - 2019 Up 24%
Industry - Chiropractic
Hood and Associates CPA's, PC

Paul Hood
www.HoodCPAs.com
2018 - 2019 Up 61%
Industry - Accountant

The Hub Gym
Luke Owens
www.TheHubGym.com
2018 - 2019 Up 66.38%
Industry - Fitness Gym

Impressions Painting
Manuel Mora
www.ImpressionsPaintingTulsa.com
2018 - 2019 Up 41%
Industry - House Painting

Inspired Spaces
Josh Fellman and Jerome Garrett
www.InspiredSpacesOK.com
2018 - 2019 Up 40%
Industry - Epoxy Flooring

Jameson Fine Cabinetry
Jamie Fagel
www.JamesonFineCabinetry.com
2018 - 2019 Up 31%
Industry - Home Improvement

Jean Briese
Jean Briese
www.JeanBriese.com
2018 - 2019 Up 90%
4. Motivational Speaker

KAE Edward Plumbing
Ron & Jacqueline Mader
www.KaeEdwardPlumbing.com
2018 - 2019 Up 46%
Industry - Plumber

Kelly Construction Group
Jon Kelly
www.KellyConstructionGroup.com
2018 - 2019 Up 42%
Industry - General Contractor

Kona Honu
Byron Kay
www.KonaHonuDivers.com
2018 - 2019 Up 14%
Industry - Diving Tours and
Scuba Instruction

Kurb to Kitchen
Lonny & Rinda Myers
www.KurbtoKitchenLLC.com
2018 - 2019 Up 126%
Industry - Home Remodeling

Kvell Fitness & Nutrition
Brett Denton
www.KvellFit.com
2018-2019 Up 35%+
Industry - Fitness Gym

Lake Martin Mini Mall
Jason Lett
www.LakeMartinCubed.com
2018 - $685,804.00
2019 - $782,551.00
14% Growth
Industry - Retail Products

Lakeshore Plumbing
Mike Boulte
www.LakeShorePlumbingOKC.com
2018 - 2019 Up 100%
Industry - Plumber

Laundry Barn
Josh Fellman
www.TheLaundryBarn.com
2018 - 2019 Up 100%
Industry - Laundromat

Living Water Irrigation
Josh Wilson
www.LivingWaterIrrigationOK.com
2017 - 2019 Up 600%
Industry - Sprinkler Install

Mennis Heating
Mike Ennis
www.MennisHeatingandCooling.com
2018 - 2019 Up 400%
Industry - Heating and Air

Metal Roof Contractors
Doug Yarholar
www.MetalRoofContractorsOK.com
2018 - 2019 Up 14%
Industry - Metal Roof Contractor

Mod Scenes
Steven Hall
www.ModScenes.com
2018 - 2019 Up 83%
Industry - Stage Design

Morrow, Lai and Kitterman
Pediatric Dentistry
Dr. Mark Morrow, Dr. April Lai,
and Dr. Kerry Kitterman
www.MLKDentistry.com
2018 - 2019 Up 42%
Industry - Dentist

Mr. Rooter
Joshua Creasy
www.MrRooter.com/New-
Braunfels/
2018 - 2019 Up 75%
Industry - Plumber

Multi-Clean
Kevin Thomas
www.MultiCleanOK.com
2018 - 2019 Up 14%
Industry - Commercial Cleaning

OK Roof Nerds
Marty Grisham
www.OKRoofNerds.com
2018 - 2019 Up 74%
Industry - Commercial and
Residential Roofer

One Way Plumbing
Chad Ward
www.OneWayPlumbing.biz
2018 - 2019 Up 11%
Industry - Plumbing

Oxi Fresh
Jonathan Barnett
Matt Kline - Franchise Developer
www.OxiFresh.com
2007 to 2019 - 400 Locations Opened
Industry - Carpet Cleaning

Pappagallo's Pizza
Dave Rich
www.Pappagallos.com
2018 - 2019 Up 21%
Industry - Restaurant

Platinum Pest
Jennifer and Jared Johnson
www.PlatinumPestandLawn.com
2018-2019 - 25% Growth
2017-2018 - 43% Growth
Industry - Pest Control

PMH OKC
Randy Antrikan
www.PMHOKC.com
2018 - 2019 Up 70%
Industry - Outdoor Living
/ Retail Products

Precision Calibration
Nathan Saylor
www.PrecisionCalibrations.com
2018 - 2019 Up 62%
Industry - Equipment Calibration

Quality Surfaces
John Cook
www.QualitySurfacesIn.com
2018 - 2019 Up 84%
Industry - Commercial and
Residential Remodeling

RC Auto Specialists
Roy Coggeshall
www.RCAutoSpecialists.com
2018 - 2019 Up 9%
Industry - Auto Repair

Rescue Roofer TX
Wesley Cannon
www.RoofingDenton.com
2018 - 2019 Up 79%
Industry - Commercial and
Residential Roofer

Revitalize Medical Spa
Lindsey Blankenship and Crista Hobbs
www.RevitalizeMedicalSpa.com
2018 - 2019 Up 36%
Industry - Medical Cosmetics

Roofing & Siding Smiths
Zach Potts
www.RoofingandSidingSmiths.com
2018 - 2019 Up 67%
Industry - Roofing and Siding

Rogers Plumbing
Roger Patterson
https://plumberinaustin.com
2018 - 2019 Up 33%
Industry - Plumber

Scotch Construction
Tim Scotch
www.ScotchConstruction.com
2017 - 2019 Up 492%
Industry - Home Builder

Shaw Homes
Aaron Antis
www.ShawHomes.com
2018 - 2019 Up 116%
Industry - Custom Home Builder

Sierra Pools
Cody Albright
www.SierraPoolsandSpas.com
2017 - 2019 Up 309%
Industry - Pool Construction

Snow Bear Air
Daniel Ramos
www.SnowBearAir.com
2018 - 2019 Up 41%
Industry - Heating and Air

Southeastern Computer Associates
Ben Miner
https://sca-atl.com/
2018 - $2,011,394.51 -
2019 - $5,531,144.01
Industry - IT Support

Spot-On Plumbing
Brandon Brown
www.SpotOnPlumbingTulsa.com
2018 - 2019 Up 120%
Industry - Plumber

Spurrell & Associates Chartered
Professional Accountants
Josh Spurrell
www.Spurrell.ca
2018 - 2019 Up 50%
Industry - Accounting

Struct Construction
Brandon Haaga
www.StructConstruction.com
2018 - 2019 Up 60%
Industry - Construction Contractor

Tesla Electric
Felix Keil
www.TeslaElectricColorado.com
2018 - 2019 Up 60%
Industry - Tesla Electric

Tip Top K9
Ryan and Rachel Wimpey
www.TipTopK9.com
1 Location - 10 Locations
Industry - Dog Training

Trinity Employment
Cory Minter
www.TrinityEmployment.com
2018-2019 Up 35%
Industry - Staffing

Turley Solutions & Innovations
Rance Turley
www.TSI.lc
2018 - 2019 Up 300%
Industry - IT Support

Tuscaloosa Ophthalmology
Doctor Timothy Johnson
www.TTownEyes.com
2018 - 2019 Up 16%
Industry - Doctor

Viva Med
Chris Lacroix
www.MyVivaMed.com
2018 - 2019 Up 90%
Industry - Primary Care Physicians

Veteran Home Exterior
James Peterson
www.VeteranHomeExterior.com
2018 - 2019 Up 145%
Industry - Window Replacement

White Glove Auto
Myron Kirkpatrick
WhiteGloveAutoTulsa.com
2018 - 2019 - 27%
Industry - Auto Detailing

Williams Contracting
Travis Williams
www.Will-Con.com
2018 - 2019 Up 33%
Industry - Construction Management

Witness Security
Keith Schultz
www.WitnessLLC.com
2017 - 2019 Up 300%
Industry - Home Security Systems

Money Is Simply a Magnifier (Both Good and Bad):

Money is just a magnifier, and I have consistently found that teaching YOU how to make more money and how to create both time and financial freedom simply allows YOU to become more of who YOU are, both GOOD and BAD.

If you are generous, having increased financial means will allow you to give even more to help those in need. If you like going out to eat, with additional income you will have the financial resources to NOW go out to eat more often. If you love traveling, with financial abundance in your wallet, you will be able to travel even more. With additional cash in the bank, if you are excited about buying exotic cars, having increased financial resources will allow you to buy even more exotic cars because money is just a magnifier. However, it is my sincere and highest desire that I haven't taught you the proven processes and success strategies so that you can become a MASSIVE ASS because the world already has enough of those (Mark Zuckerberg, Jack Dorsey, Bill Gates, etc.)

"[36] For what shall it profit a man, if he shall gain the whole world, and lose his own soul?"

MARK 8:36
KJV

So as we complete this workbook (and potentially this workshop) together, I would encourage you to sit down with yourself, with your spouse and with GOD'S PLAN FOR YOUR LIFE firmly placed in your mind and I would ask yourself the following question.

If you had all of the money in the world what goals would you have for your faith, family, finances, fitness, friendship, fun, and focus.

I would encourage you to take 30 minute to actually sketch out your ideal calendar in a perfect world where you have the financial freedom and time freedom needed to dictate what you will do with your days and whom you will spend your time with. Don't mail it in here. This is the entire point of learning how to grow a successful business. Fill in the calendar below the time that you will devote to your faith, your family, your finances, your fitness, your friend and your pursuit of fun. Don't be afraid to schedule guitar lessons, workouts, time to take your kids camping or that all important trip that you've been putting off. Every day that we are given on this planet is a gift from our God above, however what we do with each and every day is our gift to God. Remember being present is a present. But, remember, only what gets scheduled gets done.

"THE SECRET TO BUYING LAMBORGHINI'S"

Step 1: Follow Clay Clark's systems

Step 2: Buy Lamborghini's

"I own 6 Lamborghini's."

- STEVE CURRINGTON

Mortgage broker
SteveCurrington.com

WANT TO KNOW EVEN MORE?
CHECK OUT ALL OF CLAY'S BOOKS

START HERE
The World's Best Business Growth & Consulting Book: Business Growth Strategies from the World's Best Business Coach.

DON'T LET YOUR EMPLOYEES HOLD YOU HOSTAGE
This candid book shares how to avoid being held hostage by employees.

MAKE YOUR LIFE EPIC
Clay shares his journey and struggle from the dorm room to the board room during his raw and action-packed story of how he built DJConnection.com.

THE ENTREPRENEUR'S DRAGON ENERGY
The Mindset Kanye, Trump and You Need to Succeed.

BOOM
The 14 Proven Steps to Business Success.

F6 JOURNAL
Meta Thrive Time Journal.

JACKASSARY
Jackassery will serve as a beacon of light for other entrepreneurs that are looking to avoid troublesome employees and difficult situations. This is real. This is raw. This is unfiltered entrepreneurship.

THE ART OF GETTING THINGS DONE
Clay Clark breaks down the proven, time-tested and time freedom creating super moves that you can use to create both the time freedom and financial freedom that most people only dream about.

HOW TO REPEL FRIENDS AND NOT INFLUENCE PEOPLE
The epic whale of a tale featuring America's self proclaimed most humble male.

THRIVE
How to Take Control of Your Destiny and Move Beyond Surviving... Now!

SEARCH ENGINE DOMINATION
Learn the Proven System We've Used to Earn Millions.

SALES DOMINATION
Clay Clark is a master of selling and now he wants to teach you his proven processes, scalable systems and sales mastery moves in a humorous and practical way.

WHEEL OF WEALTH
An Entrepreneur's Action Guide.

WILL NOT WORK FOR FOOD
9 Big Ideas for Effectively Managing Your Business in an Increasingly Dumb, Distracted & Dishonest America.

TRADE-UPS
Learn how to design and live the life you love, how to find and create the time needed to get things done in a world filled with endless digital distractions, and more!

IF MY WALLS COULD TALK
The Notes, Quotes, & Epiphanies I've Written On Clay's Office Walls. (Hardcover).

IT'S NOT LONELY AT THE TOP
15 Keys to achieving a successful, peaceful, and drama-free life. (3/4 of this book is handwritten by Clay Clark, himself).

PODCAST DOMINATION 101
This book will show you how to prepare, record, launch, and begin generating income from your podcast, all from your home studio!

ENTREPRENEURSHIP: SIMPLIFIED, AMPLIFIED, & VISUALIZED
Throughout my career, I have been blessed to achieve tremendous success both as an entrepreneur and as a podcast host.

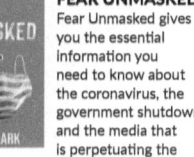

FEAR UNMASKED
Fear Unmasked gives you the essential information you need to know about the coronavirus, the government shutdown, and the media that is perpetuating the hysteria.

FEAR UNMASKED 2.0
Updated and revised for 2021. Fear Unmasked 2.0 provides more resources to kill the spirit of fear and giving YOU an action plan to save America.

THE GREAT RESET VERSUS THE GREAT AWAKENING
The Great Reset Versus The Great Awakening breaks down this EPIC battle between good and evil.